LUTHERAN QUARTERLY BOOKS

Editor

Paul Rorem, *Princeton Theological Seminary*

Associate Editors

Timothy J. Wengert, *The Lutheran Theological Seminary at Philadelphia,* and Steven Paulson, *Luther Seminary, St. Paul*

Lutheran Quarterly Books will advance the same aims as *Lutheran Quarterly* itself, aims repeated by Theodore G. Tappert when he was editor fifty years ago and renewed by Oliver K. Olson when he revived the publication in 1987. The original four aims continue to grace the front matter and to guide the contents of every issue, and can now also indicate the goals of *Lutheran Quarterly Books:* "to provide a forum (1) for the discussion of Christian faith and life on the basis of the Lutheran confession; (2) for the application of the principles of the Lutheran Church to the changing problems of religion and society; (3) for the fostering of world Lutheranism; and (4) for the promotion of understanding between Lutherans and other Christians."

For further information, see www.lutheranquarterly.com.

The symbol and motto of *Lutheran Quarterly,* VDMA for *Verbum Domini Manet in Aeternum* (1 Peter 1:25), was adopted as a motto by Luther's sovereign, Frederick the Wise, and his successors. The original "Protestant" princes walking out of the imperial Diet of Speyer 1529, unruly peasants following Thomas Münzer, and from 1531 to 1547 the coins, medals, flags, and guns of the Smalcaldic League all bore the most famous Reformation slogan, the first Evangelical confession: the Word of the Lord remains forever.

Living by Faith: Justification and Sanctification, by Oswald Bayer (2003).

Harvesting Martin Luther's Reflections on Theology, Ethics and the Church, essays from *Lutheran Quarterly,* edited by Timothy J. Wengert, with foreword by David C. Steinmetz (2004).

A More Radical Gospel: Essays on Eschatology, Authority, Atonement, and Ecumenism, by Gerhard O. Forde, edited by Mark Mattes and Steven Paulson (2004).

The Role of Justification in Contemporary Theology, by Mark C. Mattes (2004).

The Captivation of the Will: Luther vs. Erasmus on Freedom and Bondage, by Gerhard O. Forde (2005).

Bound Choice, Election, and Wittenberg Theological Method: From Martin Luther to the Formula of Concord, by Robert Kolb (2005).

A Formula for Parish Practice: Using the Formula of Concord in Congregations, by Timothy J. Wengert (2006).

Luther's Liturgical Music: Principles and Implications, by Robin A. Leaver (2006).

The Preached God: Proclamation in Word and Sacrament, by Gerhard O. Forde, edited by Mark C. Mattes and Steven D. Paulson (2007).

Theology the Lutheran Way, by Oswald Bayer (2007).

A Time for Confessing, by Robert W. Bertram (2008).

The Pastoral Luther: Essays on Martin Luther's Practical Theology, edited by Timothy J. Wengert (2009).

Preaching from Home: The Stories of Seven Lutheran Women Hymn Writers, by Gracia Grindal (2011).

The Early Luther: Stages in a Reformation Reorientation, by Berndt Hamm (2013).

The Life, Works, and Witness of Tsehay Tolessa and Gudina Tumsa, the Ethiopian Bonhoeffer, edited by Samuel Yonas Deressa and Sarah Hinlicky (2017).

THEOLOGY THE LUTHERAN WAY

Oswald Bayer

Edited and Translated by Jeffrey G. Silcock and Mark C. Mattes

Fortress Press
Minneapolis

THEOLOGY THE LUTHERAN WAY

Originally published in German under the title *Theologie* by Gütersloher Verlagshaus, 1994.

Interior contents have not been changed from prior English editions.

Paperback ISBN: 978-1-5064-2729-4
eBook ISBN: 978-1-5064-2730-0

The paper used in this publication meets the minimum requirements of American National Standard for Information Sciences — Permanence of Paper for Printed Library Materials, ANSI Z329.48-1984.

Manufactured in the U.S.A.

Contents

Contents

Contents

Editors' Introduction

Is theology theoretical or practical? That question, which is commonly asked in the church as well as in academic circles, betrays a fundamental misunderstanding of the nature of Christian theology in general and Lutheran theology in particular. The question is a product of the modern post-Enlightenment understanding of theology, which promotes a split between theory and practice. The question would never have occurred to Luther or the other Reformers, nor would it ever have been asked by the theologians of the ancient church. For them, as for Luther, theology is always both "theoretical" and "practical." The freight that these terms carry makes them basically unsuitable to describe the character of theology, at least as Luther understood it.

One of the great merits of *Theology the Lutheran Way* is that it convincingly demonstrates that the modern split between theory and practice — along with the other bifurcations of post-Enlightenment rationalism, such as the antithesis of public and private, inner and outer, theological scholarship and church spirituality — is foreign to the Reformation as well to the scriptures, and misrepresents the nature of Lutheran theology.

What then is theology? This is the question that Oswald Bayer, Luther scholar and professor emeritus of systematic theology at the University of Tübingen, sets out to answer in this book. His answer, which is also Luther's answer, comes as a shock to most Lutherans because they have drunk deeply from the wells of Protestant modernity.

But the water in these wells has been poisoned by the streams of modern secular thought.

To most people, theology is something that *we* do. However, Bayer, following Luther, argues that theology is what *God* does! It is not our work — although in one sense it is, as we will explain later — but God's work as he encounters us in various ways. First, through his civil law, by which he institutes the three holy orders of church, household (which includes marriage and family), and government in the realm of creation and through which he operates in human history. Secondly, through the preached law that unmasks us as sinners before God. Thirdly, through his hidden and terrifying presence in the world (Luther's "hidden God"). Finally, and most importantly, he also encounters us in a fundamentally different way through the proclamation of the gospel, which is crystallized in the words of the absolution: your sins are forgiven you.

Therefore, there is a basic identity between theology, understood as God's work in this broad sense, and faith. Just as faith before God *(coram Deo)* is purely passive, or (better) receptive, rather than active, so too theology, in the first instance, is not our doing, important as the academic side of theology is, but God's doing, which we passively undergo. Therefore, Luther can equate theology with the receptive life *(vita passiva)*, which is his way of saying that when we come into God's presence we come as beggars with hands outstretched who simply receive his gifts in faith (1 Cor. 4:7). When Paul says that faith is *active* in love (Gal. 5:6), he is not contradicting Luther's emphasis that faith is fundamentally *passive*. Luther says faith is passive *coram Deo,* in the presence of God, but is active, *coram hominibus,* in public, in serving the neighbor in love. In a famous passage from his tractate on freedom (1520) he says that "Christians live in Christ and in their neighbor . . . they live in Christ through faith and in their neighbor through love" (LW 31:371, trans. alt.).

Luther also says that "every Christian is a theologian" (WA 41:11), not because we have all studied books, but because we are in God's "school of life," where he sets the curriculum, and where he shapes and molds us in the crucible of suffering through the trials and tribulations of life and the times of spiritual attack *(tentatio)* so that our faith may be proved genuine and bring praise and honor to Christ (1 Peter 1:7). We bring all these experiences with us as we wrestle with God in prayer *(oratio)*, as we listen to his word in the divine service and in private devotion *(meditatio)*. Bayer's important contribution here is to stress the role of *tentatio*. He says that we only properly understand what God does through *oratio* and *meditatio* if we view it through the lens of *tentatio*. In other words, prayer and meditation, prayer and engagement with God's word, must be seen in the context of spiritual attack, which includes trial, doubt, and testing.

Theology, then, is a way of life that is stamped by prayer, listening to God's word, and spiritual attack. But Luther does not first answer the question, what is *theology?* Instead, he talks about who is a *theologian.* He concludes from his study of the psalms (especially Ps. 51 and 119) that prayer, meditation, and spiritual attack *(oratio, meditatio, tentatio)* make the theologian. Theologians (and remember he includes all Christians here) are not self-made but are made by God. And God makes theologians of us through prayer, through listening to his word, and through the cross and suffering.

The formal study of the scriptures, which belongs to the academic side of theology, is bound up principally with the question of methodology, and this in turn raises the question of the subject and theme of theology, for if theology is true to itself, its method must be appropriate to its subject matter.

What then is the subject matter of theology? According to Luther, it is nothing other than the sinful human and the God who justifies. Notice in passing how Luther does not talk in general terms about concepts and principles but deals with concrete realities. The subject of theology is not the nature of God and of human beings, but rather the human who sins and God who justifies the sinner. However, Bayer shows that ultimately the subject matter of theology is contained in God's promise, which is Luther's preferred way of referring to the gospel. The promise here does not refer to something in the future but points to the concrete presence of the triune God in the church today, and especially to Christ's bodily presence in the bread and the wine of Holy Communion. Therefore, the promise needs to be carefully distinguished from the other ways in which God encounters us, such as through the civil law and the orders in creation.

Bayer reminds us that Luther speaks of the church in two senses. Broadly, it includes all people; in that sense it is understood as a corrupted order of creation and is identical with religion in general. Although God established it, the church as an order of creation has been corrupted by sinful human beings; therefore, the general divine service of creation and creaturely religiosity result in idolatry. Luther's understanding of the first commandment fits into this, where he says that "anything that you set your heart on and cling to is really your god" (*Large Catechism,* The Ten Commandments). On the other hand, the church in the narrow sense is the baptized assembly of believers who have been renewed by the Spirit and who in worship gather around God's holy mysteries — his holy word, read and proclaimed, holy baptism, holy absolution, and holy communion.

Worship too then has a correspondingly broad and narrow sense. Broadly, worship is the general divine service of creation which embraces all people. However, here people by their fallen nature mistake Yahweh for Baal, the true God for idols. We only have to think of the terrified sailors who all cried to their different gods in their distress (Jonah 1:4-5). All human beings belong to the church, as a corrupted order of creation, and stand under God's judgment because of sin; they search for God but in their blindness they exchange the truth of God for a lie and worship created things rather than the creator (Rom. 1:24-25). On the other hand, worship in the narrow sense is the divine service in the church where the triune God serves his people through his word and they respond in prayer, which includes intercession and thanksgiving. The renewal of the church as a fallen order of creation can only occur through the renewing power of the Spirit who renews the sinner through his promise which he enacts in the particular divine service of the church. The church is the microcosm of God's plan for creation (Eph. 1:3-14).

Bayer refers to the "monastic" aspect of theology with its foundation in the divine service of the church to cover this side of theology which forms its heart and center. The term "liturgical spirituality," which is more familiar to English readers, picks up what the author means by the "monastic" element of theology. In other words, worship belongs to the heart of theology, and any so-called theology that merely engages the mind and not the heart and the affects (which includes the emotions and the senses) in the divine service is not theology.

However, theology necessarily also has an academic side. This will be most familiar to students of theology at seminaries, colleges, and universities. The academic side of theology is the scholarly study of theology (including biblical exegesis, the history of doctrine, Reformation theology, and pastoral theology) using methods that are appropriate to its content. It orders, analyzes, and reflects on its subject matter, which is provided by certain fundamental forms of speech, but these are inextricably woven together with forms of life, the orders and stations of vocation. This is important because it means that theology does not deal with abstractions; rather, every liturgical form of speech, and ultimately every doctrine, is bound to the biblical narrative, to history, and has a concrete location or setting in life. Theology focuses mainly on these forms of speech. It uses as a criterion the correlation of promise *(promissio)* and faith *(fides)* in connection with the distinction between law and gospel, for it is only through this distinction that the promise is understood as gospel in contradistinction to the law.

God in the Spirit uses these forms of speech (such as the song of praise and the complaint, the Kyrie! [Lord, have mercy!], the prayer of intercession, and the word of blessing) to enact the promise and deliver its blessings to his people; this does not happen automatically. That means that theology is first and foremost linguistics because it has to do primarily with words and language rather than with general concepts, ideas, and principles.

The close connection between worship and theology is reflected today in a distinction, common in the English-speaking world, between liturgical theology, which is primary theology *(theologia prima)* because it studies the primary texts and liturgical forms of the divine service, and systematic theology, which is secondary *(theologia secunda)* because it reflects on those primary texts and forms of the liturgy.[1]

Bayer's basic thesis is that theology has two sides that cannot be separated without theology being deformed. The one side is its "monastic" aspect, its liturgical spirituality, grounded in the divine service of the church. This is constitutive for theology because it provides it

1. Recent interest in liturgical theology mainly goes back to the work of the Roman Catholic liturgiologist Aidan Kavanagh, *On Liturgical Theology* (New York: Pueblo / Collegeville, Minn.: Liturgical Press, 1992) and the great Orthodox scholar Alexander Schmemann, *Introduction to Liturgical Theology* (Crestwood, N.Y.: St. Vladimir's Seminary Press, 1986). Two of the most important scholars today who have published in the field are David Fagerburg, *What Is Liturgical Theology? A Study in Methodology* (Collegeville, Minn.: Liturgical Press, 1992) and Gordon Lathrop, *Holy Things: A Liturgical Theology* (Minneapolis: Fortress, 1993).

with its subject matter, which systematic theology then orders, analyzes, and reflects on, making the necessary connections and distinctions. This other side of theology, its academic side, is purely secondary and regulative, because it reflects on the primary texts, the forms of speech, which are inseparably connected to forms of life.

Bayer argues that this academic side of theology is indispensable for the church's proclamation of the gospel and for defending the gospel against error and heresy. In Luther's day, this scholarly side of theology was epitomized in the tradition of the academic disputation in the university, which Luther did much to restore and strengthen. Here reason, under the guidance of faith, was honed and sharpened by rigorous debate and argumentation in order to learn how to analyze and test propositions in the light of the scriptures and so be able to distinguish truth from error, orthodoxy from heterodoxy, right worship from idolatry.

This academic exercise is always *pro ecclesia,* for the church, and so in the service of the gospel, not for its own self-glorification. However, history shows that where theology fails to reflect critically on and scrutinize the church's worship and teaching, the gospel is at risk of being lost. The close nexus between worship and doctrine is highlighted by an old rule of the church best known in its Latin form: *lex orandi, lex credendi,* which stresses that the church's worship determines its doctrine, and conversely, its doctrine determines its worship. As always, doctrine and worship are inseparable; change one and you change the other. This reciprocity is reflected in the very meaning of the word "orthodoxy," which means not only right doctrine but also right worship.

Bayer persuasively shows that when the link between academics and spirituality is broken and when theology and the Christian faith are transformed into a theory, a moral system, or an existential-psychological encounter under the *Zeitgeist* of modernity, theology is deformed and the gospel is perverted (Gal. 1:8). This represents the nadir of theology, its utter perversion and secularization.

The author shows what happens when theology renounces its own birthright for a mess of modernist pottage, allows itself to be duped by the spirit of the age and uses methodologies that are inappropriate to its subject matter. If theology is severed from the promise, or if its methods subvert it, it will mutate into ethics, metaphysics, or psychology, as has happened over the last two centuries or so, under the influence of the leading thinkers of modernity. More specifically, theology can be turned into a new form of morality and the gospel into a new law if it follows the path of Kant and the neo-Kantians. Alternatively, theology can be transformed into a general metaphysical theory, and the gospel into a religious idea, if it goes the way of Hegel. Or theology can be changed into system rooted in the psychologization of religion, and the gospel transformed into an existential encounter, if it takes the path of Schleiermacher and Bultmann. In each of these cases, theology is hijacked by an inappropriate method.

Bayer shows that any method that does not serve the gospel and is not thoroughly shaped by it is not an appropriate method for an academic discipline which, in the final analysis, begins and ends with the divine service of the church. He strikes a very postmodern chord when he argues that no method is ever neutral; the question for theology is always whether its method is grounded in its own subject matter or whether it is based on some general philosophical principle, foreign to theology, which is then foisted on it.

Existentialist approaches to theology, rejected by Bayer, are often pitted against political approaches. How does political theology fare in his work? Bayer refuses to be positioned by such dichotomies. Secular political theologies fail to honor Luther's two kinds of righteousness, the passive righteousness of faith which justifies before God and the active righteousness of doing justice to others in their need. Secular political theologies of a neo-Marxist stamp are based on a false anthropology, one that reduces the person to an agent. True, our agency presupposes freedom, but freedom is not something that we possess for ourselves; we can only receive it as a gift. Humans are fundamentally receivers, since our freedom is always *promised* and received without ever being fully possessed. In opposition to Kant's "categorical imperative," Bayer calls this the "categorical gift." His success in avoiding the Charybdis of existentialism and the Scylla of secular political theologies offers a genuine advance in theological thinking which we hope will have far-reaching ecumenical benefits.

Bayer argues convincingly that the only way to reverse the tragic deformation of theology under the shadow of modernity is to return to Luther's Reformation understanding of the linguistic nature of theology and its narrative framework so that due attention is given to the working of the triune God in time and space, through the law and creation, through the gospel and the church and the sensuous means of grace which we passively "suffer," undergo, as God molds and shapes us for his purposes. This is the *pathos* of theology, which holds the key to its proper understanding. It emphasizes the priority of God's action and the basic passivity and receptivity of human beings in his presence.

In summary, the key to resolving the false antithesis between theory and practice is to recognize the centrality of pathos in the Christian life and the role of the affects (which include the emotions, the senses, the imagination, and the desires). The answer then to the question of whether theology is theoretical or practical is that it is both and it is neither. The question can only be properly answered by introducing this third dimension that Bayer calls *pathos*, which puts the emphasis on God's action and human passivity/receptivity and therefore has fundamental significance for theology.

In the final analysis, theology is God's work, a work he accomplishes by means of a synergy between liturgical spirituality with its foundation in the divine service of the church, which provides theology with its subject matter, and academic theology, which reflects on this subject matter using appropriate methods in order to make connections and distinctions. However, the most important task of academic theology is to continue to scrutinize the doctrine and worship of the church and to enter into vigorous debate with any unbiblical teaching, idea, or ideology that threatens to subvert the promise of the gospel, which we can only keep pure if we are vigilant in properly distinguishing between law and gospel.

*   *   *

Although a systematic theologian, Oswald Bayer is first and foremost a Luther scholar whose understanding of Luther has shaped all his "systematic" thinking. Apart from the books listed below, he has also written hundreds of articles. Some of his most important journal articles have now been translated into English; many of them are published in *Lutheran Quarterly*.

His first major publication was *Promissio: Geschichte der reformatorischen Wende in Luthers Theologie* (Göttingen, 1971; 2nd ed. Darmstadt, 1989). This book incorporates Bayer's research into the nature of the promise *(promissio)* in the young Luther, which formed the basis of his doctoral dissertation as well as his post-doctoral dissertation *(Habilitationschrift)*, which is necessary to qualify as a university lecturer in Germany. The book follows Luther's journey towards his Reformation discovery of the gospel, which for him is God's word of promise. It continues to remain one of the defining books in Luther scholarship still today, but unfortunately it has not been translated.

He has also written many other significant books on Luther's theology, on Hamann scholarship, on dogmatic theology and ethics, and on the philosophy of religion.

Kreuz und Kritik (Mohr Siebeck, 1983), which he co-authored with Christian Knudsen, gives the text and interpretation of Johann Georg Hamann's last paper. Hamann (1730-1788), dubbed the Magus in the North, has played a significant role in shaping Bayer's understanding of the poetical character of theology and the importance of linguistics, poetics, and aesthetics for understanding the centrality of pathos for theology.

Aus Glauben leben: Über Rechtfertigung und Heiligung (Calwer, 1984; 2nd ed. 1990), translated by Geoffrey W. Bromiley under the title *Living by Faith: Justification and Sanctification* (Eerdmans, 2003), is the first book of Bayer's to be published in English; although only a slim volume, it goes to the heart of Luther's theology and Lutheran dogmatics. He emphasizes here that justification is not just a single doctrine but has implications for all doctrines stretching from creation to eschatology.

The other books we will simply list without comment.

Schöpfung als Anrede: Zu einer Hermeneutik der Schöpfung (Mohr Siebeck, 1986; 2nd ed. 1990); *Zeitgenosse im Widerspruch. Johann Georg Hamann als radikaler Aufklärer* (Piper, 1988); *Autorität und Kritik: Zu Hermeneutik und Wissenschaftstheorie* (Mohr Siebeck, 1991); *Leibliches Wort: Reformation und Neuzeit im Konflikt* (Mohr Siebeck, 1992); *Theologie* (HST I; Gütersloher, 1994); *Freiheit als Antwort: Zur theologischen Ethik* (Mohr Siebeck, 1995), which will be published in English (Oxford University Press); *Gott als Autor: Zu einer poietologischen Theologie* (Mohr Siebeck, 1999); *Vernunft ist Sprache. Hamanns Metakritik Kants* (Frommann-Holzboog, 2002); *Martin Luthers Theologie: Eine Vergegenwärtigung* (Mohr Siebeck, 2003; 2nd ed. 2004), which has been translated (Eerdmans).

The present volume is a translation of the two most important parts of *Theologie* (1994), the first volume in a German series of handbooks in systematic theology for use by students, pastors, and teachers of theology. The German original contains three parts. However, only the first section of the first part, which deals with Luther, and the last part, which is Bayer's own constructive proposal, have been here translated.

It may be helpful for us to briefly outline the contents of the German original. In the first section of the first part of *Theologie*, which deals with Luther's understanding of theology, Bayer develops his own understanding of Luther's theology based on Luther's famous dictum: *oratio, meditatio,* and *tentatio* make the theologian. The other two sections on Melanchthon and Calvin have not been included, although the section on Melanchthon will be published separately in *Lutheran Quarterly.* In the second part, the author considers three major twentieth-century theologians who stand in the Reformation tradition, Paul Tillich, Werner Elert, and Karl Barth, and he assesses them in the light of Luther's distinctive law-gospel understanding of theology. This section has not been translated. The third part of *Theologie,* which has been included in *Theology the Lutheran Way,* is the most important part, for it represents the author's own constructive approach to theology. Its purpose is to analyze and discuss key problems in contemporary theological methodology, but at the same time it is firmly based on Bayer's detailed and rigorous exposition of Luther's understanding of theology, which he sets out in the first part of the book. The distinctive hallmarks of Lutheran theology that Bayer notes in the author's foreword and that he develops in this book, all flow directly from his study of Luther.

This English version of Bayer's *Theologie* is not a formal translation but one that operates with the principle of dynamic equivalence. It aims to give the meaning of the original in clear accessible English without attempting to preserve every word and nuance. Since the German text is very compressed and tightly argued, there are many places where expansions have been made, with the blessing of the author, in order to assist the reader to understand better what he means. This has been done specifically for the benefit of students of theology. Apologies to academics and advanced students if some of the additions and expansions appear patronizing! The translation has not been pitched at the level of the specialist but at the level of theological students in seminaries, colleges, and universities.

This translation has been a collaborative effort between the editors, Jeff Silcock and Mark Mattes. We would both like to thank the author for his willingness to help and to offer suggestions. Mattes thanks Bayer's assistants, and especially Martin Abraham, for the help they gave him with drafting part 2, and Silcock thanks Lars Kierspel for a first draft of part 1, section 3, and acknowledges the assistance of John Kleinig, who shares with him a passion for Hamann and Bayer.

We are grateful to our institutions, Australian Lutheran College (Adelaide, South Australia), and Grand View College (Des Moines, Iowa), for study leave and financial support to complete this project. It is our hope that this translation will be of service to the church in promoting sound academic theology that begins and ends with the divine service and whose method is consonant with the gospel that it serves, to the glory of God and for the mission of the church in the postmodern world.

Jeffrey G. Silcock and
Mark C. Mattes

Translators' Preface

A number of translation problems have been addressed in the notes, making it unnecessary to discuss them here. The only word that requires some additional comment is the German word *Wissenschaft* (Latin: *scientia*), which is normally translated as "science."

To call theology a "science" may sound strange to people in the English-speaking world because we are accustomed to understanding science to mean the "natural sciences" or the so-called hard sciences. However, in German, the term *Wissenschaft* has the much broader sense of "academic discipline" or area of study.[1]

We need to remember that from Schleiermacher to the present day, theology has taken its place in the German university as a science alongside other sciences. In fact once, if not today, theology used to be called the "queen of the sciences," and on formal occasions the theology faculty led the academic procession.

However, theology is not a science in the same sense as the physical sciences. Rather, it is a science in its own right, a discipline of study with procedures and methods appropriate to its subject matter. In this sense, it has more in common with the faculty of philosophy (especially

---

1. For a discussion of the nature of "scientific theology," see Alister E. McGrath, *The Science of God: An Introduction to Scientific Theology* (Grand Rapids: Eerdmans, 2004). However, scientific theology, as understood by McGrath, is specifically, though not exclusively, the engagement of theology with the natural sciences.

if we understand that to include history and philology) than with that of the natural sciences.

In this translation, we often render *Wissenschaft* (literally: science, scholarship) with "academic discipline" and *theologische Wissenschaft* (literally: theological science) with "academic theology."

Although all possible care has been taken to produce an accurate translation, we are aware that occasional errors may occur and for that we take full responsibility.

JGS and MCM

Author's Preface

I

Who is a theologian? That is the question that this book has attempted to answer.

The understanding of theology that I present here is not "only" driven by *formal* considerations, such as methodology, the philosophy of science, and hermeneutics, but from the start it is also permeated and determined by *material* considerations, the content of dogmatics itself. We cannot therefore evade the task of also clarifying the significance of the distinction between law and gospel, the significance of the word of God, the doctrine of God, and all the other doctrines down to and including eschatology and showing how all these illuminate our understanding of theology. Conversely, it is just as important to emphasize the significance of the supposedly purely formal questions of method for the understanding of the content of dogmatics.

The understanding of theology that I have developed here is characterized primarily by its dual focus. It reveals the material dogmatic issues implicit in the formal questions, and it also clarifies the constitutive significance that formal questions have for understanding the issues of material dogmatics. In other words, I try to show that there is a mutual reciprocity between the subject matter of theology, as expressed in its dogmatics, and theological methodology. However, as the book makes clear, there is a proper order here. As indispensable as the method is, it always remains subservient to the content of theology.

II

The German version of this book, which was published in 1994 as the first volume of the series *Handbuch Systematischer Theologie* (Handbook of Systematic Theology), is different from this English version in several important respects. The German version has three main parts. The first gives an account of how the three Reformers, Luther, Melanchthon, and Calvin, understood the nature of theology. The second discusses the understanding of theology in the twentieth century as exemplified by Tillich, Elert, and Barth. The third part considers those questions that emerge from a critical comparison of the Reformers' understanding of theology with that presented in the second part. This third part is the constructive part, and in scope and character it is really an independent monograph on the main problems of prolegomena. Its general structure arises out of a critical discussion of Schleiermacher's understanding of theology. All in all, systematic theology can best discharge its responsibility through open and forthright debate with the seminal thinkers of modernity. Apart from Schleiermacher, this includes Kant, Hegel, and Bultmann.

Theology the Lutheran Way significantly reduces the size and the scope of the German original and concentrates mainly on the third part. Therefore, the book is predominantly a work in "systematic theology," which evaluates certain approaches to theology that have been very influential. Since it is consciously Lutheran, it makes sense to include the Luther section from the original in order to make clear to the reader the tradition in which this work is anchored. Likewise, the introductory section on Important Moments in the Understanding of Theology has also been taken over into this version and placed before the two main parts.

III

The following seven characteristics are the most important distinguishing marks of the concept of theology that I have developed in this book.

1. The first mark is its *dual focus* on the methodology and the subject matter of dogmatics, which I have already mentioned.

2. The second emphasizes the interweaving of the affects and the intellect, spirituality *(pietas)* and scholarship *(eruditio)*, praying and thinking. If we view the history of theology systematically, we can point to the inseparability and interconnectedness of the two sides of theology: on the one hand, its "monastic" aspect, with its tradition of liturgical spirituality grounded in the divine service *(Gottesdienst)*, and, on the other hand, its "scholastic," academic aspect, which in Luther's day culminated in the academic disputation. The first constitutes theology in that it provides its content. The second regulates it, in the sense that it provides the tools and methods that are needed to order, analyze, and reflect on its subject matter. The concept of theology consonant with this twofold emphasis could be encapsulated in the thesis: *theology begins and ends with the divine service.*

3. The third distinguishing mark is the recognition of the centrality of the *affects* and the foundational nature of *pathos*. The element of pathos in theology emphasizes that, in the presence of God *(coram Deo)*, it is God himself who is active and that we are the passive recipients who "suffer" God's work, in the sense that we passively undergo it. The recognition of the centrality of pathos and the role of the affects shatters the twofold scheme of theory and practice that has dominated theology since the Enlightenment due to its influence in the philosophy of science. Its place is taken by a threefold scheme in which theory and practice, knowledge and action, are grounded in a third dimension, *pathos,* which puts the emphasis on human receptivity and therefore has fundamental significance for theology.

4. The fourth mark is bound up with the precise way in which we understand this pathos. It is just here that there is a major difference between Schleiermacher and Luther. Is pathos in theology determined by the word or does it determine the word? Is the word the *creatura fidei,* the creature of faith (Schleiermacher) or is faith the *creatura verbi,* the creature of the word (Luther)? The concept of theology that I have set out in this book argues for the latter: that *pathos is determined by the word, by God's word.*

5. However, this word cannot be understood monistically, after the

fashion of Karl Barth. It describes the ways in which God encounters us. These ways are irreducible for us before the Last Day and cannot be integrated into a single general concept, such as God's self-revelation. Consonant with this is the realization that there are different ways in which God encounters us, and that therefore we need to *distinguish properly between law and gospel,* which is the fifth distinguishing mark.

6. The relationship between philosophy and theology, and the scientific, academic character of theology can only be properly determined in the light of the distinction between law and gospel. The *proper relationship between philosophy and theology* that is determined in this way is the sixth mark.

7. Finally, a definitive moment of the concept of theology that I present in this book is the *distinction between faith and sight.* It is especially here, in the understanding of this distinction, that we see the intertwining of the "formal" questions of epistemology and the philosophy of science, on the one hand, and "material" dogmatics, on the other.

IV

I would like to take the opportunity in this foreword to express my profound thanks to those who have collaborated in the production of this book. I am delighted that it can be published in the series *Lutheran Quarterly Books.* For that I thank the editor of the series, Paul Rorem. He and Mark Mattes were the originators of this project. Mattes worked tirelessly and selflessly on the first draft of the second part of the book, continually checking his work with my assistant Martin Abraham. Jeffrey Silcock has likewise worked unstintingly on the project and translated not only the first part of the book, but he has also assumed responsibility for the final translation of the entire book. His aim all along has been to produce a translation that is clear and accessible to the English reader. Mattes and Silcock, as joint editors of the book, have also collaborated on the editors' introduction. Lastly, I thank Paul Rorem's assistant, Amy Marga, for the list of my publications in English.

It is my hope that this book will be a useful resource for students and teachers of theology as well as for all who are interested in Luther's theology and the problems of contemporary theological methodology.

Tübingen and Hennef,   OSWALD BAYER
Christmas, 2005

Abbreviations

AC	Augsburg Confession
AGP	Arbeiten zur Geschichte des Pietismus
AWA	Archiv zur Weimarer Ausgabe
BC	*The Book of Concord,* ed. Robert Kolb and Timothy J. Wengert (Minneapolis: Fortress, 2000)
BevTh	*Beiträge zur evangelischen Theologie*
BHTh	*Beiträge zur historischen Theologie*
BoA	Bonner Ausgabe (8 Bände), ed. Clemens
BSLK	*Die Bekenntnis-Schriften der Evangelisch-Lutherischen Kirche* (Göttingen: Vandenhoeck & Ruprecht, 1976)
CD	*Church Dogmatics*
CR	Corpus Reformatum
CSEL	*Corpus Scriptorum Ecclesiasticorum Latinorum*
EG	*Evangelisches Gesangbuch*
EvTh	*Evangelische Theologie*
FGLP	*Forschungen zur Geschichte und Lehre des Protestantismus*
FKDG	*Forschungen zur Kirchen- und Dogmengeschichte*
GTA	Göttinger theologische Arbeiten
HKG	*Handbuch der Kirchengeschichte*
HST	Handbuch Systematischer Theologie
HUTh	Hermeneutische Untersuchungen zur Theologie
KD	*Die Kirchliche Dogmatik*
LBW	*Lutheran Book of Worship*
LQ	*Lutheran Quarterly*

Abbreviations

LW	Martin Luther, *Luther's Works* (American edition), ed. Jaroslav Pelikan and Helmut Lehman, 55 vols. (Philadelphia and St. Louis: Fortress and Concordia, 1955-86)
MPG	J. P. Migne, *Patrologiae cursus completus,* series Graeca, 161 vols. (Paris, 1857-1866)
MPL	J. P. Migne, *Patrologiae cursus completus,* series Latina, 221 vols. (Paris, 1844-1855)
NZSTh	*Neue Zeitschrift für Systematische Theologie und Religionsphilosophie*
PhB	Philosophische Bibliothek
SDGSTh	*Studien zur Dogmengeschichte und Systematischen Theologie*
STh	*Summa Theologiae*
TB	Theologische Bücherei
ThSt	*Theologische Studien*
TRE	*Theologische Realenzyklopädie,* 36 vols., ed. Gerhard Krause and Gerhard Müller (Berlin and New York: Walter de Gruyter, 1976-2005)
UTB	Universitätstaschenbuch
WA	Martin Luther, *Dr. Martin Luthers Werke: Kritische Gesamtausgabe* [Weimarer Ausgabe; Schriften], 65 vols. (Weimar: H. Böhlau, 1883-1993)
WABR	*Luthers Werke: Kritische Gesamtausgabe. Briefwechsel.* 18 volumes. Weimar: Böhlau, 1930-1985
WA DB	*Die Deutsche Bibel*
WA TR	*Tischreden*
ZThK	*Zeitschrift für Theologie und Kirche*

Important Moments in the Understanding of Theology

"Theology" does not suddenly appear out of the blue with the Reformation. Despite its radically new orientation, the Reformation is linked with the tradition of the church, both its history and its theology. The word "Reformation" itself means a return to the origins in order once again to emphasize them or reappropriate them. It is the consciousness of something new, a prophetic illumination, the awareness of standing at the threshold of the apocalyptic, final hour. Even more, there is the certainty that with this a new light has dawned, and that this light, which has radically enlightened a dark and perverse world, has its source in nothing else than that definitive salvific event which took place under Pontius Pilate, as we confess in the creed. The Reformation holds that this event has been definitively recorded in the words of the biblical canon, and definitively delivered to me now in holy baptism.

This entirely new thing that we call the gospel cannot do without its own particular traditions, as tradition criticism makes clear. Therefore, right from the start, we need to guard against the misunderstanding that "systematic theology" begins abruptly with the Reformation.

"Theology" certainly does not begin with Luther. In fact, Christian theology begins long before the birth of Christ. If the use of the word "theology" itself is anything to go by, we could say that Christian theology had its beginnings already with Plato. By going back to the origins of the word, we have discovered that Christian theology has its

I

location between metaphysics and mythology (section 1 below). This insight has proved decisive right up to the present time.

If we want to understand "theology" in the broad sense as including history and systematics, we cannot start out by defining it narrowly as "scholarship." Yet we cannot deny that it has a scientific, academic character. Rather, if we have to describe theology as academic, we can only properly do so in a broad general way. The precision typical of scientific, academic rigor and rationality, with its emphasis on reason to the exclusion of all dimensions of life except the cognitive, is too narrow and limited. We can no longer make any absolute claim in the name of science. Thinking is only *one* dimension of life; the heart beats before the head thinks. In the history of theology, this imbalance was corrected by monasticism, with its focus on meditation centered in the divine service. Therefore, we must view *scholastic* theology, and its subsequent forms, with its strong emphasis on scientific and academic rigor, in relationship to *monastic* theology and its tradition of liturgical spirituality. In the past, standard historiography and systematic reflection have either completely excluded it or hardly considered it. This is something we need to correct. We must constantly ask fundamental questions about the relationship between monastic and scholastic theology, between liturgical spirituality and academic theology. We therefore need to take up this question right here at the beginning (section 2 below).

There is a good reason why we must not isolate scholastic theology, but rather see it in the context of monastic theology. We cannot deny that high scholasticism, with its emphasis on Aristotle and the rise of the universities, brought a new way of understanding the concept of theology. Questions about the philosophy of science, about theological methodology, had previously been treated rather casually, if at all. Now these same questions were taken into the university curriculum and were even given precedence over Lombard's *Books of the Sentences,* which comprised the standard "textbook" in theology at the time. They have since been reformulated in many different ways and are still determinative in our day. Therefore, they deserve our attention. At the end of this introduction, we will reproduce them in the form in which they appear in Gabriel Biel's prologue to his *Collectorium* at the end of the Middle Ages (section 3 below). They provide the starting point for a perspective that allows us to look back to the very beginnings of the philosophy of science,[1] which formed a vital part of scholasticism. This is also the best place to begin our account of Luther's understanding of theology, and it is still the most helpful point of reference for considering the main problems in the philosophy of science today.

1. Christian Theology between Metaphysics and Mythology

God is a human being. This statement, made in the light of the crucified and risen Lord Jesus, describes the center of the Christian faith. This is reflected in many hymns and songs of the church. We sing, for example, in the second verse of the Christmas carol "Oh, Come, All Ye Faithful": "Born of a virgin, a mortal he comes; Son of the Father now in flesh appearing!" (*LBW* 45:2).

As the Christian faith gradually engaged intellectually with contemporary currents of thought, it began to use the word "theology." However, in doing this, theology found itself positioned between mythology and metaphysics, and had to engage both of them critically. The problem associated with the word "theology" results from the origin and history of the concept. Yet this problem enables us to make sense of the statement "God is a human being," as well as the event of justification by faith alone, which God won for us through the incarnation of his Son and his death on the cross, and which he delivers to us in the message of the cross.

"Theology" is not a biblical word but comes from Greek antiquity. The word literally means "speech about God" and, in its original usage, it is simply the stories of the gods in song and spoken form. In the Greek world, a story is a "myth" *(mythos)*. "Theology" therefore is a recital of the stories of the gods, such as we have in Homer, Hesiod, and in the Attic tragedians. At first, this recital occurs only in oral form, but then also in certain fixed literary forms. These stories recount the acts of the gods in space and time. They tell of their transformations, their "metamorphoses," how a particular god could reappear to mortals in a different form. In this way, the different, even contradictory, fundamental experiences of life in the world, such as unconscious guilt and its consequences, can be told without being forcibly reduced to a single denominator, or integrated into a coherent theory at the expense of those parts that are different and contradictory. "Theology" then refers to the stories of the gods in song and speech. It is therefore essentially polytheistic, not monotheistic.

It is worth noting that the first time the word "theology" occurs in Plato's *Republic* (379a) in this original sense as a synonym for mythology, it is strongly criticized. It is important for us to remember that here for the first time we have a metaphysics that is critical of myth. As we will see, the reason that Plato is critical of the theology of his day is because he held that theology should be a rational conception of the divine as opposed to poetic myths about the gods.

1.1. Metaphysics and Its Critique of Myth

1.1.1. Plato

According to Plato, the stories of the gods told by the poets contain "some truth" but, in general, they are lies (377a). They therefore are a danger to the state and its order. Consequently, those responsible for the education of the up-and-coming rulers must pay special attention to the stories, the "myths," they choose to tell them. Because it is "difficult to eradicate or change" certain ideas once young people get them in their heads (378d), it is of the utmost importance that the first stories they hear are "models of virtue" (378e). Therefore, the founders of the state have to know the "patterns" *(typoi),* the rules, "that poets must adhere to in composing their myths" (379a). These "patterns" are strict linguistic conventions governing what they could and could not say. The poet who does not observe them, Plato says harshly, should not be permitted to speak or be heard.

What then are the principal rules and regulations that should govern theology under the watchful eye of the philosophers? The general requirement of a myth is that it should present God the way he is (379a); it is essential to speak accurately about God's being. To that end, Plato puts forward two criteria for an orthodox theology. It must assert that God is good and that God is unchangeable.

Because God is good and is the cause of all good, we should never say that he is the cause of all that happens: "The good is not the cause of all things, but only of the good; it is not responsible for what is evil and wicked" (379b; see 617e and *Theaetetus* 176b/c). Plato regards it as intolerable and irrational that Homer in the *Iliad* (XXIV, 525-33) speaks of two urns; the one filled with good gifts, the other with gifts that are evil, as if "Zeus dispenses to us both 'good and evil'" (379e). The Greek tragedies come in for this same harsh criticism, such as in a play of Aeschylus, in which it says that God also does evil. Plato says, "If our city is to be well governed, we must do all we can to prevent anyone, young or old, either saying or being told, whether in poetry or prose, that God, who is good, can cause harm or evil to anyone. To say that would be sinful, inexpedient, and inconsistent" (380b/c).[2] God must be consistent. If he is good, he cannot be the cause of evil. Humans need to be able to be certain; they should not have to fear that God also does evil. They have to be able to expect nothing from him but good (379c). Plato could no longer tolerate the experience of suffering as presented by the tragedies. He solves the problem of theodicy by permitting people to speak only of the unity of a good cause and a good outcome. Suffering and evil are ultimately nothing but an illusion. "God is not to blame" (617e).

The second "pattern" or rule that is normative for theology deals with God's unchangeability, which is a necessary part of the good. Plato says, "Clearly, God is without deceit or falsehood in word and action; he does not change himself, nor deceive others, awake or dreaming, with visions or signs or words" (382e).[3] It is therefore not the case that God can "appear at will in different forms at different times, sometimes turning into them himself and appearing in many different shapes" (380d),[4] as Zeus did, who approached the beautiful Europa in one of his metamorphoses. Since God is perfect, he is "without deceit" and is least liable "to change or alteration by an external cause" (380d/e). He is not "changed by time or other influences" (381a). God is timeless. He is immune to time. "Time" would mean history, changeability. "Do you think," Socrates asks Adeimantus, his partner in conversation (381c), "that any mortal or god would deliberately make himself worse in any respect?" Impossible, he says. "Then it must also be impossible for a god to wish to change himself. Every god is perfect and supremely good, and remains in his own form without variation forever."[5]

Plato, in enunciating this "pattern" *(typos)* or rule, obviously had Greek mythology in mind. It has, however, also influenced the way that Christians read their Bibles, particularly the hymn to Christ in Philippians. This hymn goes to the heart of the Christian faith when it confesses that Christ Jesus, "who, though he was in the form of God, did not consider equality with God a thing to be grasped but relinquished it, taking the form of a servant . . ." (Phil. 2:6-11).

Plato does not wish to eliminate theology, which he understands as the singing and reciting of the divine myths on the part of the poets. Yet in decisive passages of his dialogue, he says that in the case of the allegorical account of the truth of the logos, even myths or fables (*Gorgias* 523-27; *Phaedo* 107-15a; see the *Seventh Letter* 335a; *Republic* 614-21; *Timaeus* 29b ff.) are a "noble risk" (*Phaedo* 114d). However, if for him truth is one, good, and unchangeable, he disciplines theology so that the myths of the gods become demythologized aspects of the concept. The relationship between the philosophical logos concerning the divine, on the one hand, and the myth of the gods, on the other, is such that the break is greater than the continuity.

I.I.2. Aristotle

We have seen that Plato wants to make the two ways of speaking about God, which we have mentioned, the rule and norm for censuring myth in the name of reason *(logos)*. His purpose in this is to ensure that people hold that the divine is in harmony with itself, and even identical with itself. However, what is only embryonic in Plato comes to full fruition with Aristotle. He wrests the word "theology" from mythology and uses the term "theologic" to designate the pinnacle of theoretical science, which includes philosophy. Poietic science, productive knowledge, knows the reasons and causes of all that has developed through human doing, human *poiesis* (*Metaphysics* 981a24-b2). Practical science, practical knowledge, on the other hand, has a twofold object: the good that people must achieve in life through practice, and the people themselves who do the good. While *praxis* (doing) and *poiesis* (making) have to do with contingent and accidental things, which may be this or that, theoretical science, philosophy, considers things that must be as they are. It represents the highest level of science and wisdom (*Metaphysics* 1025b; 1064a; *Nicomachean Ethics* 1139b-1140a).

Theoretical science, philosophy, falls into three parts: natural science, mathematics, and theologic (*Metaphysics* 1026a, 1064a/b). Natural science considers what is real but movable, while mathematics, on the other hand, deals with what is immovable but unreal. The science "which precedes both" (1026a) is theologic; it unites what is positive in both and considers only what is real and immovable. It focuses on the "divine" and sees it as "the first and most fundamental principle" (1064a/b). In other words, it focuses on the embodiment and guarantee of what is real and constant, what is immutable, reliable, and identical. In its pure reality and activity, it moves all things without itself being moved or affected by another. It is the "unmoved mover" (*Metaphysics* XII; cf. 1026a). Because it is motionlessness and independent, it is the principle, the absolute ruler: "'The rule of many is not good; let one be the ruler!'" (1076a). This is a quote from Homer's *Iliad* (II, 204) where Agamemnon is acknowledged as the one ruler and commander of the army. To quote this at the end of his account of the doctrine of God is a brilliant move on the part of Aristotle, for here he transfers the monarchical principle of sole rule to the world order, which is God's order.

Because Aristotle thinks that the divine world-principle is something immutable, he undoubtedly highlights the substance of Plato's two "patterns" *(typoi)*, his two rules, for theological discourse. It is strange, however, that he should call his theory theologic, which means rational theology, even allowing for a slight shift. It is strange because theologic has no place for sensory experience or the temporal world, yet it is the very same name that tradition had used for the stories of the gods, which appeal strongly to the senses and say nothing about the existence of one divine consistent and immutable being. Aristotle therefore robs the stories of their claim to speak about the divine and instead assigns this entirely to the philosophical term. The "theology" of Aristotle has no myth and no history. It speaks rather of "a being which is eternal and immovable and separate from sensible things" (*Metaphysics* 1073a). Theology clearly is no longer mythology. Theology is now "theologic" science. In other words, it is entirely metaphysics, the beginning and end of philosophy.

1.1.3. The Stoa

The thinking of the Stoics follows the same line of radical demythologization begun by Plato and Aristotle. They locate the decisive moment in a tripartite concept of theology, a *theologia tripertita*.[6] Theology, which deals with the true nature of God, his *physis* (Latin: *natura*), is *theologia physike* (Latin: *theologia naturalis*), "natural" theology. This differs from "mythical theology" *(theologia fabulosa)*, which must be interpreted allegorically because of its hidden philosophical sense, and from "civil" theology *(theologia civilis)*.

1.1.4. Augustine

Augustine reviews this tripartite concept of theology in his book *City of God* and in the process refers to the Roman scholar and author Marcus Terentius Varro (116-27), who follows the tradition of the Stoa. This book, written in defense of Christianity, shows that it alone of all the religions serves the true God and that therefore it alone has the right to the claim of true "natural" theology. Augustine wants to demonstrate that the philosophical concerns that Varro has about mythical theology must apply no less cogently to the civil theology that the Roman Varro considered important. For in a city, "false opinions can arise and gods can be worshipped and believed who have no real existence at all, either in the world or outside the world" (*City of God* VI, 5).

The basis on which Augustine seeks agreement with non-Christians is "natural" theology. In fact, he uses this as his basis for arguing that people should not confuse the world with its creator (compare Rom. 1:23). At the same time, there is no disputing that Augustine also rejected mythical theology; already the New Testament denies that myths are true (1 Tim. 1:4; 2 Tim. 4:4; Titus 1:14; 2 Peter 1:16).

The Christian theology of Augustine joins philosophy in opposing the untrue myths and inquiring after God's true being. Does that make it metaphysics?

1.2. The Dogma of Christ between Metaphysics and Mythology: God's Being and Coming

A text like the hymn to Christ from the letter to the Philippians cited earlier makes it clear that, according to the confession and understanding of the Christian faith, the infinite God comes in a contingent, unique, and hence finite historical event. God's eternal *being*, in which he remains faithful to himself and his promise, and his temporal *coming*, by means of which he becomes involved with his fallen creation to the point of dying on the cross, are, as the dogma of Chalcedon says

(451), "unmixed, unchanged, indivisible, and inseparable." However, God's eternal being itself is profoundly affected by Jesus' death on the cross.

In its attempt to think about God in this way, Christian theology destroyed the axiom of divine impassibility (apathy). This belief had its source in Greek metaphysics. It held that God, the unmoved mover, is immutable and therefore incapable of suffering.

On the other hand, from the standpoint of the critique of mythology, we must reject the idea of a metamorphosis, for Christian theology does not hold that God is changed into humanity and that God ceased to be God in his death on the cross. The story of the crucified God is at the same time a critique of mythology in that this story does not give fantasy the free rein that it normally has in myth. Rather, it fixes our attention on the historical fact of the crucifixion of Jesus of Nazareth. This event is decisive, both temporally and spatially, and is inseparable from the biblical narratives. These texts continue to remain the written record and witness of that event. This once-for-all event can indeed be interpreted, but it cannot be continued, at least not without losing its eschatological character.

Christian theology and the church developed the Trinitarian and Christological dogma based on the miracle of the incarnation and the resurrection of the crucified Jesus, and with critical reference to mythology and metaphysics.

Christian theology would be blind if it failed to see that it occupies a place between mythology and metaphysics.

2. Monastic and Scholastic Theology

A second important moment in the understanding of theology has to do with the relation and tension between faith and knowledge, spirituality *(pietas)* and scholarship *(eruditio)*, the affects (which include the emotions, the senses, the imagination, the memory, and the desires) and the intellect, the heart and the head. Theology would be blind if it denied this tension and tried to resolve it in favor of one side or the other.

The Hellenistic milieu did not first impose this problem on the church. Rather, the church had to face it from its earliest beginnings because the problem goes to the very heart of the Christian faith. This faith is not mute or inarticulate. It is born of the word that conquered death and it expresses itself in words: "I believe, therefore I speak" (Ps. 116:10; 2 Cor. 4:13). These words, however, should be intelligible (1 Cor. 14, esp. vv. 15 and 19). For "if the trumpet does not sound a clear call, who will get ready for battle? So it is with you. Unless you speak intelligible words with your tongue, how will anyone know what you are saying? You will just be speaking into the air" (1 Cor. 14:8f.).

Paul's stress on the *nous* (1 Cor. 14:14f., 19) corresponds to the emphasis on the mind *(dianoia)* in the "most important" commandment (Mark 12:30). This emphasis is not there in the Old Testament narrative of the Decalogue but is added by Jesus. To love God completely means to love God also with one's "mind." The Augustinian-Franciscan tradition appreciated this emphasis in a special way. Love of God and insight, faith and understanding (John 6:69), belong together and cannot be separated.

Therefore, it is not surprising that "the love of learning and the desire for God"[7] form a unity. The surprising thing rather is that these two aspects of theology were split apart in modernity. The split meant that in the universities the title "theology," in the "proper" sense, was given only to "scholastic," academic theology understood as "knowledge" *(scientia)*.[8] This highly disciplined culture of inquiry *(quaestio)* began with high scholasticism and the rise of the European universities. Only since the early twentieth century has the situation radically changed. Now scholars appreciate the distinctive nature of "monastic" theology, with its tradition of liturgical spirituality centered in the divine service, and recognize it as "theology" in its own right. Monastic theology, especially in its use of the Psalter,[9] promotes the cultivation of the affects. These affects relate particularly to our way of life and the examination of the conscience. Crucial here, as we will see later, are Luther's "three rules" for the study of theology: prayer, meditation, and spiritual attack *(oratio, meditatio,* and *tentatio).*[10] With these rules, the doctor and professor of theology, Martin Luther, who was originally an Augustinian monk, takes up "monastic" theology, with its deep liturgical spirituality, and uses it to respond to the main problems of "scholastic" theology in connection with the philosophy of science.

Leclercq[11] believes that "more and more [monastic theology] appears to be a prolongation of patristic theology."[12] However, "it was during the twelfth century that monastic theology emerges with all its distinguishing characteristics clearly delineated."[13] We find an almost idealized embodiment of it in Bernard of Clairvaux (1090-1153) and his understanding of "experience."[14]

If Bernard is the great champion of monastic theology, we find his opposite in Peter Abelard (1079-1142), who is the great champion of scholastic theology. Even though he was a monk, he sees the academic disputation — not meditation — as the heart of theology.

What is the relationship between meditation and the disputation, between the experience of faith and the knowledge of faith?

Once we see the distinction between these two basic types of theology, the danger of a one-sided emphasis becomes evident. We can fall into error on both sides. It is just as wrong to absolutize meditation and make it independent of the disputation, as it is to absolutize the disputation and make it independent of meditation.

If *meditation* becomes independent, the result is mystical darkness, that inner darkness which we can only experience but never penetrate through reading and debating. It leads to its own mystical immediacy, to things that cannot be uttered, to the inarticulate, speechless vision that transcends all distinctions and definitions. In a word, it leads to the absolute One. The one thing needful (Luke 10:42) is here identified with the neo-Platonic One.

That kind of mysticism can be combined with the pathos of pure rationality and in this combination, as advocated by Meister Eckhart (c. 1260-1337), it can become the origin of a form of atheism.[15]

On the other hand, when the *disputation* becomes independent, theology is also at risk. This can happen in a variety of ways. However, in each case, reference to the context *(Sitz im Leben)* is in danger of being lost. If that happens, scholarship becomes sterile, if not dead. We must therefore remember that all scholarly methods, including supposedly "pure" logic, have their origin in particular forms of life[16] and carry these with them, even if this origin is no longer recognized. If we remember that, we can avoid the danger of thinking that the use of scholarly methods is a purely formal matter and that the methods themselves are value-free. If scholarship understands itself properly, if it really "thinks," we would realize that it cannot exist in isolation but is connected with an experience of the world and the self, and indeed God.

Academic theology must be both academic and theological. It must be both for a basic theological reason: because the love of God includes our mind and our thinking. How then do we deal with the view that wants to absolutize either the disputation or the meditation and make the one independent of the other?

One type of combination, which brings together the meditation and the disputation, is that of mysticism and rationality. This, as we saw earlier, is exemplified by the life and work of Meister Eckhart. An altogether different type of combination is that presented by the life and work of Martin Luther and his meditation on the biblical text. This belongs to the trivium, the lower division of the Liberal Arts curriculum, and, together with rhetoric and dialectics,[17] focuses on grammar.

From the standpoint of systematic theology, the decisive thing here is not simply to see this as a unique type of theology, scholastic in name, but rather to realize that we cannot understand it apart from the liturgical spirituality of monastic theology. It is necessary to distinguish both types from each other and, at the same time, to keep them connected. This then is a fruitful way of formulating the problem of the relationship between the two sides of theology,[18] which is important not only for the history of theology but also for systematics.

Only in the light of the connection between these two sides of theology can we properly understand why Luther, who was both monk and professor, answers the classical questions of scholastic theology by turning to monastic theology with its emphasis on liturgical spirituality. This insight is crucial for grasping Luther's understanding of theology, which we shall set out in this book.

In the period following Luther, these two aspects of theology break apart again. Johann Gerhard writes his dogmatics, the *Loci theologici*, on the one hand, and the "therapeutic" theology of his sacred meditations, *Meditationes sacrae,* on the other.[19] Here a single theologian can still hold these two aspects together, despite the different ways in which he expresses them, but with Johann Salomo Semler, they become completely separated. He has no understanding at all of the monastic side of theology with its liturgical spirituality and accepts the moment of existential experience only if he can understand it in moral terms. It is in keeping with his sharp criticism of the thesis that prayer, meditation, and spiritual attack *(oratio, meditatio, tentatio)* make a theologian,[20] that he puts Melanchthon above Luther.[21] That means of course that he has to overemphasize the place of scholarship and learning *(eruditio)* in Melanchthon and reduce spirituality *(pietas)* to moral disposition, while in fact Melanchthon's appreciation of the monastic aspect of theology, with its rich tradition of prayer, meditation, and spirituality, makes him interested in the consolation of the troubled conscience.[22] This is also Luther's interest and is reflected in his first Reformation writing, which has the title *"Pro veritate inquirenda et timoratis conscientiis consolandis,"* "theses on seeking out the truth and comforting terrified consciences."[23]

In place of Semler's moral emphasis, Bultmann introduces an existential emphasis. The disjunction between the historical emphasis in theology, on the one hand, and the moral or existential, on the other, belongs to a tradition that reaches from Semler to Bultmann. This is a strong and consistent feature, especially in the work of Immanuel Kant, who ultimately reduces the Christian faith to a code of ethics. In direct opposition to philological criticism and ancient scholarship, which always emphasize the empirical and historical side of theology and therefore what is *a posteriori*,[24] he gives precedence to the moral *a priori* side.

This brief survey of modern problems also shows that without distinguishing between the monastic and the scholastic sides of theology, we cannot recognize what is crucial. This distinction is not only of historical significance but it also enables us to articulate accurately the relationship between faith and thinking, between the liturgical spirituality of the church and the academic theology of the university.[25]

3. The Main Problems with the Philosophy of Science

The best way to gain a concise understanding of the main problems for theology posed by the philosophy of science, which have immediate relevance for questions of theological methodology, is to look at Gabriel Biel's *Collectorium*. The following text represents the culmination of the scholastic development of the topic. Luther, whom we will discuss in part one, knew about Biel from his Erfurt studies. Biel clearly sets out the problems that theology has had to grapple with ever since.

Biel's exposition reads as follows:

We take up an abridged version of the prologue, with which the doctor [William of Ockham] prefaces all his books. In this [prologue] he mainly discusses three questions regarding theology: the nature of theology, the unity of theology, and the object of theology. In the first question, he asks: What kind of knowledge *(notitia)* is theology? Is it academic, scientific knowledge *(scientia)* or is it knowledge of a different kind? In the second question, he inquires into the subject matter *(subiectum)* of theology, because the unity of an academic discipline or a science is based on the unity of its subject matter. The third question is predicated on the assumption that the object of theology, like the object of any other discipline or science, is either *praxis* or *speculatio,* either practice or theory. The question therefore is whether theology is practical or theoretical?[26]

Part One

Luther's Understanding of Theology

1. Sources and Task

Luther speaks in different writings and contexts of the object and enactment of "theology," of its "subject matter" *(subiectum)* and the manner in which we speak and live it *(modus loquendi* and *vivendi)*. The disputations, especially the early ones like the *Heidelberg Disputation* (1518), and the late ones like the *Disputation on John 1:14* (1539), are not the only places where Luther makes programmatic statements. We find statements of this kind also in the prefaces: his Latin introduction to *The Freedom of a Christian* (1520) offers an exemplary treatment of the relation between the experience of faith and theological writing. With its key theological terms — faith, virtue, experience, trial, and spiritual attack *(fides, virtus, experimentum, tribulatio, tentatio)* — it is an excellent introduction to Luther's theology in general. He speaks even more programmatically about the study of theology, in the sense of the interpretation of scripture, in the preface to the first volume of the *Wittenberg Edition* of his *German Writings* (1539). Luther finds in Psalm 119 "three rules" for "the proper way to study theology": prayer, meditation, and spiritual attack *(oratio, meditatio, tentatio)*. This is what it means to live life theologically and to live as a Christian in the church catholic: to enter into the word of Holy Scripture, driven by spiritual attack *(Anfechtung)*, to pray for illumination, and to let scripture interpret us. In his 1532 interpretation of Psalm 51, which is central to his understanding of theology, it is above all the Hebrew word "to know" *(yada)* that leads Luther to the distinctive theological insight that when scripture speaks of divine and human knowledge *(cognitio dei et hominis)*, it means the knowledge of the person who sins and of the God who justifies the sinner. The relation between the sinful human and the God who justifies is the only subject matter *(subiectum)*, the object, of theology.

A useful way of ordering these different statements is to ask how Luther took up the questions that came down to him from the university tradition. If our account of his understanding of theology begins here, it will not be abstract or timeless. At the same time, this approach sheds light on several terms that Luther found useful for his understanding of theology, terms that would otherwise remain unintelligible, such as "knowledge" *(scientia)*, "subject matter" *(subiectum)*, "theory" *(speculatio)*, and "practice" *(praxis)*. All these terms appear in his programmatic statements.

Luther does not take up the questions of the tradition simply to endorse them but claims the freedom to contradict them in the name of what made him "a Christian."[1] The crucial thing to emerge from his treatment of the tradition is not his "scholastic" *academic theology* but his "monastic" *liturgical theology,* not his skill at a university debate but his pastoral use of scripture coupled with his cultivation of the affects (which include the emotions, the senses, the desires, and the imagination). This involves meditating on the text, listening to the word. This is an art that is also central to Luther's catechetical systematics. The fact that liturgical theology is foundational does not mean that academic theology is excluded. If theology is understood as meditation on the text, then from an educational point of view, Luther saw it as an essential part of the arts curriculum (trivium) which, together with rhetoric and dialectics (logic and philosophy in the wider sense), focuses on grammar. That is what Luther understands as the academic, "scientific" character of theology.

2. Luther's Response to the Philosophy of Science Tradition

We can reconstruct Luther's answer to the three main questions[2] from the philosophy of science tradition that came to him via Biel.

2.1. The Subject Matter of Theology: The God Who Justifies and the Sinful Human

The second of the three questions ("concerning the subject matter of theology") focuses on what establishes the unity of an academic discipline. We would expect this unity to flow from the unity of its "subject matter." But what then for Luther is the unifying object of theology? What integrates all its philological, historical, philosophical, rhetorical, and pedagogical elements and makes them a unity?

It is no accident that we find Luther's answer to Biel's second question regarding the "subject matter of theology" in his interpretation of Psalm 51, which was traditionally numbered among the penitential psalms.[3] This psalm has particular significance for Luther's theology. The words of the psalm compel us to speak of sin and grace.[4] Theology can have no other theme.[5] But even sin and grace can be spoken of philosophically, meaning "metaphysically," "morally," or "historically."[6] The "rule" Luther uses to judge the genuineness of theology is this: "By divine promises and laws, not by human rules, 'so that you are justified in your words'" (v. 4).[7] To speak theologically of sin and grace means to speak of God's promise *(promissio)* and of his law *(lex),* of the accusing and killing law *(Gesetz)* and the comforting and life-giving gospel *(Evangelium).*

This psalm goes beyond the story of David as the prime example of a sinful person *(homo peccator)* who experiences the God who justifies *(deus iustificans).* It speaks "of the whole of sin and its root,"[8] in all its radicalness and universality.[9] The universality applies to humankind in its totality, but also to the breadth and depth of an individual's existence.[10] The fact that we are sinners, or more precisely, the confession of our sins — Luther distinguishes between sinners who feel their sins *(peccator sensatus)* and those who are unaware of their sins *(peccator insensatus)*[11] — makes us aware of our individuality before God. Otherwise, we would only be members of the general category of "humans," not individuals. The issue at stake here is the principle of individuation *(principium individuationis).* But this is not some objective and timeless "principle." Rather, it has its root in the confession of sins, which is deeply affective (emotional) and has its own particular context *(Sitz im Leben),* as we see from Psalm 51:4: "Against you, you only, have I sinned" *(Tibi soli peccavi).*

Here we see the anthropological depth of the object of theology and at the same time catch a glimpse of the root of a theological anthropology.

This depth is disclosed and given shape in a particular medium, by the word: "in your words" *(in sermonibus tuis)* (v. 4). It is a particular use of words and language that makes the subject of theology genuine theology. God and humans are connected in the word: in the word of the confession of sins and in the word of forgiveness. Luther's definition is framed in the third person: "The subject of theology is the sinful and lost human being and the justifying or saving God."[12] However, this definition is derivative. It can easily be traced back to sentences in the first and second person, sentences of address and response. These original sentences, which form the irreducible basis of all dogmatic statements, are sentences of divine address and human response, sentences of prayer as well as sentences of confession and doxology in which God is glorified, as in the judgment doxology of Psalm 51:4: "Against you, you only, have I sinned, and done what is evil in your sight, so that you are justified in your words and blameless when you [God!] are judged [by me]."[13]

This is how we speak when we pray: We confess that God is right; we ascribe righteousness to him, we attribute it to him. A concrete situation of prayer like this is the proper "context" *(Sitz im Leben)* in which God has a right to his attributes. The copula "and" *(et)* in Luther's definition of theology: *homo peccator et deus iustificans,* the sinful human *and* the God who justifies the sinner, therefore stands for the verbal exchange between God and humans. The sinful human and the God who justifies are connected through an exchange of words.

This communicative relationship between God and humans is by no means self-evident. The amazing thing is clear from the contrast: rather than speaking about the association between God and humans, Luther speaks of the dissociation or disconnection between them. God and humans are fatally separated. Yet in this separation, "the naked God is *there* with humans in their nakedness" *(nudus deus da cum nudo homine).*[14] However, the "naked God" *(nudus deus)* is God "in his absolute majesty" *(in sua absoluta maiestate),*[15] the "absolute God" *(Deus absolutus).*[16] But we can have nothing to "do" with that God, we cannot "handle" him, we cannot "deal" with him, we cannot "speak" to him, and we cannot believe in him. Yet this disconnection does not give us naked humans *(nudus homo)* any breathing space, for we experience the naked God *(nudus deus)* as our enemy. Thus the verbal exchange between sinful humans and the God who justifies begins as a contest *(certamen)*[17] to see who will be proved right. This kind of verbal exchange is no simple correlation between our knowledge of God and the knowledge we have of ourselves. To start with, we are not even sure who our opponent is. Is it God or the devil? Did Jacob in his struggle that night at the Jabbok wrestle with a demon or with Yahweh?[18] We only know for certain whether God or the devil is our opponent from the word and its implicit Christology.

The communicative relationship between God and humans that is salvific and not destructive is grounded in the word and takes the form of an exchange of words *(in sermonibus tuis)*. When Luther emphasizes that "Christ is present"[19] in this word, he is defining the mediation more precisely. Christology explicates who is connected, the basis of the connection, and the medium of this connection. To put it more precisely, it identifies who is active and who is passive, who comes and who is brought, who makes the connection and who is connected.[20] The three "offices" of Christ are nothing else than the three interrelated aspects of the one office of mediator *(munus triplex)*. The prophetic office especially is the means of mediation (the word), the priestly office shows us who is mediated (God and humans), and the royal office is the power of mediation:[21] Christ's victory over hell, death, and devil. The saving communicative relationship between God and humans is an exchange of words. This is no harmless self-evident correlation and correspondence, but the felicitous outcome of a life-and-death struggle that is not at all self-evident.

By the same token, the category of "relation," which is the only valid category to describe the salvific connection and union between God and mortals, is also not self-evident in a vague and general way. But there is no doubt that it applies here to this salvific connection. Since the important thing is what is essential for community, we cannot think in terms of "the category of substance, but only of the category of relation" ("[*non*] *in praedicamento substantiae, sed relationis*").[22] At this point, but only here, Luther opposes the Aristotelian tradition which had privileged the category of substance over that of relation. Here Luther also brings about a revolution in logic.[23] In view of the new creation, the new being, we can speak of a "relational ontology."[24] However, it is irresponsible, theologically, to generalize this, as Hegel and Feuerbach did, and as was customary in twentieth-century theology.

Advocates of relational theology find it offensive that Luther holds on to the idea that God's being is in itself *(per se)* regardless of his insistence on the sole validity of the category of relation in the context of soteriology. God is God in his substance, in his nature, and in his person. And God is God in relation, in us, by speaking to us and addressing us. He addresses us in the word of promise, so that we can answer him in faith. "May your name be hallowed. What is this? Answer: It is true that God's name is holy in itself [in the Latin version: *per se sanctum*], but we ask in this prayer that it may also become holy in and among us."[25] God's justification by us takes place in prayer. We justify God, not "in his nature"[26] but "in and among us"! When we confess that he is right, he is justified by us.[27] In "his nature," of course, we can neither justify nor condemn God. However, he permits both in his word. "It [God's word] is condemned by those who want to be self-righteous, and it is justified by sinners."[28]

The notes to Luther's 1531 *Lectures on Galatians* are testament to the same thing: God's justification by humans in faith and the condemnation and denial of God through unbelief. This comes out in the famous statement: "Faith is the creator of the Deity, not with respect to his person but only ourselves,"[29] "not with respect to God but only us."[30] God wants nothing else "than that I make God."[31] "It is the trust and faith of the heart alone that make both God and an idol."[32]

Luther says in the same passage of the *Large Catechism* that "faith and God" belong together.[33] This is to be understood precisely in the sense of the "and" in the formula: the God who justifies *and* the human who sins *(deus iustificans et homo peccator)*, which Luther uses in his definition of theology. In other words, we are to understand it in the sense of an exchange of words. Faith and God do not belong together because there is a general basic unity between them, outside the word. For the phrase "to make God" *(deum facere)* means to give him, to attribute to him *(at-tribuere)*[34] what is his. We can only speak of God's attributes in the context of a verbal exchange *(in sermonibus tuis)*.

Let us summarize. The story of Jacob's struggle at the Jabbok shows most clearly what happens when the God who justifies meets a sinful person. In this verbal exchange, which is a life-and-death struggle for mutual recognition, faith makes God *(facit deum)*. Faith is the creator of the Deity *(fides est creatrix divinitatis)*. Unbelief, however, makes itself an idolater. Of course, this is all in us, not in the nature of God. It is in this verbal exchange between the sinful human and the God who justifies, thus between God and faith, not in the projection of unbelief and its dependence on self-made idols, that Jesus Christ is present as truly God and truly human. It is Christ's office and work to put an end to the conflict between the naked God *(deus nudus)* and sinful humans *(homo nudus)* and to overcome such a fatal confrontation so that God can speak to sinners and mercifully rescue them. He saves them from death and from being curved in on themselves, which is the origin of idolatry. Only because of this can we say that the word and faith are the subject matter and object of theology. "God does not deal [act] with us, nor has he ever dealt [acted] with us otherwise than through the word of promise. . . . We in turn cannot deal with God otherwise than through faith in his word of promise."[35]

2.2. Contemplation or Action? The Receptive Life

Biel's third and last question, "whether theology is practical or theoretical" ("an theologia sit practica vel speculativa"),[36] best sheds light on Luther's concept of theology, because for him the answer to the question is bound up with his understanding of faith, which is fundamental to his concept of theology.

Following Ockham, Biel had assumed that "theology" could generally be regarded as *scientia* (knowledge) or a science, and so he had defined theology in a way that made it no different from any other science. He emphasized that in any science the important thing is the distinction between theory and practice *(speculatio* and *praxis)*, or to use synonymous terms, the distinction between contemplation and action *(theoria* and *praxis)*. This distinction goes back to Aristotle and must be strictly distinguished from the modern distinction between theory and practice, where practice is given preeminence over theory, and the value of theory is measured against practice. Furthermore, modernity does not make the distinction within practice, as Aristotle did, between practice and poiesis (production).

Aristotle puts the highest value on contemplation. The contemplative life makes for "perfect happiness."[37] Along with the distinction between the contemplative life and the active life, Aristotle makes a similar but not identical distinction between the intellectual virtues and the moral virtues *(virtutes intellectuales* and *virtutes morales).*[38]

In order to grasp Luther's understanding of theology, we need to appreciate that he has two reactions to the distinctions made by the tradition; some he accepts and others he rejects. When he says that "theology is practical *(practica),* not contemplative *(speculativa),"*[39] he is not signaling his agreement with the Aristotelian concept of practice. Rather, he is talking there about the way theology uses God's word, which comes down to a particular practice that corresponds to the three rules for the study of theology: prayer, meditation, and spiritual attack *(oratio, meditatio, tentatio).*

However, there is a point at which Luther is open to misunderstanding: when he uses the term "practical" to designate his own understanding of theology. At first glance, this would seem like a good term to use because it is the opposite of contemplation (theory), the traditional term used by the philosophy of science to describe theology. This is important because here he breaks out of the traditional Aristotelian binary scheme that distinguishes between theory and practice, on the one hand, and contemplation and action, on the other. He does this "so that we are not led astray by the *active life (vita activa)* with its works, or by the *contemplative life (vita contemplativa)* with its speculations."[40] He does not take up either of the Aristotelian alternatives: he does not make theology a part of action *(actio),* nor does he makes it a part of contemplation *(contemplatio).*[41] Instead, Luther chooses a third option: He sees theology as an event and a path that is so different from anything else that it deserves to have its own name — so he calls it the "passive life" *(vita passiva),*[42] even though he is not as consistent as he might have been in replacing the adjective "practical."[43] Today the word "passive" is often misunderstood to mean inert. However, when Luther says that the Christian life is "passive" *(vita passiva)* he means that God is the active subject and that the Christian is the object of God's action. The Christian life therefore is *passive* in the sense that it *suffers,* it *undergoes* God's work and so passively receives it.

In any case, with Luther's understanding of theology and faith as practice, the Aristotelian understanding of practice along with its correlation of theory and practice is toppled. In Luther's understanding of theology, faith is neither identified with, nor subordinated to, the active life *(vita activa)*, nor to the contemplative life, nor even to that subtle dialectical correlation of the two forms of life, such as Meister Eckhart resorted to in his famous sermon on Mary and Martha (Luke 10:38-42) in order to avoid giving one preeminence over the other.[44] Luther, on the other hand, sees theology and faith as having their own unique life: the receptive life *(vita passiva)*. Theory and practice are no longer related to each other in a binary scheme but both are now related to faith as a third element, and it is faith that determines whether they are true or not.

This revolutionary new definition emerged from Luther's critical engagement with a particular form of mysticism that he came to know and appreciate from the sermons of Tauler.[45]

The phrase the "receptive life" *(vita passiva)* typically emerges also in connection with the reference to Tauler[46] in an excursus in *Operationes in Psalmos* (1519-21). Luther also published this separately under the title *De spe et passionibus* (On hope and suffering).[47]

The excursus contains the much-cited phrase: "The cross alone is our theology" *(CRUX sola est nostra theologia)* (WA 5:176, 32f.). However, this phrase is seldom understood in its context. The excursus is proximate to the *Heidelberg Disputation* in which Luther, on the threshold of his Reformation theology, speaks of the "theologian of the cross" *(Theologus crucis)* and the "theologian of glory" *(Theologus gloriae)* (Thesis 21; LW 31:40; WA 1:354, 21f.). The phrase "theology of the cross" *(theologia crucis)* occurs in several parallel texts: LW 31:225; WA 1:613, 22 (Explanations of the Ninety-Five Theses); WA 1:290, 39f. (Asterisci); WA 57/III:79, 20 (on Heb. 11:20; see the note in the apparatus to line 20). If faith is defined as a "virtue" *(virtus)* as in the scholastic tradition (see Luther's similar polemic against Peter Lombard: WA 5:165, 31), this obscures the important point that God is the active subject and that humans simply "suffer" *(passio)* or undergo his work.

The crucial thing about the receptive life *(vita passiva)* is that it is connected with a particular experience: an experience that I do not primarily produce but suffer or undergo: "It is by living — no, not living, but by dying and giving ourselves up to hell that we become theologians, not by understanding, reading, and speculating."[48]

In a few passages Luther understands speculation or contemplation *positively*, though admittedly only in polemical contexts ("That is truly the speculative life"; LW 26:287; WA 40/I:447, 2): ". . . illa apprehensio Christi per fidem proprie est Speculativa vita (de qua Sophistae multa nugantur; sed quid dicant, nesciunt) . . ."; WA 40/I:447, 15-28. See WA 40/III:152, 10-153, 3; WA TR 1:72, 16-73, 12 (no. 153), esp. 72, 32 ("That is truly . . . speculative theology"); LW 54:22 (no. 153); WA TR 1:302, 30-303, 3 (no. 644); LW 54:112 (no. 644); WABR 1:329, 50-2 (Letter to Spalatin, Feb. 12, 1519).

What does the passive/receptive life *(vita passiva)* or the passive righteousness *(iustitia passiva)* mean, systematically, for faith and theology? The righteousness of faith[49] is passive in the sense that "we let God work in us by himself and we with all our powers do nothing of our own."[50] "Faith, however, is a divine work in us which changes us and makes us to be born of God, John 1[:12-13]. It kills the old Adam and makes us altogether different, in heart and spirit and mind and powers" (cf. Deut. 6:5).[51] Faith then is entirely God's work and not a human achievement. We can only "suffer" it. Christian righteousness, which is passive, is entirely opposite to works-righteousness. We can only receive it. We do not work but we let another work in us, namely, God. Christian righteousness is not understood by the world.[52] It is hidden from people who are trapped in themselves and want to boast of their own achievements. It is hidden from those who not only want to make something of themselves but who want to be self-made people.

The passive/receptive life *(vita passiva)* is faith. This is neither knowledge nor action. That also holds for the passive righteousness *(iustitia passiva)* which is identical to it. Luther broke out of the Aristotelian binary scheme, which is reflected in Biel's third question, and replaced it with a ternary scheme. The decisive thing here is a completely new understanding of faith, which Luther identifies with theology. In contrast to that, we today automatically make a distinction between faith and theology, as if theology were only a reflection on faith, something cognitive. Luther, on the other hand, sees them as identical. Theology understood as faith is not an intellectual virtue, nor is it a moral virtue. In fact, it is not a virtue at all, not even a disposition. Faith is given to us as God's work alone. It "comes" to us, as Paul says in Galatians 3:23 and 25, almost as if it were an object. Faith is God's gift to me. I experience faith by letting him work it in me. The experience of faith is painful. When Luther speaks of the death of the old Adam, this is not mere picture language. "Those people who have not yet been destroyed and reduced to nothing through cross and suffering, take credit for works and wisdom and do not give credit to God. . . . But those people who have emptied themselves through suffering no longer do works themselves but know that God works and does all things in them. . . . It is this that Christ says in John 3[:7], 'You must be born anew.' To be born anew means that you must first die. . . ."[53] In a certain respect, we can understand why the pietists later insisted on a theology of the regenerate *(theologia regenitorum)* and appealed to Luther for support.[54]

The passive righteousness of faith *(iustitia passiva)*, which can only be received, comes about when justifying thinking (metaphysics) and justifying doing (morality), together with the anticipated unity of both, are all radically destroyed. We should not equate faith with knowing or doing. In other words, it is not the same thing as metaphysics or morality. We will now explicate this thesis by looking first at the limits of morality and then at the limits of metaphysics.

We begin with *the limits of morality*. Faith understood as the receptive life kills the deep-seated need in all of us to prove our right to exist. But the old self, the old Adam, wants to do more than merely exist. It wants to secure recognition for itself through what it can and does perform and achieve. This will to achieve and thus to secure recognition for ourselves has become part of our nature, our second, evil nature. For it "is very unwilling to die and to be passive, and it is a bitter day of rest for nature to cease from its own works and be dead."[55] However, this nature, in which we want to justify ourselves and make ourselves secure through our thinking and doing, through metaphysics and morality, and in which we want to be the captains of our destiny, so to speak — this nature dies.

In view of the commonly held suspicion that Lutheran theology promotes a form of quietism, we need to point out that the reverse side of this death of the old Adam is supreme liveliness and activity. This is no paradox. If I finally pin myself down and judge myself on the basis of what I have done and do, and if I let myself be pinned down by others, by their looks, their words, and their behavior, I am no longer free. But if I am liberated from this captivity, from my own absolute claims and from those of others, then this gift of freedom brings with it a sense of perspective that enables me to distinguish between person and work. This means freedom for human action, which is always finite action, for the illusion that my works can be perfect and the desire to be free of limits must die.

Luther therefore can extol the supreme vitality of faith, that work of God within us that kills the old Adam. "What a living, busy, active, mighty thing, this faith is. It is impossible for it not to be always doing good works. It does not ask whether good works are to be done, but before the question is asked, it has already done them, and is constantly doing them."[56]

Now we examine the *limits of metaphysics*. Justifying thinking more than anything else is the attempt to mediate and reconcile all things. Its driving compulsion is to prove that everything individual and particular has the general as its basis. Its thinking is based on principles. Since this kind of justifying thinking is associated with justifying action, it is ideological and blind to reality.

If it is true that Christians, together with their thinking, are determined by Baptism, that they are actually baptized into the death of Christ, then all justifying thinking is put to death through the passive righteousness of faith. Those who through cross and suffering are reborn as Christians and theologians, theologians of the cross, call things by their right names. "A theology of glory calls evil good and good evil. A theology of the cross calls the thing what it actually is."[57] The natural view of God, which we construct by our own powers, is one in which we try to fit everything into the concept of the One, the True, the Good, and the Beautiful. For the theologian of the cross, however, this view of God has been shattered by painful disillusionment. Therefore, the death of the old nature means the end of the illusion that there is a totality of meaning as well as the end of all attempts to anticipate it by postulating it hypothetically. The theologian of the cross recognizes in the deep-seated need for justifying thinking the "thoughts and strivings of the human heart," which is radically evil. Taking a lead from Genesis 6:5 and 8:21, Luther "defines" the human being as a "rational being with a fabricating heart" *(animal rationale, habens cor fingens)*.[58] As such it is continually producing images in the mind, in other words, idols.[59] Concepts of metaphysics in particular can become idols. Even a theological doctrine of the divine attributes produces idols if in speaking of God's attributes – his power, wisdom, goodness, and righteousness – it bypasses the cross of Jesus Christ. According to Luther's explanation of Thesis 20 of the *Heidelberg Disputation*, it is "not enough nor is it of any use to recognize God in his glory and majesty, unless we also recognize him in the humility and shame of his cross."[60]

Christian theology does not begin with the highest good, as all other religions do, but with the lowest depths, with the womb of Mary and Jesus' death on the cross. "The glory of our God is precisely that for our sakes he comes down to the very depths, into human flesh, into the bread, into our mouth, and into our heart."[61]

This is a profound insight of the Christian faith: we cannot speak of God's power without at the same time speaking of his weakness on the cross. However, Hegel turned this into a philosophical principle so that it ended up as a natural theology of the cross. If Luther opposed the theology of glory in his day, it is even more imperative for us today to fight against an attempt to use the cross as a principle or method for determining knowledge and reality. In other words, we are called to fight against the attempt to turn the gospel into a theory.

Luther has clearly seen that those people who regard the gospel as a theory, "a human figment and idea,"[62] are forced to demand that it also be put into practice. The scheme of theory and practice leads them into the error of saying: "Faith is not enough; we must also do works."[63] In other words, they think that sanctification must be added to justification as a second act, as the human response to God's word. Luther saw the danger of allowing the word, which establishes faith, to be turned into a theory or idea, for once that happens there is no way of escaping the demand that this idea be realized in practice. The turning of faith into a theory has as its analogue the reduction of life to a set of moral or ethical principles. In summary, when faith and the faith-creating word are reduced to a theory or idea, this will inevitably lead to the demand that the theory or idea be put into practice.

We note in this criticism that the receptive life *(vita passiva)* does not put knowing and doing as such to death, but only that knowing and doing which is aimed at self-justification. Since this limitless and self-destructive knowing and doing is drowned in Baptism, it means that knowing and doing for the Christian is something human and therefore truly finite. It no longer attempts to claim for itself absoluteness.

Faith is not a theory, nor is it the practice of self-realization or self-fulfillment, but it is passive righteousness. In other words, faith is God's work in us, which we experience by letting God work this faith in us. We do this by dying to justifying thinking and acting. This does not mean that faith is unthinking and inactive. On the contrary, it renews both thinking and acting.

2.3. Science or Wisdom? The Philosophy of Science and the Concept of God

When it comes to the question, what kind of knowledge is theology *(qualis notitia sit theologia)*,[64] Luther opts for a view of theology that sees it as being more wisdom *(sapientia)* than science *(scientia)*. This is consistent with the view of the early Luther who said that theology is "experiential wisdom" *(sapientia experimentalis)*, a view he continued to hold.[65] Wisdom does not exclude science but includes it. Wisdom takes account of the connection between science and the pre-scientific life-world. Wisdom is a path that unites theory and practice and grounds both in a third thing, an experiential life *(vita experimentalis)*, understood in the sense of a receptive life *(vita passiva)*. Since Aristotle, science operates with necessary principles *(principia)* and ultimately a single principle *(principium)*. According to the Aristotelian taxonomy of science, rational theology or theologic is the highest science.[66] This theologic science is embedded in the philosophical concept of God. Wisdom, on the other hand, has to do with experience, understood in a non-Aristotelian sense. But experience is incomplete, without being vague and indefinite *(vage)*.[67] If wisdom *(sapientia)* encompasses science *(scientia)*, science cannot become an end in itself, it cannot turn itself into a religion or make absolute claims for itself, but it must take its bearings from the pre-scientific life-world and be informed by it.

Aristotle had done away with the difference between science and wisdom. By making wisdom the highest form of science, he reconciles philosophy and theology. That means that anything historical or empirical or any type of experience is all excluded from the concept of theology. Theology in the sense of "theologic" is pure rational theology. Therefore, it is the highest science, the science of principles, or better, the science of a single principle, the principle of the divine, which moves all things but is itself unmoved and does not suffer or change.

If the pinnacle of Aristotle's taxonomy of science is the doctrine of God, the apex of this pinnacle is the absolute rule of reason: "The things that are *(ta onta)* do not want to be ruled badly. 'The rule of many is not good; let one be the ruler!'"[68]

Luther does not agree with this sole or absolute rule of reason, nor does William of Ockham whose philosophy of science Luther had become acquainted with through his Erfurt teacher and his study of Biel's *Collectorium*, especially the Prologue, which deals with the questions of the philosophy of science. Ockham is skeptical of the Aristotelian idea that science should rule supreme. His remark at the end of book 12 of Aristotle's *Metaphysics*, that there is not just one king but many kings, can no doubt be understood as a counter-metaphor.[69]

With the use of this instructive image, Ockham clearly adopted a position contrary to Aristotelian philosophy, at least insofar as the latter presupposes an ultimate unity. Ockham's position had a lasting impact on the modern consciousness, for in modernity philosophy and theology, science and church have gone their separate ways.[70] If the unity of truth is in doubt, should we be speaking of a double truth?[71]

Thomas Aquinas also cannot unreservedly agree with Aristotle in acclaiming the absolute rule of reason. But he still likes to speak of the unity of science in which there is room for the principles known by the natural light of reason as well as the principles known by the grace-given light of the knowledge of God and of the blessed *(scientia Dei et beatorum)*, without these principles being in conflict. In comparison to Luther, it is significant that Thomas, in spite of all his distinctions[72] and his cautious definition of sacred theology *(sacra doctrina)* as a subordinate science,[73] emphasizes its contemplative character[74] and the certainty of its principles.[75] Even if he has in mind the historical aspect of theological existence,[76] for him theology as a whole is a science that operates with a timeless principle. In other words, the knowledge of God is not understood within a temporal framework but is seen as something lying outside of time altogether.

Luther is different. He is aware of the sheer temporality of our knowledge of God, indeed of God himself. Therefore, he does not regard theology as a science, a study of principles, but as a study of history and experience. To Aristotelian ears, on the other hand, the term "experiential wisdom" *(sapientia experimentalis)*[77] is a contradiction in terms. According to Aristotle, nothing historical or empirical or experiential can be the object or even the ground of science. Luther, on the other hand, maintains that "theology is infinite wisdom because it can never be fully learned."[78]

This statement and its context[79] give us a remarkable insight into the meaning of theology understood as experience and wisdom. First we hear and learn this wisdom, then we no longer want to hear it and so we forget it. But then the pressures of life, with its trials, afflictions, and spiritual attack, make us learn it again in sorrow and despair. Here theology is understood as open history, almost as endless history. Time that is lived and experienced is constitutive for theology — not time as such, but qualified time, time that is either wasted or filled. Here we mean not only time in the sense of a "moment," of an unextended punctiliar event in the present, but also time in the memory of the past and time still to come in the future which is created by God's promise and can be heard already here and now.

For Aristotle and the tradition that follows him, the things I hear and learn and thus experience or fail to experience do not lead to science.[80] Rather, everything contingent, all that I happen to hear and learn, the people I meet or do not meet, all empirical knowledge *(notitia)* and experience must be judged by science, but none of it can be science *(scientia)* itself. However, Luther, as an Old Testament scholar, blows this concept of science apart and sees theology as a "science" of history and experience in which the category of passivity/receptivity *(passio)* is more important than that of action *(actio)*.[81] This means that for Luther an apocalyptic understanding of history, time, and existence is central. He has in mind an experience in which I may be tested, examined and subjected to trial and spiritual attack. Yet I am not the primary "cause" of this experience but I "suffer" it in the sense that I undergo it. I cannot master it, either through action or contemplation. Therefore, it lies outside the distinction between the intellectual and the moral virtues.

The revolutionary change to Aristotle's view of science and reality that we see in Luther's view of faith and theology comes out clearly in his understanding of the verb "to know" *(cognoscere)* in his interpretation of Psalm 51:3 (1532), which decisively influences his definition of the subject matter of theology *(subiectum theologiae)*.[82] The "knowledge" of sin and grace is not something purely cognitive but sensory *(sensitiv)*. It is dependent on sense perception and experience.[83] Whatever we encounter that is empirical, resistible, and contingent is "felt." However, for the Aristotelian tradition, scientific knowledge was by definition not a matter of experience, nor was it empirical. Rather, science — and remember that science had theology, indeed rational theology *(theologia rationalis)* at its pinnacle — had to do with what was timeless, eternal, and unchangeable. In a word, it had to do with principles. For Luther, on the other hand, "to know" *(cognoscere)* means "to feel through experience" *(sentire experientia)*.[84] This understanding of "knowing" as "feeling through experience" joins two things together that could never be joined together in the traditional view of science. Luther takes the historical character of the Bible seriously in a new way. It was not so much Luther's understanding of the philosophy of science, which we find in William of Ockham, that blew the Aristotelian view of science and reality apart. Rather, the *coup de grace* was delivered by Luther's exegetical work, such as the discovery of the meaning of the Hebrew verb "to know."[85] This was the result of an intensive study of the biblical text.

If Luther does not share the same basic assumption that is determinative for the Aristotelian view of science, the assumption that there is a separation (diastasis) between necessity and contingency, or between eternity and time, this is a consequence of an understanding of God that he learned from the Christian Bible. According to that understanding, history, time, change, and suffering are as much a part of God himself as they are of the world and human beings. However, it is precisely these things that, according to Plato's second principle of theology *(peri theologias),* should be excluded from any discourse about God.[86] Plato says that God is the highest and most perfect being, that he is supreme beauty and perfect happiness. He says that God is "the least liable to change or alteration by an external cause";[87] that he cannot "be changed by time and other influences." Indeed, it is "impossible that he should even want to change."[88]

These statements of Plato are repeated, if not always word for word then at least in a form that reproduces the substance of the argument, in book 12 of Aristotle's *Metaphysics,* and they have had enormous influence. Decisive for Aristotle is Plato's argument that it would amount to a diminution of being to become something other, something inferior or less than oneself, indeed even to see outside oneself: "It is better not to see a good many things than to see them."[89] The pure activity of God therefore consists in gazing at himself and thinking himself. He "thinks himself," "if he is the Supreme Being, in which case Aristotle's God is basically thought thinking thought."[90] Nothing else is thought except himself.

Luther makes a brief comment on Aristotle's God: "The Supreme Being sees [only] himself. If he were to see anything outside himself he would see the misery of the world. At this point Aristotle tacitly denies God."[91] The God of Aristotelian metaphysics sees in his perfection and single-mindedness only himself; he does not communicate with anyone and is totally self-absorbed. He does not love and therefore neither does he suffer. He is immune to time and change and is completely outside history. Luther counters: "If God were really like that, he would consider only himself and would not see the misery of the world outside him; but if he did worry about it, he would then be the most miserable being" *(ens miserrimum)*.[92]

Luther sharply criticizes what for Aristotle is the epitome and guarantor of human wisdom and all reality, calling it "the most miserable being." The God who is in eternal repose, who knows himself as the absolute truth,[93] and who does not make himself dependent on another, but who enjoys himself in eternal bliss — that God, Luther says, is "the most miserable being."[94]

Aristotle's concept of God, as formulated in book 12 of his *Metaphysics,* forms the keystone in the arch of his taxonomy of science.[95] "God" is what is immutable and (in a pure sense) real, the ground and source of all things, and that on which all things depend absolutely.

Aristotle attributes unchangeability and timelessness to God and in so doing follows Plato's second principle of theology for no other reason than to safeguard what is supposed to be valid according to Plato's first principle. What he says about God's unchangeability and timelessness informs what he says about God's perfection and unity, and about the one good ground of all reality, from which evil is naturally excluded. Evil is the one thing that we are forbidden to ascribe to God: "God is not to blame" *(theos anaitios; The Republic,* 617e). Therefore, the whole Platonic and Aristotelian doctrine of God and philosophy of science stand on the horizon of the problem of theodicy.[96]

Luther's "three rules" for the correct way to study theology: prayer, meditation, and spiritual attack *(oratio, meditatio, tentatio)* best show us why he defines theology as "wisdom," or, more precisely, as "experiential wisdom." This definition also shows that in Luther's thinking, liturgical "monastic" theology and academic "scholastic" theology are inextricably connected. The former, however, is constitutive, in that it provides the content of theology, while the latter is purely regulative in that it orders, analyzes, and reflects on its subject matter, making the necessary distinctions and connections.

3. The Three "Rules": *Oratio, Meditatio, Tentatio*

3.1. The Historical and Systematic Meaning of the Formula

"Luther devised a brief method of study consisting of prayer, meditation, and spiritual attack" *(compendiosam studiorum methodum Lutherus
formavit, quae constat oratione, meditatione, tentatione).* With these words,
Johann Albrecht Bengel recommends Luther's short formula for the
study of theology.[97] They were part of a valedictory speech he gave in
1741 when he left his teaching position in Denkendorf. He repeats this
formula in his proposal for the study of theology in 1742.[98] With it
Bengel stands in the tradition of Orthodox Lutheranism[99] as well as
Lutheran Pietism.[100]

The formula was able to unite Orthodoxy and Pietism. Even differences could be found and highlighted *within* this unity.[101] The common thread that united both was broken only when the scholarly side
of theology was seen as a matter of human skill and set in abstract opposition to this formula.[102] In extreme cases, the formula was used to
repudiate the need for skillfulness and scholarship and to justify a
claim to immediacy, which saw the work of thinking replaced by the
grace of prayer, and the intellectual effort of working with concepts replaced by immediate feelings and unmediated experience.[103]

Johann Salomo Semler observed such a use of the formula in the
Pietism of Herrnhut under the rubric of a "theology of the regenerate"
(theologia regenitorum).[104] He fought against it in his *Historical and Theological Explanation of the Old Saying: "Prayer, Meditation and Spiritual Attack
Make the Theologian"* (oratio, meditatio, tentatio faciunt theologum) which
was published at Halle in 1758. This was an extensive part of his book titled *A Guide to Theological Erudition* that was intended to help beginning
students of theology[105] so that "in these times . . . I may be able to keep
young minds from fanciful imagination, and from pious idleness and
laziness."[106] In his own way, Semler tried to highlight something that
was important for Luther: the connection and difference between the
"grace of the Spirit" *(gratia Spiritus)* and "knowledge of the liberal arts"
(bonarum artium cognitio),[107] between illumination, on the one hand,
and thinking, prayer, and work, on the other.[108] But he was singularly
unsuccessful.[109]

Luther's triadic formula is remarkable in the way that it could connect Lutheran Orthodoxy, Lutheran Pietism, and a theological enlightenment that, as we will see, also established itself on Lutheran soil. A formula that could connect these epochs in history and theology with the early church, particularly with the experiences and practices of monasticism, with its emphasis on liturgical spirituality, going right back to Athanasius,[110] surely deserves more than the scant attention it has received since the time of Semler.[111]

Despite some points of contact,[112] this formula represents a clear alternative to the program of "faith seeking understanding" *(fides quaerens intellectum)* that has dominated theology from Augustine through Anselm to Hegel (especially in his move against the pectoral theology of Friedrich August Tholuck)[113] and Karl Barth.[114] In contrast to the program of "faith seeking understanding," Luther's formula takes into account the historical nature of theological existence, and gives due recognition to the fundamental importance of temptation *(tentatio)*. If we understand it as Luther did, its openness makes it superior to Bultmann's idea of theology as a way of "understanding" *(Verstehen)*, which is unique to faith and related to it.[115] Luther's approach does not arbitrarily impose a general, *a priori* condition that makes possible the understanding of the gospel. Rather, it teaches us how meditation, and the use of the inexhaustible treasures of the Bible, can be a source of new experiences.[116]

The formula likewise offers a clear alternative to the view taken by Thomas Aquinas[117] and Wolfhart Pannenberg,[118] who see theology as a universal science "from the point of view of its relation to God" *(sub ratione dei)*. According to this view, theology is contemplation. Reference to a specific context *(Sitz im Leben)* is not essential to its propositions.

Any attempt to reach agreement on the nature of theology should begin with the triadic formula *oratio, meditatio, tentatio* because of its historical significance and ecumenical breadth. It not only encompasses the epochs of church history, but, as we will see, it also connects Christianity with Israel, at the crucial point, via the psalms. Furthermore, the examination of this formula is important since it shows that to frame the question of the understanding of theology in terms of the question of the relationship between the academic study of theology and the church is too narrow, although that question too must be asked. Most of all, the formula helps us recognize the critical dogmatic issues implicit in many questions that seem to be "purely" about method by exposing the anthropological, ecclesiological, and eschatological dimensions of the problems of the philosophy of science and epistemology.

We will see that the triad, because of its far-reaching significance, can shed light on all sorts of questions, such as the relationship between scripture and Spirit, word and church, time and history, experience and suffering. Nevertheless, it has its own intrinsic value.

It contains two clear negations: it excludes an understanding of theology that sees it exclusively or even predominantly as a theory as much as it excludes the view that sees it as a program of action. In short, in place of the binary scheme of theory and practice it supports a threefold scheme that besides knowledge and action takes account of faith, which establishes both and liberates them for a relative autonomy. The value of concentrating especially on the triadic formula *"oratio, meditatio, tentatio"* to answer the question — what is theology? — is evident from Semler's monograph. This offers a good starting point, especially for German-language theology, for appreciating the continuity and discontinuity of old and new Protestantism. But most importantly, Semler's book shows that the junction between them cannot be simply eliminated, as in Schleiermacher, by making certain clear distinctions, such as that between the academy and the church.[119]

We have to remember that, in the course of history, situations arise and problems become urgent that in Luther's day could still remain in the background. We cannot pursue the question, within the limits of this book, of whether Semler faced a new situation or not. In any case, he felt compelled to emphasize that the Holy Spirit does not replace the need for careful scholarly work, nor does the Spirit give us the knowledge we need while we sleep: "The Holy Spirit does not inspire us to understand books; we have to use our heads."[120] What does it mean when Semler in support of that statement appeals to Luther's insistence on the external word and to his ironclad thesis, that when God gives the Spirit, he does so only through that external word? We need to remember that Luther strongly emphasizes that none of his discoveries came without hard work.[121]

For Luther the public ministry of the word is indispensable when it comes to the external clarity of scripture *(claritas externa)*.[122] But that does not exclude the knowledge and art of philology. We would need to check whether at this point Semler is not correct in appealing to Luther. Every unbeliever, every unregenerate person, must be able to recognize and understand the meaning of the word, even if they do not let themselves be changed by it. But Luther seems to waver at this point.[123] His vacillation forces us to assume a twofold meaning of "understanding," in line with the distinction he makes in *The Bondage of the Will (De servo arbitrio).*[124]

It is instructive for our situation today to try to determine what exactly the common ground is between Luther and us. For Semler this is very important.[125]

3.2. The Place of the Formula

Luther provides the formula for the study of theology in his preface to the first volume of the Wittenberg edition of his German writings published in 1539. There he mentions "three rules," which "show you a correct way of studying theology. . . . They are *Oratio, Meditatio, Tentatio.*"[126] Luther expressly refers to Psalm 119. This is a very significant reference, as we will see later, and should not be overlooked,[127] for these rules can be learned from this psalm.[128]

We can speak of a center and two concentric circles: Psalm 119, the summary in the three terms and their interpretation (taken entirely from Psalm 119), and finally, the fate of Holy Scripture, which is explained more clearly in 1545.[129] In brief, we can sum up Luther's remarks as follows: a theologian is a person who is interpreted by Holy Scripture, who lets himself or herself be interpreted by it and who, having been interpreted by it, interprets it for other troubled and afflicted people.

For Luther, theology is the interpretation of scripture. The authority of scripture is established by the choice of viewpoints that Luther uses to speak about the proper way to study theology. He does not start with a concept of science that could be determined before considering the subject matter of theology and without it.[130] As we will see, it is true that Luther engages with traditional and contemporary understandings of science[131] and even becomes involved with questions of the philosophy of science in the narrower sense.[132] However, he does not capitulate to scholarly opinion but critically engages with questions of science and philosophy and tries to understand them by advancing contradictory arguments.

It is clear from the place where Luther condenses his whole understanding of theology into the three terms *oratio, meditatio, tentatio,* that his instruction about the correct method of studying theology[133] is not a capitulation to some preconceived notion of science, but is solely a matter of the authority of scripture. Just as theology is nothing but the interpretation of scripture, the understanding of theology is the same.[134] The authority of scripture therefore, understood as a concrete universal *(universale concretum)*, is from the start a historical *a priori*, an *a priori* which is contingently *a priori* and necessarily *a posteriori.*

First of all, we need to recount briefly the situation that gave rise to the preface.[135]

Luther was asked by his friends in Wittenberg, his house guests and his table companions, as well as by the people of Strasbourg, to agree to an edition of his collected writings.[136] But he resisted such plans as vigorously as they were put to him.

The preface is marked by this reluctance to publish his collected works.[137] It also comes out in his Table Talk.[138]

On March 29 [1538] the Strassburgers asked for permission to publish the collected works of Luther with a reliable index to the same.[139] Luther replied, "I'd like all my books to be destroyed so that only the sacred writings in the Bible would be diligently read. For one is referred from one book to another, as it happened in the ancient church, when one turned from a reading of the Bible to a reading of Eusebius, then of Jerome, then of Gregory, and finally of the scholastics and philosophers. This will happen to us too."[140]

In the same way, the preface focuses our attention solely on Holy Scripture and wants to divert our attention away from its interpreters, even from the books Luther wrote interpreting the scriptures,[141] "although it has been profitable and necessary that the writings of some church fathers and councils have remained, as witnesses and histories."[142]

Luther highly values historiography, but it does not simply serve as a general aid to memory, to prevent people from becoming like hapless mayflies, bereft of hope and experience. Rather, it serves a particular purpose. In his Table Talk, cited earlier, he says with regard to his writings: "I'd like them [my books] to be preserved for the sake of history, in order that [people] may observe the course of events and the conflict with the pope, who once seemed formidable but is now re-garded with disdain."[143] Luther is not driven by mere interest in autobi-ography. His interest in the history of his life and the history of the world is deeply connected with his interest in the course of God's word *(cursus euangelii)*, which is also the interest of the Acts of the Apostles.[144] He is interested in the history and experiences that Holy Scripture gives rise to. He is interested in the dramatic epic of the "divine Aeneid,"[145] that inexhaustible book of experiences.[146] He wrote this in his *Preface to the Catalog or Register of All Books and Writings of Luther* in 1533 about the "usefulness of learning from histories and stories, about how I fared, or rather, how the dear word of God fared, what it had to suffer from so many fierce enemies in the past fifteen years."[147]

This is the *cantus firmus* that we hear running through a series of prefaces, especially those to his own books. We can see in these pref-aces[148] a special kind of self-testimony, which is authoritative for the un-derstanding of Luther's theology. They are like reflections and refrac-tions of the divine Aeneid.[149] These prefaces, which we need to consider together with the related Table Talk,[150] give us a comprehensive view-point from which to appreciate the two justly famous prologues: the one to the first volume of the Wittenberg edition of the German writ-ings (1539), the other to the first volume of the Latin writings (1545), and, with them, Luther's approach to theology. The address to the reader, which concludes Luther's preface of 1545, is no conventional device, but is testament to the authoritative frame of reference within which we can view Luther's life, work, and also his understanding of theology:

> Pray for the growth of the word against Satan. For he is strong, evil, and furious as he gives vent to his last outburst of rage, for he knows that his time is short and that the kingdom of his pope is in danger. May God strengthen in us what he has accomplished, and perfect in us the work he has begun, to his glory. Amen.[151]

This is a characteristically "apocalyptic" view of history, in which one's life is inseparably connected with the course of God's word, marked as it is by opposition and rejection, and in which time is spanned by passionate complaint and fervent prayer for the coming of the Lord and his final judgment.

In this apocalyptic view of time and history, it would be pointless to look for a unity of speech and existence or for a pure condition that would make the experience of time, the world, the self, and God possible. Any question about transcendence, any claim to a theology of consciousness will either collapse in the face of the facts or it will have to twist them. It cannot accept the sort of experience to which Luther is testament. It simply has no language for it — it can only talk about a (re)interpretation that assumes the unity of Christian history.

Nevertheless, if we want to speak about one single history, then we have to be able to say that the history of the self-interpreting scriptures is the history of God. The open-endedness of Luther's experience, which is still purposeful in spite of its openness, comes from the inexhaustible richness of scripture that stands in marked contrast to his own poverty.[152] His experience therefore is neither blind nor empty. It is formed by praying the whole Psalter, which he calls "a mini Bible"[153] because it contains the Bible in a nutshell. However, Psalm 119 is especially important for him in shaping his experience. Luther repeats this psalm in his suffering and work, and in praying it he lives in the universal church, the community of saints.[154]

3.3. Psalm 119 as Matrix

If the study of theology has its place in the stories that tell "how I fared, or rather, how the dear word of God fared,"[155] and at the same time is located on the horizon of hope that looks forward to the victory of God's word over all opposition, then the question arises, How in this context, which is neither really intensive or extensive, are we to understand an individual like Luther and how he understands himself?

In Luther's eyes, the individuality of our own life's journey reflects the universality of the course of God's word.[156] He finds this connection between the individual and the universal prefigured in Holy Scripture, especially Psalm 119. Those who pray this psalm fully surrender their own destiny to the destiny of God's word. They see their relationship to God as nothing else than a relationship to his word.

In the psalm itself the author refers to the word of God[157] in a very individual way,[158] while Luther emphasizes its ecclesiological importance beginning with the actual use of the psalm, "which was to be sung and read daily in worship, with one psalm being read in each of [the four canonical hours of prayer]: Prime, Terce, Sext, and None."[159] But he goes much farther when he recognizes that the church is not only the one who prays during these hours of prayer, but as a creature of the word *(creatura verbi)*,[160] the church is also prayed for in this psalm. In other words, the church is the object in this psalm. For "the message of the whole psalm can be summed up in two parts: (1) that God would lead, teach, direct, and keep us in his way, commandments, and law; and (2) that he would protect us from human teaching and commands.[161]

Almost from the outset, Psalm 119 takes on fundamental significance for Luther's battle with the pope, who wants to prevent him from remaining with the word through which "I became a Christian":[162] the word of absolution. From the beginning of the Reformation, this psalm is seen as a prayer for the victory of God's word against its enemies. In fact, it is seen as a double prayer that was turned into a hymn verse in 1543:

> Lord, keep us steadfast in your word
> and curb the pope's and the Turk's sword. . . .[163]

In 1521 Luther claims Psalm 119 as the liberating (absolving) word of God against its enemy, the pope, by linking the treatise *On Confession: Whether the Pope Has Authority to Demand It*, with a translation of the psalm and a marginal note: "The one hundred and eighteenth psalm [Ps. 119], useful as a prayer that God's word might be a weapon against its great enemy, the pope and human teaching. . . ."[164]

In 1529, the year of the recess of the Diet of Speyer,[165] Luther comes out with a meditation (taking up his interpretation from 1521),[166] *Psalm 119: That God Would Preserve Us in His Word. . . . Also Psalm 83* ("Psalm 119: That God Would Preserve Us in His Word and Not Let Us Stop Praying. . . . Also Psalm 83: That God Would Save Us from All Our Enemies . . .").[167] The preface to Psalm 119 ("we should note") ends:

> . . . this psalm is from a person who stands for God and leads the cause of the divine word against Satan and his servants who, under the guise of holiness, fight against sound doctrine with violence, deception and all the tricks in the book. This is a universal, violent,

and immense battle that rages from the beginning of the world to its end.[168]

If we take such a text seriously, we avoid the misunderstanding of modern readers that prayer, meditation, and temptation are merely "individual," even "private" matters. Luther's last words are testament to the poverty and emptiness of our own existence in the face of the abundant riches of the "divine Aeneid,"[169] that inexhaustible book of experience. According to his last words, *oratio, meditatio,* and *tentatio* are about more than domestic and political life. They are about the course of God's word in the church and the world.[170] This occurs in the midst of "tumult,"[171] in the midst of a universal, violent, and immense battle, that rages from the beginning to the end of the world.[172]

This apocalyptic understanding of the world, time, and the word does not fit into any ready-made theory about theological existence, the church, or universal history. It is focused on the present in the middle of a horizon stretching "from the beginning to the end of the world." Its concentration on the present is not a form of mystical immediacy that focuses exclusively on the "moment," but it takes time into account both historically and critically. The "enemies" spoken of in Psalm 119, Psalm 83, and other psalms are the enemies of God's word, in particular the papacy as the Antichrist. The direction Luther is taking becomes crystal clear when he focuses his interpretation of the psalm to the point of making identifications that lie well beyond the literal sense of the text, but not against it. In Luther's 1529 interpretation of Psalm 119:50 he says: "We must suffer on account of the word,"[173] just as he says in his magisterial work *On the Councils and the Church* (1539) that the "cross," which we suffer because of the gospel, is a mark of the church.[174] Psalm 83:4 ("They say, 'Come, let us destroy them as a nation, that the name of Israel be remembered no more'") interprets the contemporary historical situation in which the faithful witness to the evangelical doctrine could also be linked with martyrdom: "When they have burned their bodies, they throw the ashes into the water. They hate them so much that they want to completely eradicate them so that the Lutheran cause (as they call it) will be forgotten."[175] Where the psalm speaks of "keeping" God's "statutes" (119:8: "My soul will keep your statutes"), Luther repeats it with a particular front in mind: "I keep them so that I can resist those who propagate false doctrine."[176] Luther also finds references to the "enemy" even where the psalm text does not mention it. In one place the positive expectation of salvation (119:166 "Lord, I wait for your salvation") is reflected in a polemical reference: "Help me finally to be free of them and let your word be victorious against them."[177] "The one thing I long for is that the power of your word would triumph against them."[178]

With no fewer than eight different terms for the word of God, Psalm 119 exhibits a conceptual diversity unmatched by any other biblical text. If we look over Luther's interpretations of this psalm, which focus on God's word in a wisdom-like way, it is striking how he multiplies the number of references to the "enemies" of God's word, which is already a strong theme in the psalm, and gives it a contemporary application by using it in his polemic against Rome and the spiritualists. In this particular context, "temptation" or "spiritual attack" *(Anfechtung)* becomes the specific focus for understanding "prayer" and "meditation," which are key themes of the psalm anyway.

3.4. The Three "Rules" for the Study of Theology

We will find "three rules" for the study of theology, "amply presented throughout the whole Psalm [119]. They are *Oratio, Meditatio, Tentatio.*"[179] The capital letters stand out. In addition, Luther obviously underscores the three terms by writing them in Latin in the middle of the German text of the preface.

After the title and subject are given, we have two sections repeated three times. The first in each case, in almost symmetrical fashion, describes one of the three rules. Then in each of the second sections, the respective rule is proved by reference to Psalm 119 and the general point made that the particular theological term is informed by the biblical text itself.

As we look now at the three terms, each of which describes a rule, the first thing to note is that these rules are not meant to be considered in isolation and only later reconnected. Rather, from the start they set out one single way of suffering and life, of listening and speaking, of thinking and writing. We are dealing with a single rule — a single dynamic movement, or a process that is by no means linear, in which we can distinguish three main factors, all of which are interconnected.

3.4.1. Oratio

Firstly, you should know that Holy Scripture is such a book as to make the wisdom of all other books foolishness, because it is the only book that teaches about eternal life. Therefore you should immediately despair of your reason and understanding. They will not gain you eternal life, but, on the contrary, your presumptuousness will cast you and others like you out of heaven (as happened to Lucifer) into the abyss of hell. But kneel down in your little room [Matt. 6:6] and pray to God with real humility and earnestness, that he through his dear Son may give you his Holy Spirit, who will enlighten you, lead you, and give you understanding.

Thus you see how David keeps praying in the above-mentioned Psalm, "Teach me, Lord, instruct me, lead me, show me," and many more words like these. Although he well knew and daily heard and read the text of Moses and other books besides, he still wants to lay hold of the real teacher of Scripture himself, so that he may not grasp it in a disordered way with his reason and become his own teacher. For such practice gives rise to factious spirits who allow themselves to nurture the delusion that Scripture is subject to them and can be easily grasped with their reason, as if they were *Markolf* or Aesop's Fables, for which no Holy Spirit and no prayers are needed.[180]

Luther begins with praise for the Bible. What distinguishes it from all other books is that it alone "teaches about eternal life." Other books that are clever and useful like Aesop's Fables,[181] or that are entertaining and amusing like the saga of Markolf in Bobertag's Book of Fools,[182] belong to this temporal life. The Holy Spirit is not needed to understand them. But none of us can understand the word about eternal life and salvation unless we are illuminated by the Holy Spirit.

The reason for that is sin, which accounts for the inexplicable perversion of our reason and senses. Humans "became futile in their thinking, and their foolish hearts were darkened. Although they claimed to be wise, they became fools" (Rom. 1:21f.) who "say in their heart, 'There is no God'" (Ps. 14:1).[183]

Holy Scripture liberates us from such "foolishness" and godlessness. Its work is to overcome this practical atheism, which does not need to be theoretical. The point then of Luther's praise of the Bible, perhaps surprisingly, is not to bolster its authority in a formal and general way, but to locate it materially and concretely in the justification of the ungodly. The way this happens is by no means self-evident. Luther identifies the book of Holy Scripture with the "word of the cross" (1 Cor. 1:18), or at least he speaks of its efficacy in these terms: It makes "foolish the wisdom of the world" (1 Cor. 1:20). You should "know that Holy Scripture is such a book as to make the wisdom of all other books foolishness." It does this by calling into question the "wisdom" of the "darkened heart" (Rom. 1:21) and by overcoming this darkness with its own clarity. In this way it turns practical godlessness into faith where faith knows and believes from experience that God is the creator and that I am his creature.[184]

This interpretation, together with its characteristic features, is the result of using the familiar passage from Luther's *Bondage of the Will* (1525) about the "internal clarity of Scripture" as an interpretative lens. Such a procedure is not only permitted but required by the biblical context provided by 1 Corinthians 1:20 and Romans 1:22. We now cite this passage where Luther speaks about the "internal" obscurity and clarity that must be distinguished from the "external" obscurity and clarity.

> There are two kinds of clarity in Scripture, just as there are also two kinds of obscurity: one external and pertaining to the ministry of the word, the other located in the understanding of the heart. If you speak of the internal clarity, no one understands one iota of what is in the Scriptures unless that person has the Spirit of God. All people have a darkened heart, so that even if they can recite everything in Scripture, and know how to quote it, yet they apprehend and truly understand nothing of it. They neither believe in God, nor that they themselves are creatures of God, nor anything else, as Psalm 14:1 says: "The fool has said in his heart, 'there is no god.'" For the [Holy] Spirit is required for the understanding of Scripture, both as a whole and in all its parts.[185]

With this carefully qualified definition of the internal clarity of scripture as its decisive operative principle, it is clear that Luther does not see "the wisdom of all other books as foolishness" as applying in every case. It is true only with regard to the illumination and enlightenment of human beings whose hearts have been radically darkened. In other words, it is true only with regard to the justification of the ungodly, their salvation and eternal life. However, this sharp judgment does not apply to books that serve our temporal life, nor does it apply to our rational perception of the world in general. In the same way, Luther distinguishes between "this" life and "eternal" life, especially in connection with the articulation of his understanding of theology, which he sets out paradigmatically in his interpretation of Psalm 51 (1532), and in the theses for the *Disputation Concerning Man* (1536): "Theology does not belong to this life but to the other life."[186] On the other hand, "anyone who wants to learn and become wise in secular government should read the heathen books and writings."[187]

If Luther assigns reason the first place with regard to "this" life and praises it as "something divine, so to speak" *(divinum quiddam)*,[188] this is in stark contrast to his judgment concerning reason's ability to know anything about "eternal" life and consequently about God and the self.[189] This judgment is completely negative. If what is at stake is our need to be aware of our godlessness and sin in the presence of God, who judges and justifies, and to have total confidence in him, then straightaway we have to "despair of our mind and understanding." For our mind and understanding will only lead us astray. They seek God where he cannot be grasped and do not take hold of him where he can be found.[190] The mistakes of our own mind and understanding, of blinded reason, which plays "blind man's buff"[191] with God, are of a qualitative kind. Luther's path to knowing God is neither the way of eminence *(via eminentiae)* nor the way of causality *(via causalitatis)*. Instead, he uses the way of negation *(via negationis)*, but even then he only uses it to emphasize the differences between blinded and enlightened reason. These differences call into question all talk about a quantitative view of sin: With "your mind and understanding" you will "not gain" eternal life. Those who do not despair of their own mind and understanding in regard to eternal life know nothing but an arrogant reaching up,[192] which is followed by a fall. "Such presumptuousness" will "cast you and others like you out of heaven (as happened with Lucifer) into the abyss of hell."

This dramatization of the natural search for God in the form of an (attempted) ascent and fall is found not only here. Luther repeats it so often that it becomes something like a *topos*.[193] It forcefully demonstrates the anti-speculative thrust of Luther's approach to theology. In his sermon on Genesis 28, preached in December 1520, Luther mocks the scholastic commentators of the first book of Peter Lombard's *Sentences* along with their speculations about the deepest mysteries of the Trinity. He uses an impressive, surrealist grotesque to ridicule them for their godlessness, yet he makes a serious theological point: "If they bore their way into heaven with their heads and look around they will find no one, because Christ lies in a crib and in a woman's lap. So let them fall back down again and break their necks!"[194] The speculative ascent is not only futile but, like speculating on the money market,[195] it is also uncertain and even dangerous. Speculation lacks the firm ground of experience. Therefore, even the learned and skillful disputants do not understand what they are discussing.[196] They deny God's condescension. They do not recognize the humble human form of his glory that becomes physical and that can be touched (1 John 1:1). "But the glory of our God is precisely that for our sakes he comes down to the very depths, into human flesh, into the bread, into our mouth, and into our heart." That is how Luther speaks in his important treatise on the Lord's Supper, *That These Words of Christ, 'This is my body,' etc., Still Stand Firm against the Fanatics* (1527).[197]

He uses the same argument against the fanatics and spiritualists that he uses against the students of Lombard's *Sentences* and the mystics, who stand in the tradition of Dionysius the Areopagite:[198] All have been bewitched by speculation, which for Luther means that they "deal only with ideas." They comb through their own thoughts like restless spirits, searching in their mind for what can only be found in physical things and sensory experience. Bread and wine are given in the Lord's Supper, "that our human nature can lay hold of God more certainly and fasten onto *one* sign by which it can grab hold of him, so that we do not go back and forth in endless speculation."[199] The divine creative power that has overcome the chaotic swirls of never-ending reflection is something physical, specific, and tangible, while all that is non-physical, ethereal, groundless, and intangible is an essential mark of the devil. Luther says that "all speculative theologians who deal only with ideas and have learned everything from books and nothing from experience, and who want to judge divine things on the basis of philosophy and human reason, are of the devil."[200]

Such harsh criticism of speculation (contemplation)[201] reveals an altogether different view of "reason" than that of the Platonic-Aristotelian-Augustinian-Anselmian tradition. The highest and best that this has to offer is the pure vision of the eternal. But in Luther's view, that is of the devil. For him, "pure" reason is unenlightened, blind reason. What it says about God, as we find it expressed paradigmatically in Book 12 of Aristotle's *Metaphysics,* is a tacit denial of God.[202] On the other hand, reason that is illuminated and clear-sighted does not find God up in the pure heights, far beyond all suffering, but down here in the murky depths, in the midst of suffering. He is "with us in the mud and works so hard that his skin smolders."[203]

If students of theology are aware of nothing but this condescension and humility of God, they will lose the desire to reach above and will start from below, humbly, not arrogantly. The interpretation of scripture should be consonant with its inspiration. The humility of its interpretation corresponds to the humility of its inspiration.[204] Therefore, the first rule is put most pointedly this way: "Kneel down in your little room [Matt. 6:6] and pray to God with real humility and earnestness, that he through his dear Son may give you his Holy Spirit, who will enlighten you, lead you, and give you understanding."

Anyone who prays like this does not pray like Anselm of Canterbury, "adopting the role of someone trying to raise his mind in contemplation of God."[205] As is evident from the text and its wider context,[206] the way that Luther understands prayer breaks out of the traditional subordination of prayer to contemplation as we have it in Anselm. The polemical tone here is impossible to miss. Prayer is not a mental act that could be compared with contemplation *(theoria)* or classified with it. As much as it frees reflection, it is not grounded in it. For it is not focused purely on the intelligible world (the world of ideas), which is the opposite of the sensory world (the world of the sense experience). It is focused rather on the triune God, on that event which is itself communicative and which gives the gift of communication to the world and to humans. This communicative event that is the Holy Trinity is essentially sensory and material, and as such it is a foe of that "metaphysical distinction" between matter and form, or between inner and outer.[207]

If theology had to focus on a pure form, it would be contemplation understood as prayer. But the devil uses contemplation to suck us into pure thought, which only confuses us and leads us astray. In fact, it leads us into the deadly abstract confrontation between a "naked God [. . .] and a naked human."[208] On the other hand, if theology concentrates on the triune God, who communicates himself in the physical word of Christ's promise[209] and "illuminates" us through the breaking of the bread (Luke 24:30f.), then theology, understood as prayer, is "practical," though not in the Aristotelian sense of the word, but in the sense of the "receptive life" *(vita passiva)*.[210]

The passive/receptive life *(vita passiva)* is not something that we could produce or think up ourselves. It encounters us; we can only "suffer" it, undergo it, and in this sense experience it. Only from outside ourselves and apart from all our abilities can we expect to find it, just as we "see that David always asks in the above-mentioned psalm: 'Teach me, LORD [Psalm 119:12, 26, 64, 66, 68, 108, 124, 135], instruct me [vv. 27, 34, 73, 125, 144, 169], lead me, show me [v. 33]' and many more words."

What do we pray for as we journey along the pathway of theology? What are we seeking when we pray it? Assuming that we already have faith, are we asking for insight, along the lines of Anselm's program of "faith seeking understanding"[211] *(fides quaerens intellectum)?*[212] Luther emphasizes that the author of the psalm (the pray-er) asks to be instructed and taught, even though he would have been well acquainted with the text of Moses and the other books, and would have heard and read them daily. Here we come to a difference in approach, which is crucial for Luther's understanding of theology. The theologian should try to understand through prayer what he or she already knows.

What the theologian does not yet know and is still seeking is not knowledge and insights into texts. Therefore, it is not a matter of discovering what a text is saying with the aid of grammar, rhetoric, and dialectics (logic and philosophy in the wider sense)[213] in order to be able to teach it in the school or academy. For that, of course, "knowledge of the liberal arts" *(bonarum artium cognitio)* is necessary, and Luther stresses its importance for the study of theology as much as the "grace of the Spirit" *(gratia Spiritus)*.[214] Although the work of the Holy Spirit, and therefore of the triune God to whom we pray, does not depend on human achievement and education, it does not exclude "knowledge of the liberal arts." The "grace of the Spirit" does not replace "knowledge of the liberal arts"; it sets it free. In this way, prayer and work, God's work and human work, find their proper relationship. Theology as a human project is relieved of the need to reach above, to go in search of timeless pure principles, the absolute first and last, and to be enraptured by it in a pure vision. Humans do not have to justify themselves by their knowledge any more than by their actions. Contemplation and action, theory and practice lose their claim to be the only two points of orientation. Prayer is no longer seen as being subordinate to them and as a result of this relativization they acquire a new character.

What gives them this new character is a certain kind of "experience," a "learning" that is different from the acquisition and transmission of "knowledge." Luther is amazed to find that what he knows does not come from learning: "I am surprised that I do not learn this knowledge."[215] What this learning receives and attains beyond what it knows is the certainty of what it knows, a certainty that cannot be given by knowledge and science.[216] This certainty is not within our power to create or possess. We can only seek it and wait for it from him alone through prayer. Therefore, "pray to God with real humility and earnestness, that he through his dear Son may give you his Holy Spirit, who will enlighten you, lead you, and give you understanding."

The study of theology therefore as a way of prayer is neither contemplation nor action, but from first to last it is all about waiting solely on God's work, which we can only "suffer" in the sense of "passively receive." This character of theology as the "receptive life" *(vita passiva)* will have to be considered further with the third rule, the *tentatio* and the special "experience" connected with it. Then we will also be able to explain further the distinction, noted above, that Luther makes between "knowledge" and "perception" in the sense of "experience." This perception in any case is no pure perception but is essentially sensory (the key word here for Luther is *sentire*).[217] We perceive through sensory experience, which includes the outer senses, the emotions, the imagination, the memory, and the desires. Luther's interpretation of Psalm 51 from 1532, which is important for the way he understands theology, focuses above all on the Hebrew word "to know" *(yada)*,[218] which enables him to formulate his distinctive understanding of divine and human "knowledge" *(cognitio dei et hominis)* as the knowledge of the sinful human and the God who justifies. The "subject matter" *(subiectum)* or object of theology therefore is the relationship between the person who sins and the God who justifies the sinner.[219]

Luther of course speaks explicitly about the "object" of theology (as here in the interpretation of Psalm 51) in his sermons and in his catechetical and academic instruction. In fact, he even makes it the topic of a disputation.[220] But this "object," this "subject matter," is at the same time always something enacted, an event, a path that needs time to traverse. It is not simply a known fact whose "objectivity" is such that it can be reproduced in the same way at will, by anyone in any place and at any time. We can describe this object as a path, as Luther does in the preface, which we take as our guide, but this path cannot be reduced to a method. Therefore, we today, after Descartes, cannot automatically follow Luther in talking about "rules." If we use the word "rule" with regard to the study of theology, we first have to consider the difference between Descartes and Luther, between the alleged timelessness[221] of a coercive regulation that must be followed, and the temporality (time-bound nature) of an invitation and initiation to a path. Otherwise theology would exist "only in thoughts" and would not be alive "in use and practice."[222]

If the temporal aspect of Luther's approach to theology, which we have stressed several times, is inextricably connected with things that are physical and sensory, and if it also has its own specific use of language, any reflection on his understanding of theology will have to bring this out. As we turn our attention to meditation, we will find nothing different to what we discovered with prayer. We will simply see the same thing, only from a different angle.

3.4.2. Meditatio

Secondly, you should meditate, that is, not only in your heart but also outwardly, by actually repeating and comparing oral speech and literal words of the book, reading and rereading them with diligent attention and reflection, so that you may see what the Holy Spirit means by them. And take care that you do not grow weary or think that you have done enough when you have read, heard, and spoken them once or twice, and that you then have complete understanding. You will never be a particularly good theologian if you do that, for you will be like untimely fruit which falls to the ground before it is half ripe.

Thus you see in this same Psalm how David constantly boasts

that he will talk, meditate, speak, sing, hear, read, by day and night and always about nothing except God's Word and commandments. For God will not give you his Spirit without the outward word; so take your cue from that. His command to write, preach, read, hear, sing, speak, etc., outwardly was not given in vain.[223]

With his second rule Luther takes what he had previously considered, especially in its inner aspect, and now turns it outwards. He feared that what he had said about prayer could be misunderstood in a spiritualistic and thus speculative way,[224] despite all his emphasis on the connection between inner illumination and scripture. Luther therefore points out in a sharp if not abrupt way that the book of Holy Scripture, as it is written, should not be used "in the heart alone but also outwardly." It is striking that he places the adverb "outwardly"[225] at the beginning and at the end of the passage quoted above.

The battle with the fanatics does not end for Luther in the 1520s. Spiritualism remains a constant threat to faith that lives by the external word *(verbum externum)* alone. Luther therefore emphasizes in the *Smalcald Articles* (1537), more vigorously than in the preface of 1539, that "like Münzer" there "are still many . . . today, who set themselves up as shrewd judges between the spirit and the letter"[226] and in this way make that "metaphysical distinction" between inner and outer.[227] Luther affirms that

enthusiasm clings to Adam and his children from the beginning to the end of the world — fed and spread among them as poison by the old dragon. It is the source, power, and might of all the heresies, even that of the papacy and of Mohammed. Therefore, we should and must insist that God does not want to deal with us human beings, except by means of his external word and sacrament. Everything that boasts of being from the Spirit apart from such a word and sacrament is of the devil.[228]

The indissoluble unity of inner and outer could not be emphasized more strongly. Luther also affirms in his first theological testament, the Confession (1528), that the Holy Spirit comes "inwardly" as well as "outwardly."[229] This unity of inner and outer, which goes to the heart of Luther's theology, applies also to his concept of theology, as we see now from the preface of 1539. However, since Luther uses the word "meditation" here in the sense of this unity, he is criticized by a Luther scholar who claims that "this makes the contours of meditation as a specific form of spiritual exercise unclear."[230]

It is true that Luther uses the word "meditation" in an unusual way compared with the dominant usage of the received tradition.[231] He actually gives it a meaning "which no longer fully agrees with the traditional idea of meditation."[232] In fact, Luther seems to all but reverse the normal meaning of the word, also in today's usage, when he focuses meditation on the external word.

This surprising change in accent is not the result of Luther following some chance idea. Rather, he is returning to an insight and practice of the early church that faded more and more with the passing of time, even though it was not completely forgotten.[233] We are talking here about the practice of reading and praying aloud and also — and this is even more important — the way in which this practice was connected with scripture, especially with a particular way of using the psalms.[234] Luther says that "with this book" the Holy Spirit "prepares for us the words and affects (which include the emotions, the senses, the desires, and the imagination) that we can use when we pray to the Father for those things he has taught us through other books to do and to imitate, in order that none of us misses out on what is necessary for our salvation."[235]

In Luther's opinion, the Psalter contains the whole Bible in a nutshell and can therefore be called "a mini Bible."[236] He lets it stipulate the "manner" *(modus)* and "practice" *(usus)*[237] of his relationship to God, the world, and himself, not only in general but also in particular, as in the development of his concept of meditation. It is no accident that Psalm 119, the very psalm that teaches Luther the true practice of meditation and its true understanding, is also the psalm that teaches him (as he says in his preface of 1539) how to understand theology as a whole.

Well over half of all the occurrences of the word "to meditate/meditation" in the Vulgate come from Psalm 119.[238] Luther in his interpretation of this psalm, which we talked about earlier,[239] followed the Hebrew equivalents[240] and the parallel verbs[241] in translating "to meditate" with "to interpret"[242] and then later with "to speak."[243] This was a brilliant move. Luther says: "The word 'to interpret'" in verse 15 (I will meditate = *meditabor*) "means to bring out and strike out that the meaning may be clear, just as those who gloss texts and comment on them do. Therefore, we should speak God's word and shell it, so to speak, by purging it of all human teaching so that those responsible for it may be put to shame."[244]

Luther swims against the tide of common opinion in not seeing the process of listening turned inwards but rather opened outwards. When we meditate, we do not listen to our inner selves, we do not turn inwards, but we go outside ourselves. Our inner beings live outside themselves in God's word alone. That is what establishes them. "The heart" is "essentially in the Word."[245] Meditation therefore cannot retreat behind the text of Holy Scripture, to become, as in Schleiermacher, a non-linguistic "immediate existential relationship"[246] that may be merely "expressed" or "represented" in the text and its language. From the outset, our relationship with God is enhypostatized in the word, so to speak, but we ourselves are anhypostatic. But if our essence is outside us, in God's word, then in meditation we do not turn inwards but we remain in the word that we have received and that forms our response: "My tongue will answer with your words . . ." (Ps. 119:172).[247] As we listen and meditate on the words that we have read and heard, we do not now take them back inside for our minds to consider alone *(sola ratione)*. Instead, we let those words permeate the heart and fill it to overflowing so that others might hear them as well. "I believe, therefore I speak" (Ps. 116:10; 2 Cor. 4:13).

Again, Luther discovers from Psalm 119 that the "enemies" are always the enemies of God's word.[248] Since the enemies in this psalm play such a major role, he learns that our words, which answer to God's word, will be opposed and contested. The psalm teaches him the essential connection between meditation and *tentatio*, the spiritual attack *(Anfechtung)* that the enemies of God's word will inflict on his people as they listen to his word, outwardly consider it, and publicly attest to it. At least since 1521, the conflict between "God's word" and "human traditions" belongs to Luther's understanding of meditation and so to his understanding of theology. "Therefore, we should speak God's word and shell it, so to speak, by purging it of all human teaching so that those responsible for it may be put to shame."[249]

In the light of Luther's decades-long engagement with Psalm 119, which we have seen from various examples, the opinion that the definition of meditation in the preface of 1539 is "unclear" is untenable.[250] It is not a matter of being forced to concede that, according to the preface of 1539, it "seems" (!) that "the sermon and doctrine constitute the essence of meditation."[251] Rather, Luther's understanding of meditation is determined entirely by the external word. Compared with relevant passages from Luther's earlier writings, the preface of 1539 offers no surprises. It does not blur the earlier profile of meditation, but brings it into even sharper focus.

We miss the point of Luther's understanding of theology as meditation if we buy into the modern distinction between "private" and "public," which first arose in the eighteenth century, and its related distinction between religion and theology,[252] and use that as an interpretative lens to set up an antithesis between "private reflection on Scripture" and the "public sermon and doctrine that are bound to the words of the gospel."[253] Luther's own specific understanding is lost when it is held that what is separated in this way is subsequently reunited on the basis that for him the public sermon has to "provide the content" for private reflection.[254] Such an interpretation cannot make clear that for Luther meditation is nothing but oral and public because its basis and goal, the *deus dicens*[255] (the God who speaks), is oral and public. Even meditation "in your little room"[256] is not private but that too takes place against an apocalyptic backdrop, in the sense that we participate in the universal "course of the gospel"[257] and in confrontation with its inner and outer enemies. In a word, we are involved in spiritual warfare *(Anfechtung)*.

Our neo-Protestant ways of thinking are so entrenched and come so naturally to mind that we find it hard to engage them critically enough to give us fresh access to Luther's way of thinking. Distinctions such as those between private and public, between individual subjective religion and scholarly "objective" theology, and between life and doctrine, only obstruct such access. In fact, they amount to fatal separations and do not stand up to theological scrutiny. This would gradually come out in a careful examination of Johann Semler,[258] the very theologian who promoted these separations in the first place, and who sought to test them against the formula "prayer, meditation, and attack make the theologian."

The purpose of this examination, which we can only hint at here, would be to focus attention on the crucial point in Luther, which is his understanding of the Holy Spirit. He does not expect the Spirit where there is evidence only of a purely internal word, as would be the case in the neo-Platonic tradition and its secularized counterpart, the modern concept of reason. Rather, his study of scripture, above all the Psalter and again Psalm 119 in particular, made him absolutely certain that "God will not give you his Spirit without the external Word; so take your cue from that. His command to write, preach, read, hear, sing, speak, etc., outwardly was not given in vain."[259]

Those who want to search for the Holy Spirit deep inside themselves, in a realm too deep for words to express, will find ghosts, not God. They will only be amusing themselves with baseless thoughts. As Luther said, "we all know from experience that our mind and thoughts are so uncertain, slippery and unstable, that if we want to ask a serious question or think about God without words and Scripture, we will be a hundred miles away from our first thoughts before we even know it."[260] We can all learn from such experience that

> the external word and way is useful and necessary to restrain our heart so that it does not wander but fixes its thoughts to the letter, just as our hand grabs a tree or a wall, so that we do not slide too far and go astray in our thinking. This is what our fanatics lack when they think that their high spiritual thoughts are a sign that they have made it and are too conceited to see that, without the word with its message about the way of the cross, their knowledge leads them astray. Therefore, be warned about such soaring thoughts and beware of dealing with God except through the oral word and prayer.

If Luther emphasizes in the preface, as he does in this sermon, that God "will not give you his Spirit without the external word," it does not mean that he is privileging outwardness as such. The decisive thing about his understanding of the Holy Spirit is that it excludes pure outwardness just as much as an exclusive inwardness. For this reason, he opposes Rome[261] as well as the fanatics.

Luther scholars almost immediately link Luther's insistence on the external word in his struggle against the fanatics with the preaching office *(Predigtamt)*. This is correct if this office is understood in terms of the fundamental depth and universal breadth attributed to it

by Article 5 of the Augsburg Confession.[262] But it is wrong if the external word is immediately and perhaps exclusively linked with the pastoral office *(Pfarramt)*, and thus with the special task of the person who is
"properly called" *(rite vocatus)* to it (AC 14). The temptation to collapse
the preaching office and the pastoral office into each other[263] lines up
exactly with the neo-Protestant distinctions we mentioned earlier and
is even conditioned by them. Luther, on the other hand, does not know
this temptation. This comes out with great clarity in his understanding of theology as meditation, which would be destroyed if it were divided into scientific theology, professional public religion, and silent
private piety.

Luther's idea of meditation is so broad that it cannot be limited
to the theological life and work of our professionally trained and
"properly called" pastors, who "should publicly teach, preach and administer the sacraments" in the church (AC 14), but it should include
every Christian,[264] indeed, every person.[265] If it is true that "we are creatures with whom God wants to speak eternally and immortally,"
"whether in wrath or in grace,"[266] then every person lives in meditation:
either in using God's word or, conversely, in misusing it in a wrong,
mistaken "meditation," which plays "blind man's buff" with God.[267]
There is no human being who does not belong to the order of the
church *(status ecclesiasticus)*, to the church as an order of creation.[268] But
since this order is thoroughly corrupted through human ingratitude
and sin, the law is needed to uncover sin and the gospel to overcome it.
As far as each of us is concerned, whatever is given to us must also be
appropriated by us. It must be "desired, picked up and brought to
us."[269] Meditation is the mode of this appropriation. However, it does
not happen primarily through our work of interpretation, as we apply
the text to ourselves and ourselves to the text, but it happens as the text
interprets us by drawing us into itself[270] as we appropriate it.

In view of this breadth and depth of meditation, focused as it is
on the external word *(verbum externum)*, we can see the importance of
Luther's definition of the external clarity of scripture *(claritas externa
scripturae)* that he gives in *The Bondage of the Will* and that itself may explain what he means by meditation in the preface of 1539. It is true that
the external clarity of scripture results also from a "knowledge of the
liberal arts,"[271] from the knowledge and the art of grammar, rhetoric,
and dialectics, from an education in philology and history, as well as

from hermeneutical reflection. Far from excluding such knowledge, Luther in other places even emphasizes its necessity.[272] However, here in *The Bondage of the Will* he does not focus on that but instead puts the emphasis on the instituted ministry of the external word *(externum verbum)*: "The external [clarity] is located in the ministry of the word."[273] Luther's following explanation shows that this office of the word does not refer only to the pastoral office but has a universal, even cosmic dimension embracing all people: "If you are speaking of the external clarity, nothing at all is left dark or doubtful, but everything contained in the Scriptures is brought out by the word into the clear light of day and explained to all the world."[274]

Luther's understanding of meditation has enormous breadth: it is universal and public in scope and is set within an apocalyptic time frame.[275] That is also the context for the operation of the external word *(verbum externum)* that stirs up tumult and encounters opposition,[276] but at the same time brings about that inner change and illumination of the darkened heart of people who are prisoners of themselves and therefore blind.[277] Two things belong together here. On the one hand, the experience of myself as a fool who denies God (Ps. 14:1), but who is taught by God himself, the Holy Spirit, about Christ, the One who is other and better. This is an individual experience because it makes me aware of myself as an individual in the presence of God. On the other hand, that individual experience must not be separated from the utterly universal and public nature of the same Spirit. Luther only distinguishes between the external and internal clarity in order to do equal justice to both sides of the same coin.

Since people cannot change inwardly by their "own understanding or strength,"[278] neither can they sustain that change and turn it into a disposition *(habitus)*. Even people who are enlightened by the Holy Spirit always remain totally dependent on him. They remain disciples of the teacher[279] who carries them through times of trial and spiritual attack *(Anfechtungen)*.[280] Such dependence comes out in lifelong learning, listening, and reading. This is why Luther expresses his indignation with the punctualists in the preface of 1539, as he also does in many Table Talk discourses. These are the people who think that they have to be enlightened and grasp the whole truth in a single moment, or have to understand a biblical passage after a single reading.[281] He warns: "Take care that you do not grow weary or think that you have done enough when you have read, heard, and spoken them once or twice, and that you then have complete understanding. You will never be a particularly good theologian if you do that, for you will be like untimely fruit which falls to the ground before it is half ripe."

It seems then that we have to pay particular attention to the element of *time* if we are to grasp what is distinctive in Luther's understanding of theology as meditation. The patience and constant expectation that Luther speaks of is not self-evident in the face of a Descartes, for whom only clear and certain knowledge in the timeless present is true.[282] Not even the turn in Luther's life and theology that came about with the Reformation happened "with one look" *(ad unum intuitum)*.[283] Rather, it came about while he was "meditating day and night" (see Ps. 1:2).[284] Luther's awareness of the role that time plays in his understanding of meditation comes out when he says that he identifies with "those who, as Augustine says of himself, made progress by writing and teaching. He is not one of those who went to the top from nothing, all at once, though in fact they are nothing. They have neither struggled nor suffered trials and spiritual attack, but they think that they can take one look at the Scriptures and exhaust their entire spirit."[285]

Luther naturally is not talking here about a pure search in the sense of Lessing's famous saying that the possession of truth, which belongs to the eternal God alone, makes a person lazy and indolent, while finite human beings will always be searching for it.[286] Luther of course finds truth. He is comforted in times of trial and spiritual attack *(Anfechtung)* by the promise of Christ's word. But he cannot hold on to that comfort, the "forgiveness of sins" as "life and salvation,"[287] by his own strength. He remains forever dependent on the power of God himself, the Holy Spirit, to be able to overcome once again every new spiritual attack.

Luther's rule of meditation gives us guidance as we go our pilgrim way in time, remembering that time is not in our hands[288] and that we cannot control it for ourselves[289] (Ps. 31:16). All in all, it is nothing else than a teaching about the Holy Spirit. But, as Luther insists, the Holy Spirit has bound himself to a specific form of language: to "the oral speech and the literal words of a book," to the sounds and letters of Holy Scripture. This freedom of the Holy Spirit to be bound and restricted does not exclude his immediate presence but reveals it. We see this when we compare the preface of 1539 with the tract *A Simple Way to Pray for a Good Friend*,[290] which is especially instructive for Luther's understanding of meditation.[291] While the former stressed externality and focuses on the movement from the inside to the outside, the latter has Luther pointing from the outside to the inside: The Spirit will "continue to instruct us in our hearts if they are in agreement with the word of God and cleared of alien concerns and thoughts."[292] If while this happens

> an abundance of good thoughts comes to us we should disregard the other prayers, make room for such thoughts, listen in silence, and under no circumstances obstruct them. The Holy Spirit himself is preaching here, and one word of his sermon is far better than a thousand of our prayers. Many times I have learned more from one prayer than I might have learned from much reading and speculation.[293]

This kind of internal testimony of the Holy Spirit *(testimonium spiritus sancti internum)* that we receive as we listen "in silence" (see 1 Kings 19:12) to the sermon of the Holy Spirit will not become the "Achilles heel of the Protestant system"[294] if it is "in agreement with the word of God."[295] Then it will not turn into continual unrestrained self-reflection as well as the "enthusiasm"[296] and pure anamnesis and construction of one's "own presumption."[297] For scripture is to be meditated on "not only in your heart but also outwardly," word by word, "as oral speech and literal words." It is to be worked at and rubbed like an herb,[298] read and reread, and what the Holy Spirit is saying here is to be deeply pondered.

3.4.3. Tentatio

Thirdly, there is *tentatio, Anfechtung*. This is the touchstone that teaches you not only to know and understand, but also to experience how right, how true, how sweet, how lovely, how mighty, how comforting God's Word is, wisdom beyond all wisdom.

Therefore, you see how David, in the Psalm mentioned, complains so often about all kinds of enemies, arrogant princes or tyrants, false spirits and factions that he has to put up with because he meditates, that is, because he is occupied with God's Word (as has been said) in all manner of ways. For as soon as God's Word takes root and grows in you, the devil will plague you and make a real doctor of you, and by his attacks will teach you to seek and love God's Word. I myself (if you will permit me, mere mouse-dirt, to be mingled with pepper) am deeply indebted to my papists that through the devil's raging they have beaten, oppressed, and distressed me so much. That is to say, they have made a fairly good theologian of me, which I would not have become otherwise. And I heartily grant them what they have won in return for making this of me, honor, victory, and triumph, for that's the way they wanted it.[299]

Anyone who meditates can expect to suffer. Luther once again also allows Psalm 119 to prescribe this experience. Therefore, in the light of this third rule, he expects students of theology also to see themselves in the role of the psalmist who "complains so often about all kinds of enemies . . . that he has to put up with because he meditates, that is, because he is occupied with God's Word (as has been said) in all manner of ways."

According to his understanding of meditation, Luther finds himself interpreted by the text of the psalm in his own situation. Going into the text rather than beyond it, he understands the "enemies" specifically as "arrogant princes or tyrants," or as "false spirits and factions." On the one hand, they are the fanatics *(Schwärmer)* and, on the other, the "papists" and those princes who formed an alliance with them, such as King Ferdinand and Duke George of Saxony[300] or Duke Henry of Braunschweig,[301] who tried to hinder the "course of the Gospel."[302] It is amazing that the battle against enemies such as *these* should explain the third rule, spiritual attack *(Anfechtung)*. The focus does not turn inwards, to the "interior darkness" *(tenebrae interiores),* a term that Luther was thoroughly familiar with[303] from "mystical theology" *(theologia mystica).*[304] Rather, the focus is directed completely outwards, to the spiritual and political world, which cannot tolerate God's word but opposes it to the point of causing "tumult."[305] There can be no doubt that this tumult touches a person's inmost being, the heart. Yet it cannot be seen by a spectator from a distance, but it can only be suffered by those who are deeply involved with it. "For as soon as God's Word takes root and grows in you, the devil will plague you and make a real doctor of you, and by his attacks will teach you to seek and love God's Word."[306] Luther therefore does not deny the inner realm, but here he puts the emphasis decisively on the external and the public realm, just as he did already when he introduced meditation as the second rule.

Nothing is left untouched by the great apocalyptic battle that rages through time and, simultaneously, deep in the heart of every individual,[307] for this battle is universal. This same universality that characterizes Luther's understanding of meditation is also the mark of the third rule. The battle affects not only pastors in their special office but also every Christian. In fact, from the standpoint of the theology of creation and the doctrine of sin,[308] we can say it affects everyone.

The universal claim that Luther made for his understanding of meditation and that he now also makes for his view of spiritual attack *(Anfechtung)* raises the question of whether there really is such a universal phenomenon. But before we can answer that question, we need to consider the distinctively passive nature of this spiritual attack *(Anfechtung)*, as well as the concept of experience that it entails.

This concept of experience is determined first of all by that distinction that Luther highlighted when he introduced the first rule and which we have described as the distinction between knowledge and certainty.[309] Now it turns up in the introduction to the third rule as the distinction between knowledge and experience: spiritual attack *(Anfechtung)* "teaches you not only to know and understand, but also to experience. . . ."[310] This distinction, which is representative of Luther's theology, is expressed even more sharply in the *Operationes in Psalmos:* "It is by living — no, not living, but by dying and giving ourselves up to hell that we become theologians, not by understanding, reading, and speculating."[311]

However we assess the details of the connection between Luther's concept of experience and that of the mystical tradition, especially that of "mystical theology" *(theologia mystica)* in the sense of "negative theology" *(theologia negativa)*, the decisive thing is that when Luther takes up this tradition and corrects it,[312] he highlights anew the concept of experience in New Testament apocalyptic.[313] The terms that mark out the semantic field are all found together in the introduction to *The Freedom of a Christian (De libertate Christiana)* which has not yet received from Luther scholars the attention it deserves.[314] This treatise is important for the light it sheds on Luther's understanding of the relationship between the experience of faith and theological writing. In this short introduction to the treatise,[315] the key terms "experience" *(experimentum)*, "test" *(probare)*, "trials" *(tribulationes)* and "spiritual attacks" *(tentationes)* emerge one after the other. Anyone familiar with the Greek equivalents and their usage in the New Testament writings will be introduced to a very specific way of viewing the world, the self, and God that is marked above all by a particular way of understanding time that is distinctively "apocalyptic."

The connection that Luther makes between this apocalyptic understanding of time and his idea of experience is so strong that it cannot be weakened by understanding it as a local religious-historical phenomenon peculiar to Luther, or by interpreting it existentially, or by any similar attempts to reinterpret it in terms of a neo-Protestant notion of conscience.[316] The battle against "all kinds of enemies" that "the person who meditates, the person who is occupied with God's Word has to put up with," is so public that it cannot be reduced to an inner struggle "in the conscience of the individual,"[317] as much as it might be deeply rooted there.

At stake in the whole topic of "trials, testing, and spiritual attack" *(de tentationibus)*, which Luther would like to have written a book about, is nothing else than the validity and truth of the first commandment.[318] God's unity, together with the unity of reality and its experience, is not an eternal and necessary principle that stands rock solid, but it is strongly contested by the experiences of life and in a thoroughly "external" way. When we meditate on the first commandment we are involved in the battle between the one Lord and the many lords (cf. 1 Cor. 8:5f.). We cannot withdraw from this conflict by appealing to the speculative idea of God's unity. It is not enough "to only know" about it and about God's almighty power, to see it in our mind's eye as a timeless principle. We have to "also experience" it. But to experience it we need time. It sets us on a path that wants to be tried and proved,[319] a path that we can only experience by walking it.[320]

Besides time, the affects, which depend on time, turn pure knowledge into experience and make for certainty.[321] Contrary to the misleading ideas of the modern theology of consciousness, the affects that we are talking about here, which include the senses, the emotions, the imagination, the memory, and the desires, are not primarily the affects of the believer or of the unbeliever, but the affects produced by the word of God. They are the affects of the *deus dicens,* who is not a mere mind devoid of feelings and desires, like the God of metaphysics, but he is a God who speaks through sensory means. The situation of spiritual attack makes it clear that these affects involve the senses as well as time. "This is the touchstone that teaches you not only to know and understand, but also to experience how right, how true, how sweet, how lovely, how mighty, how comforting God's Word is, wisdom beyond all wisdom."

Spiritual attack *(Anfechtung)* itself is not the touchstone of the genuineness of faith, if by faith we mean the truthfulness and credibility of the believer. Rather, it is the touchstone[322] of God's word, which demonstrates its credibility and power in times of spiritual attack and in the fight against it. "For only spiritual attack teaches us to listen to the Word." Luther understands Isaiah 28:19 in this way and, although he misses the meaning of the Hebrew text,[323] he focuses his understanding of scripture and theology on the crucial point.

Only spiritual attack *(Anfechtung)* teaches us to attend to God's word, which is necessary before we can experience it. Therefore, to experience God's word we *do* nothing; we simply *"suffer"* it in the sense of letting it do its work with us.[324] Scripture and experience do not stand alongside each other as "two touchstones."[325] They neither complement each other, nor can they be thought of as the two focal points of an ellipse. If Luther distinguishes between them,[326] he does so only to make it clear that the scriptures are not simply printed words to be read off a page but life-giving words that stimulate our senses and emotions, our memory and imagination, our heart and desires. He says that the Holy Scriptures "are not . . . mere literature; they are words of life, intended not for speculation and fantasy but for life and action."[327]

Luther's famous sentence "experience alone makes the theologian"[328] excludes high-flown thoughts and speculations and therefore pure knowledge,[329] but it should not be used to support a principle of pure experience that could only be the principle of a vague openness and incompleteness. What makes the theologian a theologian is not experience as such, but the experience of scripture.

The way I experience scripture is that it interprets me and thus provides for its own interpretation. Indeed it is its own interpreter, *sui ipsius interpres,* as Luther neatly puts it with reference to Psalm 119.[330] He insists that "the words of God are more intelligible and certain than the words of all human beings . . . so that they are not informed, tested, understood and confirmed by human words but human words by them."[331] It means letting the author, the triune God, work in me through the scriptures. That is the passivity that is unique to the experience of faith. It is primarily the passive life, the receptive life *(vita passiva).*[332]

Passivity is the main characteristic of Luther's view of experience, and experience in turn belongs to his third rule and so to his understanding of theology. However, passivity is a complex phenomenon and cannot simply be taken into a definition that posits a universal epistemology and anthropology, such as the feeling of absolute dependence.[333] Admittedly, a text like the following might suggest that Luther held there was such a phenomenon: "Note that we must suffer divine things more than act. In fact, the faculty of feeling and perceiving is by nature also passive."[334] This comment combines theology and philosophical anthropology in a remarkable way. The impact of its implied Aristotelian[335] and neo-Platonic[336] elements on Luther's theological thinking should not be underestimated. However, these philosophical elements are located within a scriptural context that makes it clear that God cannot be "simply the expression of the passive constitution of the mind in general."[337] For the threefold distinction between the law, through which God kills, the gospel, through which he makes alive, and the crushing hiddenness of God's work beyond law and gospel, cannot be resolved for us into a final unity, not even into that of a feeling of absolute dependence.[338] The gospel acts on us very differently than the law and even more differently than God's hidden work, which can plunge us into the worst kind of spiritual attack: the attack by God himself.[339] Overcoming this by means of the *deus praedicatus,* the proclaimed God,[340] which is the opposite to the hidden God, lets us "experience" in a profound way "how sweet, how lovely, how mighty, how comforting God's Word is."

With that in mind, we can come back to the question of whether Luther's third rule can be understood in a universal way, which we raised earlier.[341] This question is bound up with his understanding of theology as a whole. To seek the answer in Luther's understanding of scripture is consistent not only with his preface of 1539, which is by and large in praise of the Bible, but also with Luther's work in general.

In the *Assertio*[342] cited above, Luther relates his understanding of scripture, which he gets expressly from Psalm 119, to what Aristotle says about the "first principle" *(principium primum).*[343] In this way, Luther relates his understanding of scripture to the way in which science was understood at the time.[344] According to that, scientific knowledge can claim absolute necessity. But everything that exists "of absolute necessity is eternal, and what is eternal does not come into existence or perish."[345] Therefore, it comes as an enormous shock when Luther calls the temporal, contingent, historical Bible a "first principle" *(principium primum),* given that by its very nature it is so closely bound up with the sensible world. However, there is a paradox here that no one speaking about Luther's "scriptural principle" should overlook.[346] This term is only meaningful if it is understood as denoting a conflict, a conflict involved in understanding theology as a science or academic discipline that has continued unabated since Luther's day and that will continue into the future. If we talk about the "scriptural principle," we can only do so by radically criticizing an understanding of science, particularly of philosophy, that sees it as a timeless, pure *a priori.* We, instead, insist that it is an impure, historical *a priori.* We hold, as theologians, that truth is accidentally *a priori,* but necessarily *a posteriori.* Here theology can also be a stimulus to the other sciences, particularly to philosophy.[347]

The question about the universal nature of the experience of spiritual attack *(Anfechtung)* and our victory over it is therefore answered in a specific way. This victory can never be taken for granted but has to be sought once again in every new situation. As in the case of Luther's understanding of theology generally, it led us to the point where we realized that we can no longer express it using the general, supposedly timeless categories that were previously used. Luther's idea of spiritual attack and its defeat is alien to modern thinking and is as much in conflict with it as it is with Aristotelian categories. Its specificity and breadth militate against a universal historical construal, just as its specificity and depth resist an existential interpretation.[348]

3.5. The Ecclesiological Understanding of Theology

If we want to describe Luther's understanding of theology in one word, it can best be called "ecclesiological." The justification for that comes from the preface as a whole as well as its context,[349] but especially from a comparison with a treatise that was published in the same year (1539), *On the Councils and Church.* Surprisingly, it shows that the three marks of theology *(notae theologiae)* are identical in structure with the marks of the church *(notae ecclesiae),* a fact consistent with the truth of the thesis: "Where the word is, there is the church" *(ubi est verbum, ibi est ecclesia).*[350] An examination of the two documents reveals the following structure:

On the Councils and Church	*Preface*
1.1 word[351]	1.1 *meditatio*
1.2 prayer[352]	1.2 *oratio*
2.0 cross[353]	2.0 *tentatio*

The seventh mark of the church, the cross, which is suffered on account of the gospel, is often only considered an appendix. However, in the light of the preface, the importance of this mark becomes clear. Again, although the public aspect comes out in the preface, the treatise on the church emphasizes this even more strongly. The two-part division coincides with that of the epilogue to the Psalter of 1525, which highlights God's word and the way we should use it as well as the cross as the "two parts" to which we must pay attention.[354]

A Table Talk discourse confirms that the three marks of theology are identical in structure with the marks of the church: "Satan is conquered and the church protected in three ways: by (1) faithful teaching; (2) earnest prayer; and (3) perseverance in suffering."[355]

Luther's understanding of theology is thoroughly "ecclesiological" while it receives breadth and depth from the theology of creation. This comes out very impressively in the preface to the Psalter of 1528:

> In a word, if you want to see the holy Christian church painted in living color and shape, comprehended in one little picture, then take up the Psalter. There you have a fine, bright, pure mirror that will show you what the church is. Indeed, you will find yourself in it also and the true *gnothi seauton* (know yourself), as well as God himself and all creatures.[356]

4. Catechetical Systematics

Since Luther was a monk, priest, and university theologian, he tried to hold academic theology and liturgical spirituality together without tension. He took up the catechetical tradition of the medieval church's spirituality and combined it with the liturgical spirituality of monasticism, based on meditation, and its emphasis on the affects (which include the emotions, the senses, the desires, and the imagination) to produce a thoroughly pastoral theology.

In the *Large Catechism* he addresses the "preachers and pastors."[357] Because they are now free from the useless, bothersome babbling of the seven [canonical] hours, they could instead "read a page or two from the catechism, the prayer book, the New Testament, or some other passage from the Bible morning, noon, and night and pray the Lord's Prayer for themselves and their parishioners."[358] All baptized people, in fact all people generally, should grow up and become fluent with the *Small Catechism*, come to faith themselves, be certain of their faith, and be able to articulate it in a clear and precise way.

The awareness of each person's individuality before God, which resulted from the daily examination of the conscience and the frequent confession of the monk, is now expected of every Christian. Through his sermons on the catechism, which he preached at least four times a year and two weeks at a time,[359] as well as through the writing of the *Small Catechism*, Luther made sure, as Karl Marx so wittily and pithily put it, that the monks became the laypeople because the laypeople all became monks.[360] Behind this was his understanding of Baptism. Luther in no way rejected the monastic vow but gave it a new interpretation in the sense of Jesus' call to radical discipleship. We can sum up his whole ethics by saying that he understood what was true about obedience, chastity, and poverty because he saw them in a new light. By listening, the basic stance of all people before God, we learn what God has given us and what he expects from us. That holds for every baptized person as well as for the monk. Training in the catechism, which was one of the positive aspects of monastic life that Luther wanted to see preserved, is necessary for the salvation of every person. Luther tried to inculcate this throughout his life, perhaps never more urgently than on March 9, 1522, at the beginning of his first Invocavit Sermon: "The summons of death comes to all of us,[361] and no one can die for another. Each of us must fight our battle with death alone. We can shout into another person's ears, but each of us individually must be prepared for death when it comes, for when the summons comes, I will not be with you or you with me. Therefore, we all need to know and arm ourselves with the main parts of the Christian faith."[362] Here of course Luther has in mind the catechism.

It is necessary for salvation to know and use the catechism. Faith clings to the word and all the individual words. The rhythm and structure of the words cannot be divorced from the content of the catechism. Both are essential and belong together.

The amazing thing, and this is typical of Luther's theology, is that he wanted to connect three things in a dynamic way: (1) All that was true and good of monasticism, with its liturgical spirituality; (2) the catechetical tradition that was alive in the spirituality of the medieval church; and (3) university theology with its tradition of the academic disputation, which the university had cultivated since the time of high scholasticism.

Luther wanted to avoid creating a gulf between the spirituality of the church and theology of the university. He taught the *one* truth in the language of the sermon and in the language of the catechism. We can learn from him how university theology, pursued on the basis of the seven liberal arts, especially grammar, dialectics, and rhetoric, cannot be separated from church spirituality. Luther criticized the scholastic theologians and their distinctions where they became blind to their own shortcomings, forgot the truth of the catechism, or, as he ironically says, where "they never even knew it in the first place."[363] No wonder he says in the Latin preface to his tractate on freedom (1520) that even those learned and skillful disputants do not understand what they are discussing![364]

However, the polemic against scholasticism[365] is never motivated by contempt for rationality and scholarly work in general. Luther knows that the sin-darkened heart[366] also affects our reason and perverts its use so that reason becomes a whore.[367] However, knowing this does not lead him to oppose reason and science in the abstract but to practice and demand a good and right use of reason. This is clear from the fact that Luther obviously made use of the seven liberal arts. He even wrote an essay on "dialectics," "logic,"[368] in which he treated the terms concept, proposition, and judgment.[369] In this way he cultivated the three fields of the Aristotelian *organon*.

The remarkable functionalism of Luther's theology is evident from the fact that his academic work is never an end in itself. It is always related to a specific context. We see this clearly from the title of the first Reformation text of Luther's theology, a set of theses titled "On seeking out the truth and comforting terrified consciences" *(Pro veritate inquirenda et timoratis conscientiis consolandis)* from the early summer of 1518.[370] The theses set out conclusions and opinions that Luther wanted to have debated at the university. He hoped that the dispute over the proper understanding of repentance would bring to light the true meaning of confession and absolution so that troubled and frightened consciences would be comforted. The title of the theses made it clear that the search for the truth is no self-serving academic exercise but is intended to help troubled consciences. Although this was carried out in the context of a university disputation, where arguments were advanced for and against a position according to the rules of debate developed by the medieval scholastics, the aim of the exercise was that consciences would be instructed, roused, and comforted.

"My advice," said Dr. Martin, "is that you should not dispute about secret, hidden things but simply stick to God's word, especially the catechism, for in it you have an excellent, accurate, and brief account of the Christian religion and its main articles."[371] The catechism offers "the most exact method of any religion."[372] For "God himself has given us the Ten Commandments, Christ has taught us the Our Father, and the Holy Spirit has summed up the articles of faith with great brevity and accuracy. These three parts are written in such a way that they could not be more excellent, comforting, and succinct. But people despise them and regard them as simple and trivial because children have to recite them every day."[373]

What Luther, as a professor at the university, posted for debate and wanted to have discussed in the interests of the truth *(pro veritate inquirenda)* lies right at the point of intersection of kerygma and didache, of the kerygmatic and didactic forms.

The kerygmatic forms are the forms of God's address to us and our response to that address, which has its original form in the gospel preamble to the Decalogue: "I am the Lord, your God!" The forms of the answer are the forms of faith. Faith is nothing else than prayer, which embraces praise and complaint, confession of sins, petition, intercession, and adoration.

The didactic forms, on the other hand, are more concerned with instruction than address. In both cases, however, the emphasis is on listening and attending. It is really all about "knowledge" *(notitia)*.[374] But this term needs to be nuanced. In terms of church history, the didactic forms, which do not so much address as instruct, have their context *(Sitz im Leben)* in baptismal instruction. In the preface to *The German Mass and Order of Service* of 1526, Luther offers this definition: "Catechism means the instruction in which the heathen who want to be Christians are taught and guided in what they should believe, know, do, and leave undone, according to the Christian faith. This is why the candidate who had been admitted for such instruction and learned the creed before his or her Baptism used to be called a catechumen *(catechumenos)*. This instruction or catechization I cannot put better or more plainly than has been done from the beginning of the Christian church and retained till now, that is, in these three parts, the Ten Commandments, the Creed, and the Our Father. These three plainly and briefly contain . . . everything that a Christian needs to know."[375] Luther already emphasized how important this knowledge is in his first Invocavit Sermon of 1522.

Three years later, in 1529, Luther's *Small Catechism* appeared in the form of wall charts with each main part printed on a separate placard. This catechism now contained two further parts: one on Baptism, the other on the Lord's Supper. Between them in 1531 came an instruction on "How simple people are to be taught to confess."[376] However, this addition is no mere appendix. Further parts that were added later, on the other hand, are clearly meant to be seen as appendixes: Morning and Evening Prayer,[377] and the Household Table,[378] which teaches all the members of the household how they are to conduct themselves: fathers towards their children, children towards their parents, slaves towards their masters and masters towards their slaves, as set out in the so-called "Household Tables" of the New Testament, which gets its name from Luther.

The two parts of the catechism dealing with Baptism and the Lord's Supper are the most kerygmatic because it is just here that the kerygma is presented in its most concrete form. The instruction of the household and family in the catechism was helped by having the placards hung up in the living room so that people could always see them and learn them by heart. This instruction is related to the kerygma and worship, not only to family worship with its practice of morning and evening prayer, but also to the public worship of the church, especially to Baptism and the Lord's Supper.

Let us now clarify the web of relationships that exist within Luther's catechism and then focus on what could be called its "systematics," which we will explain later.

After Luther had expounded each of the traditional parts of the catechism, the Decalogue and the Our Father, in his sermons, he put these parts together in 1520 to form a catechism with three parts: *A Short Form of the Ten Commandments, the Faith, and the Our Father.*[379] In the preface Luther reflects on the connection between the three parts. While their number and sequence varied in the tradition, Luther now fixed the order: The Ten Commandments, the Faith (Creed), and the Our Father. "These three parts contain all that is in Scripture" and that needs to be preached. They also contain a complete and thorough summary of "everything that a Christian needs to know."[380] There are three things that "we need to know" in order to be saved. "First, we need to know what to do and what not to do. Secondly, if we find that we cannot by our own strength do or not do what God asks of us, we need to know where to turn to find that strength to be able to do or not do what he says. Thirdly, we need to know how we are to seek and get that strength."[381]

At first glance it seems as if the catechism has a three-part structure. But in reality there are only two parts to it, the distinction between law and gospel. The Creed and the Our Father are meant to be taken together. Then the distinction between law and gospel represents the sum of the scriptures and the Christian life. Baptism and the Lord's Supper, the parts that were added later, fit into the gospel-side of the catechism, along with the Creed and the Our Father.

The Credo (creed) and the model prayer, the Our Father, belong together and constitute the gospel as distinct from the law. They permeate the catechism more than we would expect from reading the preface. The explanation of the Creed is nothing but a confession of what is believed in the prayer, with the certainty of being heard, for confession itself is already prayer. Prayer belongs to the gospel, not the law, because it is a gift, not a work. The certainty Luther has that God will answer prayer comes out in his explanation to the conclusion of the Lord's Prayer: "I believe . . . and do not doubt that the Father will give me all that I pray for in this prayer, through the Son Jesus Christ, with and in the Holy Spirit — that is the meaning of the AMEN, that it is really and certainly true."[382]

Luther's catechetical systematics, in general terms, is an engagement with God's performative word in our human response, on the basis of the distinction between law and gospel. There is a precise correlation between this response and the word that precedes it. The focus is on what God has given me, what he expects and demands from me, what I should thank and praise him for, what sins to confess, what complaint to make, and what requests to make.[383] Luther makes all the parts of the catechism into "a garland of four strands,"[384] with each part becoming for him a textbook, song book, penitential book, and prayer book.[385]

These different ways of using God's word, or our response to it, cannot be identified with particular parts of the catechism, as if we hear the Decalogue only as demand and not also as outright gift and promise, as in the preamble. The Creed too speaks not only of what we have received from God but also of our duty "to serve and obey him."[386] And the Our Father is not only petition but, as in its address, also thanksgiving. It also leads us to recognize our sin and therefore, like the Decalogue, acts as a mirror for confession.

Prayer incorporates different linguistic elements from various contexts insofar as it is based on God's command to pray and his promise to hear. Furthermore, it relates to a situation of need and boldly claims God's promise to hear.[387]

It is clear that the catechism is to be not only learned by heart but also practiced inwardly every day by praying it and meditating on it, since *meditation* means nothing else than engaging with God's word. Over the course of time, the whole catechism is prayed so that when any one part, such as the article on creation, becomes the focus of attention, the other parts still speak in the background and no part is ever isolated from the rest. Nor does catechetical meditation proceed discursively along a linear path that could be left behind, once it has been traversed, and the information stored and retrieved at will from our store of memories. Rather, this kind of catechetical meditation, which engages with God's word in a fourfold response to it, is a daily practice of rumination (Ps. 1:2) that involves remembering and repetition.[388]

In spite of all the succinctness and precision of language, we should not expect Luther, especially in his explanation of the catechism, to give us final and definitive formulations. Rather, what he gives us are open sentences that stimulate our thinking and imagination and that we can take up and develop further. Since our response will draw its inspiration from the *Small Catechism,* our sentences too should have a poetic character. Apart from the aphoristic and rhapsodic elements, responses could go in two different directions. On the one hand, we could formulate sentences that function as an organizing principle that subsumes all diversity under the idea of a rigid unity. But that monarchical kind of response flattens out all differences. On the other hand, these sentences could suggest all sorts of connections that might be helpful in different situations, although often these connections can only really be made in a concrete situation.

Luther's catechetical systematics offers a third way. It reminds us that life is open and incomplete this side of the grave. This approach tries not to close what life leaves open. It takes into account our real life situation and does not go beyond this context *(Sitz im Leben).* Catechetical systematics therefore is strictly related to the complaint but always within the framework of theodicy. Knowledge of the complaint does not eliminate the need to make it known.

The distinction between knowledge and certainty has already been discussed.[389] We will now consider it in the light of catechetical systematics, which culminates in the distinction between law and gospel. It is, of course, essential that we know about the distinction between law and gospel. However, just knowing about it is no guarantee that we can actually distinguish between them. This distinction between knowledge and certainty must also come out in the formulation of dogmatic propositions. "This art, namely, the proper distinction between law and gospel . . . is easy to learn as far as the words are concerned. But when it comes to experiencing it and putting it to the test in our heart and life, it is a high and difficult art and we cannot begin to understand it."[390] "There is no one on earth who knows how to properly distinguish between the law and the gospel. We may think we understand it when we are listening to a sermon, but we're far from it. Only the Holy Spirit can master the art. Even the man Christ lacked this art at the Mount of Olives so that an angel had to comfort him. Though he was a teacher from heaven, and the Holy Spirit was on him in the form of a dove, yet he was strengthened by an angel. You'd certainly think that I'd have mastered the art because I've been writing so much and so long about it, but when a crisis comes I can see that I am still a long way from it. God alone then must be our most holy master and teacher."[391]

When Luther refers to his discovery of this distinction, he calls it a breakthrough: "When I discovered that the law is one thing and the gospel another, then I made a breakthrough and I was free."[392] But this liberation is not the kind of experience that you can simply leave behind as you take with you certain ideas about freedom that you can call up at any time. Therefore, it will always be an art and a stroke of good luck to be able to get the distinction right in a time of spiritual crisis.

This presents a special difficulty for the tradition of the academic disputation in which precisely formulated theses are put up for debate. Admittedly, the authors of the Lutheran confessions tried to formulate precise doctrinal statements giving "rules" for the proper distinction between law and gospel, as we see from the *Formula of Concord*. But the proper application of these rules to the Christian conscience in a time of spiritual crisis depends on the particular situation. Because this situation varies from person to person and cannot be known in advance, it is very difficult to make the proper application of law and gospel the topic of a disputation which, by its very nature, demands precision of formulation and has no room for the element of the unknown. God himself is the Lord of both the distinction and the unity of law and gospel, not we. However, in order not to forget this, we must dare to teach law and gospel theologically. By this I mean that we must teach it in such a way that the distinction between them is considered in the light of its context *(Sitz im Leben)*.

5. Philosophy and Theology

5.1. The Critical Nature of Theology as an Academic Discipline

The fundamental importance of the problem of the relation between philosophy and theology cannot be overestimated. It is as significant as the problem of natural theology. Luther, like Paul in Romans 1:18–3:20, regards every human individual as being in a relationship with God, a relationship that in reality and practice is flawed. The problem is human reason, not so much theoretical reason but practical reason guided by the imagination. It always reaches out for God, but it always falls short of the mark. Consequently, Luther (thinking of Jonah 1:5: "All the sailors were afraid and each cried out to his own god") can say quite emphatically, "These men in the ship all know of God, but they have no sure God."[393] The office of Christ is to make us certain of God.

Luther's distinction between knowledge and certainty is along the same lines as that between "holy" and "saved" that we find in his *Confession* (1528). This distinction is highly illuminating for his definition of the relationship between philosophy and theology. God orders his creation within three orders.[394] The basic order of all human life is "holy" because it is "grounded in God's word and commandment."[395] "However, none of the orders is a way of salvation. There is only one way beyond all these, the way of faith in Jesus Christ. For to be holy and to be saved are two entirely different things. We are saved through Christ alone. But we become holy through this faith as well as through these divine institutions and orders. Even the godless can have much about them that is holy, but they are not for that reason saved inwardly."[396]

This clear distinction between "holy" and "saved" implies a distinction between humanity in general and Christians in particular. The specific issue at stake is how Luther uses the traditions of the ancient world, such as the economic and political wisdom of an Aristotle or a Cicero, in his interpretation of the Decalogue and primal history of the Bible.

The relationship between philosophy and theology, understood in this way, cannot avoid controversy. Luther never sees theology operating in a private realm cut off from conflict, but he sees it rather as a discipline in which conflict, argument, debate, polemic, and criticism are the norm. In other words, theology has to be fundamentally critical and polemical because that is essential to its nature as an academic discipline. This way of seeing theology has found classical expression in the *Disputation Concerning Man* (1536),[397] as is clear from theses 1-19 on "philosophy" and theses 20-40 on "theology."

The scope of Luther's work in the *Disputation Concerning Man* is broad, yet the focus is clearly on anthropology. He used exactly the same approach a few years earlier (1532/33) in the interpretation of Psalm 127 ("Unless the Lord builds the house . . .") where the focus was on social ethics.[398]

The logic of this interpretation of Psalm 127 sheds light on the exact meaning of that sentence in Luther's great *Confession*, that "even the godless can have much about them that is holy, but they are not for that reason saved inwardly." In his interpretation of this psalm he not only makes the necessary distinction between heathen humanity, although still created by God, and the rescue ("salvation") accomplished by Christ, but he also connects them. To do that, he has recourse to the Aristotelian schema of the four causes, just as he does in the *Disputation Concerning Man.*[399]

Luther admits that Aristotle, Demosthenes, and Cicero have some knowledge of the material and formal cause *(causa materialis* and *formalis)* of social life and the arts; in short, they know about the use of reason. "They treat this matter most admirably."[400]

However, this praise is not without qualification. "They only know about the material and formal cause of politics and economics. They do not know anything about their final and efficient cause. In other words, they do not know either the origin of politics and economics or who sustains them; neither do they know about their end."[401] They are to blame, like every other godless person, because they themselves want to be the efficient and final cause. They themselves want to be the creator and perfecter of economics and politics. "But this," Luther says, "is not up to you." Your job is "to be the instruments."[402] People who are not content to be God's instruments and appointed representatives destroy the way that God intended reason to be used, through their ingratitude and self-glorification. A man like Cicero speaks and acts well, but not when he wants to boast of his achievement and says: "I have done it."[403] "Because he says, 'I have done it,' they [God's gifts] become dung."[404] "Their [heathen] actions do not issue purely and simply from the heart for the sake of God, but they search for some other end [their own] because they lack a real faith in and a true knowledge of God."[405]

However, even if the heathen do not fear and love God, they cannot extinguish the light of reason entirely, because God established it at creation with his promise and blessing. In fact, they fulfill the second table of the Decalogue so brilliantly that "at times [they certainly] appear holier than Christians."[406]

It has become clear that Luther sees the relationship between general and Christian humanity, between philosophy and theology, to be one of radical conflict. In fact, to do theology means to become involved in this conflict. The sharpness of the conflict is not toned down, as in Thomas Aquinas, who concedes that philosophy has a relative independence. This allows him to say that grace surpasses and perfects philosophy and nature. On the other hand, we must guard against interpreting Luther's theology from the angle of transcendental philosophy, according to which grace does not surpass nature but deepens it, so that God and his freedom are made the condition of human freedom.

5.2. Distinction Rather than Separation, Identification, and Analogy

"Every single art [and science] has its own terms and words, which it uses. These words are valid in their [respective] areas. Jurists have their own, doctors theirs, and likewise philosophers."[407] Each group has its own understanding of certainty, which matches its own concept of knowledge and its own method of proof.[408]

Does that mean that Luther approves the idea of a conflict-free plurality, the idea that different terms can peacefully coexist alongside each other? Yet what actually happens is that terms and concepts are transferred and the area of their validity expands. In the disputation just cited on Romans 3:28, Luther warns against the indiscriminate transference of "physical" concepts, by which he means philosophical and natural concepts, into theology. For example, the Aristotelian concept of justice is perfectly correct in its own field of ethics, as well as in politics and economics, the area of civil righteousness. However, when we transfer this concept into the doctrine of sin and grace, it takes on a meaning that is foreign to the Bible with disastrous consequences: God becomes our business partner, and his righteousness is no longer seen as a gift that he bestows by faith alone, without human works. Luther therefore insists that when we take concepts from philosophy over into theology, we must examine them critically. "If however you want to use these words, you must first give them a good bath and purge them."[409]

When Luther stresses that words become "new" words, words with a wholly different meaning, when we transfer them into a different sphere, a different situation, a different context,[410] he is not being positive and constructive but negative and critical. It seems that, in his opinion, we can only purify these concepts in a negative way, by distinguishing one from the other. In other words, we must distinguish between civil righteousness and divine righteousness and not make them into parallel concepts. Luther is not interested in making "physical," natural concepts more natural in their field. He does not offer any positive constructive example of how to purify terms used in the area of civil righteousness. When Luther looks at the fields of the jurists, the economists, and the doctors, as a theologian, it is not with the intention of justifying their concepts anew, reordering them, or even aligning them with Christ and the gospel. Rather, just as he vigorously demanded that concepts transferred from the secular realm into the spiritual be critically examined, so too he equally insists that secular things be allowed to remain secular and not be qualified anew retrospectively, on analogy with soteriology.

Instead of this kind of retrospective, Luther insists on making a clear distinction.[411] "I distinguish":[412] "There are two different kinds of righteousness: one is based on the law and produced by our own strength and effort. The other is imputed to us by God through faith because of divine mercy. This is how we must purify these words of the scholastics. A coin is valid where it is minted. . . . Before God our works count for nothing, if we do them with the intention of meriting eternal life, but in the eyes of the world they count [absolutely]."[413] The Aristotelian idea that justice is communicative *(iustitia commutativa)* and distributive *(iustitia distributiva)* has its rightful place in the political realm and should not be criticized. However, we must criticize and condemn it in the strongest terms if this idea is transferred into the theological realm. Luther insists: "There is a double realm, one theological, the other political."[414]

Is Luther promoting here the thesis of a double truth?

5.3. Double Truth?

"The theologians of Paris thunder [and decree]: 'What is true in philosophy is also true in theology.'"[415] However, the thesis of the one truth is an abstraction and departs from the path of history. We cannot jump over it nor can we ignore it. That is why the thesis of the one truth is strangely abstract and governed by an inappropriate eschatology,[416] for every epistemology has its own eschatology.[417]

"For all created things such as the sun and moon, are for Christ and are not against him, because all things work together for good with the godly [Rom. 8:28], even the devil, death, and hell. But you cannot conclude from this that truth is the same in theology and philosophy, for they will continue to be different in kind and in matter,"[418] until the eschaton.

Luther persistently refuses to teach that there is a double truth. He denies that "the same proposition can be true in philosophy and false in Christian theology, and vice versa."[419] Yet he rejects the speculation that everything is one, even if that speculation is grounded in the confession to Christ. What does this mean? Luther does not hold to a theory of double truth because even the political realm, and the philosophical realm if we understand it in the broadest sense, is the arena in which God is at work as creator and preserver. By distinguishing between the preservation of the world and its redemption, Luther refuses to accept a concept of truth that bridges the real distinction between God's spiritual and secular governance and that tries plausibly to eliminate it through the use of analogies. Luther does not make "mediation" into an all-encompassing principle, even though in the context of soteriology it is determinative. He therefore does not generalize the category of "relation" *(relatio)*[420] or transfer it to all realms, even though in a soteriological context it is the only appropriate one. In the realm of civil righteousness and cosmological entities, the category of "substance" is justified.[421] Luther does not end up with the idea of total mediation, but he maintains the tension between these two realms. The understanding of theology that lies behind this found programmatic expression in the *Disputation Concerning John 1:14,* held January 11, 1539.[422]

After the *Disputation Concerning Man* (1536), this disputation gives the most thorough treatment of the relation between philosophy and theology. It even makes a special point of dealing with the agreement between philosophy and theology, a topic that the *Disputation Concerning Man* does not treat. The Wittenberg theological faculty consciously opposed the Sorbonne, the stronghold of scholastic theology. In the disputation, they argued against the proposition put up by the Paris theologians that "the same thing is true in theology as in philosophy, and vice versa."[423] They mounted the counter-thesis "that the same thing is not true in theology and philosophy. For we know that it is one thing to understand, another to believe. Therefore, philosophy and theology are to be distinguished. It is the task of philosophy to understand by the use of reason; it is the task of theology truly to believe what is above all reason."[424]

That sums up the essence of the disputation.[425] It is necessary to see a difference and not to dissolve this into a unity of truth, or to make philosophy and theology mesh with each other. Luther insists that philosophy and theology have different objects, just as "you will never discover that the same thing is true in all [realms]."[426] Here Luther takes up an idea that was important to Ockham.[427] "For as God has established distinct spheres in heaven, so also he [has established different realms on earth], so that every single work and skill may retain its place and form and may not move outside its own center in which it has been placed."[428] That means there is no peaceful coexistence and no correspondence.[429] As long as philosophy wants to control theology, it will contradict it. We will therefore have to develop our theology in conflict with philosophy. The very nature of theology demands that we do it that way and not leave it to chance. Given this situation of conflict, it is essential that theology engage seriously in philosophical and logical argumentation in order to fight the opponent with the opponent's own weapons.[430]

It is not by accident that the thesis advanced against the Sorbonne is tested against John 1:14 ("The Word was made flesh"). In other words, it is tested against the union of God and humanity. This is the main topic of Luther's theology, along with the union of bread and wine in the Lord's Supper and the relationship between sinful humans and the God who justifies them.

In Luther's eyes, the conflict between theology and philosophy involves a concrete negation, not something abstract. Theology does not contradict philosophy if philosophy attends to the "wisdom that comes from the law" *(sapientia legalis)*.[431] It contradicts it only if moral and metaphysical claims are allowed to determine theology in its totality.

5.4. The Grammar of the Holy Spirit

The *Disputation Concerning the Divinity and Humanity of Christ* (1540) follows on closely after the two disputations that we have just noted, especially the last one.

In the *Disputation Concerning John 1:14*, the question of the relation between philosophy and theology emerged as a special theme, which was then discussed in the light of the key proposition that "God is human." However, in the *Disputation Concerning the Divinity and Humanity of Christ*, it is the Christological question that occupies center stage, but not to the exclusion of the "methodological" questions. Philosophy therefore plays a lesser role in dialectics than in grammar.

Even the study of grammar that Luther praised so highly and gave pride of place to in the trivium[432] is not something that theology can follow uncritically, for it also reflects certain biases and the linguistic conventions of the day. The way that key theological terms are used, such as the words "God" and "human being," "creator" and "creature," proves disastrous for theology. The world of sin, the old world, also has its own "old language." "A 'creature,' according to the old language, is someone the creator has created and from whom he has separated himself. But this meaning has no place in Christ according to his human nature as a creature. There the creator and the creature are one and the same."[433]

In this sense "the Holy Spirit," who makes the old world and its old language new, "has his own grammar."[434] Indeed, "grammar operates in all fields, but when the subject is greater than can be comprehended by the rules of grammar and philosophy, it must be left behind."[435] Grammar confirms and strengthens the "philosophical argument," that "there is no relation between the creature and the creator, between the finite and the infinite," between a beginning in time and eternity.[436] "We, on the other hand, assert not only a relation, but [even] the union of the finite and the infinite."[437] "There the Holy Spirit has prescribed formulas for us. Let us walk in that cloud [Exod. 13:21f.]."[438]

From statements like these, Bengel and Hamann formed the opinion that for Luther "theology" is a "grammar of the language of Holy Scripture."[439] Hamann and Luther are also united in their recognition that the role of terms and sentences will vary according to their situation.[440]

The formulas of the new language are a gift of the Holy Spirit. They focus on the way we talk about the communication of attributes.[441] We must, however, protect them against rash generalizations, the work of enthusiastic eschatology, aided and abetted by human reason.[442]

Again, Luther achieves this by thoroughly philosophical means: through the distinction between the concrete attributes *(concreta)* of Christ's being and the abstract attributes *(abstracta)* of human nature in

81

general, creation and the world as such.[443] Luther stresses the importance of this distinction, which seems to anticipate the criticism that is
necessary today in the face of a post-Christian natural theology, with its
distinctively Hegelian stamp, which dominates, for instance, the theology of Barth and Bonhoeffer. The hallmark of these forms of post-
Christian theology is the endless and lavish use they make of the proposition "God is human" or "the creature and the creator are one and the
same."[444] However, in what is surely a countermove to this, Luther pleads
for a "spare use" of this kind of talk.[445] The thesis that "all words receive a
new meaning in Christ" is not true if we expand it in a speculative way,
but only "if they have the same referent."[446] People who do not see this
clearly and who fail to distinguish between the concrete attributes of
Christ's being and the abstract attributes of humanity and the world,
"do not know how to distinguish between equivocal words."[447] In their
enthusiasm, they relish the fog of equivocation and refuse to let the
cloud (Exod. 13:21f.) of the Holy Spirit and his grammar be their guide.

Because Hegel understands the new being of Christ and in Christ
as a universal reality, "he does not elevate a particular truth to the level
of a general truth. Rather, he brings the new back under the conditions
of the old."[448] Luther's understanding of theology, on the other hand,
is distinctively anti-speculative. He persistently denies the thesis "that
the same thing is true in all realms,"[449] and he emphasizes the importance of the historically irrevocable distinction between philosophy
and theology, between the political realm and the theological realm,
and between civil righteousness and the righteousness of God.

Given this distinction, the context into which we proclaim the
word is not one that is characterized by the peaceful coexistence of differences or by their absolute separation. Rather, it is characterized by a
relationship marked by conflict and dispute. It is just as unnecessary to
fabricate an identity as it is to posit a separation (diastasis). We must
not attempt to avoid conflict or soften it by means of analogy. Rather,
we need to see it in a concrete way. Theology is a discipline in which
conflict is essential to its very nature. If we lose that insight, it will simply become speculative or positivistic. If it becomes a positivistic science, theology will simply end up plowing one field alongside other
fields. However, if it chooses to go in that direction, it cannot appeal to
Luther's distinction between the faculties and the different fields of
learning for support.

Part Two

Understanding Theology Today

The Problem

"Is not the vitally necessary distinction between faith and theology one of the great achievements for which theology . . . has modernity to thank?"[1]

The distinction between faith and theology is an invention of modernity. Since Johann Salomo Semler,[2] and Schleiermacher[3] a generation later, this distinction has become so natural that we take it to be self-evident and for the most part no longer reflect on it critically. Hence, contemporary thinkers are scandalized when a study of Luther's understanding of theology leads to the thesis that theology and faith should not be fundamentally distinguished, let alone separated. Similarly, Luther does not make the sharp distinction, usually made today, between professional theologians and other Christians: "All are called theologians as all are Christians" *(Omnes dicimur Theologi, ut omnes Christiani).*[4] Luther holds that the "monastic" aspect of theology with its liturgical spirituality grounded in the divine service is constitutive, in that this provides theology with its content. On the other hand, he says that its "scholastic" academic aspect is purely regulative in that it orders, analyzes, and reflects on the content of theology and makes the necessary distinctions and connections. These two sides of theology are kept united in a special way by meditation *(meditatio).*[5] However, since Semler, this unity has been lost and theology has been split into several spheres: academic theology,[6] professionalized public religion (the public ministry of the church), and private religion.[7] Yet the only place where Semler's distinctions are "essential" is in the area of constitutional law and politics.[8] Apart from that, these distinctions have proved to be unhelpful separations, and in cases where this has led to an actual disjunction between theology and faith, the results have been catastrophic.[9]

If Luther's understanding of theology is sound in holding together the "monastic" side of theology with its liturgical spirituality, on the one hand, and the "scholastic" academic side of theology, on the other, then we today can no longer accept that the distinctions, or rather separations, perpetuated since Semler are self-evident. Rather, they will need to be carefully examined and reconsidered. However, we cannot ignore the modern understanding of theology without injuring both theology and the church. A pure repristination of Luther's theology would not do justice to the task of systematic theology, which has to work responsibly within the present situation. Luther's understanding of theology, however, presupposes a different context. Therefore, if we are going to use Luther's theology as an orientation, we will have to undertake a *meta-critique* of modern theology. This critique is presupposed in all that follows. However, space will not permit us to discuss this in detail.[10]

The point of the meta-critique is to deal with the much-criticized separation of church spirituality from university theology, life from doctrine, and a theologian's personal faith from the issues that impinge on that faith for which the theologian is publicly responsible. However, the meta-critique we are proposing does more than deal with the symptoms of these separations. It attempts to bring about a radical healing by going to the root of the problem. The experience of more than two hundred years of church history, the history of theology, and the history of ideas shows that Semler set theology on a fundamentally wrong course when he made these separations. It is time therefore to take a fresh look at the concept of theology, both historically and systematically. That is the purpose of the second part of this book. This new look at the understanding of theology within the context of a meta-critical engagement with the classical problems of modernity will shed new light on Luther's understanding of theology. It will also illuminate the traditions of the Middle Ages and of the ancient church, and at the same time of Judaism, insofar as these have a bearing on the heart of Luther's theology: the crucial importance of prayer *(oratio)*, meditation *(meditatio)*, and spiritual attack *(tentatio)* in the formation of the theologian.

If we affirm Luther's understanding of theology in the context of a critical engagement with the problems of modernity, we will not try to resolve one-sidedly the tension between faith and knowledge, spirituality and scholarship, the affects (which include the emotions, the senses, the imagination, the memory, and the desires) and the intellect, the heart, and the head. In short, we will not try to resolve the tension between its monastic and scholastic aspects. Rather, we must preserve this tension and focus on meditation, which for Luther always means engaging with the biblical text, for this is central to understanding theology as a "grammar of the language of the Holy Scriptures."[11] This is the only way to overcome the modern attempt to treat theology as if it had no substantive object,[12] without resorting to the kind of scientific objectivity advocated by positivism.

We take as our starting point the crucial question: What is the object of theological reflection? What should we choose as the object of theology? The problem begins already here, for we do not choose the object of theology. It is given to us and it is the task of theology to recognize it. The decisive thing after all is not what we think the object of theology should be, but what we discover it is. For in the final analysis, we do not choose it but we recognize it as the only object possible. But how can we describe the object of theology (and here our initial question comes to a head) without it appearing either too vague in its breadth or too narrow in its specificity?

In response to this question, we will begin with worship, or as we prefer to call it, the divine service *(Gottesdienst)*. This means starting at the beginning, for whatever passes for theology grows out of the divine service.

Instead of looking first at the particular divine service in the church (the public liturgical assembly), we will begin with the general divine service in creation, which is identical with religion in general. In identifying the distinction and connection between the general and the particular divine service, we must neither let the general become too vague in its breadth nor understand the particular too narrowly in its specificity.

I. Divine Service and Theology

I.I. Divine Service

I.I.I. General Divine Service:
The Church as an Order of Creation

According to the second narrative of creation, God's first word to humankind is the promise of life (Gen. 2:16): "You may eat . . ."! This promise of life, however, is guarded by a threat of death (Gen. 2:17): "But of the tree of the knowledge of good and evil you shall not eat, for in the day that you eat of it you shall die."

In his *Lectures on Genesis* (1535), Luther comments on this passage in lapidary fashion: "Here we have the establishment of the church before there was any economic or political order."[13] Prior to household and government, God instituted the church, not a particular church but a universal church, a church without walls.[14] It exists in the word and in faith, by the fact that God calls Adam (and so all humankind), into life, and in this way "preaches" to him, "sets his word before him."[15] Accordingly, "God wants only this: that he [Adam] praises God, that he thanks him, and that he rejoices in the Lord."[16]

There are three basic forms of life, three orders *(Stände)*. Although they are interconnected, they also need to be distinguished. God the creator has established these orders and he orders human life in them by his word. Of these three basic forms of life: the church, the household (including marriage and family), and the state, the church is the first. It is the basic order. It includes all people, since all are addressed by God and are called to offer him a free and thankful response. We are humans precisely because God has given us life, because he has addressed us, because we can hear him, and because we can and must respond to him. God's address and our human response are the essence of worship. Indeed, they are the essence of religion, cult, and church, if we understand church here as an order of creation. All people and all religions belong to it. Every human being as such belongs to the church, as an order of creation. In fact, this is what defines us as humans. But this order is now corrupt due to human ingratitude and sin, so that it is no longer in fact the church.

Luther holds that divine service, the church, is meant to be an "order of creation," and not, in the first place, something specifically Christian. That may at first strike us as a strange thesis! But its value will become evident as we proceed.

The scriptures provide us with the basis for a particular kind of "natural" theology and at the same time a phenomenology of religion. We find it in the primordial promise of life, valid for all people (Gen. 2:16), as well as in God's self-introduction, "I am the Lord, your God!" (Exod. 20:2). We also find it in the first commandment, that we should have no other gods besides him (Exod. 20:3), where the threat of death guards the promise of life (Gen. 2:17). Like Romans 1:18–3:20, natural theology assumes that every human being lives in a relationship with God, which, in practice, is always being broken from our side, and so is fundamentally disordered. Reason, not so much theoretical but practical reason, guided by the imagination, always tries to grasp hold of God, but it is always wide of the mark. Luther (commenting on Jonah 1:5: "The sailors were afraid and each cried to his god") could say quite emphatically: "these men in the ship all know of God" "but they have no sure God."[17] The office of Christ is to make us certain of God.

The community that arises from God's self-introduction to his creation is always flawed, and so the church, as an order of creation, is corrupt. The whole of creation has fallen captive to this corruption and "groans" (Rom. 8:18-23). Therefore, the God who speaks, the "God who addresses the creature through the creature" (Hamann), is present and effective only in law and gospel. But he is also active outside of law and gospel in his terrifying hiddenness. Here, in the form of the hidden God, I can no longer hear him, and in any case, I can no longer "understand" him. Where God acts outside of law and gospel, his "voice" terrifies me. I experience him as overwhelming, frightening, and uncanny. In terror, I flee to the gracious and merciful God, the Father, who has shown me through his Son that his fatherly heart is nothing but love.

Because we begin with the general divine service in creation and its basic corruption, rather than with the particular divine service in the church, we are confronted at once with the problem of how theology relates to the world religions. We cannot, of course, assume that any general theory of religion could form "the appropriate framework for Christian theology and all its disciplines."[18] Yet while we cannot avoid the "perspective of a history of world religions,"[19] we need to note that this perspective has its origin solely in the "center" (Gen. 2:9) that in primeval history is tied to the promise of life that is given to every human, as well as to all creatures. And nowhere do we hear it more critically (in the sense of the second use of the law) and more comfortingly than in the preamble to the Decalogue and the first commandment: "I am the Lord your God. You shall have no other gods besides me!" (Exod. 20:2f.).

Luther's explanation of the first commandment in the *Large Catechism* is impressive in showing the incredible breadth of the concept of religion that comes out clearly in his interpretation of this commandment. If we take this concept of religion together with the theology of creation that we have just described, and if we see it in connection with an elementary experience of the world that embraces both the social and individual aspects of existence, as explicated in the teaching of the three orders, then inevitably it has both a cultural-anthropological dimension as well as a sociological one. This then means that the study of religion also becomes a study of its institutions.[20]

This is sufficient to outline what we mean by the general divine service in creation. Theology cannot avoid the task of examining this teaching, not only because of its contact with the world religions, but also because it is already embedded in its own sources, the biblical texts. It was important to briefly outline it here, so that the particular divine service of the church, to which we now turn, can be seen in context and does not appear isolated and arbitrary.

1.1.2. The Particular Divine Service

The restoration of the church from its corruption, as an order of creation, which God accomplished through Christ, is given and distributed to us as a gift in the Christian divine service. "Distribution"[21] is something altogether different from mere "representation,"[22] for it is no symbolic expression but a gift; no statement but a promise. Everything depends on God's performative word for the enactment of the promise of the forgiveness of sins and the healing of our ingratitude towards the creator. Since this word precedes our faith, our response of faith and prayer can never lead us to understand the divine service as a "self-realization of the church."[23] Even as the response of the church, faith remains God's work.

The standard arguments from ecclesiology and sacramental theology resort to the category of "representation," and speak of the "self-realization of the church" and of the church as the "original sacrament."[24] It is clear from this that the criterion of the particular divine service, which Luther vigorously promoted from the beginning of his Reformation theology, is not at all self-evident. For him, worship has to do with the enactment of the word and faith, of *promissio* and *fides*. This is classically formulated in the treatise, *The Babylonian Captivity of the Church* (1520): "For God does not deal, nor has he ever dealt, with us except[25] through the word of promise. We, in turn, cannot deal with God except through faith in the word of his promise."[26] This asymmetrical correlation between word and faith, where the word always comes first and faith follows the word, is for Luther the criterion of the true divine service. At the end of his life he preached a sermon at the consecration of the castle church in Torgau in 1544. There he gave his famous definition of the divine service that beautifully exemplifies this criterion. He calls on the people to join him in the consecration "in order that the purpose of this new house may be this: that nothing else may happen in it except that our dear Lord himself may speak to us through his holy word and that we respond to him through prayer and praise."[27]

Two things belong together and must not be separated: the public word and inward prayer, in which "the heart speaks with God in petition and intercession, thanksgiving and adoration."[28] From this viewpoint, it is unthinkable to regard "religion as a private matter."[29] The word that creates faith is an "embodied word," as Article 5 of the *Augsburg Confession* emphasizes with its anti-spiritualizing thrust.

The externality of this word can be seen in the Lord's Supper, which has four interconnected aspects (italicized below). First, *the social* aspect of communal eating and drinking which is constitutive; this of course includes *the natural and cultural* dimension. However, for this meal to be the *new covenant*, the renewal of creation, the final community between God and humanity along with all creatures, this real, present, physical event that can be experienced and even seen, must be accompanied by the word of Jesus Christ by which he gives us his body and blood according to his promise. This eschatological community of course is not possible without a physical coming together of God's baptized people. But they come together first of all as sinners who have become, and will become, the eschatological community only through a *performative word* that addresses them through bread and wine, and that derives its *competence*, its authority, from the resurrection of the crucified Jesus.[30]

If the constitutive aspects of the "embodied word" are evident from the event and enactment of the Lord's Supper, we do not need to locate the authority of God's word and the Holy Scriptures in a rigid positivism of revelation. But neither should we let it sink into an inexhaustible sea of ever-new and far-reaching interpretations and applications. The Lord's Supper then frees us from the need to lay claim to the historical world of modernity in its totality as an institutional counterweight to subjectivity, a totality that says nothing because it tries to say everything.[31] Instead, we only have to look to an event, a meal, which we can experience as a present reality. This meal highlights the mutuality of the word and the body, where the body functions verbally and the word operates bodily, and where both work in a way that has at once anthropological, Christological, ecclesiological, and eschatological dimensions.

This is enough for a basic understanding of the "particular divine service."[32] There are only two aspects that still need to be mentioned that are decisive for a general understanding of the particular divine service as well as the restored general divine service: (1) sacrifice and gift, and (2) celebration.

Sacrifice and Gift Divine service *(Gottesdienst)* is first and last God's service to us, the sacrifice he made for us in Christ, which he distributes to us in the particular divine service: "Take and eat! I am here for you!" (compare 1 Cor. 11:24 with Gen. 2:16). We misunderstand this divine service, which is meant to delight us, if we want to give as a work what we are meant to take and receive as a gift.[33] Here we "are not offering a good work, we are not *actively* receiving the Lord's Supper," as if our actions could bring about the self-realization of the church. Rather, we receive through the "priest," as the servant of the divine word, "the promise and the sign, and we receive the Lord's Supper *passively.*"[34] The sacramental gift-giving word is not a prayer; and the gifts that we are to take and receive are not to be offered to God as a sacrifice.[35] The Lord's Supper is not a "sacrifice that we offer to God."[36] Rather, God in his gracious condescension and self-surrender gives himself to us in this meal. We are the recipients; we simply *receive* his sacrifice.

The mystery of Christian godliness does not consist of services, sacrifices and vows, which God demands of us, but of promises, fulfillments and sacrifices which God has made for our benefit. Again, the mystery of Christian godliness does not consist of the finest and greatest commandment that God has imposed, but of the supreme good that he has given us. Once again, the mystery of Christian godliness does not consist of laws and moral teachings which merely have to do with human dispositions and actions, but of the enactment of divine decrees by means of divine acts, works and measures for the salvation of the whole world.[37]

In the particular divine service, we can hear, taste, and see, through the word, that what holds the world together in its inmost essence is the categorical gift rather than the categorical imperative (*contra* Kant). *The particular divine service* does not cultivate its own separate religious sphere, but it *discloses the world as creation*. In the light of his Reformation discovery that the Words of Institution spoken over the Lord's Supper are fundamentally performative words that give what they say, Luther developed his characteristic understanding of creation as God's gift. Luther has these gift-giving words of the Lord's Supper in his ears, before his eyes, and in his heart when he confesses that every action of the triune God is a promise that gives and a gift that promises.[38]

The universal character of the categorical gift finds its counterpart in the universality of the response, for which we are empowered by the gift and promise: "For all of this I am bound to thank and praise, serve and obey him." An ethos of giving and love is included in the response. It is included but is not identical to it. Thus, it is a mistake to conclude from Romans 12:1-2 that "the doctrines of worship and Christian 'ethics' coincide."[39] It is even less possible to understand this *Magna Carta* of the new obedience (Rom. 12:1f.) in the sense of the Roman Catholic idea of the sacrifice of the faithful together with Christ in the Eucharist.[40] This proposal is no better than the claim that worship coincides with ethics.[41] Neither proposal has any place for the indispensable distinction between faith as God's service to us, and love as the service of the faithful to their fellow creatures. This distinction is so necessary for salvation that we cannot do without it.

In the overall context of the letter, the "sacrifice" and the "worship" that Paul speaks of in Romans 12:1-2 explain the significance of

Baptism, which Paul sums up as living a new life (Rom. 6:4). This not only has ethical implications but it goes beyond ethics and includes the whole physical perception of the world which needs to be worked out in a comprehensive aesthetics that looks at how our senses, emotions, memory, and imagination are all involved in our experience of reality. We can only view creation properly through that judgment and "death" which is enacted in Baptism; otherwise all talk about creation is idle chatter.

This brings us to the second aspect of the church's particular divine service: the aspect of celebration.

Keeping the Festival: "The Day of Rest" Festivals and holidays (holy days) make harsh demands on the old nature, for it means that we must cease from our work: "For our sinful nature is very unwilling to die and to be passive, and it is a bitter day of rest for it to cease from its own works and be dead."[42] This has been a bitter pill for modern theological anthropology, right up to the theology of Barth[43] and Bultmann,[44] in which humans are always seen as active subjects, as doers (for Barth analogously to God). We see this most clearly in Karl Marx. For him, the world exists only in "self-production" through human "work."[45] However, this overlooks the power of the Sabbath, of Sunday, to establish life, because on the Lord's Day human work ceases and God is active. If we receive this power as a categorical gift, the urge to realize ourselves, not only in our work but also in our actions, even in the act of faith,[46] must die. This is the harsh side of the divine service, understood as a festival, a holiday. We emphasize it when we say that preaching is a "remembrance of Baptism" *(memoria baptismi)*[47] and that Baptism itself is constitutive for the divine service as a whole. It is impossible then to ignore what Paul says about dying in Romans 6.

This kind of dying, however, makes room for life: "Keep hand and heart from labor free, that God may do his work in thee."[48] When we keep the festival, observe the Lord's day and cease from our work, the result is sheer delight, for he removes our burdens so that we can relax in his presence and "enjoy God forever" *(Westminster Catechism)*. It means that God, and God alone, does his work in us. Faith, of course, is nothing but "a divine work in us which changes us and makes us to be born anew of God, John 1 [12-13]. It kills the old Adam and makes us altogether new persons, in heart and spirit and mind and powers."[49]

If it is true that we must rest from our work, die to the old self, to let God do his work, faith is primarily neither theory nor practice, neither a speculative life *(vita contemplativa)* nor an active life *(vita activa)*, but, to use Luther's term for it, a receptive life *(vita passiva).*[50]

In the summary below, which anticipates the detailed exposition to follow, we will show what this means for the understanding of theology.

1.2. Theology

If the divine service has this universal dimension that we have demonstrated, then theology, understood in the narrower sense as a disciplined way of thinking, cannot go beyond it. It can never outstrip it, nor even catch up with it. *Theology begins and ends with the divine service.* As a disciplined way of thinking, it is closely connected to faith, which comes from hearing (Rom. 10:17). Faith loves God not only with all one's heart, but also with every power and vitality, including the mind (Mark 12:30). Broadly speaking, theology is identical with faith. At any rate, that is the way Luther sees theology, even though today, in the wake of Semler and Schleiermacher, it may sound strange to our ears. If we want to think of it in terms of "rules," there are none better than the three rules Luther described with the triad: *oratio, meditatio, tentatio* (prayer, meditation, and spiritual attack).[51] It was not his intention that any of these rules should be used as a distinct method in isolation from the others, but he saw them as one rule. We will show later exactly how these rules are to be properly understood.

In this way, *sapientia* and *scientia,* wisdom and knowledge, as well as life and doctrine do not fall apart. Modern models of understanding theology, on the other hand, are characterized by this very kind of separation which goes hand in hand with an approach to theology that denies it has any substantive object. So theology is no longer a doctrine of the word but becomes a doctrine of faith, as in Schleiermacher.[52] Or it is transformed into a philosophy of mind and identified with thought, as in Hegel. For him, "philosophy coincides with religion; philosophy is . . . worship itself, it is religion."[53] He forgets that people live in their bodies and not just in their heads, that they have passions and not just minds. So in Hegel, the passion of the complaint is replaced by "the passionless calm of purely intellectual knowledge."[54]

Modern theology has understood Christianity in three different ways. One follows Hegel and understands it theoretically; another follows Schleiermacher and sees it existentially, while the third follows the Kantian tradition and understands it morally. In view of these transformations,[55] I believe that there is only one way in which systematic theology can come to a responsible understanding of what theology is, and that is to see it linguistically or, more precisely, to see it as a doctrine of forms. Although we will keep in mind the general divine service in creation and the church, where the church is understood as a corrupted order of creation, theology focuses specifically on the liturgical forms of the particular divine service which shape human life and human speech, such as the songs of praise and the complaints, the cries for help (like the "Kyrie!"), the prayers of intercession, and the words of blessing.[56]

The important thing therefore is that theology focuses on the forms of speech that are used in the divine service. In view of the great variety of forms and their relationship to each other, a doctrine of forms such as I am proposing will need to use as a criterion the correlation of promise *(promissio)* and faith *(fides)*, or more precisely, the distinction between law and gospel, for this is the only means of arriving at a precise understanding of the promise.[57]

If theology, or more specifically systematic theology, is understood in this way as a doctrine of forms, it will no longer be able to simply follow the outline of the creed, as most textbooks do, beginning with creation and ending with eschatology. In order to avoid the danger of abstraction and speculation as much as possible, it makes more sense to locate the organizing principle of systematic theology in the distinctions and connections between the different parts of the *Small Catechism.*[58]

Theology, understood as a doctrine of forms, is a "grammar of the language of the Holy Scriptures,"[59] of the language of the interpreted and interpreting Bible, of the living and life-giving voice of the gospel, which is related to the law that kills and, in a different way, to God's terrifying hiddenness. Theology therefore is not primarily concerned with morality, as in Kant,[60] or with "concepts," as in Hegel,[61] or even with "motivations," as in Schleiermacher and Feuerbach.[62] It does not try to elevate "forms" into "concepts" or reduce them to "motivations." Rather, theology is a doctrine of forms and as such it preserves the findings of form analysis *(Formgeschichte)*. It takes up Franz Overbeck's insight that forms of speech are inextricably woven together with forms of life.[63] "Forms" embody the social as well as the individual modes of existence, and both are bound up with an elementary experience of the world. This is not only implied but always presupposed in both theory and practice. Theology and its ethics therefore cannot be made to fit the Procrustean bed of the theory-practice scheme, nor can theology be primarily a theory of action.[64] For people can act only because they have the freedom to act. However, this freedom is not the result of their action but its presupposition. This presupposition of course does not take the form of a postulate or implicate but of a promise which is mediated by worldly means.

Theology not only studies forms but it also studies history, which it sees in the light of the promise. In that light, we can say that history is shaped by the knowledge of sin and the longing for forgiveness. If theology views history in any other way, it would have to develop the idea of a unity of history and speak of God as the unity of reality, as a totality of meaning. It would then have to try to grasp that by means of hypotheses, unless of course it sees history as a series of natural cycles, or sinks into skepticism and despair. However, if theology sees history in that way, eschatology becomes nothing more than a theoretical idea subordinated to the modern concepts of projection and hypothesis.[65] But if theology holds that history is shaped by sin and forgiveness, it renounces the idea of a unity and refuses to try to make sense of history, for it cannot give meaning to something that has no meaning.

Theology does not gloss over the painful discrepancies between the promise of life, which is unconditioned and unconditional, valid for all people at all times, and our daily experiences that contradict this promise. Rather, it resonates with the passion of the complaint, which echoes this discrepancy. Thus, theology is a *theology of Anfechtung: it involves trial, testing, and spiritual attack*. It renounces the idea of a unity of history and all attempts to offer a theodicy. In other words, it gives up any attempt to justify God and his goodness in the face of radical evil. Theology has to face the fact that God is inaccessibly remote and at the same time uncomfortably close. As Luther says, he "does not give you a definition of himself in his word," but rather "is hidden in majesty and does not lament or remove death, but brings about life, death, and all things."[66] In the face of this God, theology can only speak of the God who speaks to us through the history of Christ. It refuses to reconcile the inscrutable hiddenness of God and his tangible promise, which does lament death and brings about life through death. It does not try to comprehend God's hiddenness rationally but recognizes that it will always remain a mystery to us this side of the grave. Theology cannot even identify it with his wrath and judgment, because God's wrath and judgment are forms of his love. Therefore, theology cannot even understand it in the light of the distinction and inseparability of law and gospel, the gospel's promise of life and the law's threat of death.

Nor can theology explain away the discrepancy between God's promise of life and all that contradicts it simply by contemplating the unity of history. It cannot even create that unity or make history with freedom as the regulative idea. It cannot resort to either speculation or action. It is neither speculative nor moralistic but practical. But what does that mean? Theology is practical in the sense that it is an experience. It is the experience that we encounter in meditation, as we listen and learn by engaging with the biblical text, in prayer, and in the context of spiritual attack *(Anfechtung)*. In this experience God is the active subject. He works at shaping and molding us. And we are the passive recipients who "suffer," who undergo his work. For that reason Luther calls theology the receptive life *(vita passiva)*.

2. The Main Problems with the Philosophy of Science

If "theology," understood as a disciplined way of thinking, begins and ends with the divine service, it has two sides. First, there is the monastic side that embraces liturgical spirituality. This is grounded in the divine service, which is constitutive. Secondly, there is the academic side, which orders, analyzes, and reflects on the content given by its monastic side. This therefore plays only a regulative role.[67] Matters relating to the philosophy of science then belong to this regulative side of theology and so are not left to hang in the air or become independent. On the other hand, the fact that the philosophy of science is related to theology in this way should not be allowed to short-circuit its own legitimate contribution to the theological enterprise. Since the main focus of theology is on the object itself, it has a relative degree of freedom to pursue its own scholarly inquiries.[68] But this freedom is never absolute, because the academic side of theology must always remain subservient to its monastic liturgical spirituality centered in the divine service. However, as a disciplined way of thinking, theology shares the dignity of theoretical reason, within the limits mentioned above. In other words, it shares its relative freedom and autonomy.

Heinrich Scholz, in 1931, raised the question: "How can Protestant theology be an academic discipline?"[69] However, it was not possible for the Protestant theology of his day to launch into a full-scale discussion of the question. Only in the 1960s and 1970s was the question raised again, this time with even greater urgency, whether and to what extent theology can be an academic discipline.[70] At present, however, interest in academic theology seems to have waned again and is limited to what is considered to be the bare minimum necessary for the prolegomena of systematic theology. However, the situation is different in Roman Catholic theology, which has its own discipline, called fundamental theology, which formally introduces questions dealing with the philosophy of science.[71]

In what follows, we will deal with questions relating to the philosophy of science by concentrating first on the three major problem areas set out in Gabriel Biel's *Collectorium*.[72] Our aim is to compare the work done in these areas since the medieval scholastics and, in order to offer a contemporary account of theology, to look at them in relation to the most important questions of modernity. Our ultimate aim is to highlight the truth of Luther's understanding of theology. Our assumption is that Biel's three questions take up all the problems, or at least the essential ones, connected with the philosophy of science and theological methodology also in our day.

The specifically modern questions, which in the main we can only consider briefly in this second section, will be given thorough attention in the sections that follow. All sections constantly refer to each other, both implicitly and explicitly, with later sections taking up themes from earlier sections and developing them further.

2.1. The Object of Theology

We begin with Biel's second and most important question. From Thomas Aquinas to Wolfhart Pannenberg, many consider that "God" is the object of theology, without any further qualification. Thus, Pannenberg says, "God" is "the true object of theology."[73] Every topic in theology is discussed "in the light of its relation to God *(sub ratione Dei)*."[74] In this sense, we can say that theology is the "science of God."[75]

On the other hand, Luther's definition,[76] that the object of theology is the sinful human and the God who justifies, is criticized by many for being far too narrow. Furthermore, from a logical standpoint, this definition seems to presuppose that "God" and "human" are general terms that lack specific content. Does this then mean that Luther's definition also presupposes and implies a general concept of God, which is initially indeterminate?

We cannot here enter into a proper discussion of this implication, which really has its place in a fully developed doctrine of the Trinity. In any case, when it comes to understanding Luther's definition of the object of theology, the important thing is that we understand the qualifiers (the *sinful* human and the *justifying* God) as essences rather than as accidents, but that does not imply that humans were created sinful in their being. We mean that "sinful" and "justifying" are not simply qualities that we might add to the general concepts "human" and "God" in order to distinguish them from other members of the same species. Rather, they define the very essence of both God and humanity. Therefore, human beings, theologically, are essentially people who are accused and absolved by God. Conversely, the defining characteristic of God is that God is the one who accuses and absolves us. Cosmological and political questions then only have theological significance in relation to this definition of the object.[77]

If we are correct in defining the object of theology this way, it will have enormous consequences, for it will affect every theological statement, from the doctrine of creation, through Christology and the doctrine of the triune God, to eschatology.[78]

If the sole object of theology is the sinful human and the God who justifies, theology cannot be anything but critical. To begin with, it means that we cannot understand its object in the same way as in positivism, as if the relationship between a sinful human and the God who justifies is open to scientific verification! But since this is not the case, has this insight robbed the object of theology of its certainty and turned it into a problem? However, we cannot go along with those who talk of "the openness and inconclusive state of the question of God," because to do so means that we would have to say that the object and theme of theology is "the *problem* of God"[79] rather than "God." Anyone who holds that the object of theology is not a given but a matter of inquiry had better be prepared for where this quest will take them. It will not simply lead to the realm of the indeterminate or, as Pannenberg[80] thinks, to the harmless open horizon of meaning, to that serene philosophical no-man's land, where the finite coexists with the infinite in a relationship of correspondence and correlation, which he finds, for example, in the third Meditation of Descartes.[81] Rather, it will lead to Mount Moriah (Gen. 22:1-14) and to the Jabbok, where an unknown figure struggles with Jacob in the night, and where it is only clear to him *after* the struggle that the stranger he had wrestled with was none other than God himself (Gen. 32).[82] Jacob's opponent had offered fierce resistance and Jacob's lame hip was a constant reminder of this life-and-death struggle for mutual recognition.

As for indeterminacy, we know from Romantic nihilism and atheism that a vast open expanse can also cause angst.[83] However, the indeterminacy that is not just ideological but directly existential is experienced more forcefully in the confined space of that struggle at the Jabbok. The fact that Jacob escaped with his life from that mortal confrontation with God was a sheer miracle and cannot be extrapolated into a general principle and applied to every human encounter with God. Jacob escaped; another person may not. His experience therefore cannot be assumed as a self-evident truth and made the starting-point for theology. In fact, the opposite is the case: We should make the uncertainty and indeterminacy of the divine-human encounter part of the definition of theology itself. If this is removed from the broader understanding of theology so that there is no longer any living memory of the fear and terror ("primal dread"[84]) associated with that encounter, the definition we are left with is dead. Therefore, we must reject this positivistic *praecisio*[85] that wants to excise this element of primal fear and dread from the human encounter with God because it is not scientifically verifiable. We must be careful, however, not to go too far in the other direction. Just because the primal fear and dread associated with this encounter cannot be verified, we dare not trivialize it into a harmless indeterminate correlation of the infinite with the finite.

Let us summarize: We started out by saying that the object of theology is the sinful human and the God who justifies. Putting it another way, we could say that the object of theology is the word of the law that kills and the word of the gospel that gives life. However, this does not mean that the object of theology is a datum in the positivistic sense. It is not a dead object that is open to scientific investigation and verification. Rather, the object is a living, dramatic event that is as difficult to describe as a bird in flight, and yet it must be taught.[86]

If theology seeks its own object, it moves along a dangerous ridge and could easily fall off on either side. It could fall into a form of positivism that demands scientific verifiability, or into a mysticism that demands that I am silent about that of which I cannot speak.[87] It could also fall into the trap of attempting to understand its object in terms of total mediation.[88] Alternatively, it could fall into the activist trap of attempting to define the object of theology in terms of the realization of its essence.[89] Or yet again, it could fall into the subjectivist trap of attempting to understand its object in a "non-objective" way[90] in the context of a faith that understands itself as a "leap" in the "moment" of "decision."[91] Theology therefore must maintain a proper balance, otherwise it will not remain faithful to the biblical text, which always needs to be interpreted in the light of the distinction between law and gospel. A failure here will result in people either understanding the Bible in purely moral terms,[92] or interpreting it existentially,[93] or seeing it in terms of a total mediation, according to which the object thinks and interprets itself, leaving no room for language and history.[94]

In the case of a total mediation, such as we have in Hegel and his theological followers, every opposition is overcome. The other is understood as the other of myself, so that by relinquishing myself, by going out of myself and immersing myself in the other, in that which is alien to me, I return to myself enriched. In other words, I only gain myself by losing myself and becoming immersed in the other. But finally one always remains with oneself. In any case, the spirit remains in this movement with itself; nowhere do I find the resistance of an opposite. I cannot encounter God, and he cannot encounter me or find me. He neither affects me nor concerns me.

On the one hand, therefore, the dependence of faith on the word is to be recognized, objectively and concretely, as history *(Geschichte)* and not, subjectively and abstractly, as historicity *(Geschichtlichkeit)*. But, on the other hand, we must oppose the idea of a total mediation, in which the dependence of faith on the sure and certain word is no longer important.

Since the sinful human and the God who justifies are connected through the word and faith, we cannot define theology either as a doctrine of the word or as a doctrine of faith. Yet if we take into account the priority of the word to faith, it would be better to speak of theology as a doctrine of the word than as a doctrine of faith. That means that we must not overlook the specific textual structure of this object. This needs to be emphasized over against the hermeneutical strategies of modernity that are not oriented to the text. Therefore, we must be just as strong in our opposition to understanding the object of theology (which is the same as its subject matter) ethically as we are to understanding it theoretically or existentially.

The latter happens in the Schleiermacherian tradition. We adopt a critical stance over against Schleiermacher's understanding of theology and its implied hermeneutic. According to Schleiermacher, the object of a theological statement is located in "the emotions of the religious self-consciousness."[95] We do not agree with the prevailing hermeneutic of regression, the attempt to get behind the text to discover the original emotions that give rise to the text, nor do we take the object to be "the emotions of the religious self-consciousness" or the believing self-understanding[96] but the written and oral texts that establish it.

We must stress against Schleiermacher and his followers that the object of theology is essentially bound up with language. Negatively, this means that theology is not primarily related to knowing or doing. Nor is it related to words that necessarily express some deeper, more original phenomenon lying behind them.[97] Rather, it is related to those elementary speech acts in which law and gospel are concretely enacted. There is a very close relation between theology and speech acts. This is evident from the fact that theology is entirely dependent on them and is enacted in them.[98] This means that we must do justice to the vitality of the object. This, of course, flies in the face of that form of positivism which insists, in the name of scientific objectivity, that the object to be observed must be dead. The object of theology, on the other hand, is very much alive, even if it is not a bird in flight! For the Logos became flesh (John 1:14) and encounters us in the "embodied word."

Because of the peculiar vitality and physicality of its object, theology is forced to develop its own understanding of the objectivity of its object, which does not fit the mold of the current alternatives of either a subject-object scheme or an objective experience as distinct from a non-objective experience, nor does it fit the scheme of total mediation advocated by a philosophy of spirit, such as we have in Hegel, whose fundamental tenet finally is the identity of thinking and the object of thought, in other words, the identity of the subject and the object. Theology can only develop its own understanding of the objectivity of its object if it takes seriously the following three ways in which God encounters us, which are irreducible and cannot be subsumed under a general concept, not even the self-revelation of God.

God encounters me in three ways: (a) through the opposition of the law that points its accusing finger at me, convicts me of sin, and hands me over to death; (b) through the promise of the gospel, in which God himself speaks for me, indeed takes my place in Jesus Christ; and (c) through the assault of God's incomprehensible, crushing hiddenness that radically contradicts the gospel and is more than merely an effect of the law.

(a) The first encounter with God is linked with the law. In it God confronts me and asks me hard questions that I cannot escape: "Adam, Eve! Where are you?" (Gen. 3:9). "Where is your brother?" (Gen. 4:9). Questions like these convict me. They make me aware of what I do not know. In fact, I am actually unmasked for the first time: "You are the man"; you are condemned to death (2 Sam. 12:7 and 5). I cannot say that to myself but I have to hear it from another. Nevertheless, I stand convicted, and like David before Nathan, the prophet of God, I pronounce judgment on myself. The law that confronts me convicts me at the same time from within. Its externality is no heteronomy, no alien voice that I do not recognize. But then again, neither is it simply an echo of myself.

(b) While God speaks *against* me in the law, he speaks *for* me in the gospel. Therefore, the gospel is a "different" word, a second word of God, which cannot be fused with the word of the law to form a third overarching concept such as God's one self-revelation. These two words are irreducible and cannot in any way be combined. The distinction between law and gospel must not be eliminated by subsuming it into a higher or deeper unity.

The second, decisive, and final word of God is the gospel, which speaks for *me*. However, we cannot consider this within an epistemological framework, as commonly happened in the neo-Protestantism influenced by Kant, where the "for you" of the Reformation was understood as "for me" *(pro me)*. This was modeled on Kant's propositions in the methodological section of his *Critique of Pure Reason.*[99] If this way of reading Kant is coupled with the intention of rejecting or even playing down the objectivity of the object of faith in order to insist solely on my own certainty, it blatantly contradicts the Reformation, even though its self-understanding is entirely different from what we find, say, in Wilhelm Herrmann.

In any case, the *pro me* of Luther's Reformation theology was the communicative being of Jesus Christ himself, in which the triune God promises and gives himself "in the external word"[100] with Baptism and the Lord's Supper, as well as with every baptismal and eucharistic sermon. In this encounter, in which we receive the promise of the forgiveness of sins, we sinners are created anew and have our permanent identity outside ourselves, in another, who is alien to us and who has taken our place in a wonderful exchange, where human sin is exchanged for divine righteousness. This event of Christ's vicarious atoning death and his bodily self-giving gives theology the criterion of truth it needs to critique both the ancient "metaphysics of substance" and the modern "metaphysics of the subject," since neither allows us to think of an "'ex-centric' being" or of the permanent identity of the self in another person.

Therefore, Luther's understanding of Christ's vicarious representation of sinful humanity is the rock of bronze that shatters the desire for identity of the modern Narcissus.[101] This desire for identity can of course also be expressed Christologically. We see this in transcendental thought, in the pure, rational Kantian archetype,[102] as well as in the pure, historical Schleiermacherian archetype.[103] We also see it in idealism's law of identity, particularly in the Hegelian doctrine of reconciliation that generalizes Lutheran Christology into a post-Christian natural Christology.[104]

Here we discover the decisive point of controversy in the conflict between Luther's theology and modern thought. In focusing on this, theology needs to define the relation between the being of the self and the being of the other. The philosophical tradition since Plato's

Parmenides has understood this relation in accordance with monarchical[105] reason, but this is now being revised by Emmanuel Levinas who, in contrast to this tradition, clearly stresses "otherness" (*altérité*, which comes into English as alterity).[106]

Theology views this relationship between the being of the other and the being of the self from its own perspective and so in *its* own way. It insists that the righteousness given to me as my own is and remains the righteousness of another *(iustitia aliena)*. It cannot therefore follow Hegel in conceiving this relationship between the self and the other as the "identity of identity and non-identity."[107] If it did, theology would once again bring the relationship under the rule of the law of identity, and thus subordinate itself to monarchical reason and its desire for unity.

The ultimate reason why theology cannot do this but must instead suppress the desire for identity on the part of the modern Narcissus lies in the third way in which God encounters us, to which we must now turn: the assault of God's incomprehensible, crushing hiddenness, which radically contradicts the gospel and is much more than just the effect of the law.

(c) We are confronted by this hiddenness in events such as the senseless catastrophes of nature, unrectifiable injustice, innocent suffering, starvation, murder, war, incurable illness, and the tragic death of the young. "God" for the most part remains anonymous in all this, almost always concealed in passivity. He is not for life but against it, not a preserver of life but its destroyer, who contradicts his revealed will and the gospel. This is the cause of the most profound testing, trial, and spiritual attack *(Anfechtung):* that the one who presents himself "for you!" in the promise of life and of eternal community, vouching for it with his own death, is the same one who, as Luther says with the Old Testament, "neither deplores death nor takes it away," "but works life, death, and all in all."[108]

Who can comprehend this? No one! God is not consistent but contradicts himself. Here we see God against God! We can see it in the book of Job. Hence, the only thing left for those who cannot remain silent or resign themselves to the situation is the complaint: "When can I come and see the face of God?" (Ps. 42:2). When will I see him no longer as "a dim reflection," as some enigmatic figure, but "face to face" (1 Cor. 13:12)?

The gospel promises that this complaint will be answered. Therefore, Luther can preach: "Set God's promise of life against your fear of death!"[109] The certainty of the promise that God will answer makes it even more difficult to endure the discrepancy between that promise and our present trouble. As we try to ride it out and take hold of God in his promise, we are stretched to the limit by the gulf that separates the anguish that we feel now from the joy of the promise. All we can do is hope. The complaint culminates in the certainty that God will answer us. On the strength of that promise, we can persistently pester (Luke 11:8), pressure, and badger God with our request for justice, justice for ourselves and our fellow creatures against the last enemy, death (Luke 18:1-18). In asking God for justice, we are only asking him to remain faithful to his own justice established with the promise of life.

The theology that we do en route as pilgrims *(theologia viatorum)* is stamped by these three irreducibly different ways in which God encounters us.[110] They resist being subsumed into the concept of a unity and are a stumbling block to reason's monarchical desire for unity and to a theoretical concept of God's unity that goes with it, even if this is developed trinitarianly. They show therefore that the question of the object of theology confronts us with an insoluble dilemma (aporia). We are assuming of course that this question is identical with that of the *unity* of theology, understood as an academic discipline, and that "the unity of an academic discipline is based on the unity of its subject matter" (Biel).[111]

Some think that they can escape this dilemma by refusing to think of the unity of theology as a system, in the sense that it "unites our manifold cognitions under one [single] idea."[112] They think that they can find this unity in God's self-revelation, understood trinitarianly, or in the correlation and correspondence between self-consciousness and God-consciousness. However, the weakness of the great theological theories of the last two hundred years or so is that their authors succumbed to the pressure of the Enlightenment to make their work conform to a nice neat system. This blinded them to the fact that the three ways in which God encounters us, which we mentioned above, are so different that they cannot be fitted into a single concept or system. If we take account of these insuperable differences, we should really speak of at least a threefold definition of the object of theology.[113] That way we might avoid both a theoretical dualism and a theoretical monism.[114]

But as we shall see, we should speak not just of a threefold definition of the object of theology, but rather of a fourfold. It would be very difficult to unite the first or political use of the law *(usus politicus)* with the second or theological use *(usus theologicus: elenchticus)* to form a single concept called "law" without causing misunderstanding. That would mean ignoring the distinction between the grace of preservation and the grace of the new creation, which is the gospel. In the interests of clarity, we should keep the political use of the law, which is more a gentle presence of God than a fourth way he has of encountering us, absolutely separate and give it special emphasis. In line with that, we should really speak of a fourfold definition of the object of theology.[115]

This fourfold definition of the object of theology does not contradict Luther's binary formula that we took up at the outset, according to which the subject matter of theology is the sinful human and the God who justifies. It rather explicates what is implied by this formula and what in any case can be known from Luther's theology as a whole.

Finally, in view of the fourfold definition we have described, the question of theology cannot be reduced to the simple alternative: Does theology start with a particular concept in order to demonstrate its universality,[116] or does it begin with a general indeterminate concept[117] in order to fill it with a specifically Christian content? Both ways fail, the first in its point of entry, the second in its development, because neither of them sufficiently differentiates the relation between specificity and breadth. In this regard, the fourfold definition of the object of theology that we have presented is superior.[118]

2.2. Contemplation, Action, Receptivity (passio)

The sort of *access* we have to the object of theology depends on the nature of the object. It depends on the manner in which this object presents itself to us, forces itself on us, suggests itself to us, and communicates with us. If it fits the fourfold definition just described (2.1), there can be no one single way of perceiving it. We cannot simply say that the faith that grasps hold of the word addressed to us gives us access to the object. It is more complex than that. The convicting law creates anxiety, the liberating gospel joy, the hiddenness of God terror, and his preservation thanksgiving. The object of theology encounters us in different ways: it can oppose us, seize us, and liberate us. But at no time can we ever gain control of it, press it into our service, or make it fit our predetermined system. We can neither establish it nor be certain of it. We can do nothing with it except receive it. We can neither determine nor define it, but, on the contrary, the object of theology determines and defines us.

Schleiermacher's attempt to take this into account as he grappled with the questions of modernity is laudable. With his demonstration of the "feeling of absolute dependence," he wants to emphasize the pure passivity, the pure receptivity of consciousness and existence. We cannot acquire this, let alone account for it, by any sort of "knowing" or "doing." In the second of his speeches *On Religion* (1799) Schleiermacher, in a threefold typology, distinguishes the third category, which he calls "religion," from that of "metaphysics" and "ethics." He takes up this threefold typology in *The Christian Faith* (§3), where he puts forward the proposition: "The piety [spirituality] that forms the basis of all ecclesiastical communities is, considered purely in itself, neither a knowing nor a doing, but a modification of feeling, or of immediate self-consciousness."[119] In §4 this feeling is defined more exactly as the "feeling of absolute dependence" or the "consciousness of absolute dependence."[120]

With this, Schleiermacher takes up the substance of that question of the medieval scholastics in relation to the philosophy of science and theological methodology: Is theology *contemplatio* or *actio*? Is it theoretical or practical?

Ever since theology began to be thought of as a philosophy of science in the thirteenth century, the question has been asked: How do we know what we know? Is our knowledge only theoretical? Or is it also practical? Or is it also affective, involving the senses, the emotions, the memory, the desires, and the imagination?[121] The question has been predominantly answered with the twofold scheme of theory and practice *(contemplatio* and *actio)*. As for the "affects," they seem to be placed, as in Bonaventure,[122] between *contemplatio* and *actio*, between theoretical and practical knowledge.

Luther rightly torpedoed the traditional twofold scheme and corrected it. Adopting the experience and language of the mystic Tauler, he speaks rather of the "receptive life" *(vita passiva)*,[123] "so that neither the active practical life *(vita activa)* with its works nor the contemplative theoretical life *(vita contemplativa)* with its speculations should lead us astray."[124]

Monasticism essentially handed on the spirit of antiquity and especially the Aristotelian understanding of science, which included philosophy and academic theology. However, under the motto "work and pray!" *(ora et labora)*, it accepted the theoretical life *(bios theoretikos)* as well as the practical life *(bios praktikos)*, the contemplative life *(vita contemplativa)* and the active life *(vita activa)*, but not without considerably reshaping them. Anyone who wants to develop a broad-based concept of theology that takes account of the history of science, particularly as it has developed in Europe, cannot afford to neglect a careful consideration of the distinction we have mentioned and the twofold scheme that reflects it.

This twofold scheme was itself riddled with tension. On the one hand, the Aristotelian distinction privileges contemplation *(theoria)* over action *(praxis)*,[125] theory over practice, and especially over production *(poiesis)*.[126] At first glance, the story of the two sisters Mary and Martha (Luke 10:38-42) seems to support this. It seems to be saying that our love for God, which corresponds to *theoria*, is the "one thing needful" *(unum necessarium;* Luke 10:42), and that this therefore should be valued more highly than our love for the neighbor, which corresponds to *praxis* and *poiesis*. On the other hand, any privileging of *theoria* is opposed by the double command to love God and to love the neighbor (Matt. 22:34-39). For here Jesus, in answer to the question, which commandment is the greatest, puts the command to love the neighbor on the same level as the command to love God ("the second is like it"). Therefore, the story of the two sisters invites us to see the unity of theory and praxis, of *vita contemplativa* and *vita activa*, which they personify. Furthermore, the privileging of *theoria* over *praxis* and *poiesis* is also opposed by the high value God gives to human work, especially manual work, with its *Magna Carta* in the biblical story of the Garden of Eden (Gen. 2:15).

In his famous sermon on Mary and Martha, Meister Eckhart resolved this tension in a way reminiscent of the wisdom of Solomon, not, of course, by simply deciding for one against the other, but by means of a subtle dialectic. In order to be who she really is, Mary must first become Martha. She must adopt the active life *(vita activa)* in such a way that it no longer finally excludes the contemplative life *(vita contemplativa).*[127] In this way, the question of which takes priority is overcome. The active life (practice) is given a higher value without seeing the contemplative life (theory) in purely functional terms, as so often happens in modernity.[128]

The twofold scheme serves as a basic model right up to our own day. An impressive example of this is the motto of Taizé: *contemplation et lutte,* "prayer and engagement." However, this is reversed if we turn it into the purely functional slogan "spirituality for combat" in keeping with Seneca's famous maxim: *"non scholae, sed vitae discimus"* ("we do not learn for school, but for life"). The Roman Catholic tradition has at its best maintained the twofold scheme up to the present in the sense of Meister Eckhart's dialectic. Karl Barth has also followed this twofold scheme in his strongly cognitive and contemplative understanding of faith, which of course is connected to the modern emphasis on construction. However, this scheme, together with the Platonic-Aristotelian concept of science that always goes with it, was dealt a fatal blow by Luther's concept of theology. For him, faith is no longer subordinated to theory, but it is a unique and distinctive kind of life, a receptive life *(vita passiva).* Theory and practice are no longer related to each other in a twofold way. Rather, both are related to faith, and it is this *third* element that determines whether they are true or false.

What, according to Luther's new understanding, does "faith" mean for "science," for academic theology and philosophy, if it is a matter neither of "knowing" nor of "doing" but precedes both? And what is the significance of the fact that faith turns both the contemplative life *(vita contemplativa)* and the active life *(vita activa)* into a receptive life *(vita passiva)* because it "suffers," undergoes *(pati)* God's work.[129] This understanding of faith completely revolutionized the way that the Reformation understood science, which included academic theology and philosophy, particularly in its Aristotelian form. It also fundamentally criticizes many things that pass for science today. Luther's understanding of faith has never been superseded and its claims still challenge us today. In what follows we will attempt to outline the main aspects of this impressive thesis.

The righteousness of faith, which has its basis in God's word and work, is essentially passive. In other words, it is donated righteousness, the righteousness that God gives to faith as a gift. The passivity/receptivity of faith radically destroys justifying thinking (metaphysics) and justifying action (morality) and their alleged unity.

Protestant theology has learned from Luther, the interpreter of Paul, that in matters of morality, it is necessary to distinguish between faith and action, between person and work. It knows, for instance, from the *Treatise on Good Works* that people by their fallen nature want to justify themselves by their works. It knows that this nature is "very unwilling to die and be passive, and that it is a bitter day of rest," when it has to "cease from its own works and be dead."[130] However, when it comes to metaphysics and science, and here we remember that metaphysics is always determinative for science, things are different. The insight that theology needs to make an equally necessary distinction between faith and knowledge has received comparatively little attention since the Reformation. The *Treatise on Good Knowledge* has not yet been written.[131] Hegel, who could have written it, did not give any serious consideration to the distinction between faith and knowledge but, on the contrary, tried to overcome it together with the distinction between faith and sight (2 Cor. 5:7).[132] Paul and Luther are not to be blamed for this shortcoming. In fact, the general chapter of the German Augustinian order, meeting in Heidelberg in 1518 under Luther's presidency, debated theses about wisdom and the cross, the theology of glory and the theology of the cross *(Heidelberg Disputation)*. According to Paul, the Greeks who seek wisdom are just as much enemies of the cross and of the receptive life *(vita passiva)* as the Jews who demand proof through moral vigor (1 Cor. 1:22f.).[133] Luther says that faith kills not only works if they are misused for self-justification, it also kills reason if it is wrongly used for the purposes of self-justification.[134]

Paul and Luther are testament to the incredibly sharp conflict between faith, on the one hand, and a knowledge and action that do not proceed from faith, on the other, and therefore are sin (Rom. 14:23). However, Schleiermacher and his Berlin antipode Hegel, the author of *Faith and Knowledge* (1802), both found a way around the sharpness of this conflict. Hegel very cleverly stripped the cross of its offense and only brought it in as a speculation about Good Friday. He completely transformed the Pauline theology of the cross into a natural theology of the cross *(theologia crucis naturalis)*[135] to make it acceptable in philosophy and especially in theology and the church.

What Paul says about the cross of Christ in relation to Greek metaphysics and Jewish morality applies even more to people of modernity. They understand themselves primarily as doers and actors. According to Karl Marx, they "produce themselves" through "work."[136] This makes them different from the people of the ancient world with their cosmic spirituality, and radically different from people of the Middle Ages. But as doers and makers, the people of modernity fail to honor the Sabbath and do not rest from their work. They claim to "do" everything, even what happens to them, what they experience. They find it intolerable to think that they do not produce these things but simply have to undergo them passively. At least they want to understand in theory what they can no longer understand in practice, for they are scandalized by suffering and theodicy. Here they are different from the people of former times.

Since Plato,[137] the problem of theodicy refers to the farthest horizon of all forms of scientific theology and theological science, including all conceivable forms of related knowledge that deserve the name "science." This needs further explanation.

The scientific enterprise essentially involves remembering (anamnesis) and making connections, in the hope of eventually finding one single connection for everything, and thus a unity. The drive for this comes from a primal human need to construct a harmonious picture of the world and the self as the self sees it. This can happen in a contemplative (speculative) way or, as in modernity, in an active way.[138] This finally includes the subordination of practice *(praxis)* to production *(poiesis)*, which itself is made to serve knowledge; for the power of modern science is knowledge.[139] Contemplative and active science are both a struggle, a struggle against chaos, against the contradictions we experience in life, against dissonances, against any fragmentation that threatens coherence and unity. Science, and the metaphysics that forms its pinnacle, join forces in the human struggle against chaos. The question, of course, is whether science and metaphysics have really been able to overcome these contradictions once and for all by searching for an underlying unity. Can they ever be overcome? And if not, do we simply ignore them and pretend that they will go away? Or is there another way? Can science educate itself to be more open and not so intolerant of all the irritations and inconsistencies that we encounter in our world of everyday experience and that come to a head in the problem of theodicy?

Science is worthy of its name only if it is prepared to listen to Payne, who Georg Büchner has say in the first scene of Act III of *Dantons Tod (Danton's Death)*: "We can deny evil, but not pain. We may be able to prove God with our reason, but our feelings rebel against it. Think about this question, Anaxagoras, why do I suffer? That is the bedrock of atheism. The slightest twinge of pain, even if it could hardly move an atom, rends creation from top to bottom." If science refuses to listen to this, on the grounds that it is unscientific, it is no longer truly science.

The only science that deserves to be taken seriously is a science that listens to words like these, addresses the problem of theodicy that they articulate, and then relativizes itself accordingly. The position taken by any science (and that includes academic theology and philosophy) on the question of theodicy provides a necessary touchstone for proving its true worth. Christian theology does not enter philosophical discussion with this thesis as an outsider but rather sees itself tackling a common problem that philosophy, for its part, has been debating since the time of Plato and Aristotle. Both these philosophers, of course, like many of their successors right up to our own day, tended to play down the problems associated with theodicy.

The threefold scheme implicit in Luther's concept of theology does not immediately address the problem of theodicy, nor does it refer to the word of the cross. This becomes clear when we take a look at Schleiermacher, for the scheme is equally decisive for his systematic theology *(Glaubenslehre)*. We now need to enter into a critical discussion with him to further clarify the question of access to the object of theology.

If theology is to retain its integrity, it must follow Schleiermacher in making certain fundamental distinctions. For example, it must distinguish religion from knowing, on the one hand, and from doing, on the other, although religion is the basis of both. Furthermore, theology must uphold these distinctions unconditionally against every attempt on the part of the academy to transform religion into either knowing or doing. The attempt to see it as knowledge (theory) is modeled on Hegel's philosophy of religion,[140] while the attempt to see it as action (morality) is based on Kant's philosophy of religion[141] or Karl Marx's critique of religion.

However, even Schleiermacher's approach cannot defend itself against a transformation critical of religion if this is carried out in the sense of Feuerbach and Freud's secularization of religion that ends up psychologizing it. This secularization extends not only to the way that people experience society, but also to the way they experience themselves. Here it becomes most problematic for theology. The experience of the self seems to be the final refuge of apologetic theology. Therefore, the neuralgic point is the way in which the secularization of religion entails its psychologization.[142]

The secularization of religion in psychological terms has enjoyed an easy victory over Schleiermacher's transcendental-dialectical thinking and its related hermeneutic. According to this, faith must express itself in words, but these words are only of secondary importance. Therefore, exponents of the secularization of religion only have to insist on the inauthenticity of the verbal expression to be released from any obligation to its specificity and to claim the right to give it its "interpretation."

We need to avoid this danger of a secularization of Christianity in religious psychological terms, so that the Christian faith is not identified with knowing and doing, for it is prior to both and undergirds both. But we can avoid this danger of secularization only by refusing to remove the transcendental element of the Christian faith from the medium of language and by locating it instead *in* language. Hence, we cannot follow Schleiermacher's hermeneutic, which we can call a "hermeneutic of regression,"[143] because it is bound up with this transcendentalism.

According to Schleiermacher, the object of a theological proposition is located in "the emotions of the religious self-consciousness"[144] or, in the final instance, in the "feeling of absolute dependence." Luther, on the other hand, holds that it is bound up with those basic speech acts in which law and gospel are enacted. This then represents another profound difference between Luther and Schleiermacher, in spite of the fact that they both operate with a threefold scheme.

This difference has to do with the kind of passivity that determines the basis of the threefold scheme, which Schleiermacher and his disciples understand monistically in the sense of a single anthropological ground of existence. However, if the passivity *(passio)* is related to the work of the law and the work of the gospel, it is a different *passio* and not simply an expression of the passive nature of existence and consciousness in general. The difference then cannot be accommodated by one single anthropological definition, such as the basic "feeling of absolute dependence." For the gospel, which gives life, is received differently than the law that kills. The way in which we receive the liberating gospel is totally different from the way in which we encounter the oppressive, hidden work of God, outside of law and gospel, who can hurl us into the most profound spiritual attack *(Anfechtung):* the attack by God himself, where God becomes our enemy.

The theology that we do en route as pilgrims *(theologia viatorum)* is stamped by these three totally different and irreconcilable ways in which God encounters us. Each has its own unique kind of passivity. Therefore, if these different kinds of passivity are to retain their distinctive form, they cannot be lumped together into one single general category called passivity. In view of this, the concept of the passive, receptive life *(vita passiva),* which we have already used approvingly, is not without its problems. The idea of a single concept will have to be immediately set aside. At most, it can serve as a category for the three different kinds of passivity/receptivity.

The passivity associated with the political use of the law *(usus politicus legis)* should be understood differently than the other three passivities. For when God works through his law to preserve his creation, the human agent *(homo agens)* works with him. Indeed, he uses people as his masks *(larvae).* However, even here we are passive *(passio)* in the sense that we receive his gifts. The specific connection between this human receptivity *(passio)* and the free action *(actio)* of the human agent is normally covered in the teaching about the "cooperation with God" *(concursus divinus)* which is part of the doctrine of providence.

These different dimensions of the receptive, passive life *(vita passiva)* correspond to the different ways in which God encounters us and which in turn constitute the object of theology. However, we must always ensure that the human recipient *(homo recipiens)* is defined by the God who speaks *(deus dicens),* and not the other way round.[145]

2.3. Theology Understood as Wisdom

2.3.1. Is Science the Path to Wisdom?

Since the time of the medieval scholastics, the question has been asked whether theology is wisdom or science, and how the relationship between wisdom and science should be understood. The same question has also been asked in philosophy.

Kant makes the problem crystal clear in the closing sentences of his *Critique of Practical Reason*, in which he reveals the intent of his whole philosophical project. He sets out the issue at stake in the following, beginning with a negation.

> [We need to prevent] *the leaps of genius,* by which, as happens with the adepts of the philosopher's stone, visionary treasures are promised and true ones are thrown away for lack of methodical study or knowledge of nature. In a word, science (critically undertaken and methodically directed) is the narrow gate [Matt. 7:13f.] that leads to the *teaching of wisdom,* if by this is understood not merely what one ought *to do* but what ought to serve *teachers* as a guide to prepare well and clearly the path to wisdom that everyone should travel, and to secure others against taking the wrong way. Philosophy must always remain the guardian of this science and, though the public need take no interest in its subtle investigations, it has to take an interest in the *teachings* that such considerations first make clear to it.[146]

Kant is right in opposing an appeal to mere intuition or even to mere feeling that tries to escape the rigor of scientific discipline. We also have to agree with his rejection of that enthusiasm which he calls the "leap of genius." However, while we can agree with his negations, his own position comes at too high a cost.

According to Kant, the science that leads to wisdom should be "critically undertaken and methodically directed." Philosophy's "sole preoccupation is wisdom; and it seeks it by the path of science" — "through the mediation of a rational cognition from mere concepts, which, call it what one will, is really nothing but metaphysics."[147] Kant, professor of logic and metaphysics, tried to present a metaphysics that would appear as science and that would have to be able to be counted as science. The decisive thing here is the rational knowledge from "mere" concepts which are obtained, analogously to the method of chemistry, by the art of separation. Kant wants to follow "a method similar to *chemistry*" and to undertake the "*separation* of the empirical from the rational."[148] In a word, he sets "the rational against the empirical."[149]

Any theologian who wants to follow Kant in the art of separation had better be clear about the impact that Kant's concept of science has on the interpretation of the Bible. That "reason has insight only into what it itself produces according to its own design,"[150] means that the Archimedean point in Kant's understanding of reason, the law of pure practical reason, determines everything. Kant also sees in it the condition for the possibility of understanding biblical texts generally, so that the word speaks "not to an ineffectual faith but to a faith that is relevant to our moral destiny and [therefore] intelligible."[151] For "the only thing that matters in religion is *action,* and this ultimate purpose, together with a meaning consistent with it, must be ascribed to every biblical doctrine."[152]

Formally, Bultmann says exactly the same thing with even greater precision. Since he makes a split between understanding *(Verstehen)* and explanation *(Erklärung),* he is interested only in understanding biblical texts existentially, and not in explaining them historically. Hence, he excludes or precludes (= *praecidit*)[153] anything that does not promote the understanding of their present significance, in other words, anything that cannot be interpreted existentially. For Bultmann, as for Kant, this elimination of certain biblical passages enhances the scientific character of the method. Only in this way can the "purity of the concepts" and our "obligation to strive for conceptual clarity"[154] be safeguarded, the very thing Bultmann repeatedly demanded of Barth.

The clarity that Bultmann and Kant strove for comes at the cost of an enormous impoverishment. For Kant, the science that is "critically undertaken and methodically directed" is the narrow gate that leads to the teaching of wisdom. But if this is constrained by a prior separation of the empirical from the rational, history from reason, a subsequent attempt to relate them cannot heal this broken marriage, not even through the aesthetic of the *Critique of the Power of Judgment.* The wisdom teaching of Kantian philosophy, the cosmic aspect of his philosophy,[155] filters out anything that is not consistent with the pure concept of morality in the inexhaustible, highly complex, and even dissonant textual world of the Bible.[156] In the same way, Bultmann's "existential interpretation" excludes texts that supposedly have no existential reference, on the supposition that they cannot be understood or preached. For, according to Bultmann, the kerygma "as kerygma" can be understood "only when the self-understanding awakened by it is recognized to be a possibility of human self-understanding."[157] Consequently, for Bultmann the horizons of creation theology and apocalyptic eschatology fade into insignificance or disappear completely. And Kant interprets the primal history of the Bible (Genesis 1–11), "the end of all things," as well as the heart of the Christian proclamation, Christ's vicarious action for us, in purely moral terms.[158] He does this in order to preserve the unity of the self-consciousness and the identity of the self, the "I."

If that is the price to be paid for a science that is meant to lead to wisdom, theology cannot adopt Kant's understanding of science. However, if it does not want to give up its status as a science altogether, and in the German university theology is still regarded as a science, it will have to develop its own understanding of science. If theology does not want to be understood as a science merely on the basis of intuition or even feeling, in other words, on the basis of the "extravagance of genius" that Kant rightly rejected, it must at least share his criticism in its opposition to that kind of enthusiasm. It can affirm the manner in which Kant, with the help of Hume's skepticism, disciplines the excessive use of reason common in dogmatism.

But since Kant's criticism once again becomes dogmatic,[159] the only option open to theology, if it wants to establish itself as a science, is that of a meta-critique between dogmatism and skepticism.

Positively, this meta-critique can only be described as a meta-critical *middle*. Any critique of reason that operates only within its own framework is in reality uncritical. This is evident to anyone who does not deny the historicity and relativity of reason. According to the kind of radical enlightenment thinking that we should follow, we always find ourselves in a middle position that oscillates *between* authority and criticism, thus preventing us from ever identifying with an absolute beginning that always allows us to begin anew, or with an absolute end that we can anticipate just as speculatively.

The price Kant pays for his criticism is especially evident from the leading role he plays in the dispute between the faculties of philosophy and theology over the interpretation of the Bible. He ends up having to deny history. Kant's anamnetic and constructive[160] reason demands on principle that the "divine nature" of the "moral content" of the Bible be systematically separated from "the humanity of its historical narrative."[161]

If theology cannot accommodate itself to a concept of science that operates with this distinction, we need to give up the term "science" in favor of "wisdom." This term is more appropriate to theology because it is more comprehensive, both in its breadth and its depth, and so is better able to express coherence and embrace difference. However, if the concept of science employed by Kant and Bultmann is too narrow in its precision, we need to be careful that the concept of wisdom we are seeking is not too vague in its breadth.

2.3.2. Meta-Critical Wisdom

The meta-critique of Kant contradicts the motto "science is the path to wisdom!" However, the wisdom we seek respects science and abhors "misology" (the hatred of reason or scientific knowledge),[162] even though we cannot acquire it through science. Wisdom does not exclude science but makes room for it.

Wisdom reflects on the connection between science and the pre-scientific life-world. Wisdom unites the theoretical and the practical. It grounds both in the receptive life *(vita passiva)*.[163] Since Aristotle, science has worked with necessary principles *(principia)*, or better still, with a single principle *(principium)*. This means that science, including modern positivistic science which wants to exclude all contradictory elements that do not fit the system,[164] is closed. By contrast, wisdom has to do with experience, whether we are the active subject of the experience or the passive recipient of another's action. However, experience is not closed but open, without being vague and indefinite. If wisdom encompasses science, we cannot allow science to enclose itself in its own world, but we have to relativize it in the light of the pre-scientific life-world.

There is then a given that precedes scientific knowledge and this cannot be excluded without that knowledge becoming sterile, even dead. The wise recognize that the ground and goal of their understanding is given, and that this is something they cannot control.

The wisdom of Israel knew this. Therefore, its basic principle is: "The fear of the Lord is the beginning of wisdom" (Prov. 9:10),[165] along with the recognition that I have not created myself and that I am finite and dependent. With this principle the wisdom literature is basically nothing else than a repetition of the first commandment: "I am the Lord, your God. . . . You shall have no other gods besides me!"

Wherever twentieth-century theology has been influenced by the philosophy of existence *(Existenzphilosophie)* and personalism, it has seen the first commandment, and God's accompanying address, in purely personalistic terms. The decision of faith as an act of obedience is above all removed from life in the world. However, our worldly existence, which unites us with our fellow creatures, is only possible in bodily form, or to use the language of Descartes, as *res extensa* (matter, extension). Yet according to Bultmann's understanding of theology, for instance,[166] human existence has always fallen victim to objectifications, and its continuous extensity or bodily form is foreign, if not inimical, to the intensity of faith's moment of decision.

Since Bultmann provides us with such a complete theological orientation, we can assess the significance of a meta-critical understanding of theology, along the lines of wisdom, that does not force us to choose between a personal decision and a comprehensive view of the world based on wisdom, but holds both together, as do the texts of the Old and New Testaments. In these texts, address[167] and observation, understanding and interpretation, explanation and narrative[168] are not separated. Thus, the wisdom texts of the Old and New Testaments urge us to avoid the modern alternative of choosing between a subjective understanding of personal existence, on the one hand, and an objective scientific explanation of the world and an objective way of dealing with it, on the one hand. The former is typical of the social sciences, the latter of the natural sciences. More precisely, these biblical texts urge us to reunite our perception of the world and our perception of ourselves, through a meta-critique of this subject/object split, which is the distinctive hallmark of modernity.

We are still to discover what it means that the first commandment is repeated in the biblical wisdom texts and is therefore also applied to that area of knowledge that modern science and technology is revising based on the assumption of a "methodological atheism."[169]

If the first commandment, and the personal relationship between God and humanity that it entails, is considered in connection with the wisdom arising from a complete sensory perception of the world, then the object of theology *(subiectum theologiae)*,[170] which is also its subject matter and theme, can no longer be defined personalistically in a twofold way, as a pure correlation between the knowledge of God and the knowledge of the self. This, of course, is how it has been defined since

Augustine,[171] and especially since Descartes and Kant, while in the twentieth century it characterized, among others, the theology of Bultmann.[172] Rather, the object of theology must be defined in a three-fold way, with reference to God, the world, and the self. In other words, it must be defined by the God who *addresses* us using worldly means and likewise by humans who, together with the whole created world, *respond* to God using worldly means. Without the wisdom we gain from the experience of the world, the first commandment would be empty. On the other hand, without the first commandment, wisdom would be blind.

The primordial promise of life and the threat of death (Gen. 2:16f.) that applies to all people is an essential part of the first commandment (Exod. 20:2f.). The voice of wisdom that addresses us opposes the voice of foolishness that leads to death.[173]

2.3.3. The Historical *A Priori:*
The Understanding of Time and the Concept of Science

The meta-critical wisdom we are advocating needs to be developed in connection with a critique of modernity. This means a critique of the Cartesian method of explanation and demonstration, a critique of the idea that we can create a unity of self-consciousness. It means giving up the idea that we can discuss the whole or the unity of reality, or even God as the "unity of reality." Since modernity has privileged reason, a critique of modernity promotes all that is other than reason: the senses and the emotions, the imagination, the memory and the desires. This locates theology between mythology and metaphysics and in critical relation to both.[174] Finally, it means emphasizing the importance of the human body and our elementary bond with all fellow creatures, and not letting instrumental reason rupture it.

It might seem we have picked up the impulse of "postmodernity," and in some specific senses we have. Yet the meta-critique we are proposing has no connection with that arbitrariness and non-commitment, or with that spiritual and physical rootlessness that is typical of the so-called "postmodern" quest.

Admittedly, anyone committed to this meta-critique will have no hesitation in speaking of the "crisis" of the Enlightenment and its "dialectic." In fact, they will even go further and speak of an "end" of the modernity that has so shaped our culture that our fellow humans have become cannon fodder, while our non-human fellow creatures have become either the hapless victims of our consumerist culture, or, in reaction, idols adored by nature-loving romantics.

However, this kind of meta-critique of modernity, which is in essence a critique of modernity's own critique, is not only postmodern but also pre-modern, in the sense of Hamann's conclusion to his *Aesthetica in nuce* (1762): "Let us hear the sum total" of this "newest aesthetics, which is also the oldest of all: Fear God and give him glory, for the hour of his judgment has come. Worship him who made the heavens, the earth, the sea and the springs of water."[175]

The oldest aesthetics is enshrined in the first commandment: to fear, love, and trust solely in God above all things. But the oldest is at the same time the eschaton, the last thing, the newest of all, the absolutely new, which never becomes old.

In short, we see from this that the threefold definition of the subject matter of theology *(subiectum theologiae)* that we have described offers a completely different way of seeing the relationship to God, the world, and the self than that given in the prevailing tradition. For Augustine, as then also for Kierkegaard, our relationship to the world ultimately had only negative significance for our relationship to God and the self, since at the crucial point he wanted to know nothing apart from God and the soul.[176] His only concern was to be free from the world. We, on the other hand, are advocating a return to the world, a new "aesthetics," a new way of perceiving the world in a comprehensive sense, which embraces the moral, the physical, and what we mean today, in a limited sense, by aesthetics. This includes the senses, the emotions, the imagination, the memory, and the desires.

In this way, the public reading and hearing of the Old and New Testament, as living tradition, creates the irreversible condition for the possibility of understanding the world and the self within the communicative community of justified sinners. But is this condition a necessary condition? Here our answer reflects our non-foundationalist starting point. The condition is necessary only *a posteriori,* that is, in the light of experience. We cannot say that it is necessary at the outset based on first principles. Hence, *a priori,* the condition is thoroughly contingent. In the light of this understanding, we can therefore say that the Bible, which creates this condition, is a historical *a priori.*

The voice of the law that kills and the voice of the gospel that gives life, that voice which addresses us in a different way, and is "for us" in a different way, than the law, must not be abstracted from the letter of the scriptures which have been handed down through the ages. We do not have the voice without the letters, just as we do not have the ear without the eye, or hearing without seeing, or time without space. "The Holy Scriptures should be our dictionary and grammar, the source and basis for all Christian words and concepts."[177]

If we let the Bible be our concrete historical *a priori,* we are introduced to an infinitely vast breadth of experiences that cannot simply be brought under our control, either by interpreting them morally or existentially, on the one hand, or by understanding them in terms of general history or process philosophy, on the other. The book that leads us into this incredibly vast breadth of experience is the "divine Aeneid," Luther's term for the Bible, because the experiences that it records are of epic proportions. Its treasures are so rich and vast that it needs more than a lifetime to mine them. "For the wisdom of this Scripture is greater than the ability of the whole human race to comprehend it."[178] However, the Bible is not vague and indeterminate in its breadth and depth. On the contrary, it is very precise in its own way, yet this precision is far removed from the ideal method of Cartesian philosophy, for while the Bible's method does not exclude logic, it rightly connects it with history and poetry. This also ensures that the question of method is never isolated from the question of truth.[179]

A method that does not ignore the question of truth, a science that is not abstracted from the inexhaustible "wisdom of experience" *(sapientia experimentalis),*[180] will not isolate the realm of observation, hypothesis, theory, and system, what we usually regard as "science," from the past and the future, from history and poetry.[181] All three dimensions, past, present, and future, belong to science and must be kept together if science is to be productive rather than sterile, living rather than dead.

2.3.4. Science Is Wisdom Understood as Law

If a living science is to be understood as wisdom, those who work with it must handle it with due restraint. They should not indulge in "leaps of genius" or despise the rigor of sound methods. But can wisdom discipline its freedom? How can that happen if the path to wisdom is not critically undertaken and methodically directed by science as Kant proposed?

The answer to this question lies in the Pauline-Lutheran distinction between law and gospel. But to apply this to the philosophy of science, not only to questions of method in theology, but also in philology and philosophy, indeed, in every science, including the natural sciences, may seem bold if not strange.[182] Is it possible to generalize a genuine theological distinction after the manner of the philosophy of science? Would that not color it with a post-Christian natural theology that cannot be justified theologically?[183]

However, the path we are taking is not that of a generalization. The gospel is not a general idea but a concrete word that addresses a specific person in a particular situation. For the gospel, in its precise sense, is the word with which the triune God himself appears before me, defends me against his own accusing law, and intercedes for me. As Christians, our knowledge and action remain bound to the place of the divine service, which essentially means bound to the enacted word and to faith. It cannot be understood as a general principle of knowledge and action that could also be applied to non-believers. However, where insights of the gospel are clear to unbelievers and become moments of thought and impulses for action, God's life-preserving law is at work in its political mode *(usus politicus legis)*.

Therefore, we should not use "wisdom" as a general concept but only in a differentiated way, guided by the distinction between law and gospel.[184] For a more detailed description of this, we can only refer the reader to the fourfold definition of the object of theology that we discussed earlier (2.1). But here we want to focus on its importance for the understanding of science.

Understood as gospel, wisdom disallows an unqualified trust in science as well as any absolute claims to a worldview made in the name of science. Through its personal address,[185] which locates us in a particular context and addresses us as individuals, wisdom creates a *subject* that is critical of ideology as well as of the *self*. Without this *self-critical subject*, critical knowledge is impossible.[186] "The fear of the Lord is the beginning of wisdom and his evangelical love is the goal and purpose of wisdom. I know of no other Archimedean point — the point about which Archimedes is supposed to have said: 'give me a place to stand,

and I will move the earth' — than the Lord's word, his oath, and his *'I am,* and *will be.'"*[187] The being of God is his name (Exod. 3:14), in which he reveals himself and speaks his promise (Exod. 20:2). Through this promise to listen, he calls people into being who are endowed with reason, but more than that, he calls them to think. Therefore, the *"I think,"* which must *"be able* to accompany all my representations (ideas),"[188] can never be a final foundation but only a response.

Old Testament wisdom is taken up by the New Testament in such a way that wisdom understood as gospel is sharply distinguished from wisdom understood as law. For example, Paul uses the passage Deuteronomy 30:11-14 to substantiate and unfold (Rom. 10:5ff.) the central statement of his theology: "Christ is the end *(telos)* of the law" (Rom. 10:4). However, in order to bring out the contrast between law and gospel, Paul has to turn the single unified statement in Deuteronomy into two opposing statements, one that speaks of "the righteousness which comes from the law," and the other that speaks of "the righteousness which comes from faith." In a comparable way, John emphasizes the same distinction at John 1:17. Therefore, the law that convicts us of sin is to be distinguished from the gospel that sets us free.

A philosophy of science and hermeneutics has to take sin seriously. Human sin is certainly also determinative in our knowing and understanding. This obviously has important ramifications for what is said to be "objective" knowledge.[189]

It is all the more surprising then that in spite of sin, reason, "the inventor and guide of all the [liberal] arts, of medical science, of jurisprudence, and of whatever wisdom, power, ability, and honor humans possess in this life,"[190] rules in human affairs and that, through it all, God miraculously preserves this passing world for its future. For "God, even after the fall of Adam, did not take away this majesty of reason," the commission to rule and take care of the world (Gen. 1:28; 2:15), "but rather confirmed it."[191] Wisdom, understood as law, does not convict us of sin in our God-given reason but works rather in the sense of the political function of the law *(usus politicus legis).*[192]

That is a clear definition of the space-time framework of science, of every science: *science is wisdom, understood as law, in its political, secular use.* And just as justice and the legally constituted political order are determined by two fundamental factors, freedom and constraint, so too is science. Constraint, discipline, respect for rules and verifiability are just as determinative for science, which includes theological methodology, as the freedom and relative independence that we spoke of at the beginning of this section[193] and will speak of again in the concluding section ("Faith and Sight").[194]

3. Promise and Faith

In our discussion of the definition of the object of theology (2.1) we saw that God encounters us in ways that are irreducibly different. We cannot therefore accept a monistic doctrine of the word of God, as advocated by Karl Barth. In the midst of the contradictory and complementary ways in which God encounters us, which are laden with tension and conflict, the gospel stands out in its uniqueness as God's decisive, final word. The gospel, strictly speaking, is a promise without any demand,[195] a pure promise *(promissio)*, a gift.

In what follows, we will concentrate on this crucial way in which God speaks to us and will consider the unique objectivity of the promise *(promissio)* from the standpoint of hermeneutics and the philosophy of science. Its objectivity of course cannot be understood in a positivistic sense,[196] as if it were a scientific datum open to empirical verification. But, on the other hand, neither can we go to the other extreme of surrendering the objectivity of the promise on the grounds that God and faith are not objective realities that we can grasp but are inaccessible and beyond our reach,[197] as the disciples of Kant maintained, especially in dialectical theology.[198]

3.1. Analysis of Existence or Analysis of Language?

Theology, in the narrower sense, understood as a disciplined way of thinking, refers to an object that it participates in but is other than itself. It is related to it in the same way as ordinary language philosophy is related to ordinary language. At the end of his *Tractatus Logico-Philosophicus* (6.54), Wittgenstein makes a provocative assertion: "My propositions serve as elucidations in the following way: those who understand *me* eventually recognize *them* as nonsensical" (emphasis added). They have to throw away the ladder, so to speak, after they have climbed up it. Elsewhere, he puts it in a way less prone to misunderstanding (4.112): "The result of philosophy should not be the production of 'philosophical propositions' but the clarification of propositions."[199] If we applied this thesis to theology, we could avoid much futility. It would then read: *The result of theology should not be the production of theological propositions but the clarification of propositions of proclamation in their particular context (Sitz im Leben).*

The definition of the task of theology implicit in this thesis, with its reference to the analysis of language, does more justice to its object than a definition that builds on Heidegger's analysis of existence in *Being and Time* (1927). This work has had considerable influence on theology generally and the Bultmann school in particular. If Heidegger says in *Being and Time* that philosophy, understood as the analysis of *existence,* fastens the end of the connecting thread of all philosophical inquiry at the point from which it arises and to which it returns,[200] and if the corresponding sentence in Wittgenstein says that philosophy, understood as the analysis of *language,* fastens the end of the connecting thread of all philosophical inquiry at the point from which it arises and to which it returns, then the answer to the question about the task of theology can be formulated programmatically as follows: *Theology, understood as the analysis of the language of proclamation, fastens the end of the connecting thread of all theological inquiry at the point from which it arises and to which it returns.*

However, this means that the object of theology cannot be found either by attempting to go beyond the word in knowing (Hegel) and doing (Kant and Marx) or by attempting to go deeper than the word to something behind it that is more original (Schleiermacher). Rather, understood as gospel, it is the medium of a language that establishes communication, that liberates us from distorted and destructive communication, and that wins the victory in the struggle for mutual recognition in the spirit of God's paradoxical condescension in Christ, who though he was rich yet for our sake became poor, so that we through his poverty might become rich (2 Cor. 8:9; see also 1 Cor. 9:19).

3.2. Austin's Theory of Speech Acts

How to Do Things with Words: this is the title of the 1962 posthumous publication of the lectures of the British philosopher John L. Austin. At the same time, however, the words represent a program that can be understood in the light of the later Wittgenstein's remark about how words are connected with situations, or how a given language game is interwoven with a particular way of acting or a particular form of life.[201]

In his lecture on performative and constative utterances,[202] Austin distinguishes between these two types of speech in order to develop a general theory of speech acts against the background of the question: "How to do things with words?" "What we need is . . . a new theory that gives a complete and general account of *what we are doing when we say something* [. . .]. It needs to take into account all variant meanings of this ambiguous expression. It has to be a theory of the 'speech-act' in its totality, which does not merely take account of one or other aspect and disregard the rest."[203] The purpose of the lecture comes out in the way he formulates the task: to find a category that embraces the two kinds of utterances without overlooking their differences. The constative utterance is certainly also a speech act and therefore also has a performative aspect. But it is performative in a different sense from the performative utterance that Austin distinguishes from the constative.

We can summarize Austin's explanation and at the same time sharpen it by saying that a constative utterance refers to a state of affairs that has already been constituted. It gives us information about it but it does not itself bring it about. The constative sentence therefore manifests and discloses what already is. It is a *logos apophantikos,* a declarative sentence,[204] the classical judgment of the Aristotelian logic of the statement.[205] But something different occurs with the performative utterance, which Austin distinguishes from the constative. It itself constitutes a situation. It does not simply establish, disclose, and confirm it as already existing, but it actually brings it about. It is not by accident therefore that Austin explains a performative utterance by referring to what in legal parlance are called "operative" clauses.[206] These are "the clauses by which the legal act is actually executed, as opposed to those (of the so-called preamble) that describe the circumstances of the legal act."[207]

As a key example of a performative utterance Austin cites the promise. Again, this is not by accident. What do I do when I say: "I promise you . . ."? What happens when this is said or heard? I enter into an obligation. This is an act, but not the act of description. It is not the statement of a detached observer who reports: "X promised Y," but it is an act that brings it about. Through it a relationship is established which previously did not exist. However, this relationship will be destroyed if the promise is broken and not kept. The promise is also misused if the person making it is not in a position to keep it. If I make a promise without being authorized and empowered to do so, the promise is null and void. It is nothing but a deception and a lie.

It is clear from this that a speech act, a performative sentence such as "I promise you . . . ," is of a quite different kind in that it is more multidimensional and wide-ranging than a premise in the sense of traditional logic. It is also "true" or "false" in a different way than a premise. The promise is a function of time. It cannot be falsified in a moment by disregarding the time factor, as we do, for example, when we check the needle of a measuring instrument. When, for instance, is a marriage vow verified or falsified?

In summary, we can say that a performative sentence which has the same structure as the example "I promise you . . ." does not refer to a preexisting situation whose existence the sentence merely reveals. Rather, it constitutes and creates a relationship and incorporates features that are both personal and objective. The main function of linguistic analysis is to assist in the clarification of this and similar performative sentences. However, in relation to its object, the analysis itself is merely a constative speech act.

Wittgenstein and Austin provided the stimulus for an "analytic jurisprudence" that developed chiefly in England but also in Scandinavia, which inquires into the verbal conditions necessary for a legal sentence and its semantic implications.[208] Theology in the English-speaking world, as well as in Scandinavia, especially Sweden, has also continued to be influenced by linguistic analysis, which is also called analytic philosophy.[209]

We will now try to define the object of theology in relation to the gospel, for this is its crucial aspect. Although we will not specifically use linguistic analysis for this, we will refer to it as we retrieve Luther's Reformation hermeneutics.

3.3. Speech Acts Liberate and Give Certainty

Luther's Reformation rediscovery of the gospel focuses on certain kinds of sentences, such as: "I am with you always, to the end of the age" (Matt. 28:20). Sentences of this kind are promises *(promissiones)* and pledges. We can describe them in the same way that Austin described the performative sentences in the example of the "promise" by comparing them to the operative juridical clauses, which are not premises, by which the legal act itself is executed.

Luther came to understand the gospel as a performative speech act, or as an "effective word," as he called it, by a difficult path.[210] It happened in connection with a careful study of the function of the sacrament of penance, which was necessitated by the controversy over indulgences. At first, Luther understood the priestly words of absolution, *"Ego te absolvo!"* ("I absolve you of your sins!"), as a declarative act, or to use Austin's language, a constative speech act: the priest sees the remorse, takes it as a sign of the divine justification, the divine absolution that has already occurred in the penitent, without that person knowing it. He discloses it, makes it evident, and acknowledges it for the assurance of the penitent. The declaration then is a disclosure, a description of a present state of affairs, rather than the actual performance of forgiveness. The word of absolution therefore is understood as a "judgment" *(iudicium)* in the precise sense of the classical logic of the statement, in the sense of the *logos apophantikos*. In a word, the absolution is a declarative statement.

Luther, therefore, initially remained within the framework of this ancient understanding of language, which came mainly from the Stoics and which was determinative for Augustine's hermeneutic of signification. Still today, this continues to be the most common way of understanding language. According to this understanding, language is a system of signs that point to an object or a state of affairs, or that express an emotion. In either case, the sign *(signum)*, understood as a statement or an expression, is not the reality *(res)* itself.

However, Luther's great hermeneutical insight, his Reformation discovery in the strict sense, was that the verbal sign *(signum)* is itself the reality *(res)*. This new insight turned the ancient understanding of language on its head. He first came to it, as we have already noted, in reflecting on the sacrament of penance. He realized that the sign means what it says. With reference to absolution, the sentence "I absolve you of your sins!" is not a judgment that merely states what is true already. It does not assume that an inner, divine, proper absolution or justification has already taken place. Rather, the absolution is seen as a speech act that first constitutes, brings about,[211] a state of affairs, by creating a relationship between the one in whose name it is spoken and the one to whom it is spoken and who believes the promise. Such a speech act establishes communication, liberates and gives certainty. Luther calls it *"verbum efficax,"* an active and effective word. In Austin's terminology, it is a performative speech act.

Luther also discovers this kind of performative word in the sacraments of Baptism and the Lord's Supper, as well as in the Christmas story ("To you is born this day a Savior!"), the Easter story, and many other biblical passages.[212] As we said before, he regards these sentences as promises *(promissiones)*. They are the concrete way in which Christ is present, and his presence with us is clear and certain: it clearly liberates us and makes us certain. I cannot remind myself of this freedom and certainty in isolation; I cannot have a monologue with myself. These gifts are given and received only by means of the promise spoken by another person (and not only by the official priest or preacher), who addresses it to me in the name of Jesus. I cannot speak the promise to myself. It must be spoken to me. For only in this way is it true. Only in this way does it give freedom and certainty.

What this certainty is all about is clear from a short passage in the *Lectures on Genesis* that Luther virtually offers as a theological legacy: "I have been baptized. I have been absolved. In this faith I will die. No matter what trials and problems confront me, I will not waver in the least. For he who said: 'The one who believes and is baptized will be saved' (Mark 16:16), and 'whatever you loose on earth will be loosed in heaven' (Matt. 16:19), and 'this is my body; this is my blood which is shed for you for the forgiveness of sins' (cf. Matt. 26:26, 28), cannot lie or deceive. This is certainly true."[213] In the *Lectures on Galatians* (1535) Luther writes, "And this is the reason why our theology is certain: it snatches us away from ourselves and places us outside ourselves *(nos extra nos)*, so that we depend not on our own strength, conscience, mind, person, or works but on what is outside ourselves *(extra nos)*, that is, on the promise and truth of God, which cannot deceive."[214]

In contradistinction to every metaphysical construct of the doctrine of God, God's truth and will therefore are not abstract properties but are a concrete promise, made orally and publicly, to a particular person in a particular situation. "God" is the one whose promise to us in the oral word is such that we can depend on him. God's truth lies in his faithfulness to the word that he speaks. Because he has bound himself to the promise that he made to us at our Baptism, we are emboldened and empowered through the oral word of the sermon, when we are spiritually attacked, to lay hold of him once again in that same promise. We are made confident that he will snatch us out of ourselves whether in pride *(superbia)* or in despair *(desperatio)*.

A theology that reflects its central object, the gospel, in sentences that, from the standpoint of form analysis *(Formgeschichte)*, have the same structure we have described, will exclude from the first a biblicism that makes everything in the Bible of equal importance. It is critical insofar as it attends to all the form-critical peculiarities and takes seriously the coincidence of form and content. Furthermore, it does not draw out of the Bible isolated concepts and "ideas," even if they are concepts like "justification by faith alone," "love of neighbor," or "freedom," or themes like "a new heaven and new earth, in which righteousness dwells." It is also not the task of theology to engage in an infinite regression that works its way back from what the author said to what the author meant, back to the history that lies behind the text or to a specific concept of human existence that underlies the text, as is the case in existential interpretation from Schleiermacher down to the Bultmann school. Equally, it should not cling to the letter in a kind of biblicistic legalism as in theological positivism. In fact, theology is guided only by particular sentences, particular speech acts, none of which, it can be shown, has been chosen arbitrarily and none of which is derived from some principle behind the text. For the Bible itself is full of promises and sentences that can be easily converted into these particular kinds of sentences and speech acts without doing violence to the texts.

However, in this we do not recommend the practice of reciting whole slabs from the Bible in preaching and pastoral care, even if they are clear promises like "I am with you always," although in certain situations the reading of biblical texts, such as Psalm 23 read at the deathbed, is very appropriate and can communicate very powerfully. However, it is important for us to take particular note of statements such as Matthew 28:20, which are examples of the promise of the gospel. For they teach us that when we address people with the gospel, we should not tie them down to themselves and their relationships, we should not demand anything of them, but we should promise them something unexpected, undeserved, something that they are not and do not have, something impossible, at least not possible for them. Through such a promise, they belong to Jesus through the faith that it creates. And we can appeal to this same Jesus because he is the Lord, the one who has the first and last word. Most of all, we should appeal to him if ever we are asked "by what authority" we perform a speech act of the said kind. For we have no authority to claim anything for ourselves but our authority comes from the Lord (see 2 Cor. 3:5).

Let us now look more closely at the problem of authorization and legitimation, or, in other words, the problem of verification. This is not the first time that theology has had to face up to this problem.

If the subject matter of theology is the promise, as we have said earlier, there are two negative factors connected with the problem of verification. First, the promise is not a statement giving information and cannot be transformed into such. If it was a statement, we would have to be able to check it against what it says. In that case, it would be true only if the statement, in the sense of the "understanding" *(intellectus)*, corresponded to the object or reality *(res)* that it discloses. This is the classical definition of truth *(veritas* is *adaequatio rei et intellectus)*. According to it, truth is the equivalence, correspondence, or conformity between the intellect, the judging mind, and the thing *(res)* perceived (where *res* can be an object, fact, situation, or state of affairs).[215] However, the promise is not a statement and so must not be understood in this way. Secondly, the promise is not a prescription and cannot be transformed into such. If it were a prescription, its criterion of truth would be whether the action prescribed is fulfillable or has been fulfilled, whether it is doable or has been done. In that case, it would be true only if, so to speak, the thing *(res)* done corresponded to the understanding *(intellectus)*, only if the prescription was carried out. The truth would then lie in its performance.[216] A transformation of this kind, based on the scheme of performance, presupposes that the words spoken with the promise are ineffectual. Where theology unfortunately did go down this wrong path, the transformation went in two directions, one forward ("progressive"), the other backwards ("regressive"). The former assumes the latter and is pursued by Marx,[217] the latter by Feuerbach. The anthropology that he discovered in Christianity with the help of his "hermeneutic of regression" is a *"realized idea — the truth* of Christianity."[218]

The truth of the promise, on the other hand, and no dialectic can overlook this fact, lies only in the realm that is opened up and so first constituted by the promise itself. It therefore lies in the relationship between the speaker and the listener. The speaker introduces himself in the promise and makes himself known. He is not there for us apart from the promise, because he does not want to be there for us in any other way. And we, as listeners, cannot isolate ourselves from our situation, our life history in the midst of world history. If the relationship constituted by this promise makes us into listeners and verifies us,[219] then we cannot verify the promise ourselves. If we could, we would have to presume to be also the secret subject of the promise in the sense of the idealist premise of identity, which posits the identity of the subject and the object. Then we would hear nothing more than we ourselves could say. Then, as Feuerbach saw,[220] the promise made by the other would be nothing else than the actualization of our own possibilities, or the fulfillment of our own needs. It would be merely a means of self-discovery, a means of becoming identical with ourselves.

In this sense, the modern philosophy of identity has altogether perverted the promise and made it into a form of self-referentiality, directed back reflexively to the human ego, which thus claims to be able to verify itself. But that is pure atheism. It boils down to the same thing whether I verify myself in my subjective spirituality, or in my quest for God as the unity of reality, or even in explicit atheism. People want to speak the truth about themselves but in the process they make God into a liar: *homo verax — deus mendax* (see, on the other hand, Rom. 3:4). In their self-referentiality and self-reflection, the modern followers of Narcissus lose both their individuality and their freedom, which God has promised us and which he has given us as a gift. They lose them, as Luther says in his *Freedom of a Christian* (§16), like that dog in Aesop's fable who, while carrying a piece of meat in his mouth, snapped at his reflection in the water and as a result lost not only the meat but also his reflection.[221]

Theology must not capitulate to the idealist premise of identity and its implied critique of religion. Any capitulation at this point is tantamount to acknowledging that this critique is true.[222] Rather, theology will remain true to its brief if its own critique of the idealist's critique of religion is accurate, for then it will contradict it at the decisive point, which is its premise of identity. If theology does not challenge it here, people will become so obsessed with the gift of their individuality and freedom that they will end up losing the gift as well as the giver. Therefore, theology's dispute with the critique of religion is not just over its denial of God or its "interpretation" of God, but over its understanding of humanity, according to which human beings define themselves by taking themselves as the fundamental point of reference. Theology, therefore, attacks this critique of religion at the very point where it thinks it is strongest but is in fact weakest, in its anthropology, or more specifically, its self-referentiality.

In view of the present situation, theology must launch its attack at the very place where people today generally think there is no longer any dispute in theology and the church, and that is in relation to psychotherapy. This is often identified with a modern interpretation of the Christian faith. Its premises, however, have never been thoroughly scrutinized. Yet these very premises are all linked to the idealist principle of identity, which lies at the core of atheism.

3.4. Promise or Catalyst?

If the central object of theology is the gospel, and if this is located in the promise that gives freedom, then theology seems to be in direct competition with psychotherapy, in which liberation from distorted communication is likewise "no solitary movement, but is bound to the intersubjectivity of a verbal communication with another person."[223] However, if we overlook the difference between theology and a psychotherapeutic conversation, it will be at the cost of totally mistaking its own subject matter. Given the present situation, we need to make a sharp distinction between them, just because the similarity between them leads many people to assume, incorrectly, that they are identical.

In order to clarify this distinction, let us stay with our model of the performative word, which we are taking as the subject matter of theology, specifically the word of absolution.

When we speak the word of absolution, the promise, the advocates of the psychotherapeutic approach raise the objection that the speech act, "your sins are forgiven," is of absolutely no use. In fact, they tell us that to understand the words of absolution in the strict sense of a promise, as we have described it, rather than as a statement of information, is utter nonsense. According to psychotherapy, the client who is addressed must also speak; it must be a two-way conversation. This can be facilitated by the intervention of the therapist, but even then the support offered by the therapist is supposed to be minimal. The therapist, of course, is the necessary catalyst for self-discovery, the midwife, like Socrates in Plato's *Meno*, who elicits latent ideas from others by a logical process of question and answer (the Socratic method).[224] This, in substance, is also the Kantian "Methodology of Pure Practical Reason" which tries to help people discover their inner capability, their *inner freedom*, which they would not otherwise know they had.[225]

Therapist and client collaborate in the clinical conversation in order to search for the truth together. But, properly speaking, only the patient is supposed to seek and find the truth. The other, the therapist or teacher, only provides the necessary stimulus. In the final analysis, the truth can only be sought and found in anamnesis, in remembering the past. A person has to find it in oneself, through a reflective process that sheds light on one's own life history. They have to consciously revisit decisive moments of the past and relive them verbally and dramatically. This process of self-reflection is long hard work for the patient, even if it is eased by moments of play and relaxation. The outcome, if successful, is twofold: patients are not only healed, they also find themselves. They learn to become identical with themselves and accept themselves.

Within the textual world of a psychotherapeutic conversation, the only significant thing that can happen is that people can learn to "accept" their guilt or "work it through." There is no place for the forgiveness of sins that comes from the promise, "your sins are forgiven!"

Within psychotherapy, such a promise must appear as a foreign intrusion, an instance of heteronomy, in which the therapist imposes his or her will on the client. The promise is held to create a space or refuge, external to the clients, which they can retreat into to escape from themselves. The promise of course may simply be dismissed from the outset because it is something merely external and therefore is supposedly unable "really" to change anything in the person addressed. We need to remember that according to modern thinking, and Freud's psychotherapy works with these assumptions, an external thing cannot change anything inside us until it is remembered, appropriated, and seen as a possibility latent within. This is the only logically consistent critique that can be offered by anyone who accepts the idealist premise of identity.

The psychologization of religion offers the perfect recipe for secularizing the Christian faith[226] with its center in the forgiveness of sins, understood as the promise of freedom. All it would take is for the all-important distinction between the promise, on the one hand, and the word as catalyst and midwife, on the other, to disappear from the theology and the practice of the church. If, however, we safeguard this distinction, we can be quite objective in considering the promise of the forgiveness of sins and its relation to the psychotherapeutic conversation. We then need to make a distinction between faith and work and properly value the psychotherapeutic conversation as "work." If, however, we understand the conversation in the sense of a work born of faith and determined by faith, its premise of identity is blown apart and it takes on a new character.

We have already said that the promise, understood as the central object of theology, does not state a fact, nor does it prescribe an action. It is therefore neither a statement nor an appeal. Now we can add that neither does it act as a catalyst, like a midwife in the process of childbirth.

We can now further clarify the thesis that the promise, in the sense of the performative word, lies at the core of the subject matter of theology, by expressly relating the thesis to the question of the essence of Christianity. This question has influenced the history of the church and its theology since the beginnings of Pietism and the Enlightenment. Since the development of our thesis, so far, has been implicitly connected to this question already in our discussion, we can refer back to what we have said earlier.

3.5. The Essence of Christianity

The search for an essence of Christianity has led to the "realization that it is impossible to encapsulate the essence of Christianity in a formula. For the distinction between appearance, and here we have to include all formulations, and what lies behind it led to the development of the concept of essence. For this reason, all attempts to promote verbally fixed dogmas, confessions, or fundamental articles as a sufficient expression of the essence of Christianity were utterly fruitless and will remain so in the future."[227]

Luther's hermeneutic, on the other hand, excluded any distinction between "essence" and "appearance." The speech act with the promise of the forgiveness of sins in the name of Jesus is not an "appearance" but the "essence" itself. Therefore, in view of the definition of the gospel, the central object of theology, which we have taken over from Luther, we can say with Wittgenstein: "*Essence* is expressed by grammar."[228] However, the question of an "essence of Christianity" assumes the validity of the distinction between an "essence" and its relativized "appearance." In this sense it reflects the influence of the Augustinian hermeneutic of signification which is determined by the distinction between reality *(res)* and sign *(signum)*. But Luther overcame this distinction and in doing so shares something in common with the linguistic analysis of the later Wittgenstein.[229]

There is a suspicion that by insisting that theology is primarily concerned with a particular speech act, we could be making it into a "doctrine" that stands in the way of "life." However, this will prove unfounded if we take the speech act as it stands and do not try to isolate it from its context, which includes the ensemble of speaker and listener together with the listener's changed situation resulting from the speech act. Understood in this way, the speech act overcomes the unfortunate antithesis between "doctrine" and "life." We can describe this as a middle position that stands in critical relation to Hegel, on the one hand, and to Feuerbach, on the other.[230] On the one hand, we cannot theorize the speech act in the sense of the Hegelian transition from the religious representation *(Vorstellung)* to the philosophical concept *(Begriff)* without destroying it. But neither can we psychologize it in the sense of Feuerbach's "hermeneutic of regression" without destroying it. We must reject both ways of dealing with the speech act, because they do not do justice to it but turn it into something that it is not. On the one hand, Hegel's theorizing approach wants to transform (sublate) the speech act into a "concept" while, on the other hand, Feuerbach's psychologizing approach wants to reduce it to a "motivation," to something lying behind it that makes it necessary. In short, Feuerbach wants to reduce the speech act to a psychological datum or behavior that in itself is non-linguistic.

This second approach, which Feuerbach uses to determine the essence of Christianity, is the same, in structure and intent, as Schleiermacher's hermeneutical move and is consistent with his transcendental philosophy.

On the other hand, if theology is convinced of the truth of Luther's Reformation hermeneutic and wishes to retain it, it will take account of the fact that its object needs to be expressed in time-related formulations and considered in the light of linguistic analysis, especially that of the later Wittgenstein and Austin, rather than in the light of the analysis of existence. The existential interpretation of the Bible and dogma, taken up by Bultmann and Hans Jonas, via Dilthey and Heidegger, which can be traced back especially to Schleiermacher, is inappropriate for promoting Luther's hermeneutic. This is because it begins with the pre-linguistic realm, where it locates the original source of life, rather than with the external word *(verbum externum)* in the sense of the promise, understood as a speech act.[231]

If we do theology on the basis of linguistic analysis rather than the analysis of existence, we will still preserve what existential interpretation considers important in its privileging of proclamation over theology.[232] But in contrast to Bultmann, we can now focus directly on the event of proclamation without taking anything away from the event itself. Theological reflection always objectifies its object. The question is only whether it focuses attention primarily on the effect of the proclamation in the believing subject,[233] whether it goes from the "content of faith" back to the "ground of faith" (Wilhelm Herrmann[234]), from the secondary theological explication of the believing self-understanding back to the self-understanding itself (Bultmann), or whether it approaches this primarily in the light of the speech act, uses it to discern the ground of faith, and distinguishes it carefully from theological reflection.

Our thesis is that the gospel, understood as a particular speech act, is itself the ground of faith. Since the "essence of Christianity" is a speech act, it must be illuminated, not primarily by an analysis of existence, but by an analysis of language. This, however, needs further clarification, but it will have to wait for our critical analysis of Schleiermacher's transcendental thinking and Bultmann's existential interpretation.[235]

4. Transformations: The Problem of Secularization

When we dealt with the object of theology (2.1) we considered the different ways in which the God who speaks *(deus dicens)* encounters us. This in turn has as its counterpart the multidimensional *passio* or receptivity of the human recipient *(homo recipiens)*. In discussing this, we noted that the "suffering" *(passio)* of these divine encounters refers to the way in which we passively undergo them, where the *passio* reflects an old meaning of the English word "suffer" (2.2). In the last section (3) we noted that the ultimate way in which God encounters us is in the gospel. If we consider this encounter from the standpoint of its most concrete form in Baptism and the Lord's Supper, we could describe the gospel more accurately as the "embodied word."[236]

If theology focuses on this "embodied word," it can avoid the three problematic and dangerous approaches that we have already briefly anticipated in our earlier discussion (3): the *ethical,* the *theoretical,* and the *existential.* Theology then does not refer primarily to a "doing" or "knowing" or "feeling," but to a word. Not to word and language in general, but to a particular word which, corresponding to the three negations we mentioned, is neither an appeal, nor a statement, nor an expression.

This cannot be stressed strongly enough. For what we say of the word we can say also of faith. If the word becomes an appeal, faith becomes its performance in action. If the word becomes a demonstration, faith becomes insight; if it becomes a statement, faith becomes knowledge. Finally, if the word becomes an expression, faith becomes a ground of existence or a ground of experience given with human being as such. Only if the word is promise *(promissio)* is faith really faith.

One way of understanding the theological and intellectual situation that has influenced theology for the last two hundred years or more is to see it through the lens of the threefold typology that we have introduced. We will not simply write off modern Christian thinking as "fate," as Emanuel Hirsch does,[237] but we will work at accurately understanding it, even if, for the sake of truth, we have to criticize it or oppose it outright.[238]

We therefore have to oppose those transformations of Christian thought in modernity that absolutize either the ethical, the theoretical, or the existential element of theology, because they not only obscure and distort the character of the promise, but also end up destroying it.

The threefold typology that we have chosen as an interpretative lens for understanding theology (the ethical, theoretical, and existential approaches), which takes up the threefold scheme that we introduced earlier (theology as contemplation, action, or passivity) (2.2), allows us to reflect critically on the intertwining of the Christian faith and the modern world with all the conflicts that this entails.[239]

Since the term "transformation" can connote a stable identity in spite of any change, it might be more appropriate, given the acuteness of the problem, to use the word "secularization" instead. Admittedly, the word has such different meanings that we really have to ask whether we would not be better off giving it up altogether. However, it may serve a useful purpose after all, since it might be able to keep alive a necessary conversation that furthers both understanding and communication by clarifying references that would otherwise remain unclear.

However, the concept of secularization will only be useful if we do not expect it to express a simple fact or give the definitive answer to an insoluble problem. Every time we reflect on it, we are attempting both to describe a problem and to form a judgment at the same time. But this is not a problem that can be easily solved, and it will need to be tackled afresh again and again. The idea of "secularization" is used in quite polemically pointed ways by each of the different parties to the debate. This indicates a dispute about legitimation, which inevitably involves the justification of positions by means of accusations and counter-accusations, and includes the problem of accepting each other's different theological and political criteria. In the debate about secularization, thinkers make and dispute claims to totality. The debate is all about comprehensive judgments of a philosophical and political nature.

The use of the word "secularization," which has different connotations, always refers to a process of change in understanding the world and the self. Depending on our perspective, "secularization" may be seen negatively as a defection, a loss of what is specifically Christian to the sinful "world." Or, on the other hand, it may be seen positively as the use of the Christian faith to shape and change the world. Hence, depending on the context, "secularization" can mean either the loss or the gain of what is essentially Christian. In fact, we can even talk of Christianity gaining itself by losing itself, in the sense of "relinquishing" itself to the world.

The real value of the idea of secularization lies in the way it can facilitate a discussion of realities that would otherwise be seen as irreconcilably opposed. For instance, modern people, in the strict sense of the word, claim they are "rational," "come of age," "religionless," or "atheistic" in their self-understanding. But we could ask them if they are aware of how the very religious elements that they claim to have outgrown and eliminated from their thinking continue to live on or come back in new forms and under new guises. It can easily be shown how people who abandon religious authority, ostensibly because they find that the creeds and dogmas of the church rob them of their freedom, are soon willing to worship at another altar and to offer "faithful" allegiance to new creeds and ideologies. These new authorities are even more unrelenting in their demand for unconditional submission, which they justify on the grounds that their demands are perfectly reasonable and are no more than could be expected of any person. Indeed, it is clear that modern ideologies have all the elements of a religion when people look to them for ultimate meaning and ascribe to them unconditional validity and authority.

If the Christian faith rejects such a usurpation, which it must, it has to do more than formally negate it in the abstract. We can begin by looking at its main line of argumentation. We need to check whether the proponents of the various secularized versions of the Christian faith, who oppose it with arguments drawn from the critique of religion, do not use the very same arguments that Christianity itself uses against its opponents who usurp Christian elements and then use them in the service of secular ideologies.

For our use of the term "secularization," we propose the following definition: secularization is the dissolution of religion's autonomy and the dispersal of its legacy in a way that limits it to the forms of "doing" and "knowing" or holds that its functions are taken over by these forms. These two forms of secularization represent two different approaches to religion, the ethical and the theoretical, both of which are to be distinguished from the existential. This third approach destroys theology and transforms it into anthropology, but not primarily into the forms of knowing and doing. Rather, the transformation occurs on theology's own home ground, in the area of faith, understood as the feeling of absolute dependence, which is different from both knowledge and action.

These three forms of the secularization of the Christian faith have received classical shape in the thinking of Kant, Hegel, and Schleiermacher. These thinkers propose transformations in which the ethical, the theoretical, and the existential aspects respectively are absolutized and thus disconnected from the promise. We have already discussed the details of this in section three.

4.1. The Ethical Approach (Kant)

The danger of an ethical approach to theology exists wherever the unity of law and gospel is stressed for the sake of truth.[240] We find this, for instance, in Karl Barth. However, the danger of turning theology into ethics is not always avoided even when we follow Luther and relate theology to the distinction between law and gospel.

We see this danger in the *Ethics* of Wilhelm Herrmann,[241] where the ethical approach to theology appears almost as an ideal type. Its two-part structure, "Natural Life and Moral Thinking" and "The Christian Moral Life," reflects a particular way of linking the "natural" and the "Christian."[242] For him ethics, which is autonomous, "natural," and general, forms the basis of Christian dogmatics because it raises questions without providing answers. "Only a morality based on independent knowledge . . . brings people to the point where they can understand that the appearance of Jesus Christ in this world and their encounter with him is their redemption."[243] This one sentence stands for an entire concept of theology, in this case a *type of ethicized theology*. Here ethics is the fundamental discipline of theology insofar as ethics and its irresolvable dilemmas (aporias) provide the necessary framework for understanding theology and making it understandable to others.[244]

This type of theology is unthinkable apart from the philosophy of Immanuel Kant. According to Herrmann, his significance for Christianity is that he has "clearly seen" "that the certainty of faith . . . is based on the fact that all people can understand the demands of morality and grasp their eternal necessity."[245] An ethicized theology, as advocated by Herrmann, affirms the core of Kant's philosophy. We see this from the three questions: What can I know? What should I do? What can I hope for? For Kant claims that in answering these three questions, we in fact answer the one question: What is a human and what is the nature of humanity?[246] The first question is asked in order to set the stage for the second, while the answer to the third comes from working through the second. Hence, the second question is the most important. "Morality therefore leads inescapably to religion."[247]

This ethicized theology is broadened and deepened, but not fundamentally altered, in Helmut Peukert's *Science, Action, and Fundamental Theology*.[248] He makes special use of critical theory to develop a "fundamental theology understood as a theory of communicative action and of the reality of God in this action."[249] He holds that theology as a whole must be developed in terms of the fundamental structure of this action. Peukert's "analysis of the beginning and status of theological theory formation" (the subtitle of the German original)[250] compels us to clarify how the term "action" is used in theology.

If we follow Kant and his successors by making the question "What should I do?" the most fundamental and important question about human nature, we fail to remember that practical reason is not ultimately autonomous but is guided by the power of the imagination. In other words, to go the way of Kant is to fail to realize that we are primarily "aesthetic" beings who are governed by our perceptions. It does not recognize that we are, first and foremost, moved by the power of those images that, consciously or unconsciously, guide what we do and determine our desires. The crucial thing is to see that our desires — think of Kant's question: What should I do? — are governed by this stratum of impulses with their linguistic disposition and that the intensity and orientation of our affects and passions are governed by the images that we have stored away in our memories. In short, we are determined by pathos, by what we "suffer," by what we passively undergo.

We cannot therefore begin with the question, "What should I do?" Rather, the first question must be: "What is done to me? What do I undergo?" For human action does not begin with the self, but is made possible by the prior gift of freedom. We can act only because God gives us the freedom to act.

How do we obtain this freedom? Does it belong to us naturally? Can it be established empirically? Can it be conceived theoretically? Can it only be postulated for practical purposes? Or do we owe it to a particular promise?

Theology, understood as a linguistic discipline and a doctrine of forms, reflects on our *promised* freedom. It reflects on it as a "form" in which the social and individual modes of existence are part of the elementary experience of the world. This "form" is not only implicit in theory and practice but it is always assumed and accordingly must be distinguished from both.[251]

The question we have to debate with Kant and his theological successors is: *How* is human freedom given? Kant says that the moral law, which presupposes and demands freedom, is grounded in the "fact" of pure reason.[252] If being human and living in the world constitute an endless task, at least the task as such is *given*. This givenness of the task is sufficient to justify speech about God for theologians who worship at the altar of transcendental philosophy. But the question of the how, how this task is given to us, fades into the background. For the sake of a possible gain in the plausibility stakes, theologians are willing to accept that, within the perspective of transcendental philosophy claimed by fundamental theology, the word of God the creator can be reduced to the cryptic assertion: I do not set the task for myself, but I always find within me that it has been set already.

This fails to take into account that poetics and aesthetics always come before ethics.

4.2. The Theoretical Approach (Hegel)

To love God wholly means that we must also love him with our mind or *thinking* (Mark 12:30). Therefore, if we have a non-theoretical outlook in principle, we will hardly do justice to the Christian faith, which draws its life from intelligible words, which are in turn closely linked with the mind *(nous)* (1 Cor. 14:14f. and 19). The word of forgiveness and life, which overcomes sin and death, gives us something to think about. It empowers and compels us to think freely, boldly, and outside the circle.

Hegel has attempted to do this and to that end appeals to God's self-revelation. God fully discloses himself and thereby sets human thinking free. The individual and the particular are not passed over, at least in theory. This kind of thinking embraces all individual things, all separate things, and reconciles them by virtue of the Spirit who raised Christ from the dead (Rom. 8:11), who is the "negation of negation" *(negatio negationis)*.[253] This kind of thinking always makes connections and eventually develops into a system.

The significance of Hegel's system is set out impressively in his essay, "Who Thinks Abstractly?"[254] He shows that the "nothing but" of the fatal abstraction is conquered by the "still also" of concrete thought. "In quite a different manner, I once heard a common old woman, a hospital maid, kill the abstraction of the murderer and bring him back to life to honor him. His severed head had been placed on the scaffold, and the sun was shining. 'How beautifully,' she said, 'the sun of God's grace shines on *Binder's* head!' — 'You are not worthy of having the sun shine on you,' we might say to a rascal who has made us angry. But this woman saw that the murderer's head was lit by the sunshine and thus was still worthy of it. She raised him from the punishment of the scaffold into the sun of God's grace. She did not bring about the reconciliation with violets and sentimental vanity, but she saw him received into grace in the higher sun."[255]

Should we not follow Hegel?[256] Does not his philosophy reflect the radical universality evident in the event of God's incarnation and death on the cross?

Our doubts are justified in the light of what we have already said above about the object of theology (2.1) and our fundamental passivity/ receptivity *(passio* of *homo recipiens)* in the face of the different ways in which the God who speaks *(deus dicens)* encounters us (2.2).[257] We have doubts about Hegel's understanding of sin and evil, *Anfechtung* (trial, spiritual attack), and the way in which he sees the difference between faith and sight.[258] But our main concern here is with his understanding of the word.

Hegel transformed Luther's understanding of the word into a philosophy of spirit. The new Protestantism that he represents is distinguished from the old by the fact that it no longer holds to the word of God in the sense of the "embodied" word (*Augsburg Confession,* Article 5), but turns it into a theory. The claim and intention of this theorizing is to transform faith into knowledge. The result is that the contradiction between the law that convicts me of sin and God's liberating promise in the gospel fades into a way of thinking that claims to be aware of the externality of the embodied word and grasps everything alien as the other of myself. Hegel offers impressive proof for his theory in those numerous passages in which he considers the Lord's Supper, where he emphasizes the full appropriation of the gifts bestowed and the consumption of all the external elements.[259]

In this form of self-referencing and self-reflection the modern

Narcissus[260] loses his subjectivity and freedom. These, however, are not his by right, nor can he lay any claim to them, but God gives them to him freely as a gift. Yet he loses them, a bit like the dog in Aesop's fable, which while carrying a piece of meat in his mouth, snapped at his reflection in the water and so lost not only the meat but also his reflection.

It is certainly not Hegel's intention to destroy Christian freedom or the word of Christ that establishes it. He only wants to destroy its external *form* with its fixed objectivity, not its *content*. He actually wants to preserve the content and elevate it to its true importance, to show it off to its best advantage. This is what Hegel means by the "sublation" of the Christian religion, in the threefold sense of the German word *Aufhebung*: abolition, elevation, and preservation. And this is what he accomplishes in his philosophy of religion with the transition from the religious representation, image *(Vorstellung)*, to the philosophical concept *(Begriff)*. In the first step, the infinitely deep, subjective, religious feeling attains an external form in which it imagines, symbolically represents, the Christian faith. However, this representation must be negated again and its external form relinquished. Only in this way can its content be appropriated and understood. Only by the process of conception and by means of the "concept" that it produces, does its content become real.

In his philosophy of religion, Hegel assumes what he mistakenly praises as Luther's "great principle": "that all externality disappears at the point of the absolute relation to God."[261] The sensory form of religion, even if it is a speech act like the promise of the forgiveness of sins, is, for Hegel, an external thing and as such must be negated. The content can be separated from the form and, once separated, it can be appropriated.[262] At first it appears only as a feeling, then as a representation. After its externalization and manifestation, Hegel demands, as the final stage of his logic, that the religious representation *(Vorstellung)* is transformed into the philosophical concept *(Begriff)*.

This kind of theoretical approach to Christianity negates all particularity as sinful narrowness, in order to be able to stand in absolute relation to the absolute. It does not recognize the distinction between sinful narrowness and the divinely willed particularity and limitation characteristic of God's creation. This distinction is fundamental to theology and cannot be given up. Indeed, Hegel's theoretical approach sees religion as a sure means of transcending the finite and approaching the infinite.

The subject matter of Christian theology, however, consists of the concrete speech acts in which God is at work through law and gospel in a twofold way that both obligates and liberates. These speech acts highlight the distinction between God and us, and therefore limit us. Because they appeal to our senses they have an inbuilt resistance to being transformed into concepts. Religion is not about rising above the finite to the infinite, but it brings us to the point where we recognize and accept the finiteness of our human existence as determined by God.

How is the transition from religious representation to philosophical concept understood in Hegel's thinking? Is the content preserved? Does it really only come into its own, as Hegel claims, with this transition? Or is it not in fact destroyed?

Feuerbach saw clearly that this transition to the philosophical concept actually destroys the content of religion.

"I have attacked *speculative* philosophy at its most vulnerable point, its own *point d'honneur,* by showing . . . that it robs religion of its true, essential content when it tries to bring it into harmony with itself.[263] Feuerbach polemicizes against that "philosophy which claims that it has the same content as religion, but stripped of the sensory form into which religion lowers it." He argues that "this form cannot be separated from the content of religion without religion itself being destroyed. It is absolutely essential to religion."[264]

Franz Overbeck's polemic against the "false theological idealism that holds religion to be indifferent to its particular forms,"[265] runs along the same lines.

Anyone who recognizes the importance of the form-critical insights of Old and New Testament exegesis, as well as Luther's understanding of the gospel, will agree with Feuerbach's criticism of Hegel's philosophy of religion. However, Feuerbach was mistaken in his opinion of Christianity even though he was perfectly correct in his criticism of Hegel. This is clear from the fact that he saw the "absolutely essential" form of Christianity as an analyzable psychological phenomenon, in the sense of a depth hermeneutic, according to which theology should be "treated as a psychological *pathology*"[266] for the purposes of therapy.[267]

We happily join Feuerbach in criticizing Hegel at the most decisive point. That, however, does not give a blanket approval to Feuerbach's critique of theology. On the contrary, we have to oppose him also by again stressing that God's spoken word appeals to our senses (2.1).[268] This criticism of Feuerbach applies in a specific way also to Schleiermacher.

4.3. The Existential Approach

So far we have considered those types of transformations in which either the ethical or theoretical element is absolutized. We now turn to a completely different type of transformation in which the existential element, human subjectivity, is either absolutized or at least allowed to predominate by becoming a principle of knowing (ratio *cognoscendi*),[269] according to which the God who speaks *(deus dicens)* is defined in terms of the human recipient *(secundum hominem recipientem)*. The classical form of this transformation is found in Schleiermacher. Neo-Protestantism, as represented by Schleiermacher, differs from old Protestantism at a crucial point. It transforms the doctrine of the word of God into a doctrine of faith.

4.3.1. Schleiermacher

Schleiermacher's systematic theology[270] is a doctrine of faith *(Glaubenslehre)*. As the full German title says, it is an account of the Christian faith as a coherent whole according to the principles of the evangelical Protestant church. Schleiermacher says that he can only describe what is given. In his systematics, he presupposes faith as something given, and as always, in the case of human beings, as something living. He understands it as spirituality. Therefore, "Christian doctrines" are nothing other than "accounts of the Christian religious affections set forth in speech" (*The Christian Faith* §15[271] [hereafter CF]). Every doctrine "is only what is derived, and the inner affections are the original" (*Letter to Lücke*, p. 40; CF p. 77 note). "All religious emotions" (CF p. 77) are in themselves non-linguistic. They are concerned with "an immediate existential relationship."[272] Logically, but not temporally, secondary, they must "manifest" themselves "outwardly" (CF p. 77). They "express" themselves (CF pp. 77, 78, 82ff.) in a "statement" (CF p. 107 etc.) in a secondary, though no less necessary way.

Only the inmost being of a person, the most individual thing that characterizes a person as a whole, manifests itself outwardly in order to become at once an inner reality by "acting" on another. The "inner" speaks to the "inner." It must therefore use the external word for the purposes of "communication" and "mediation." This is the external means that "evokes the same inner experience in another" (CF §14). The word is "but the short distance that the spirit has to traverse through a region which, though familiar to human nature as such, is alien to the spirit as the inmost core of this nature, in order to come from itself to itself. The word 'proceeds from . . . another human interior and therefore always points back to an interior.'"273

This understanding of the relationship between faith and word is typical of Schleiermacher's whole theology. It defines how he understands the "*one* source, from which all Christian doctrine is derived," the "self-proclamation of Christ"274 as well as its corresponding ecclesiology. It is repeated in Schleiermacher's practical theology, his Christian ethics, his hermeneutics, and his aesthetics.

In comparing Schleiermacher with Luther, it is especially instructive to look at how Schleiermacher describes "the service of the divine word." It is characteristic of his understanding of the word that he does not use it in its basic dogmatic form, but in one of its two secondary forms! It is helpful to see how in this way he transforms the Lutheran "distribution" of the "external word" (AC 5). For him the "communication" of the faith amounts to a "self-communication" on the part of the minister of the divine word *(minister verbi divini)*. There "can be no self-communication except through a self-presentation acting as a stimulus. The movement of the self-presenting person, which is received through imitation, becomes a force in the person who is open to receiving this stimulus, and this in turn evokes the same movement" (CF §133, p. 612; translation altered).

Schleiermacher's theory of language is unmistakably a *hermeneutic of regression,* or we could also call it a *hermeneutic of expression.* Regardless of the differences between a "poetic," "rhetorical," and "didactic" expression ("where the latter is a derivative and secondary form made up from the other two" [CF p. 79, translation altered]), *every* word can only be understood as an "expression" or "statement." In its unequivocal character and specificity, the word is an objectification, which can be understood only by going back, regressing, to an original word that underlies it and evokes it.

This is true not only of the relationship between preaching and theology, in which theology, understood as reflection on preaching, is derived from preaching. Rather, Schleiermacher holds that this also applies, in a structurally identical way, to the relationship that exists between any type of preaching and the ground of faith present in the immediate religious self-consciousness. "Preaching" is "utterance and presentation" (CF §18, p. 87).

Therefore, we can already see from an initial glance at Schleiermacher's systematic theology *(The Christian Faith)*, as well as from supplementary texts, that the word for him has indeed a necessary function, but only in a secondary and derivative sense.[275] He cannot say that the word prior to faith is the external word *(verbum externum)*. Faith is not a result of the word, as it is for Luther. Therefore, Schleiermacher's theology is not a doctrine of the word, where the word is final and ultimate. Rather, it is a doctrine of the "feeling of absolute dependence," which we can never get behind. While for Luther faith is a "creature of the word" *(fides creatura verbi)*, for Schleiermacher the word is a creature of faith *(verbum creatura fidei)*.

This is Schleiermacher's hermeneutic of regression, by which he deconstructs the object of theology and rids it of any substantive content. We can see from this that his reductive method is similar in approach to Feuerbach's method with its critique of theology.

Feuerbach holds that the absolutely essential form of Christianity is sensory, dependent on the senses rather than the intellect or spirit, and that we find it in psychological phenomena, in the elementary forms of experience, especially in the emotions of fear and love, of thankfulness and trust.[276]

Luther's explanation of the first commandment in the *Small Catechism* ("We should fear, love and trust in God above all things") comes close to Feuerbach's critique of theology and hence to the theory of secularization based on the psychologization of religion. But Luther's understanding of the first commandment is more challenging for a theology that is not "Lutheran" than a theory of secularization that transforms theology completely into forms of knowing and doing.

If, as we saw earlier, the secularization of religion means turning it into a theory, this, according to Hegel, has implications for the *content* of the Christian faith (especially for "reconciliation") because it means transforming it into something that can be grasped with the mind, or, following Marx's adaptation, removing it from the theoretical realm and applying it to the area of social praxis. Here the Christian faith is wholly drawn into the forms of knowing and doing, into the scheme of theory and practice *(praxis)*.[277] However, if the Christian faith is viewed through the lens of Hegelian or Marxist philosophy and seen in the light of knowing and doing, we fail to recognize that vital third dimension, the *passio*, which makes it clear that we are not primarily actors in life but the passive recipients of the actions done by another (2.2).

On the other hand, the secularization of the Christian faith, based on the psychology of religion, has in view something that, according to Schleiermacher, must be distinguished from knowing and doing and that underlies both.[278] It interprets Christianity neither in the sense of the hermeneutic of the Hegelian philosophy of religion, nor in the sense of the economic hermeneutic of Marx, but is in substance comparable with the depth hermeneutic of Feuerbach and Freud. It changes not the content of the Christian faith but its *enactment*, if we may be permitted to use such a problematic distinction. Here the content of the faith is seen as a secondary objectification that conceals its motivation, and as a rationalization of our primary drives, emotions, and needs that has to be decoded. This hermeneutical approach is interested solely in the *form* of faith, which it regards as an act, and interprets it as the general human psychological behavior of one, in a certain sense, timeless individuality. This reduction of the content of faith to the form of a motivation is Feuerbach's way of eliminating theology and transforming it into anthropology.

The hermeneutical method implicit in this reductive approach to theology, which reduces content to form, is the same type of "interpretation" as that of Freud's psychoanalysis. This observation is supported by the preface to the first edition of *The Essence of Christianity* (1841), in which Feuerbach programmatically formulates the hermeneutics governing his critique. There it says, as we have already seen (4.2), that theology is to be treated "as a psychological pathology" for the purpose of therapy. Feuerbach says, "I let religion *speak for itself*; I see myself only as its listener and interpreter."[279]

Schleiermacher shares with Freud and Feuerbach the hermeneutical method of regression that interprets a symbolic expression by tracing it back to the psychological experience that conditions it.

This would suggest that the next thing we need to do is to look in more detail at Schleiermacher's relation to Feuerbach. This opens up a fundamental problem of contemporary theology that we can no longer ignore. It goes back to Karl Barth's judgment that he made in connection with his discussion of Feuerbach, especially the latter's interpretation of Luther. Barth accuses Schleiermacher and the theology that followed in his footsteps, right up to the Bultmann School, of committing the cardinal sin of turning theology into anthropology.[280]

Schleiermacher's transformation of theology, which we are calling an "existential approach," is intended to eliminate the object of theology. This approach, though understandable from the perspective of the political history of modernity,[281] is highly problematical from a theological standpoint. He relativizes the biblical texts by understanding them as merely expressive phenomena, expressions of the authors' inner soul. Through a process of regression, he goes back behind the words of the texts to the expressions that lie behind them, for the words themselves are seen as mere objectifications. In going behind the texts, however, he has not reckoned with their relative autonomy and their resistance to relativization.

Our critique of this hermeneutic is offered from the standpoint of the subject matter.[282] It will have to pay attention especially to that point which puts everything else in perspective and which is the focus of all Schleiermacher's philosophy and theology, the point at which everything converges, or more precisely, from which everything originates, for this point is not the summit of his thought, but its root or ultimate depth. This point is the one common transcendental ground of our certainty[283] both in willing and knowing, in the sense of the leading propositions in §§214f. in the *Dialectic* of 1814: "We need a transcendental ground for our certainty in willing as much as for our certainty in knowing, and the two cannot be different. Accordingly, we now have this transcendental ground only in the relative identity of thinking and willing, which is located in the feelings."[284] This ultimate certainty placed in the "feelings" is immediate certainty. That does not mean it is unmediated. It is simply not bound to any specific linguistic means but discloses itself in all possible means and through all possible means. In other words, it is universal, in the sense that it is the depth dimension of each and every individual human existence.

However, is there not an elementary uncertainty at work here rather than this ultimate immediate certainty? Are we humans, by ourselves, always conscious of our radical finitude, our creaturely being, and do we always recognize God as the creator and give him the honor? Or do we not seek by all possible means to give this honor to ourselves, appointing ourselves as judges of our life and of all its successes and failures. And, depending on how we answer that question, do we not fall into pride *(superbia)*, or despair *(desperatio)*, or both, either one after the other or simultaneously? Rather than the feeling of absolute dependence, are our lives not stamped by revolt, rebellion, and its correlative, resignation?

"Humans are by nature unable to let God be God. Indeed, they themselves want to be God, and do not want God to be God."[285] "What greater rebellion against God . . . is there than not believing his promise? For what is this, if not to make God a liar or to doubt that he is truthful? Surely this is to ascribe truthfulness to one's self but lying and vanity to God? But don't people who do this deny God and set themselves up as an idol in their heart?"[286] Humans "deny" God "with such unfaith" and set up "an idol of their own understanding in their heart against God" — "as if it knows their heart better than God."[287] Such an interpretation of the first commandment[288] makes it immediately clear that theology is basically ideological criticism from the standpoint of its subject.

Theology cannot encounter its object externally, so to speak, in a supposedly objective, neutral way. It cannot assume the generality of the "feeling of absolute dependence" and then proceed to act as if our thinking and doing is grounded in an ultimate certainty, on the basis of which we can be addressed, because it is immediately given with our human existence. The uncertainty that in fact prevails and the certainty mediated by the particular word of Christ, understood as promise, are not ontologically convergent. These two kinds of certainty are not the same. They cannot be formalized into a single ontological certainty that would always be prior to ontic uncertainty and certainty, to sin and grace, and so would always be part of both. Otherwise, we play a philosophical game with real, ontic uncertainty, in which humans themselves want to be God, and so we end up playing a game with sin. We overlook the fact that people who are locked up in themselves and their own world for the most part do not even recognize their real uncertainty. Therefore, they do not respond to anyone who talks to them about this and points them to the certainty that they need. The natural ideological blindness, which is a mark of the human condition, is played down and covered over by regressing to a formalized ontological transcendental (the feeling of absolute dependence), which is said to be an abstract integral that must be assumed in order to secure anthropological continuity.

If we refuse to go this way, it is because theology as an academic discipline cannot proceed from a scientific consensus regarding a primal anthropological datum, nor can it establish that datum scientifically. However, no such consensus existed either in Schleiermacher's day. Why then did he assert the universality of his transcendental-dialectical demonstration, in spite of the differences that he knew existed between himself and Schelling and, above all, between himself and Hegel? Finally, the only way to understand this is to see it as a missionary strategy in which the challenge of the gospel is expressed in the demand made on each of them to always let action and knowledge, which result from inquiring into the truth, be accompanied by the confession of the radical finitude of human existence.

Schleiermacher's demonstration therefore is really an assertion *(assertio)* that expects people to change their way of thinking. It amounts to an ideological critique since it radically questions Hegel's ideology of absolute idealism and his thinking about self-realization.

But if the "essence of the Christian faith" cannot be seen as self-realization, its rival interpretation from within the scheme of self-realization wants to see it as a matter of self-understanding. This, however, seems to offer no objection to Schleiermacher who distinguishes faith from knowing and doing and sees both grounded in faith, understood as pure receptivity *(passio)*. For that very reason he says that faith cannot be identified with knowing or doing or both. But we must insist, *contra* Schleiermacher, that this distinction comes about concretely. It occurs in particular performative statements of Christian proclamation, of the kind that we have in the promise of the forgiveness of sins.

We cannot, however, extrapolate from this concrete event to a supposedly generally valid definition that forms the vanishing point of a phenomenology of religion so broad in its conception that it can accommodate all religions. In Schleiermacher's view, Christianity would be situated closest to that vanishing point, where all religions are distinguished from it in degree and kind. He makes this clear in the propositions he borrows from the philosophy of religion (§§7-19 of *The Christian Faith*), but they always stay within the whole realm of "ethics"[289] (as given in §§3f.). The real decision, that against atheism, which identifies human existence with its action and work, comes *prior* to even entering this realm. Atheism is excluded from the broad field of religion from the start, even though it manifests religious elements. Here Schleiermacher differs from Luther, who includes atheism in his understanding of religion. We only have to think of his graphic explanation of the first commandment in the *Large Catechism*. For Luther, atheism comes to full flower in the religions, and we see this most pointedly in the religion of self-realization, where humans aim to make themselves dependent on the self rather than on God.[290]

Admittedly, Luther also seems to reduce the ontic antitheses of faith and unbelief, "both sides of the antithesis" (Schleiermacher), to a single ontological denominator: to the "trust . . . of the heart," that "makes both . . . God and an idol."[291] It is tempting to see in this formal integral of "trust" the same basic human emotion or state that we find in Schleiermacher's "feeling of absolute dependence."

But if Schleiermacher's thinking really agreed with Luther's on this matter, he would have to take into account what he excluded in §§3f. of *The Christian Faith*, that self-realization is a form of spirituality. In other words, he would have to accept that one's "feeling of absolute dependence" is a form of self-realization. But Schleiermacher did not do this, no doubt because of a Christian pre-commitment: the assumption that life is first of all a gift. However, what he *has* done is turned a simple ontic reality (being as such) into something ontological (which presupposes a theory of being) without admitting it. But in doing this, he has excluded from this ontological, transcendental dimension "trust" in works or "false trust," the very thing that for Luther exists as an ontic reality in strict opposition to "genuine trust." Therefore, for Schleiermacher, nothing can stand on the "one side of the antithesis," the side of sin, which is *qualitatively* different from the "other side," the side of grace. Since for him sin belongs to the perspective of the same transcendental as that gained by the transformation of grace into an ontological entity, it is only *quantitatively* different from it. In other words, if grace represents the clarity of the God-consciousness, sin is not *qualitatively* different from grace, as for Luther, but simply a diminution of grace weakened by sin.

With this doctrine of sin, Schleiermacher pays the price for his method of formalizing specific theological data, by turning them into general abstract concepts, so that they seem to become a philosophical antechamber to theology, in order to make them appear more plausible than they would be as theological doctrines. However, theology should begin with its own subject matter, not by any sleight of hand, as in Schleiermacher, but openly and transparently, as Luther does.

In contrast to Schleiermacher, Luther does not start with a general concept in order to make the first commandment intelligible to his readers. In fact, he does the very opposite. He comes to an understanding of what "religion" is from the first commandment: the "trust of the heart" (compare the wording of Deut. 6:5!). This "trust" therefore is not something transcendental but is created concretely by God's self-introduction and demanded by the first commandment. It cannot be conceived in a formal ontological way but only in a material ontic way. The opposition to God's self-introduction and the first commandment is likewise concrete in the form of "false trust." It is so concrete, material, and ontic that it cannot be relativized by a transcendental in order that it might have something in common with "genuine trust." This has implications for the relationship between the two kinds of "trust." It means that we can only know what false trust or unbelief is in the light of genuine trust or faith, not vice versa. It is precisely this irreversible direction in the definition of this relation that leads to the extraordinary breadth of Luther's concept of religion which comes from his interpretation of the first commandment.

Schleiermacher wants to work towards a scientific understanding of what we generally call "religion." To do this he turns to transcendental philosophy to develop a formal preconception or logical general concept[292] of the Christian faith by first demonstrating its basic ontological structure. However, the remarkable thing is that Luther's interpretation of the first commandment shows that Schleiermacher's method actually works against him. That is, in his attempt to secure the greatest possible breadth for his notion of religion, Schleiermacher ends up narrowing it down, since, by definition, he has to exclude self-realization as a "way of faith." For him the way of faith is rather the refusal to derive a broad concept of religion from the Christian faith, and the conviction that this faith must instead be based on a phenomenology of religion grounded in a supposedly general *a priori*.

Can transcendental philosophers then really exclude the notion of self-realization from the definition of religion? Can they exclude it in advance in a purely theoretical way? Or does not the distinction between faith and knowledge, and above all, between faith and action, which is part of this exclusion, take place concretely in those elementary speech acts like the promise of the forgiveness of sins?

In fact, the distinction that constitutes the "essence of Christianity" is only made in these concrete speech acts. This distinction is between God, the creator and judge, and humans, who no longer want to usurp God's place but are content to live as his creatures. That means that they do not have to prove themselves in success or give up in times of failure. It means that they are liberated from pride *(superbia)* as well as despair *(desperatio)*.

This definition of the "essence of Christianity" is something that I can only speak of theologically as one who is already personally involved, and even then only with the intention of criticizing and renewing the elementary speech acts that occur daily, so that these sentences that convict and liberate may be for me life-giving words that are absolutely dependable.

This contradicts Schleiermacher and his hermeneutical intention, which if not implied by his transcendental philosophy, is at any rate in perfect agreement with it. However, this contradiction does not mean that we cannot or must not adopt essential elements and polemical references that belong to his concept of theology, assuming that we correct the approach of his transcendental philosophy and hermeneutics.

A path similar to that of Schleiermacher was taken by Gerhard Ebeling, especially in *God and Word* (1967).[293]

According to Ebeling, because theology knows that the universal claim of the gospel is valid for Jews and Greeks and so for all people, it cannot permit the gospel to be confined to the language of an ecclesiastical "ghetto." Theology therefore must do everything to help proclamation speak in a way that is generally understood and relevant. The message of the church must address people's most basic needs; it must talk about essentials and not about things that they can do without.

We rely unconditionally on language. We could say that we are absolutely dependent on it. Since we have the gift of language, we can pin others down with our words and, conversely, others can pin us down with their words.

But we are called to use words responsibly, as those who will have to give an account.

The breadth of the field of the many linguistic phenomena that Ebeling describes is nothing other than the interpretation of a single depth, for also that breadth can be accounted for by the thesis that our basic human situation is a "word-situation." The common characteristic that embraces all people is language.

From this it is clear that Ebeling shares significant common ground with Schleiermacher, but also that there are important differences. Both speak of a single basic human situation, which is that of absolute dependence. The difference is that, for Schleiermacher, the feeling of absolute dependence does not involve words. More precisely, its verbalization is only secondary. For Ebeling, on the other hand, language belongs immediately to the transcendental side of our humanity, although it cannot be denied that he also shows a tendency to inquire behind language, to ask about the condition for the possibility of speech. This is especially evident when he reflects on what compels us to speak.

However, we need to look at Ebeling's basic anthropology, which he understands in terms of a phenomenology of language. We can easily see[294] that the structures he regards as universal are specifically Christian or post-Christian, but not generally human. They may well become that. If they do, we would be in the epoch in which Christianity becomes a worldwide general phenomenon. But Ebeling does not think in terms of this evolutionary model but instead proceeds in a transcendental direction. His concern is for the origin of human being, for the source, which is in danger of being lost. This means that he is not thinking about a fundamental situation that will only become generally human, but one which is that already.

But it is precisely here in connection with this universality that there is no unanimity. Ebeling claims to have demonstrated that this fundamental situation he has described is a situation in which the word is paramount *(Wortsituation)*. However, there is a significant counterclaim that proceeds from the notion of self-realization and only moves gradually to the situation described by Ebeling. In light of this, Ebeling's supposed demonstration of a general phenomenon already appears to be nothing more than an assertion.[295]

In the same way as Schleiermacher's fundamental anthropological demonstration of the feeling of absolute dependence is determined by the Christian faith in creation, Ebeling's equally fundamental demonstration that the basic human situation is from the start a "situation of the word" has to be specifically informed by that which is supposed to be understood only in the light of this demonstration, that is, in the light of the Christian proclamation. Therefore, what we said above about Schleiermacher applies here also. The methodological procedure is not entirely tautological insofar as the criterion of the intelligibility of what is to be understood is its *formal* characteristic.

What stopped Schleiermacher and Ebeling from expressly acknowledging the specifically Christian elements of their fundamental anthropology as such is a deeply rooted fear of a revelatory positivism that is not readily communicable and cannot be understood by everyone. They abhor the statement "God verifies himself." This theological proposition therefore is applied to humans and transformed into an *anthropological* proposition: "Human beings are verified and can understand this verification." However, there is a secret assumption here that needs to be declared: this capacity to understand depends on humans themselves "being verified." But here we must reaffirm what we have already said in opposition to the thinking of Hegel and Marx. We cannot verify ourselves, nor can we realize ourselves. If that is the case, there is only one other possibility. God is the one who verifies us. If we go back to the anthropological turn we mentioned above, we notice that God is not spoken of here directly, but indirectly, in terms of human "passivity/receptivity." "We are verified" is simply an indirect way of saying that "God verifies us." We are passive in the sense that we receive our verification from God. We can see in this a modern variation of the typically Jewish way of speaking about God that is also reflected in the New Testament. Here the direct use of God's name is avoided and God is spoken of indirectly using the passive voice, the so-called divine passive *(passivum divinum)*.

4.3.2. Bultmann

The essential feature of the existential approach that we saw in Schleiermacher is repeated in Rudolf Bultmann's theology, although his concept of the kerygma claims to take up Luther's theology of the word. We see it in his reluctance to talk directly about the God who speaks *(deus dicens)* and his preference for talking about God in the mirror of the human recipient *(homo recipiens)*. Bultmann also approves an indirect way of speaking about God: "The only thing we can say about God is what he does with us."[296]

Bultmann insists that we cannot speak of God objectively; we cannot make God the object of our discourse. Here he differs from

Schleiermacher in that Bultmann's thinking is stamped in a special way by the philosophy of Kant. The Kantian legacy is also evident in the way in which Bultmann understands faith as obedience, as an act. Hence, the existential type of approach that we find in Bultmann has links with the ethical approach that we have already considered (4.1).

The following presentation and discussion[297] takes up a point made at the beginning of the book where we said that theology has its place "between metaphysics and mythology."[298] We now want to apply this to Bultmann's theology in order to outline as clearly as possible the essence of his existential approach and to show how it transforms Luther's understanding of the promise.

Bultmann's critical attitude towards *mythology* is easy to spot. He holds that a radical demythologization of the New Testament is indispensable for properly understanding it. However, at the crucial point he is unable to carry out his project to its logical conclusion, the point at which he, as a Christian and a theologian, comes to speak of the resurrection of the crucified Jesus. For here he is compelled to speak of God's "action" in raising his Son from death.[299]

But how does he fare with *metaphysics?* Nowhere in his *New Testament and Mythology* does Bultmann describe his position as "metaphysical." Yet the problem of metaphysics is there, even if he does not refer to it by name. Admittedly, it is somewhat concealed. Bultmann does not follow the Stoics, for instance, in critiquing myth on the basis of natural theology. Hence, he does not speak of the true essence of God or of the nature of God, but he speaks rather of the true essence of human being. He inquires about the true "self,"[300] and its "authenticity."[301] But it is just here that we are confronted by the question of metaphysics, but in its modern form, as a philosophy of the subject, although in Bultmann's case, it would be more accurate to call it a "philosophy of existence," or better still, an "existential interpretation."

In the context of modern thinking, the problem of natural theology for Bultmann is bound up with the metaphysics of existence and the question of the true human "self" and its "authenticity." It is no accident therefore that Bultmann originally published his *New Testament and Mythology* with the essay on "The Question of Natural Revelation" (Rudolf Bultmann, *Offenbarung und Heilsgeschehen, BevTh* 7 [Munich: Lempp, 1941], which was later published in

Glauben und Verstehen II, 3rd ed. [Tübingen: Mohr Siebeck, 1961], pp. 79-104. See *Anknüpfung und Widerspruch* [1946], ibid. [117-32], 120: "The point of contact with the word of God can be found in the human quest for authenticity that stirs the heart of the person who has lost his or her self and wants to be a self." See also *Glauben und Verstehen* I, 4th ed. [Tübingen: Mohr Siebeck, 1961], pp. 294-312 ["The Problem of 'Natural Theology'"]).

This kind of metaphysics is just as sharply opposed to myth as that of Plato and Aristotle. However, Bultmann's metaphysics is not interested in the world with its beauty and order. Hence, it has no interest in the *cosmos*. Its interest rather centers round the true essence of humanity, what it means to be *human*. It centers on my *self* in its *authenticity*, and considers this in distinction from the cosmos and the world. Here Bultmann's fundamental philosophical decision becomes evident, the fundamental decision of his metaphysics of existence, which he cautiously calls an "existential interpretation."

With his fundamental philosophical decision, Bultmann takes over Immanuel Kant's separation between what is and what ought to be, without giving any justification for it. What "is" can be experienced, in space and time, through the collaboration of intuition and concepts; it can be grasped objectively. But what "ought to be" belongs to a completely different dimension, not to that of nature generally, which is causally determined, but to that of freedom, which is known through the unconditioned law.

This is always intertwined with a general view of reality, as things are now, which can be understood in terms of the category of causality. For Bultmann, therefore, as for Kant, everything hinges on preserving human freedom and with it the true historicity *(Geschichtlichkeit)* of human existence. "Freedom" is the "ability to . . . begin a state of affairs";[302] it is "absolute spontaneity of action," which is the "proper ground of imputability itself."[303] Yet freedom can have no extension, nor can it be experienced empirically. We can think of it only, if at all, as a virtual point, or, to use the language of geometry, the point at which a tangent touches a circle. In other words, human freedom, which is the mark of our true humanity and the true self of every human being, is only possible, as Bultmann learned from Søren Kierkegaard's reading of Kant, in the "moment,"[304] by seizing the moment, the moment in which eternity breaks into time. Human freedom exists only momentarily, at given points. It has its being solely in the act of each new deed. The "being of the moment" is our "authentic being."[305]

What we do not find in this freedom of the moment, which alone constitutes the essence of our being, we can perceive only by "objectivizing representations."[306] This is exactly how Bultmann describes myth.[307] What we perceive as an object is something "present-at-hand" *(Vorhandenes)*, a natural and historical continuity, which, understood as a date and fact, belongs to the past. Things, however, are different in the case of a free, truly historic existence. This is not based on something fixed which, for that reason, belongs to the past, but it is based on a future possibility. That means that true existence lives by the moment and *in* the moment. "Existence is in every case an *event* that occurs in the decisions of the moment. It is never something static, present-at-hand, but always something dynamic, something that happens *(Geschehendes)*. My being as a father or a son, as a spouse or a friend . . . is always being called into question and can be gained or lost only in my decisions. The continuity of this kind of being is not natural but historic *(geschichtlich)*."[308]

Bultmann in his thinking consistently separates the natural from the historic, where "the historic" is understood as a free decision of the moment. He therefore concludes with a thesis that grounds both the necessity and the legitimacy of his demythologization of the New Testament: ". . . a peculiar contradiction that runs throughout the New Testament: on the one hand, human beings are cosmically determined, and on the other hand, they are summoned to decision. On the one hand, sin is fate, and on the other, it is guilt. Alongside the Pauline indicative there is the imperative, and so on. In short, human beings are understood, on the one hand, as cosmic beings, and on the other hand, as independent persons who can win or lose themselves by their own decisions."[309]

This passage from Bultmann's *New Testament and Mythology* clearly shows that he stands in the Kantian tradition and how he uses this legacy to establish, on the one hand, the necessity, and on the other, the legitimacy, of his demythologizing project. His commitment to Kant's dualism is so strong that it automatically excludes, on principle, other possibilities of understanding. Above all, it excludes the *aesthetic* possibility of understanding which, of course, does not demand a detached examination of the object or a neutral, uncommitted enjoyment of it.

The alternative way of understanding that we want to promote, *contra* Kant and Bultmann, is bound up with an "aesthetics," which has to do with the perception of the world in the most comprehensive sense, embracing the moral, the physical, and what we mean today in a limited sense by aesthetics. We learn about such aesthetics from Johann Georg Hamann, particularly from his meta-critique of Kant (for an overview, see Oswald Bayer, *Zeitgenosse im Widerspruch. Johann Georg Hamann als radikaler Aufklärer* [Munich: Piper, 1988]). Its corresponding concept of theology no longer defines the object of theology, its subject matter *(subiectum theologiae)*, in a personalist twofold way. This twofold approach, which has held sway since Augustine (see above note 171) and has become even more dominant in the modern era since Descartes and Kant, is characteristic of Bultmann's theology. It defines the object of theology as a pure correlation between the knowledge of God and the knowledge of the self. In Hamann, on the other hand, the object of theology (its subject matter) is always determined by *three* things: God, the world, and the self. In other words, theology is determined by the God who always addresses us mediately through worldly means, and by humans who, in the midst of their fellow creatures, likewise always respond mediately through worldly means.[310]

We begin our fundamental critique of Bultmann with a small but highly significant point. In the passage cited earlier, he makes a clear parallel between the Pauline indicative, our being in Christ, which, by virtue of the divine incarnation, is also every bit as much a being in time and space with its own historical narrative, and the "cosmic nature of our humanity," which is separated from the "call to decision." Because of his prior in-principle philosophical decision, Bultmann does not view creation and the new creation as a gift to be seen, beheld, observed, and indeed enjoyed. If he speaks of gift, and he does so quite emphatically, especially in connection with Paul's words in 1 Corinthians 4:7,[311] the crucial point for him is that it is the gift of a task. He could never say with Johann Georg Hamann, for instance, that "the cross" is "the great *delight* of our existence."[312] Because for him "to believe in the cross [means] . . . to make the cross of Christ our own, to undergo crucifixion with him."[313] Therefore, the word of the cross, for Bultmann, is essentially nothing else than the demand[314] to let our self be crucified to the world, to die to it, in the act of the decision of faith. Again, it is the demand to surrender the old self-understanding, which anxiously safeguards itself and extols its good works, and to live solely from the possibility presented by the kerygma, to live from the future.

Bultmann has argued for decades, especially in critical discussion with Karl Barth, that theologians have a responsibility to speak clearly. He demands from them "purity of concepts" and speaks of the "duty of conceptual clarity." By this he means that theologians have the task of making the New Testament kerygma understandable to modern people.[315] The problem, however, is that he assumes that modern people, by definition, affirm the Kantian dualism. Hence, he uses Kant to explain and proclaim the New Testament.

If we are going to criticize Bultmann, we must chart a different course than that laid out by Kant. But then again, we can only understand the path Bultmann takes in the light of Kant. Admittedly, his reception of the later Schelling, with his stress on the underivability of the fact, the "that" of revelation, together with the influence of both Kierkegaard and Heidegger, produced important changes in Bultmann, but they were not sufficient to make him revise his fundamentally Kantian approach.

Bultmann's links with Kant can also be seen in his quest for a clear truth, as evidenced in his *New Testament and Mythology,* where he attempts to show that the "truth" of the biblical texts is intelligible only after we "strip the mythological framework from the truth they enshrine."[316] This is the equivalent to Kant's art of separation,[317] which focuses on "distinguishing," indeed separating "the [linguistic and sensory] *outer shell,* useful and necessary for a time, from the thing itself."[318]

Bultmann, like Paul and Luther, recognizes the word of the cross as the canon of truth. Admittedly, he understands it in the sense of the Kantian dualism mentioned earlier, which permits no aesthetics[319] but knows only the *demand* for decision in the realm of historicity *(Geschichtlichkeit).* The word of the cross, in which the kerygma is concentrated, is an address that confronts us with the moment of decision: are we going to safeguard our life, or freely surrender it? If we surrender ourselves, we believe, and to believe means that we have realized in faith the possibility of understanding our life anew,[320] a possibility offered to us in the word. Word and faith, for Bultmann, are almost always related to each other in such a way that the word has the potential to create faith, but faith is necessary to enact the word.

The word, the gospel, is the power of God *(dynamis theou)* (Rom. 1:16). This means that it is not merely a possibility that still remains to be realized. It is the power of God because through it he empowers those who hear it. Our basic criticism is that Bultmann, unlike Aristotle, gives ontological priority to the modality of "possibility" rather than to that of "reality." Here he follows in the footsteps of Heidegger.[321] But this privileging of "possibility" does not do justice to the *"dynamis"* of Romans 1:16, since this cannot refer solely to time in its future mode. Furthermore, the *dynamis* of the gospel is robbed of its potency because the condition for understanding it is given fundamental ontological priority over the gospel itself.

Bultmann gives fundamental ontological priority to the condition for the understanding of the kerygma rather than to the kerygma itself, the word that addresses us in an ontically contingent way and is never at our disposal. And the condition for understanding the kerygma is that it must open up the possibility of human self-understanding. He says that the "kerygma is understandable as kerygma only when the self-understanding awakened by it is recognized to be a possibility of human self-understanding."[322]

The understandability of the kerygma, for Bultmann, is given with the general validity of the "hermeneutic of existence *(Dasein)*" that he took over from Heidegger, who worked this out in the form of the analysis of existence in his *Being and Time*. Bultmann never departed from the assumption that this analysis of existence *(Dasein)* is *neutral* because of its fundamentally ontological character.[323] For him the analysis is the formal *a priori* of all possible ontic realizations of human self-understanding. In exactly the same way, Schleiermacher holds that the feeling of absolute dependence, which theologians presuppose but philosophers must demonstrate, is something purely formal and ontological which is always given and presupposed in all ontic realizations. This commonality between Bultmann and Schleiermacher becomes most apparent when we compare the outline of Bultmann's account of Paul in his *Theology of the New Testament* with that of Schleiermacher's systematic theology in his *The Christian Faith*, although Bultmann himself never comments on it.

The formal ontological section of Bultmann's account of Paul that deals with "the anthropological concepts" corresponds to the first part of Schleiermacher's dogmatics that deals with the "development of that religious self-consciousness which is always presupposed and contained in every Christian religious affection." The first material ontic section, which deals with "the flesh, sin, and the world" in Paul's account, corresponds to the second part of the dogmatics, the "explication of the facts of the religious self-consciousness, as they are determined by the antithesis of sin and grace," specifically the first sub-section ("first aspect of the antithesis: explication of the consciousness of sin"). The second material ontic section that deals with "man under faith" corresponds to the second sub-section ("second aspect of the antithesis: explication of the consciousness of grace"). Only in a purely external sense has Bultmann's structure shifted away from that of Schleiermacher's, which is clearer: A, 1.2; B compared with I; II, 1.2. (See Oswald Bayer, *Was ist das: Theologie? Eine Skizze* [Stuttgart: Calwer Verlag, 1973], p. 43.) Bultmann has "frequently made tacit reference to central thoughts in Schleiermacher" (Martin Evang, "Rudolf Bultmanns Berufung auf Friedrich Schleiermacher vor und um 1920," chapter in *Rudolf Bultmanns Werk und Wirkung,* ed. B. Jaspert [Darmstadt: Wissenschaftliche Buchgesellschaft, 1984], p. 23 [together with note 64!]).

An important difference between Schleiermacher and Bultmann is that, according to the latter, the "pure," formal ontological analysis of existence "simply cannot take into account the 'God-human' relationship" (*Zum Problem der Entmythologisierung,* chapter in *Kerygma und Mythos II,* ed. H. W. Bartsch [Hamburg, 1952], p. 194). Schleiermacher, by contrast, knows that God is always implied as the author of the immediate self-consciousness, "which is always both presupposed by and contained in every Christian religious emotion"; he expects others to know this too.

We have now had a critical look at the decisive aspects of Bultmann's metaphysics of existence as it comes out in his existential interpretation. In his lecture on demythologization *(New Testament and Mythology),* it is not only implicit, but he sets it out in a very accessible way. The fact that Bultmann himself, as already noted, does not use the term "metaphysics of existence," but speaks only of "existential interpretation," should not stop us from describing the matter in this way. The use of the term "metaphysics of existence" will enable us to make a sounder judgment than would otherwise be the case.

We need to engage in Christian theology in a way that situates it between metaphysics and mythology. However, in the light of our discussion of Bultmann, we can now go further than that and say that theology needs to be *more critical of metaphysics* and *more conscious of mythology.* For just as Bultmann gives too much room to metaphysics (of existence), so also he pays too little attention to mythology.

But how can theology be more critical of metaphysics and at the same time more conscious of mythology?

1. Even a stance that is critical of metaphysics does not have to deny its necessity. It is after all implanted ineradicably within us as creatures endowed with reason.[324] It is alive in us by virtue of God's creative will and expresses itself either as an interest in the cosmos or as an interest in our own existence. It only becomes a problem if we try to satisfy this metaphysical desire by resorting to purist separations. This happens especially in the philosophy of Kant and his followers, but also in Bultmann's demythologization and existential interpretation with its separation of cosmos and existence. Existence cannot be separated from the cosmos without being destroyed. If our freedom from the world, our renunciation of it, is not at the same time a return to the world or a new way of experiencing it, the result is a fatal abstraction. The triune God calls us out of the world only to send us back into the world in freedom. Freedom from the world and a rejection of it *(Entweltlichung)* that is not also a return to the world or a new way of experiencing it is a fatal abstraction.

It is entirely understandable that Bultmann developed neither a doctrine of creation nor an eschatology, except for his construct of the "moment." Even if he had a desire to do so, his approach would not allow it.

2. We have already indicated why and where Christian theology must be more conscious of mythology than Bultmann. If it is not, it will not be able to take seriously God's act, his work of salvation, and the word or kerygma that distributes, imparts, and communicates this act. This is precisely what Bultmann wants to draw attention to but does not succeed, because his Kantianism leaves no room for that elementary aesthetics, according to which even the appropriation of Christ's vicarious work for us takes place in a promise that involves our senses (see Ps. 34:8). Through this promise, faith takes hold of Christ's work and experiences it with great delight without succumbing to a kind of thinking that sees it purely as an objective event in the distant past.

The Christian faith, as part of its intellectual responsibility, has adopted the word "theology" and in doing so has located its theology between metaphysics and mythology, so that it always remains critically linked to both. We have tried to confirm this thesis by considering

Rudolf Bultmann's program of demythologization or, said positively, his "existential interpretation." We have shown that Bultmann is neither sufficiently critical of metaphysics nor sufficiently conscious of mythology. From the beginning of his theological thinking, he followed the Kantian separation (diastasis) between the recognition of what is and the thought of what ought to be. In other words, he separates the extensive, space-time dimension and the intensive, ethical dimension. The latter, he says, is grasped in the "moment" of existential decision, which is opposed to objectifying thinking. At this decisive point, he is a Kantian. A critique of Bultmann therefore has to face up to his Kantianism.

4.3.3. Jonas

The best theoretical clarification of Bultmann's demythologization of the New Testament message, or, in positive terms, his "existential interpretation" of the kerygma, was provided by Hans Jonas, in his analysis of the hermeneutical structure of dogma, more than a decade before Bultmann even gave his lecture on demythologization *(New Testament and Mythology)*. Our aim in what follows is to set out this analysis, in which Jonas, like Schleiermacher, appeals to "an immediate existential relation."[325] At the end of this section (4.3), in which we are dealing with the existential approach to theology, Jonas's analysis will appear with such clarity that we could almost call it an ideal type. The analysis comes in the essay titled *"Über die hermeneutische Struktur des Dogmas"* (in Hans Jonas, *Augustin und das paulinische Freiheitsproblem. Eine philosophische Studie zum pelagianischen Streit,* 1st edition 1930, Appendix I; in what follows, the 2nd edition will be cited [Göttingen: Vandenhoeck & Ruprecht, 1965], pp. 80-89). This can be regarded as a classical text of the history of modern theology.

The two decisive assertions made by Jonas, or the two assumptions from which he proceeds, form a definition, first of the outer form of dogma and secondly of its inner ground.

"In their outer form, dogmas are statements that have the rational structure of the apophantic ('theoretical') subject-object statement and as such their content is located in an objective realm that has a general logical connection to them" (p. 80).

The theoretical structures of dogmatic statements have their inner ground in the phenomena of existence *(Dasein)*. They are "hyposta-tizations of something that was originally a demonstrably inner exis-tential reality" (p. 80).

The relation between outer form and inner ground only becomes a problem if we concede (with Jonas, p. 80) that it involves no temporal succession, so that "a phase could be isolated in which a phenomenon could first be immediately experienced for itself and only then undergo the process of dogmatization." Jonas therefore does not simply sepa-rate the outer form from the inner ground but clearly indicates how they are connected when he speaks of "the primacy of the original un-derlying existential stratum" (p. 84).

The formation of dogma therefore has its origin, as far as content goes, in the phenomena of *Dasein*, existence. Naturally, *Dasein* wants to interpret itself. The formation of dogma therefore is not accidental or arbitrary, but necessary. However, it is clear from this necessary relation what the source of that necessity is, and what has fundamental onto-logical priority. "The basic act" "that makes the formation of dogma possible is an objectification of the phenomena of existence *(Dasein)* which is driven to express itself in language. In other words, it is funda-mentally a self-objectification of existence that has an inner compul-sion to interpret itself" (p. 81). Dogma therefore has a "particular inter-pretative and cognitive function in connection with the self-illumination of a general historical existence" (p. 25, note 1). The forma-tion of dogma is therefore necessary. It "arises inescapably from the fundamental structure of the human spirit as such. That it interprets itself in objectifying formulas and symbols, that it is 'symbolical,' is what is most essential to the spirit. . . . To come to itself, it must take this detour via the symbol" (p. 82). (Here, at last, the philosophical and historical background that Jonas has concealed becomes clear. It is a fusion of Hegel's understanding of language and Schleiermacher's transcendental hermeneutic, the latter being the starting-point and lasting center for Jonas's work — in far-reaching agreement with Cassirer's philosophy of symbolic forms.[326])

However, under certain conditions, the thing that "is most essen-tial to the spirit" may at the same time be highly dangerous. That would be the case if the "fundamental ontological transformation of the phenomena, a 'translation' that reaches down to the deepest struc-tures and transforms them into another form of being, is not reversed.

It would be highly dangerous if the hypostatization of these phenomena from merely existential realities into quasi-material concretions, analogous to worldly beings" (p. 81),[327] is not transformed back to its origin and the transformed phenomena become autonomous in its rational sphere, so to speak. That would lead to those well-known insoluble questions of compatibility, such as: "How can this be reconciled with . . . ? For instance, how does human freedom square with divine omnipotence and providence, or predestination with human responsibility?" (p. 83; Jonas's study is concerned with the Pauline problem of freedom in Augustine's dispute with Pelagius and thus with the dogma of predestination and original sin).

According to Jonas, these questions of compatibility should be taken as reminders that although dogmas are the products of the rational objective world they are "not originally ontological" (p. 84). Questions like these should force us back to their origin, back to the "genuine phenomena" (p. 85), which "originally, at some level of inwardness, we experience as a fact of existence" (p. 85).[328] And, "only by a lengthy reversal of the process," using a hermeneutic of regression, "is it possible for a demythologized consciousness to directly approach, also conceptually, the original phenomena concealed under this covering" (p. 82).

In contrast to this kind of existential approach and its associated hermeneutic of regression, theology has its place "before" the text, out of respect for its otherness and its relative autonomy.[329] Theology is not interested in any "immediate existential relation"[330] but sees human existence as first and foremost linguistic, in the sense that it is constituted by particular sounds and letters,[331] and therefore by space and time.[332] In other words, theology is "a grammar of the language of Holy Scripture."[333]

4.4. Conclusion

By means of the threefold typology that we have presented in this section, we can understand the main aspects of the theological and intellectual history that have influenced theology for more than two hundred years. This is the context in which we offer our contemporary account of theology and of how it has been understood.

We have considered several transformations of the Christian faith in which either the ethical, the theoretical, or the existential element has been absolutized and so detached from the promise that we discussed in section 3. Such absolutizations teach us to attend carefully to the precise form of the word that creates faith and to the divine service generally. For theology, understood as an academic discipline, always does its scholarly work in the service of the church's worship and the proclamation of the word centered in the promise.

We have said that the subject matter of theology forms its liturgical "monastic" side, which is anchored in the divine service. This is constitutive for theology in that it provides it with its content. Theology, however, also has an academic "scholastic" side which, while playing only a regulative role, gives it the tools it needs to reflect on its subject matter, to clarify and test its thinking, and to refute error through rigorous debate and argumentation. Up to this point, we have been considering the academic side of theology, understood as a disciplined way of thinking. Like any science, academic theology also needs to ensure that its methodology is appropriate to its object or subject matter. The question now is: How do these two sides of theology relate to each other? What is the relationship between the academic side of theology, with its questions of methodology, and its constitutive side, which emphasizes its liturgical spirituality grounded in the divine service? In short, what is the relationship between the disputation and meditation?

5. Theology and Methodology

5.1. Performative Speech Acts and "Scientific" Theological Propositions

How can theology verify its propositions? For the sake of clarity, it is necessary in our discussion of this problem to distinguish between two levels or spheres. On the one hand, there is the primary sphere of the performative speech acts, the sphere of the word and faith. On the other hand, there is the secondary but related sphere of the constative speech acts, the sphere of theology (in the narrow sense) and its propositions. The statements to which the theological propositions refer, the promises that create faith, are not premises, as we stressed earlier (3). Therefore, they are not propositions that can be checked against what they assert. Rather, their truth and certainty are located in what they are, in what they bring, and in what they constitute. I cannot verify them because they verify me, because they embrace, permeate, and carry my knowledge and actions. I am entirely dependent on them.

We must make a distinction between these propositions of proclamation and the propositions of scientific, academic theology. The latter are constative speech acts and therefore statements. As statements, they must be able to be checked against what they say. We must be able to establish whether or not they are commensurate with their object, the subject matter that they reveal. Verification in the sense of the philosophy of science only makes sense in connection with the constative speech acts, and so in connection with the propositions of scientific, academic theology.

The importance of this distinction can be assessed more clearly if we review Schleiermacher's idea of the scientific character of theological propositions. In the light of that, we will see more clearly both the commonality as well as the differences between our understanding of theology and that of Schleiermacher's.

5.2. Schleiermacher's Concept of Science

Science for Schleiermacher is a single enterprise but with two modes, one transcendental-dialectical, the other technical-dialectical. On the one hand, the transcendental-dialectical mode of science deals with the principles of history and nature. Understood as "the science of the principles of history," it is "ethics."[334] On the other hand, the technical-dialectical mode of science deals with distinctions and connections and has to focus on defining concepts and making judgments.[335]

To say that propositions are "scientific" is the same as saying that they are "dialectical." This means that there is a constant dynamic between statement and contradiction, thesis and refutation, hypothesis and falsification. Therefore, there is no end to the dispute about the appropriate way to understand a fact. It is the endless quest for truth in the sense of the *adaequatio rei et intellectus*. According to this dictum, truth is the correspondence between a thing (which may be a fact, object, or state of affairs) and its understanding.[336] "The game of science is, in principle, without end." That is the principle of Karl Popper's *The*

Logic of Scientific Discovery,[337] which we can compare to Schleiermacher's *Dialectic,* owing to their common philosophical heritage.

The propositions that comprise the back-and-forth movement of the dialectical process are, for Schleiermacher, of a different kind than the propositions of faith (doctrines).

What the scientific, dialectical propositions do not have themselves, but what they assume and indirectly rely on, is ultimate certainty, in the sense of the leading propositions of §§214f. in the *Dialektik* of 1814 cited above.[338] According to Schleiermacher, science recognizes this, at least in its transcendental-dialectical mode. It sees in this dependence its ground and limit, but this recognition is at the same time an acknowledgment. In Popper's view, on the other hand, this transcendental-dialectical dimension no longer has any place in science. For science is concerned solely with establishing and testing hypotheses and therefore has no interest in their origin and discovery[339] or even their application. The only science that Popper would acknowledge in Schleiermacher is what the latter calls its second dimension, its technical-dialectical mode.

Even if a few abstract transcendental-dialectical propositions state that that ultimate certainty, which underlies all knowledge and action, is an important part of knowledge itself, this is never said in so many words in any scientific propositions, but only in statements of faith (doctrines).

Doctrines are the objectification of specific religious emotions in which that ultimate certainty, the feeling of absolute dependence, appears ontically. By the same token, it is also true, especially in the light of the Christian faith, that "Christian doctrines are accounts of the Christian religious affections set forth in speech" (§15 of *The Christian Faith,* leading proposition).

Schleiermacher distinguishes three "forms of doctrine." They correspond to the three different types of speech: the "poetic," the "rhetorical," and the "descriptively didactic."[340] Those doctrines of the "descriptively didactic" type, which aim at the highest possible degree of certainty, are dogmatic propositions (§16 of *The Christian Faith*). But dogmatic propositions are theological propositions. And it is consistent with Schleiermacher's whole concept of theology when he says that theological, especially dogmatic, propositions have "a twofold value — an ecclesiastical and a scientific" (§17 of *The Christian Faith*). "The ecclesiastical value of a dogmatic proposition consists in its reference to the religious emotions themselves."[341] "The scientific value of a dogmatic proposition depends . . . upon the specificity of its concepts and of their connection with each other."[342] (In a hand-written note Schleiermacher clarifies what he means by "scientific value" when he says "not for science, but through it."[343]) According to Schleiermacher, theology, apart from its transcendental-philosophical foundation, is therefore a science in the sense that its concepts and connections are highly specific.

5.3. A Critique of Schleiermacher

Clearly, there is considerable common ground between Schleiermacher's approach and the one we used earlier (3) when we distinguished between the performative speech acts that create faith and the constative speech acts of scholarly theological propositions which, in principle, are open to revision because they are dialectical. But regardless of this common ground, there is one crucial difference. We do not see the theological scientific propositions referring to "the religious emotions themselves." We therefore oppose Schleiermacher's strategy to move behind the word in order to focus on what is necessary to produce it.[344] We reject this move, the hermeneutic of regression, because to go behind the word and join the transcendental quest for the immediate means abandoning the space of intersubjective communication. If, for the moment, we use Schleiermacher's terms, inadequate as they are, this means abandoning the poetic and rhetorical realm. In other words, to go behind the word is to go inside the human psyche, and that means abandoning the external realm of communication between people.

Schleiermacher would not accept that argument and would certainly not see it as applying to him. He says that it is precisely in our intersubjective linguistic communication, in the dialogue that belongs to our transcendental-dialectical quest for the truth, that we come to understand what is decisive, the primal human datum of the feeling of absolute dependence. He holds that it is not something that we first experience in intersubjective linguistic communication, but we find it deep inside us, and this feeling forms the basis of our communication. This depth of our existence, in which we become aware of our radical finitude, is "not an accidental element . . . nor even something that varies from person to person,"[345] but it is "the same in all,[346] a universal phenomenon.[347]

However, we must stress, *contra* Schleiermacher, that the universal nature of the experience of the radical finitude of our existence, which makes us all aware that we are individuals, is precisely the teaching and claim of the Christian doctrine of creation. This experience is not a primal human datum that precedes its linguistic expression. Rather, it is the response to a word. Consequently, it is a determination that is given to us. We cannot remember it through self-reflection. The only way we can remember it is through the public and oral promise that is spoken to us by another in the name of Jesus: "Do not be afraid, only believe!" "You do not need to sit in judgment on yourself!" Words like these are related to such statements as "Adam, where are you?" "Where is your brother, Abel?" These are but a few examples of statements that demand accountability and promise freedom, statements in which law and gospel are concretely enacted.

The field to which the theological scientific propositions refer is the linguistic field common to everyday speech and public discourse. They do not, however, refer to the depth dimension of the religious emotions themselves, because they relativize them and rob them of their interconnectedness and specificity. Rather, the emotions, the affects, are *in* such propositions and *in* the response to them that we can either give or withhold. That is where they belong, not behind them at some supposedly deeper and more concrete level of the soul, which is accessible only through the hermeneutic of regression. There is no truth deep inside the religious consciousness.

Since the object of theology does not lie in a subculture below the speech acts, theology cannot explain them psychologically or existentially. Likewise, it cannot theorize them, it cannot reach beyond the speech acts in a speculative way to develop its own independent supraculture in a higher spiritual realm, in which one theological proposition could be established from another. That would be nothing more than a "case of treating thoughts as if they were self-contained entities that developed independently and were subject only to their own laws."[348] On the contrary, we must emphasize with Schleiermacher, after making the necessary changes, that "no dogmatic proposition has its ground in another. Rather, each can be found only by considering the Christian self-consciousness" (§17 of *The Christian Faith*).[349]

Here, of course, we have to make a change to that part of his thesis that says that a dogmatic proposition "can be found only by considering the Christian self-consciousness." In light of our criticism of Schleiermacher, we would now have to say something like this: it (indeed, any theological proposition) can be found only in relation to the performative speech acts of the kind that we cited earlier, in other words, only in relation to law and gospel.[350]

5.4. The Necessity of Theology as a Science

Should we not simply let the language games of these performative speech acts play themselves out? Do we even need theology at all? And if so, why?

Schleiermacher says that theology is unnecessary. He says that "the Christian faith actually does not need such a thing [as theology] to be effective, either in the individual soul or in the life of the family."[351] For Schleiermacher, therefore, the Christian faith is not necessarily dependent on theology, because, at a deeper level, it is not necessarily dependent on the speech acts. Rather, for him it is the other way around. The speech acts actually have "their ultimate ground so exclusively in the emotions of the religious self-consciousness, that where these do not exist the doctrines cannot arise" (§15 of *The Christian Faith*, concluding sentence).

However, if Pauline and Lutheran hermeneutics are correct, according to which faith comes from the word and not, as in Schleiermacher, the word from faith,[352] then theology, in principle, is always necessary because it refers to this word and is needed to settle disputes about the word and to overcome heresies. It is not something of only secondary importance, as Schleiermacher holds, to facilitate "the united leadership of the Christian Church."[353] It is as if for him, and this has to be said against the explanation of §2 of the *Brief Outline*, "a small community has no need of proper theology!"

The elementary speech acts that create and preserve faith are disputed precisely because they are not meaningless utterances. Rather, they claim to be concrete alternatives to the propositions that deny the distinction between God and humanity, between the creator and the creature.[354]

The basic lesson of church history is that the word which creates faith is continually disputed, misinterpreted, and misused not just by those who do not want to be Christians, but most of all by Christians themselves. It is not so much attacked from without as perverted from within. Theology therefore is necessary because of the constant threat of heresy.

If we are ever going to be able to discover any new heresy, we need to take a step back, so to speak, from the immediate business of the church and, through discussion with others, try to establish the facts and come to some conclusions. To do that, we must deal objectively with the speech acts and make the events they refer to an object of reflection. In other words, we need to isolate them into parts in order to be able to analyze them and compare commensurable elements. This raises several methodological questions. Might the approach we use be arbitrary? Has the point of contention been properly located? What viewpoints and rules could be useful in helping us locate it? How can the dispute be resolved or ended?[355]

This area that we have briefly mentioned, with all its connections and complexities, belongs to the scientific character of theology, or, at any rate, to what Schleiermacher calls its technical-dialectical aspect. It is the realm in which hypotheses can be advanced and tested in discussion on the basis of a set of agreed rules. These rules require us to give an account of the formation and use of concepts and demand logical consistency in a given context.

We need constantly to reaffirm that this sort of theory should not serve the academic side of theology but its subject matter. However, this is not to deny that theology, understood as a scientific discipline, has relative freedom to pursue its own goals. But it means that the scientific character of theology should always be subordinated to its monastic foundation with its tradition of liturgical spirituality. As necessary as scientific theology is, it has its limit, which is identical with its ground.

5.5. The Limit of Theology as a Science

The question of the limit of theology as a science can be dealt with by reflecting on the rules[356] we follow, or should follow, in pursuing it.[357] We can distinguish between various kinds of rules, the main ones being the rules of the historical critical, the ideological critical, and the empirical critical methods. Admittedly, this distinction is purely artificial because the methods themselves are not mutually exclusive. Nevertheless, it has to be made, if only because many theologians identify with one of these main methods and dispute the legitimacy and scope of the others.

Because different systems of rules compete with one another in their claim to be legitimately recognized as academic theology, the situation in which theology finds itself is much the same as the position of science generally with its discussion about the philosophy of science.

Confusion arises from the fact that even the practitioners of a certain method cannot fully agree on the rules and how they should be applied. This is true, not only for the question of what we are to understand by "the"[358] method of ideological criticism and "the" method of empirical criticism, but it even extends to "the" method of historical criticism, which by now, one would think, would have been well and truly settled.

If there is no agreement within any one of these three "systems,"[359] the same holds true to an immeasurably greater degree for the rules governing the way in which the three competing methods are supposed to work together, assuming, of course, that we do not advocate a chaotic power struggle, a "Darwinism of methods," so to speak.

The main difficulty with these methods is that they are not merely formal or technical but, for the most part, have to do with content. The use of a method is not arbitrary. It affects the purpose for which it is used. It would therefore be an illusion to think that a method could be used in an unbiased way, which, if followed properly, would constitute the subject matter of theology. If "the development of an unreservedly historical view" is "a dynamic principle for attaining a comprehensive view of everything human,"[360] we need to be aware of the factual assumptions embedded in every method and to determine its limits by working out where these assumptions are in conflict with the subject matter of theology.[361]

Understood as a science, theology has no methods that are not also the methods of other sciences, or at least could not become so in principle. The "secularization" of Schleiermacher's hermeneutics is an impressive example of that.[362]

What we have said about methods applies also to the texts and knowledge of theology. As a science, theology has no knowledge that is not also the object of another science, or that could not become so, at least in principle. For example, the New Testament can also be a field of study for ancient philology and the history of ancient religions; contemporary church life can be studied by sociology; and above all, the performative sentences, which we discussed earlier (3), can be a topic of study for linguistics and linguistic analysis.

Theology has no special knowledge and no special methods. And what it has bequeathed to the realm of generalities, which is quite considerable, it can no longer call its own, so that in using its own, it is using what is general. We can agree with Schleiermacher, after making the necessary changes, when he says: "When this same knowledge is acquired and possessed without relation to the government of the church, it ceases to be theological and devolves to those sciences to which it belongs, based on its content. Depending then on the subject matter, these sciences are linguistics and history, psychology and ethics, together with the general theory of art and the philosophy of religion, both of which are disciplines that proceed from these sciences" (*Brief Outline*, §6, translation altered).

5.6. What Makes Theological Science Theology?

What makes theological science theology, according to Schleiermacher, is its "relation to the government of the church" (*Brief Outline* §6), its "will to be effective in the leadership of the church" (*Brief Outline* §7). "Without this will, the unity of theology disappears and its parts disintegrate into its various elements" (*Brief Outline* §7).

On the basis of the argument previously developed, we can agree with this thesis of Schleiermacher's only to the extent that it denies the uniqueness of theology's knowledge and methods and makes its organizing principle one that is not already included in science itself. However, regardless of any agreement, we must criticize it at two crucial points.

First, we must restate the thesis in §6 of the *Brief Outline* even more radically in the sense of Schleiermacher's overall intent: when this same knowledge is acquired and possessed without relation to a "feeling of absolute dependence," which is presupposed in the transcendental-dialectical demonstration, it ceases to be theological and becomes general and thus devolves to each of the sciences to which it belongs, based on its content.

The critique proposed by this version of §6 concerns Schleiermacher's concept of theology, particularly its root in transcendental philosophy. This root of course is unaffected by the positive way in which his theology is shaped by practice. The "root"[363] can influence the apex or "crown,"[364] but the crown cannot influence the root. If, however, we assume such a mutual interaction by understanding theology as an analysis of the language of proclamation that fastens the thread of its inquiry at the point from which it arises and to which it returns,[365] then Schleiermacher's definition of the organizing principle of theology as the "relation to church government" proves inadequate because it is too narrow. Then theology is given a fundamental significance and necessity that it does not have for Schleiermacher, as we saw earlier (5.4).

Secondly, if we accept Pauline and Lutheran hermeneutics as determinative, the answer to the question, what makes theological science theology, is far more compelling than its "relation to the government of the church." It is the confession of our absolute dependence on the speech acts, which we described earlier as the subject matter of theology (3), and our necessity and will to be active in them. Whoever takes them as their point of reference has already begun to be a theologian. Although all Christians as such have already begun to become theologians, academic theologians differ from them at one point, and this is their unique vocation. They have to be able to explain, in academic terms, why the speech acts are their primary point of reference. In other words, scholars need to be able to describe clearly and precisely the significance of the speech acts and the role that they play in theology.

Hence, the following thesis is an answer to the question: What is theology? It follows Schleiermacher closely (see especially §§5-8 of the *Brief Outline*) but at the same time it also contradicts him: *what makes theological science theology is its relation to those elementary speech acts in which law and gospel are concretely at work in the binding and liberating of the conscience. This relation is seen in theology's confession to be absolutely dependent on them and in its will to be active in them.*

This form of the organizing principle of theology, as stated in our thesis ("its relation to those elementary speech acts . . ."), also avoids the striking vacillation of Schleiermacher's definition in §§6-8 of the *Brief Outline*. According to §§6 & 7, what makes theological science theology is its "relation to the government of the church," or its "will to be effective in the leadership of the church." But according to §8 it is its "interest in Christianity."[366] Both cannot be, or at least do not have to be, the same. Thus, in the nineteenth century, the confessional theologians of the church appealed in substance to §§6 & 7, while the liberals appealed to §8.[367] In our thesis, we have avoided this ambiguity[368] without letting theological science, academic theology, become lost in the vague generality of an "interest in Christianity" or, seen from the other side, without having to limit it to a "relation to the government of the church," which is too narrow to be appropriate to the subject matter of theology.

We can basically avoid and overcome this ambiguity with its divergence and rivalry, which is still a problem today, only by adopting an approach that is committed to Luther's Reformation hermeneutic. Let us underscore what we said earlier. It means that the basic propositions of theology, which are identical with the speech acts we spoke of earlier, cannot be understood theoretically (here we agree with Schleiermacher against Hegel), but neither can they be understood existentially or traced back "to the religious emotions themselves"[369] (against Schleiermacher). In other words, the basic propositions themselves cannot be accounted for again, by means of any experience, either perception or conviction.[370] This hermeneutical approach means at the same time that a regression to the realm of transcendental philosophy, such as we have in Schleiermacher, no longer makes sense because the distinction made by faith between knowing and doing is a *concrete* distinction. It cannot be pushed back to the realm of transcendental philosophy, antecedent to theology, but it takes place only in those elementary speech acts in which law and gospel are at work.

5.7. What Makes Theological Science Science?[371]

Our summarizing thesis, which answers the question What makes theological science theology?, also clearly gives us our point of orientation when we inquire into the necessity and limits of the use of the historical critical, the ideological critical, and the empirical critical methods in theology. Therefore, we will assume from the start that these methods are not sufficient in themselves and that they must be supplemented by a meta-critique. This meta-critique, formulated in our thesis, comes at exactly the place where, for example, in Hans Albert we have the decision to use critical reason as a "way of life,"[372] and in Schleiermacher the recognition of our radical finitude, emphasizing the fact that we do not even have control over the beginning of our thinking. However, this recognition, which marks the way we begin, and which Schleiermacher expected not only of theologians but of every scientist, cannot be generally assumed. This is because, according to our concept of theology, we can only come to this recognition, or better, it is only given to us, in a linguistically *concrete* way.

But the relativization of all scientific methods and the general awareness of their limits does not mean that we can use whatever method we choose or choose to use no method at all. Academic theology is a science only if it uses a method. Methods are necessary, at least in their regulative function. We need them to help us order, analyze, define, and reflect on the subject matter of theology. But methods themselves cannot legitimate or constitute the subject matter itself.

Therefore, we must add a second thesis to the first: *what makes theological science a science is its use of contemporary scientific methods. These methods do not legitimate or constitute the subject matter of theology, but rather they regulate our reflection on it. This reflection is necessary especially in order to work through and overcome heresy.*

The two theses are tightly interwoven and produce, via the political use of the law *(usus politicus legis),*[373] a single concept of theology. This is no static concept but is kept in flux by the distinction between what makes theological science theology and what makes it science. In other words, it is energized by the distinction and vital correlation between the two sides of theology. On the one hand, the "monastic" side, with its tradition of liturgical spirituality centered in the divine service, is constitutive. On the other hand, the "scholastic" side of theology with its academic disputation, which orders, analyzes, defines, and reflects on its content, is regulative. In short, theology receives its dynamic from the distinction between the subject matter of theology and its methods.

6. Specificity and Breadth

We must now treat in more detail the problem that we already touched on right at the very beginning (1.1) when we spoke of the distinction and connection between the general divine service in creation and the particular divine service in the church. At the same time, we will take up the thesis we mentioned earlier (at the end of 2.1) but have not yet explained: that the fourfold definition of the object of theology (see 2.1) does not lead to the simple alternative: Does theology start with a particular concept in order to demonstrate its universality, or does it begin with a general indeterminate concept in order to fill it with a specifically Christian content?

The one problem of the relationship between specificity and breadth, seen from the standpoint of the fourfold definition of the object of theology, can be dealt with under the following headings: the question of the relationship between history and reason (6.1), and between philosophy and theology (6.2), the problem of natural theology (6.3), and the question of the extent to which theology can be understood as religious studies (6.4).

6.1. History and Reason

"History is always a better matrix for science than logic."[374]

Is the science of theology history or logic; is it historical analysis or logical synthesis? Is it a science of history or a science of nature, a science of existence or a science of essences? Rahner[375] tries to find it in a balance of both and here he agrees with Schleiermacher for whom theology can no more be construed purely scientifically than it can be conceived merely empirically.[376] But in this approach to theology, the transcendental question of the condition for the possibility of understanding the empirical dimension is given formal priority over the historical.[377] However, if we privilege the logical we give supremacy to the question of the unity and essence of God and of humans within God's world. In this way, theology becomes, at least at its foundation, a science of essences. According to this view, the essence of humans is their openness to the world and to God's self-communication, which for its part presupposes the openness and receptivity of humankind.

But how is theology to be pursued if we cannot begin with a general concept of human openness in which general "closedness" or sin is always overcome (Rom. 11:32; Gal. 3:22)? In that case, we cannot posit any *a priori*, not even a logical one, before or after, in or under the antithesis of sin and grace. Its theme and object[378] then is nothing other than the God who justifies and the sinful human being.

In order to view this object of theology in such a way that it does not appear to be too vague in its breadth or too narrow in its specificity, we have stressed that the decisive thing, in the context of the four-fold definition of the object (2.1), is that the category of "promise" is understood not primarily as something in the future, but as a present reality (3). In every promise, God repeats his original words of self-introduction: "I am your God. And, therefore, you are my people." It opens up for us a reliable community in which even now, in the midst of all threats, we can be free. We should understand this promise not in an abstract personalistic sense, but in a concrete worldly way. When we hear it, it is always intertwined with covenant and creation.[379] The gospel preamble of the Decalogue, the so-called "first commandment," has its counterpart in the promise of life, valid for all, which we find in the primal history. It is through this promise that we are given space and time, nature and history. The "first commandment" is: "you may freely eat . . ." (Gen. 2:16). "But of the tree of the knowledge of good and evil you shall not eat, for in the day that you eat of it, you shall die" (Gen. 2:17). Like the prohibition against having "other gods besides me" (Exod. 20:3), this threat of death protects the prior gift of freedom and the promise of life: I must fear God, if I refuse to trust his love. We cannot speak of God, or humans, or the world, apart from this fear and love, apart from grace and judgment, law and gospel, faith and unbelief, death and life, and all that contradicts God's promise for reasons we do not understand.

In this sense, theology is not a science of essences, but a science of history and experience. The word, of course, contains not only past times but also future times: "truths of history not only of past times but also of future times."[380] History is the criterion not only for the way in which we speak of humanity and the world, but also for the way in which we speak of God. For God himself has entwined his eternity with time, not only in his incarnation and death on the cross, but likewise as the creator, who "addresses the creature through the creature," and as the Spirit who, through ordinary, particular, temporal events and narratives, kills and makes alive. By the same token, we cannot construe the object of theology purely scientifically. Rather, we should grasp it purely empirically. We should understand it through hearing, learning, and experiencing the history brought about by the promise as well as by the suffering caused by the things that contradict it. In that sense, theology is a science of experience because God is the active subject and we passively "suffer" *(passio)* what he does, we undergo his work on us (2.2).

If theology is a science of history and experience, understood in the sense we have described, doing theology cannot mean the pursuit of a general concept that can be thought of prior to this history in order to make sense of it or even justify it. Thus, the young Schelling and Hegel maintain that revelation is a necessary idea that presupposes its historical realization.[381] They hold that the precedence of the *idea* of the incarnation over the *event* in time secures the general validity of the philosophical proof of the truth of revelation.[382] However, theology, understood as a science of history, has nothing to do with such a "purely scientific construction," including its inherent compulsion to search for a theodicy, but rather it operates with a "purely empirical conception."

In characterizing theology as a science of history, we have used definitions that Schleiermacher uses to develop his concept of theology. We can clarify what we have said if we compare it directly with his concept of theology.

Schleiermacher's attempt to maintain a balance between a purely scientific construction, on the one hand, and a merely empirical conception on the other, implies the negation that "the distinctive nature of Christianity no more allows of its being construed purely scientifically than of its being apprehended in a strictly empirical fashion." The negation of these two extremes gives him the scope to move dialectically between them. Therefore, "the distinctive nature of Christianity" can "only be defined critically":

> The distinctive nature of Christianity no more allows of its being construed purely scientifically than of its being apprehended in a strictly empirical fashion. Consequently, it admits only of being defined critically [compare §23], by comparing what is historically

given in Christianity with those contrasts by virtue of which various kinds of religious communities can be different from one another.[383]

For Schleiermacher, a "merely empirical conception" is out of the question. In this respect, he follows Kant. This is clearly seen in the explanation of §21 in the *Brief Outline:* "That the essence of Christianity is attached to a particular history determines more precisely what mode of understanding is required." Finally, then, the fundamental thing for Schleiermacher is "philosophical theology." The empirical conception can only determine "more precisely" the mode of understanding given from the start, but it cannot also lay the logical and conceptual foundation itself.

In contrast to Schleiermacher, we do not seek a general concept of religion, apart from God's promise, in order afterwards to specify its distinctively Christian character *(differentia specifica christiana).* We do not consider the history created by the promise as a purely empirical conception. Rather, we wish to develop theology principally as a linguistics, or more precisely, as a doctrine of forms[384] which has its *a priori* in the biblical texts, from which we also derive the categories of logical and conceptual analysis. As Luther says, "The Holy Scriptures should be our dictionary and grammar, the source and basis for all Christian words and concepts."[385]

We can focus theology more sharply on the question of the relationship between history and reason if we realize that philosophy has also had to deal with the same question for over two hundred years, but in its own way. Philosophy itself has recognized, at least since Kant, that even transcendental reflection is historically conditioned and that it has its origin in a particular historical situation. However, it wants to be regarded as general. Furthermore, it has to ask how "the unconditioned, which is mediated to us through history, can again be mediated in history."[386]

In the conversation that theology must have with philosophy at this point, it will be able to learn most from engaging with the later Schelling.[387] This will improve its possibility of articulating the significance of that historical event which happened "once for all" (Rom. 6:10; Heb. 7:27; 9:12; 10:10) in Christ and of reflecting on this as a concrete universal.[388]

6.2. Theology and Philosophy

Theology, for its own sake, cannot afford to surrender to philosophy but needs to engage with it seriously and impartially. The compulsion to do this does not come from outside but arises from the inmost ground of the Christian faith and its universal claim, which theology is called to reflect on. It is "systematic" theology, in all its disciplines, if it tests truth claims in conversation with philosophy, understood in the broadest sense, and ventures to offer an intellectually responsible opinion as to what constitutes Christian faith and action today in the light of the past and the future.

This necessary conversation of course is inevitably a debate. By entering it, theology not only develops its relationship with philosophy, but it really constitutes itself. Theology is not a conversation that faith has with itself, it is not a monologue, but it is a critical engagement with doctrines, ideas, and ideologies inimical to the faith of the church. It is the very nature of theology to be fundamentally critical and polemical. It only becomes what it is meant to be by engaging with objections and entering into disputes. It cannot ignore anything that attacks the lived faith of the church in the realm of understanding and thinking. But then faith should be no stranger to conflict and dispute if its charter is: "I am the Lord, your God. You shall have no other gods besides me!"

The confession of the *one* God and Lord (Deut. 6; 1 Cor. 8:4-6) is the church's response to this promise. The Jewish and Christian faith begins and ends with a unity, the one name of God. That is what constitutes its being.

But now the question arises, how is this *unity* related to *that* sought by Greek philosophy and its metaphysics, with its search for the true essence of the divine, for the *natura dei?* This is not a question that is foreign to the faith. It is asked because the Christian faith, as part of its intellectual responsibility, has engaged with the word "theology" since the time of the ancient church. This engagement locates theological reflection between mythology and metaphysics, and brings it into critical relationship with both.[389] Before that, this question was raised by the Greek form of the Hebrew name of God in the Septuagint. God's name in Hebrew has a verbal form that can be taken as a reliable promise that God is freely present with us: I am/will be who I am/will be

(Exod. 3:14). However, in Greek this dynamic is lost and the divine name is petrified into the self-predication of an absolute being: *ego eimi ho on* (where *"on"* is the word in Greek metaphysics for "being").

In Greek thinking, immortality, the absence of emotion and its accompanying impassibility (apathy), all belong to being, pure and simple, to being itself. However, where the biblical texts are taken seriously, there will be a grave conflict with Greek metaphysics and ontology. The event described in Hosea 11:7-11[390] is ontologically unthinkable. Ancient metaphysics rejects it as mythology because it cannot abide the thought that there is a "coup," a change in God himself. Here God is not identical with himself; he is not consistent with himself:

> . . . My heart is changed within me, I am full of remorse. (9) I will not execute my fierce anger; I will not again destroy Ephraim; for I am God and no mortal. . . .

Clearly, there is a strong tension between theology and philosophy that we cannot minimize or even try to harmonize.[391] On the other hand, for the sake of the claim to truth and general validity that both philosophy and theology make, this tension must not be allowed to collapse in such a way that there is no longer any relationship between them. Without this connection, theology and the church would exist in a linguistic and intellectual ghetto.

In view of this danger, we cannot emphasize strongly enough that Israel did not articulate its confession to God as creator in any other way than by engaging with the questions and challenges of its surrounding world. And Paul (Rom. 1:18-3:20), when he speaks about sin, stresses the responsibility and inexcusability of all people by taking up the language of the Stoics. Substantially the same general claim is made in the prologue of the Gospel of John. All can know God, praise him, and live life as a thankful response to him, but none do it, except the person who has been reborn with a new heart and whose eyes have been newly opened.

The universal breadth therefore can only be seen in conjunction with the specificity of a doctrine of sin and Christology. If there were no sin, there would be no difference between the gospel and the voice of nature, between theology and philosophy. In that case, all people, according to Melanchthon's delightful description of the paradisal university *(locus amoenus)*, would be theologians taught by God, who respond to him in praise and who, with all other creatures, including the co-philosophizing angels, are students of the one teacher.[392] But sin ruptures the unity of theology and philosophy and tears them apart. A warning such as Colossians 2:8 becomes necessary: "See to it that no one takes you captive through philosophy and empty deception, based on human tradition and the basic principles of this world rather than on Christ."

On the other hand, philosophy cannot be rejected out of hand as empty deception. We simply need to distinguish its misuse from its proper use (compare the classical distinction between the magisterial use of reason and its ministerial use). But even the misuse of philosophy and all the attempts at self-justification in philosophy and ethics have not hindered the course of the gospel but have actually promoted it. In the second of the philosophical theses of the *Heidelberg Disputation,* Luther says provocatively that, outside of Christ, philosophizing is the same as committing fornication [with the whore Madam Reason]: just as people do not use sexuality "properly unless they are married, so too no one philosophizes well unless that person is a fool, in other words, a Christian."[393] "Those who wish to philosophize by using Aristotle without danger must first become thoroughly foolish in Christ."[394] Luther cites as proof *(probatio)*[395] 1 Corinthians 3:18: "If you think that you are wise in this age, you should become fools so that you may become wise."

If you have let yourself become a fool through the word of the cross, you will not seek your own good in philosophical knowledge. Rather, you have been liberated from such an inversion, and in love you will let your knowledge benefit the neighbor and their needs. You will not seek fame or aspire to the heights, but you will associate with the lowly (Rom. 12:16). You will see history, for example, from below, from the perspective of the lowly and humble.

Therefore, philosophy and theology (of the cross) should be distinguished from each other as sharply as possible, yet they should also be connected. The consequences of this can be stated briefly since we have already considered them in detail above (2.2). As thinking beings, we seek clarity and transparency, we want to see a connection between things, we want to discover it, even establish it. Anyone who does not ask about the beginning or the end of all things does not think properly. The metaphysical necessity that we are born with, the need to ask ultimate questions, simply cannot be rooted out.[396] Hence, the temptation to engage in justifying thinking is especially strong for a systematic theologian, for this kind of thinking develops the idea of a "unity" of reality.

From a metaphysical standpoint, justifying thinking and knowing is in league with justifying action (morality). Justifying thinking is preoccupied with the desire to mediate and reconcile all things. It is driven by the compulsion to demonstrate that every individual and particular thing is based on something general. By allying itself with justifying action, justifying thinking misunderstands and perverts the truth of things and their relationships.

Insofar as metaphysics is justifying thinking, which is in league with morality in the sense of justifying action, it is put to death by the passive, donated righteousness of faith. The person who is reborn a Christian and a theologian through the word of the cross and is a "theologian of the cross" says what a thing is: "A theologian of glory calls evil good and good evil. A theologian of the cross calls a thing what it actually is."[397] Why is that so? People by nature have their own natural idea of God, in which they flatten everything out to make it fit the concept of the One, the True, the Beautiful, and the Good. But the theologian of the cross has had that false idea of God shattered through painful disillusionment.

The death of the old self therefore also means that our illusion of a totality of meaning is destroyed, even if it was only hypothetically anticipated. Humans have a deep-seated need to engage in justifying thinking. But the theologian of the cross recognizes in this the "thinking and striving of the human heart," which is radically evil (Gen. 6:5 and 8:21). In its justifying thinking the human heart is a "fabricating" heart *(cor fingens)*[398] that constantly produces and projects images in the mind, idols, on which we hang our hearts, archetypes, prototypes, hopes of happiness and success. Each of us has such images on which we hang our heart, which the heart itself has produced. Therefore, Calvin, like Luther, says that the human heart is an "idol factory" *("fabrica idolorum")*.[399]

The concepts of metaphysics especially can easily become idols. Even a theological doctrine of the divine properties can end in idolatry, if it bypasses the cross of Jesus Christ when it speaks of God's "attributes," his power, wisdom, goodness, and righteousness. This is what Luther means in his explanation of thesis 20 of the *Heidelberg Disputation* when he says that it is "not enough, nor is it of any use, to recognize God in his glory and majesty, unless we also recognize him in the humility and shame of his cross."[400] Christian theology does not begin with the highest good, as all other religions do, but with the lowest depths, with the womb of Mary and Jesus' death on the cross. "But philosophy and the worldly-wise have wanted to start from above because they have become fools. We must start from below."[401]

Conversely, of course, the cross cannot be made into a principle, as has happened also in theological thinking and in the church's discourse since Hegel's philosophy. Making the cross of Christ into a principle comprehensible to everyone, and so into a "natural" theology of the cross, is the danger of *our* time. Therefore, the task of the church's proclamation and theological reflection today is to steer a course between the Scylla of the natural theology of glory, which Luther in 1518 exposed in his *Heidelberg Disputation,* and the Charybdis of a natural theology of the cross, which is the greater danger today.

In order to determine the relationship between theology, on the one hand, and general thinking and knowledge, indeed humanity generally, on the other, it is of the utmost importance that theology deals properly with the specifically Christian contribution to the history of thought. For Christian thinking together with its center, the theology of the cross, has in a certain sense become generalized and has changed and deepened philosophical questions in several important ways. Think of the refutation of the axiom of impassibility, that God cannot suffer. Think of how the use of the term "category" in theology went from being Cinderella to queen. Again, think of the rise of the concept of "contingency" and that of haecceity (that which makes something the kind of thing it is and makes it different from any other), and with it the concept of individuality and personality. Think, too, of how "freedom," "history," and "evil" have become serious philosophical problems. We can also speak here of "analogies." The word of the cross not only sets limits but also creates analogies. However, these analogies must not be treated as gospel but as law, in the sense of its first *(primus usus legis)* or political use *(usus politicus).*[402]

Here theology and philosophy, gospel and culture, must be carefully distinguished. It is true that many aspects of our Western thinking (and ethos) cannot be understood apart from the gospel. But even that general thinking which has grown out of the gospel, out of the word of the cross, is different from the gospel. It is different from the new world of divine righteousness *(iustitia dei)*. It is still part of the sinful world that is passing away. Even the actions and thinking of Christians in this world are not free from ambiguity and still have to face the judgment of works (2 Cor. 5:10; Matt. 16:27).

The distinction between law and gospel will not be overcome this side of the grave. It determines the life of the Christian and the theologian, and the life of the whole church. It is especially determinative for the way in which we understand the relationship of theology to philosophy and science. The truth of the unity of law and gospel has not yet been revealed to us (see 1 John 3:2).

Melanchthon rightly emphasized that sin makes it necessary to distinguish between the gospel and philosophy, and so to keep theology as a separate discipline of its own. In the original state of innocence, theology was not an individual science but a universal science and identical to philosophy. And of course, it will be that also in the eschaton. But for now it is *theologia viatorum,* the theology we do en route as pilgrims.

Because our theology is the theology of pilgrims *(theologia viatorum),* its relation to philosophy and to the general view of human nature is going to be one of radical conflict. Classically, this conflict appears in Luther's *Disputation Concerning Man* (1536), in which theses 1-19 deal with philosophy and theses 20-40 with theology. This division, however, does not mean that theology played no role in the first part or philosophy in the second. Luther's anthropology emerges "in the dispute over whether it should be basically philosophical or theological in nature."[403] The conflict is not resolved by going the way of Thomas, who holds that grace elevates and perfects nature.[404] Nor do we find the answer to it in transcendental philosophy, according to which grace does not in fact elevate nature but deepens it, so that God and his freedom become the condition for human freedom. Again, it is not resolved by the abstract separations (diastases) typical of Barth's early dialectical theology, nor is it even softened by Tillich's method of correlation or Barth's model of analogy and difference in his later theology.

If, like Luther, we see theology as a discipline that by its very nature is involved in conflicts and disputes, we will be aware of the tension that exists between wisdom and the cross.[405] This tension that Paul paradigmatically describes in 1 Corinthians 1:18–2:16 will not be overcome on our journey through life. Theology therefore should not confine itself to the circle of believers, whether this is the self-reflection of faith or the conversation between the churches. Rather, it is meant to engage with the other, with whatever stands in conflict with it. In a word, theology, if it is true to its charter, will be involved in dispute and conflict.

6.3. The Problem of Natural Theology

The problem of natural theology was not simply imposed on the church from outside. If, however, we understand natural theology as the question of the true nature of the gods or of the *one* God, the question of his *"physis"* or his *"natura,"* it is true to say that, in its philosophical and metaphysical form, this question did not have its origin within the Christian church but came from the Greek metaphysical tradition with its critique of myth. The church, however, did not take up the question at the philosophical level, but approached it from its inner core, the confession of Christ (1 Cor. 8:4-6; Gal. 4:8). In the service of the church, natural theology serves to articulate the universality of the gospel, which is to be proclaimed not only to all people, but also to all creatures (Mark 16:15). Jesus is the one and only Lord. "There is salvation in no one else, for there is no other name under heaven given among mortals by which we must be saved" (Acts 4:12).

This might seem to suggest that we should think of the person of Christ as the unity of reality or, conversely, of the unity of reality as the person of Christ, based on such key texts as the New Testament Christ-hymns, for example, Colossians 1:15-20, Hebrews 1:1-4, and the prologue of the Gospel of John. It is in this sense that especially Dietrich Bonhoeffer[406] and Karl Barth have asserted that Jesus Christ is the *one* Word of God.[407] But in order to demonstrate its claim to truth or its claim to general theological validity, we do not have to begin with an indeterminate, general concept, which would have to be assumed or anticipated, but rather with the particularity of the Christ event.[408]

Certainly, this necessarily critical task cannot be undertaken in any other way than from the standpoint of the particularity of the

Christ's incarnation, death, and resurrection. But the question is, what should we take as our points of reference? For it can hardly be denied that we cannot examine the claim in isolation but only *with reference to other things*. Without such points of reference, we cannot even articulate the necessary contradictions. For proof of this, we only have to look at I Corinthians 1:18–2:16, Romans 1:18–3:20, and Acts 17. Only an *a priori* Christological construct, divorced from all connections with life and suffering, could exist in glorious isolation because it spins everything out of itself. However, such a construct would imply the annihilation of the world *(annihilatio mundi)*, which in any case could never be anything more than a thought experiment, for it would imply that everything is godless and must be destroyed so that it can be reconstructed anew through Jesus Christ as the one word of God.

If we look to history for examples of the articulation of a "pure" Christological argument, we could take Hegel's philosophy of religion, with some modifications, but we also need to look at Karl Barth. We recall that Barth's initial treatment of the problem of natural theology resulted in his outright rejection of it with his famous "No!" to Emil Brunner in 1943. But then in 1961 Barth says, "Later I retrieved natural theology via Christology."[409] Therefore, we must examine his natural theology, which he rehabilitated on the basis of Christology, because of its connections with Hegel's philosophy of religion. We need to see what it achieves theologically and where it is problematic.

A new approach to the problem of natural theology, which had been pioneered by Lessing and Kant, emerged with Hegel. The significance of this change cannot be overestimated. *Before* the change, natural theology had focused on what came prior to the truths of revelation. Its focus therefore was on the truths of reason, which had been classically formulated by Hermann Samuel Reimarus (1694-1768) in his book published in 1754, *Die vornehmsten Wahrheiten der natürlichen Religion (The Principal Truths of Natural Religion)*. These truths are the "existence of God, the world's dependence on God, the manifestation of the divine attributes in nature; the dualism of body and soul and the destiny of humans for the highest perfection possible for a rational, sensory being; the special providence of God for humankind and its defense in the form of a theodicy; immortality as the means by which the virtuous are permitted to ascend to a higher state of blessedness than that attainable in this world."[410] On the other hand, "sin, guilt, grace,

and redemption" are strictly separated from these truths of reason because "they belong to the realm of positive religion."[411]

This separation, or at least distinction, has its counterpart in theology. A Lutheran dogmatics, such as that of David Hollaz, has the
mixed articles *(articuli mixti),* which are also accessible to reason, coming prior to the pure articles of faith. These mixed articles are the
teaching of the existence, power, and goodness of God in relation to his
creation, preservation, and governance of the world.[412] They are distinguished from those parts of Christian doctrine that deal with the divine "mysteries,"[413] such as the incarnation and Christ's atoning death,
Baptism and the Lord's Supper.

The new approach we mentioned can be first seen with Lessing.
In a series of theses in *The Education of the Human Race* (1780), he makes
an important comment in relation to the doctrine of the Trinity (§73),
the doctrine of original sin (§74), and the doctrine of satisfaction (§75):
"The development of revealed truths into truths of reason is absolutely
necessary" (§76). We are now no longer to think of the truths of revelation in contrast to the truths of reason but rather as comprehended by
reason so that they themselves become truths of reason. Thus, revelation is illuminated by reason (§36).

Lessing has his disciple in Kant, at least in method even if not in the
details. Kant's essay, *Religion Within the Limits of Reason Alone* (1793), does
not deal with God's existence, with the contingency of the world or providence, but instead with sin, Christology, soteriology, and ecclesiology,
including the means of grace: prayer, divine service, Baptism, and the
Lord's Supper. "Thus, it deals with just those articles that dogmatics
usually reserved for the theology of revelation."[414] Reason is no longer re-
pelled by history, as it is in a very pronounced way in Reimarus.[415] Rather,
it now takes hold of history and draws on it; in any case, it tries to demonstrate its rationality. To put it more precisely, reason seeks to discover
and identify reason within history by means of a critical method.

With Hegel, the way pioneered by Lessing and Kant reaches its
completion. The cross becomes "rational" in that the historical Good
Friday is understood as an idea and so is transformed into the speculative Good Friday, while Christ's resurrection becomes the negation of
negation.[416] The concrete attributes *(concreta)* of the being of Jesus
Christ are tacitly transformed into abstract attributes *(abstracta),*[417]
into general definitions that delineate reality as a whole and as a unity.

In this kind of natural theology of the cross, *theologia crucis naturalis*, the problem of the old natural theology has disappeared, insofar as it was characterized by the essential distinction or even separation between the truths of reason and the truths of revelation. But the claim to universality, which was so much a part of the old natural theology, is still there. In fact, it is brought into prominence in a wholly new way so that now natural theology achieves the unity and harmony that previously seemed possible only through thinking.

We can also see the character of this new, post-Christian natural theology by looking at the change in the usage of the two concepts *theologia* (theology) and *oikonomia* (economy). Since the fourth century, and especially since Eusebius of Caesarea, *theologia*, as distinct from *oikonomia*, has been applied to the doctrine of God itself. *Oikonomia*, on the other hand, means the enactment of God's plan of salvation, his salvific action, which is focused on his incarnation and death on the cross. Therefore, *oikonomia* refers to the "mysteries"[418] and truths of revelation, which at the time of the Enlightenment, before Lessing and Kant, were distinguished from the truths of reason in natural theology.

In the new form of natural theology perfected by Hegel after Lessing and Kant, the old distinction between theology and economy is set aside and transformed into the *one* reality of Christ. Dietrich Bonhoeffer, speaking wholly in the sense of the Hegelian philosophy of religion, says: "There is . . . *only one reality*, and that is the reality of God, manifest in Christ, in the reality of the world."[419] Karl Barth says the same thing, theologically, especially in his "doctrine of lights" in *Church Dogmatics* IV/3. Responding there to the problem endemic to the tradition of natural theology, he says that he retrieves "natural theology via Christology"[420] on the basis of Jesus Christ as the one Word of God.

Hegel and Barth have consistently tried to remove the difference between "theology" and "economy," or more specifically, between a general experience of God and a Christian experience of salvation. Schleiermacher also planned to remove this distinction but it did not materialize; the time for it was not yet ripe.[421] So he gives up the idea of a Christological construction or reconstruction of his whole systematic theology and lets the two-part division stand, which the leading proposition of §29 of *The Christian Faith* describes this way: "We shall exhaust the whole compass of Christian doctrine if we consider the facts of the religious self-consciousness, first, as they are presupposed by the antithesis expressed in the concept of redemption, and secondly, as they are determined by that antithesis." Accordingly, the first part of *The Christian Faith* offers the "development of that religious self-consciousness which is always presupposed by and contained in every Christian religious affection." In this respect, Schleiermacher has a prominent successor in Rudolf Bultmann who, in his account of Paul's theology, starts with a discussion of the (formal-ontological) anthropological concepts.[422]

In this way, the intention of the old natural theology has been taken up, but in a much-transfigured form, certainly quite differently than in Hegel and Barth. Indeed, the idea of unity is also there in Schleiermacher and Bultmann. But they do not approach it through a speculative expansion of the economy. For them it is not a matter of an ontological unity in Christ but of a fundamental anthropological unity, which Schleiermacher ultimately locates in the feeling of absolute dependence.[423] If Deism had assumed that natural religion, with its truths of reason that applied to all people, was a historical phase prior to the concrete positive religions, Schleiermacher and Bultmann preserve the general intent implicit in such a construct. We see this in their concern for an anthropological unity that tries to explain the transition from unbelief to faith or from the consciousness of sin to the consciousness of grace. This unity, they say, must at least be understood in a formal ontological sense, even if not in an ontic factual way. The "kerygma is understandable as kerygma only when the self-understanding awakened by it is recognized to be a possibility of human self-understanding."[424]

While the distinction between Schleiermacher and Barth may be ever so great, they agree with each other in their thinking about unity.[425] While Schleiermacher, of course, thinks of unity anthropologically, as the one fundamental state, Barth approaches it Christologically, by holding that Jesus Christ is the one Word of God.

If we criticize Barth's thinking about unity, we will have to ask ourselves whether the unity of God is something that we can only confess, as when we confess Jesus to be the one and only Lord, or whether it is something that we can also conceive with our minds. But this can happen only in the sense of 1 Corinthians 8:4-6 and of the prayer of the Isaiah Apocalypse: "O Lord our God, other lords besides you have ruled over us, but we acknowledge your name alone" (Isa. 26:13; cf. Micah 4:5).

Yahweh's lawsuit with the other gods must not be glossed over even by systematic theology through an abstract monism. At stake is the truth of the first commandment: "I am the Lord your God, you shall have no other gods besides me!" Nevertheless, the other gods have their reality in their promises and enticements, as either something fascinating *(fascinosum)* or frightening *(tremendum),* in the sense of a power that is given to them by the human fabricating heart *(cor fingens).*

The unity of God that we confess can only be believed. It cannot be conceived, if that means to possess the idea of the unity of God as a datum that we could summon at will as we do our hopes and memories. It is not a piece of information that we can store away and retrieve. The question, however, is whether what we believe can only be believed or whether it can also be conceived, and if so, how? In any case, God's unity is not like an idea that can be remembered or construed. It will always be a matter of dispute. Even thinking cannot escape this conflict between the *one* God with the many gods. Therefore, this situation must be made clear also in thinking and in theology, especially in systematic theology. We cannot skip over the distinction between law and gospel, which is at stake here, for the sake of the idea of the unity of gospel and law.

If we speak of a "unity" in connection with law and gospel, life and death, judgment and grace, it must be clear that this is meant in a strictly eschatological sense.

The critical point in dealing with the problem of natural theology is the question of the distinction between law and gospel or of the unity of gospel and law.

6.4. Theology and Religious Studies

Theology is a study of religion in the sense outlined at the beginning (1). That means that it begins and ends with the general and particular divine service.

The concept of "religion," understood as divine service, which we are focusing on here, is derived entirely from texts of the Bible. If, however, we combine the promise given at creation (Gen. 2:16) with the gospel preamble of the Decalogue (Exod. 20:2), we get a broader, though more specific, concept[426] that makes room for a general study of religion and for a phenomenology of religion, and certainly for Christian missiology. Therefore, we must not attempt to seek a supposedly neutral concept of religion. Such a concept could only be developed in abstraction from the concrete religions with all their specificity, and would therefore not do them justice. The history of the quest for a neutral, general concept of religion has taught us that we not only can, but also must, for the best outcome, "understand the reality of the non-Christian religions from the standpoint of the fundamental insights of Christian theology. That means that we have to judge how Christian theology is related to the non-Christian religions from the perspective of Christian theology's own self-understanding."[427] Conversely, it is important to recognize that "in all questions of dogmatics and ethics, Christian theology needs the religions to be able to understand clearly its own convictions."[428]

The relation of the Christian faith to the other religions is not only problematic but also full of opportunity. Its claim to universality, however, does not give it the right to regard the truth claim of the other religions as indicative of an unbridgeable chasm separating them from Christianity. Indeed, the existence of the other religions is a reminder to us that Christian theology does not exist in a vacuum and that there is no such thing as a pure theology that dialogues with itself in isolation from the conflicts and struggles of the world and its religions. On the other hand, the clear certainty of the Christian claim makes it impossible to transform this relationship into an apparently already existing *identity*, even if it is as Christologically grounded as Karl Rahner's assumption of an "anonymous Christianity" in all religions.[429] His assumption is problematic for two reasons. It has its basis in transcendental philosophy[430] and is driven by the hope for an evolutionary perfection of the world. These two factors serve to abstract his assumption from the context *(Sitz im Leben)* of the *promise*[431] and its historical foundation in the event that took place under Pontius Pilate.[432] Therefore, his assumption is thoroughly speculative and fails to recognize the importance of sin.[433] We must avoid the identification that Rahner makes, as in his thesis of the anonymous Christian, just as strongly as the disjunction that others make, and recognize that we are in a situation of *conflict* in which truth and error are in contention.

The "communicative form of judgment,"[434] which is to be tested in this conflict, emerges from that event in which the old person becomes a new person, which still has to relate to the old. That means that we will only escape the compulsion to think in terms of a unity[435] if our thinking is not determined by an origin or goal but rather starts from a given center. Our thinking therefore must proceed from a key event that discloses the meaning of all the events that come before and after it and at the same time proleptically fulfills them. "All philosophical contradictions and the whole historical riddle of our existence, the impenetrable night of its *termini a quo* and *termini ad quem*," its origin and end, "are resolved by the primal message of the Word become flesh"[436] (John 1:14).

A key event, especially for the history of religion, and one that is very specific as well as being universal, is the union of divinity and humanity.[437] This event is God's physical and verbal self-communication in Jesus Christ. That explains why the image of God in humans is to be understood in a concrete physical way rather than as an abstract personalistic opposite to God, or as a mediation, as in Plato, between the world of ideas and world of matter. The physical and sensory form is essential to religion. Even understood as a study of religion, theology attends first and last to the "form" by appreciating the bodily aspect of the word as much as the linguistic aspect of the body.

If, in light of the Christ event, God's self-communication and its appropriation involves our senses, and if God's goodness can be "tasted" (Ps. 34:8), it follows that one of the tasks of mission is to take seriously the rites and myths of the ethnic and world religions that in themselves are responses to God's address with its appeal to the senses. However, in doing so, we must avoid the mistake of starting with the idea of a general openness, in which the general closedness of humankind to God, which scripture calls sin (Gal. 3:23; Rom. 11:32), is not recognized.[438]

This general closedness makes dialogue with other religions impossible insofar as a dialogue, at least according to the conventional understanding, assumes that the hidden truth, which always drives us to ask questions, will reveal itself to us little by little as we search for it together. This assumption of a general openness succumbs to the same illusion as the anticipation of a common understanding. Paul, at any rate, does not carry on a dialogue with the Corinthians. Rather, he freely becomes their slave (1 Cor. 9:19) and involves himself with them so deeply that he himself takes their place (1 Cor. 4:6). In this way, he does not exalt himself above the level of dialogue by presuming to be their master, but he humbles himself as their slave. The alternative to dialogue is not domination but intercession in the solidarity spoken of in Romans 9:3. In the congregation's intercession that grows out of learning through suffering, the church is there for others. Here the illusion, conjured up by the word "dialogue," is shattered, the illusion that the two parties in dispute can find a center around which they will reach agreement and arrive at a consensus. Asymmetries and dissensus should not be glossed over. The dispute within the Christian community at Corinth, for example, or that between Christians and Jews, or even more broadly, the dispute between Christianity and other religions — all these are part of world history, part of a life-and-death struggle of all against all for mutual recognition. If, with Paul, we let this battle be decided in the Spirit of the one who was free yet became the servant of all (compare 2 Cor. 8:9 with 1 Cor. 9:19), we cannot simply conduct our conversation with the Jews and regard our conversation with the religions as a dialogue.[439]

Hence, the question about the freedom of theology is decisive. What understanding of freedom does it develop? How does it hear, conceive, and test its own freedom? Because of its history, semantic field, and present relevance, the idea of freedom is the best catalyst for a productive debate about the truth of the Christian faith and the proper interpretation of nature and history in general.

Theology, understood as an academic discipline, proves its own freedom through debate, dispute, and polemic. It does not advance the truth it is called to consider by trying to adapt it prematurely to contemporary society and the global community, or by abstractly opposing the truth of faith to the prevailing currents of thought, but by engaging in controversy. It does not seek to minimize conflict but clearly to express itself in and through it. *Theology is primarily critical and polemical; its first task is not to try to integrate itself with philosophy (in the broad sense) but to look for differences.* It gambles on the fact that the only way to unity is through argument and dispute.

The "communicative form of judgment," which provides the basic structure of this dispute, has deep and far-reaching significance for all aspects of the church's work: preaching and catechesis, pastoral care and diaconal work, mission and ecumenical engagement. It has fundamental theological significance and is the critical political way of referring to nature and history as that reality which God has created by his unconditional promise, which he has preserved from the chaos due to sin and corruption, and which he will perfect through the final judgment.

7. Faith and Sight

7.1. The Problem

Every systematic theology has to face up to three ruptures and transitions: (1) the transition from the created to the fallen world, (2) the transition from the fallen to the redeemed world, and (3) the transition from the world already redeemed, but still contested, to the world indisputably redeemed.

As the title of this concluding section "Faith and Sight" suggests, we are concentrating on the third transition, the transition from the world already redeemed but still contested, to the world indisputably redeemed. We can approach it in various ways. The formulation of the topic comes from Paul (2 Cor. 5:7): "We walk by faith, not by sight" *(dia pisteos gar peripatoumen ou dia eidous).* We as Christians go our *way*, but this path needs *time* to traverse. We walk by faith in the word of Christ which always accompanies us, by a faith that does not see (Heb. 11:1). Even if we "see" Christ by hearing him and trusting him as the Word already now in his "glory" (2 Cor. 3:18), this is still very much a seeing of faith, for the presence of the Lord and the perfection of the world is still contested. Because we see God as present only in the word (see Deut. 4:12), Paul can say in 1 Corinthians 13:12, which at first glance appears to be in contradiction to 2 Corinthians 3:18, that we do *not yet* see God, that only then will we see him "face to face." We are already known by him, he *has* already known us, but we and the whole perfected world with us will only know him then.

In both passages, Paul refers to Numbers 12:8 in the Septuagint (LXX) where Moses is distinguished from all the other prophets by an incomparable immediacy with God: "I [God] speak with him directly (literally: mouth to mouth) and he [Moses] sees the Lord in his form, not through dark words or riddles *[en eidei kai ou di' ainigmaton].*"

The various references to the same passage in the Septuagint, which at first glance seem contradictory, draw our attention to both the visibility and the invisibility of God revealed in Jesus Christ. The *invisible* God is not invisible in *every* respect; for the Son is the image of the invisible God (Col. 1:15) and is of the same essence as God. Conversely, the visible God is not visible in every respect; people can fail to recognize him in unbelief and in this sense he can remain hidden. And precisely because God has revealed himself, we as believers are challenged by those things that contradict this. But when we encounter his terrifying hiddenness, we can turn away from this and flee to his mercy, which has ultimately been revealed to us through the Son in the Spirit.

By means of this contrast, "by faith, not by sight," Paul delineates our present status, which of course is no state, but a path. We are on the way *(in via)*. Our theology is a theology of wayfarers *(theologia viatorum)*, the theology of those who are still on the journey, not the theology of those who have already arrived at the goal and *see*.

This suggests that we should treat the difference between faith and sight in our discussion of the meaning of theology, and therefore in connection with prolegomena, the philosophy of science, and epistemology. It is in this context that, ever since medieval scholasticism, the question has been asked whether theology, in the sense of knowledge, be it science or wisdom, has a contemplative character, the character of *sight*, and if so, what exactly that means. But, not surprisingly, the main place it comes up, apart from the discussion of the nature of faith in eschatology, is in the article concerning the beatific vision *(de visione beatifica)*, that joyous vision of God granted to all believers in heaven. A careful treatment of the question about the "vision of the divine essence" (the *visio divinae essentiae*), which according to Thomas Aquinas is the main hallmark of the blessedness of the blessed, can be found in the final section of his *Summa Theologiae*, posthumously added from his commentary on the *Sentences*.

What is striking there, in question 92, is that the references to anthropology and epistemology are not only strong, but also essential to his argument and therefore also essential to the principal questions of theology. Here the following sentence from Thomas's conclusion will have to suffice as proof: "since knowing is that activity most proper to humans, it follows that a blessedness appropriate to this activity must be conferred on them in which this activity will be perfected in them."[440]

The relationship of material dogmatic eschatology (its subject matter) to the question of theological principles (prolegomena) is, not only in Thomas Aquinas, a mutual relationship, just as any supposedly "merely" formal, methodological question in relation to the philosophy of science and hermeneutics is not really "pure" at all but is thoroughly permeated and determined by the subject matter of dogmatics or its philosophical equivalents.

Those who want to see a clear distinction, or if possible, even a separation between questions of method and subject matter are irritated by this mutuality and go around in circles in the game of *quid pro quo*.

But it is not only theology that goes around in circles with this question. This mutual relationship is *not* unique to theology; any other academic discipline has to deal with it too. Likewise, no philosophical approach to a topic can dispense with discussing the question of eschatology, what comes last, and, its counterpart, protology, what comes first. Thus, for Jürgen Habermas and his philosophy of emancipation, the eschaton is the attainment of dialogue free from coercion. He claims this is possible because of the *a priori* of reason embedded in language. Each "act of speaking" already contains "the telos of understanding."[441] And for Popper, openness and inconclusiveness promise the best outcome, relatively speaking, for human history. This openness, which is demanded, methodologically, by the principle of falsification, corresponds to his basic, quasi-religious decision to opt for critical rationalism. But the demand for rationality can be met only on the basis of a "moral decision."[442]

Even the unavoidability of the questions of protology and eschatology, and their counterparts in the area of the philosophy of science and epistemology, which deals mainly with the inscrutable mutual relationship of formal and material matters, cannot produce a conclusive answer. So then the way of dealing with the problem is also in dispute among philosophers.

This is especially clear from the opposite position, such as we have in the contrast between Kant and Hegel. It is important for Kant that limits are recognized and respected and that we do not go beyond them. Hegel, on the other hand, holds that if thinking encounters limits, it should go beyond them. He therefore makes no distinction between faith and knowledge, or between faith and sight. This is also the case for Fichte. In his *The Way towards the Blessed Life,* he says that philosophy supersedes "all faith" and "changes it into sight."[443] Here, clearly, he is referring to 2 Corinthians 5:7. "True and perfect humans," who use philosophy to its full potential, "ought to be thoroughly clear in themselves; for" — and here we should hear echoes of 2 Corinthians 3:18 in the background — "universal and perfect clarity belongs to the image and likeness of God."[444] Fichte, and even more so Hegel, cultivates the "dream of a total mediation," at the end of which reflective thinking is again equated with intellectual intuition, in its *transparency* for the self as an absolute subject.[445]

It comes as a surprise that Kierkegaard, Hegel's stiff opponent, also insists on transparency. This comes out in *The Sickness unto Death* in which he gives his "definition of faith, by which I steer my course in the whole of this work, as by a sure mariner's mark. Faith means that the self, in being itself and in willing to be itself, is grounded transparently [!] in God."[446]

Kierkegaard emphasizes the faith of Abraham who does not see,[447] yet he still expects that we will "see clearly" not only at the eschaton but already now in faith. If therefore even a Kierkegaard insists on an adequate reflection, correspondence, and correlation between our relationship with God and our relationship with the self, it becomes patently clear that the task of philosophy as well as theology is to determine the relationship between faith and sight.

7.2. A Solution

Our task then is to end the circularity of the mutual relationship between material and formal considerations, between questions of prolegomena (form) and questions of dogmatic eschatology (subject matter) in order to find a point as fixed as possible from which we can determine the relationship between faith and sight in a theologically responsible way.

Our solution to the problem begins with the observation that in every treatment of the eschatological doctrine of the beatific vision *(de visione beatifica),* whether in Thomas Aquinas[448] or David Hollaz,[449] Job 19:26 and 27 occupy an important place, especially the words "I will see God," whether now *"in* my flesh" or, as Luther translated the difficult text, *"without* my flesh." Verse 27 continues: "I myself will see God with my own eyes — I, and not another."

For Thomas as for Hollaz, epistemological questions, the questions of the subject, the act, the type, and the object of the seeing and knowing, are dominant. As a result, the main point of the immediate context as well as the dramatic theme of the whole book are completely ignored: Job's lawsuit with God, his complaint, his protest, his struggle, culminating precisely here in chapter 19 with his appeal *to* God *against* God, Job's suffering under God's enmity and hiddenness, his longing for a justice that cannot be blunted by any form of rationalizing wisdom. These emphases form a vital part of the text, yet they do not even rate a mention in the thinking of Thomas and Hollaz about the beatific vision. Hence, there is little chance that they would be taken seriously or made the focal point.

Thomas and Hollaz represent a broad consensus that needs to be contradicted. In order to clarify the significance of our counterproposal, we need to look a little further into the Old Testament, especially the Psalter.

For the peoples of ancient Greece and the Near East, apart from Jews and Christians, the sight of God or the divinity, which was represented by the idol in the temple, was certainly something astonishing but not altogether foreign. The situation, however, is completely different when we consider it in the context of the prohibition of idols in Israel. The ardent desire of the devout Israelite in the Psalter who asks to see God's face (Ps. 11:7; 17:15; 24:6; 27:4, 8f.; 42:2f.) calls to mind the longing of the pagan worshipers to see the image of their god in the non-Israelite cult, but in the Psalter the devout Israelite longs to see the image-less temple in Jerusalem.

In order to understand this passionate expectation to see God, it is crucial to realize that its context *(Sitz im Leben)* is the complaint. Psalm 17 is especially instructive for our question. The psalmist, who has been wrongly accused and persecuted by his foes, expects God to intervene and vindicate him, to prove publicly that he is innocent (righteous) beyond any shadow of doubt. This intervention is the "wonder" (Ps. 17:7) of the new creation, God's help at daybreak. "I — in righteousness I will see your face; when I awake, I will be satisfied with seeing your likeness" (Ps. 17:15). This epiphany of God's saving grace, this act of deliverance, demonstrates God's divinity, in that "the true

God will be seen in Zion" (Ps. 84:7). God himself overcomes the satanic attack *(Anfechtung)* implicit in the taunting question of the enemy: "Where is your God?" (Ps. 42:3, 10; compare Ps. 79:10).

However, the severest spiritual attack is the one God launches against me when he becomes my enemy, when he "turns cruel" to me (Job 30:21). The boldest statement in the Bible about seeing God comes from the book of Job. The beatitude in Matthew 5:8, "Blessed are the pure in heart, for they will see God," for instance,[450] becomes empty and lifeless like the generic saints in the medieval pictures of the Last Judgment, if we forget Job 19:25-27 and 16:19-21. These are the key texts: "I know that my redeemer lives, and that in the end he will stand upon the earth. And after my skin has been destroyed, yet in [or: without] my flesh I will see God; I myself will see him with my own eyes — I, and not another" (Job 19:25-27). "Earth, do not cover my blood; may my cry never be laid to rest! Even now my witness is in heaven; my advocate is on high" (Job 16:18-21).

Job's lawsuit with God focuses on an extreme point. Job's complaint is that God hides himself and that he is unjust. He claims that God has become a cruel enemy and owes him an answer. Job appeals to an advocate, an avenger, a deliverer. In a defiant "nevertheless" (compare Ps. 73:23-26) he is certain that this redeemer (19:25: *goel*) will help his cause and that in the struggle of God against God, justice will finally prevail.

Job's revolt is an extreme contrast to that stoic resignation which has largely influenced the history of Christianity and which has promoted the obedient surrender to God's will without complaint as the hallmark of the Christian life. Because of this, the Christian church has been alienated from its own tradition, which includes Job's complaint, protest, and appeal to God. Interestingly, James remembers Job for his patience in suffering (James 5:11), not for his complaint and accusation against God. Because the church has not understood the importance of complaint, its understanding of the life of Jesus has often suffered from distortion. The passages in the New Testament that are decisive for Christology, the temptation of Jesus, his prayer in Gethsemane as he struggled over the cup of suffering, and his crucifixion, have all been robbed of their emotion and passion under the influence of Stoicism; the same has happened to the miracle stories with their emphasis on Jesus' compassion; see Mark 1:41. These distortions overlook the fact that "God despises apathy,"[451] and above all, that in both Jewish and Christian thought, the vision of God always occurs in a *forensic* context (see the martyrdom of St. Stephen, Acts 7:55).

In Luther's day, this understanding was still alive. Erasmus Alber, Luther's student and friend, ends his Advent hymn, *"Ihr lieben Christen, freut euch nun, bald wird erscheinen Gottes Sohn . . ."* ("Dear Christians, now rejoice, God's Son will soon appear . . .") with two pleas, both of which arise from the sighs and groans of a person under attack: "Help us, dear Lord; our judge, make haste. Show us the glory of your face." These two pleas not only parallel each other, but they say the same thing (*EG* 6:5).

To see God is to become aware of his righteousness and justice. "The light of glory [. . .] will one day reveal that God, whose judgment [now] is of incomprehensible righteousness, is a God of the most just and manifest righteousness."[452] This light will clear away the hiddenness of God which is incomprehensible, not only in the light of nature, but even in the light of grace. The light of glory, which is identical to the last judgment, will end the lawsuit with God and resolve the question of theodicy. "In that day," the Christ of John's Gospel promises in his farewell discourse, "you will no longer ask me anything" (John 16:23). With these words he provides a brief but sufficient answer to the question of the relationship between faith and sight.[453]

The understanding that to see God is to become aware of his righteousness and justice makes it fundamentally impossible to separate individual from universal eschatology. It would be just as difficult to imagine the perfected world of God's new creation inhabited by impersonal and anonymous beings as to imagine a person with perfect eyesight having no world to see. In that light, even a hymn such as "Jesus Christ, my sure defense . . ." takes on a different meaning. This hymn, which appeared in Berlin in 1653, like Martin Schalling's verse, "Lord, let at last your angels come . . ." (*LBW* 325:3; *Lutheran Worship* 413:3) takes up Job 19:27:

> Then these eyes my Lord will know,
> my redeemer and my brother;
> in his love my soul will glow —
> I myself, and not another! (*LBW* 340:5; *Lutheran Worship* 266:5)

7.3. Consequences

The consequences of our discussion for eschatology and for questions of prolegomena would have to be explained separately. Here it will be enough to indicate the consequences that it has for prolegomena, particularly for the problems of the philosophy of science, which includes theological methodology. This will bring to a close our discussion of the understanding of theology today.

What is striking in the book of Job and the Psalter, and finally reaches its climax in the *Maranatha!* (I Cor. 16:22; Rev. 22:20), the prayer for the coming of the Lord who has come, is the utterly theological nature of the questioning *(quaerere)* that we find there. This is a type of questioning that arises most pointedly for a faith that is certain of its salvation but is ever and again challenged and attacked and therefore does not live by sight. It is precisely the objective certainty of faith *(assertio fidei)* that is questioned. Believers never cease to question. In fact, it is only when people come to faith that they really begin to ask questions, radical questions. For the discrepancy between the promised life and all that contradicts it within and around us makes us cry out, complain, and ask: "Where are you, God? Why have you forsaken me? How long will you hide your face from us? When finally will I see your face? When finally will the light of your glory arise on us?"

Questions of complaint such as these arise from the experience of feeling attacked and abandoned by the very God who promised us victory. They arise from knowing that our present sufferings stand in stark contradiction to the glory of God that already shines decisively in the face of Jesus Christ (2 Cor. 4:6). Yet strange as it may seem, these questions are connected with the great sense of wonder that is right there in the midst of the complaint in the book of Lamentations (3:22 and 23): "The steadfast love of the Lord never ceases, his mercies never come to an end; they are new every morning; great is your faithfulness."

This sense of wonder that we *are,* that we and all creatures really *still* are, that the forces of chaos have not devoured us and that, after this night, day has come again, that there is something rather than nothing at all — this great sense of wonder gives birth to all sorts of questions. If we can stand in awe of the goodness of God, we will think more deeply than those who have forgotten it. For the person who is filled with wonder is inspired to think.

Our proposed solution to the problem of how faith and sight are related to each other presents us with a task. We must consider the elementary and irreducible acts of wonder and complaint, of complaint and wonder, and the questioning they give rise to. In short, we must consider *that kind* of questioning *(quaerere),* and its context *(Sitz im Leben),* in the divine service, if we want to appreciate the place of our 2500-year-old philosophical and scientific culture of inquiry *(quaestio)* and debate *(disputatio).* Within the framework of that elementary questioning *(quaerere),* this philosophical and scientific questioning *(quaerere)* has its legitimate place and its relative autonomy, the autonomy of the penultimate. Philosophy and science then are not eclipsed or overburdened by religious claims and expectations regarding salvation but are liberated for their worldly splendor and earthly dignity.

The relation of these two different types of questioning *(quaerere)* can be better understood if we expressly employ the distinction between law and gospel. This questioning, more than anything else, compels us to distinguish properly between faith and sight so long as we are still on our earthly pilgrimage *(in via).*[454]

The distinction between law and gospel makes it clear that philosophical and scientific questioning belongs to the realm of the law, not the gospel. Where the gospel not only sets limits, as it does over against soteriological claims and expectations, but also finds parallels and analogies in philosophy, science, and in the whole secular realm, which is the domain of human reason, it does this not as gospel, but as law in its political use *(usus politicus).*

The law in this sense rules that entire secular realm that Luther speaks of in the *Small Catechism* in his explanation of the petition for bread in the Lord's Prayer. This realm is the domain of theological ethics, after it has been considered by dogmatics. It is especially the doctrine of creation that reminds us that space and time belong to the passing world, which God preserves every moment for its future, in spite of sin.

Philosophy and science, and that includes theology as a scholarly pursuit and an academic discipline, belong to this life-preserving realm of the law, this secular realm that God preserves through the gift of reason which he gives all people. And just as civil law and the legally constituted political order are determined by two fundamental factors, freedom and constraint, so too are philosophy and science. Constraint, discipline, and respect for rules govern them as much as, hopefully, that freedom, that disinterested thinking and seeing (observing) which have always been the hallmark of the academy *(schole)* ever since its beginnings in ancient Greece. This academic tradition stretches all the way from the contemplation *(theoria)* that marked the philosophy of Greek antiquity, via the pure disputation, which led to the foundation of the universities in the Middle Ages, to the idea of the Humboldt University, the model for the modern German university, and to Hegel's "passionless calm of purely intellectual knowledge."[455]

We should not cast suspicion on this pure, beautiful seeing — the German *"Schauen"* (seeing) is etymologically related to *"schön"* (beautiful) — even though it is common to question the value of anything that seems to have no useful purpose. It does not first have to prove its moral worth before it can be enjoyed and developed. True science is beautiful, not instrumental — an end in itself, a luxury like the nard that was poured out on Jesus in Bethany (Mark 14:3-9). "What is beautiful" *(schön)*, Eduard Mörike wrote in his poem "On a Lamp," "seems delightful in itself." This delight that we have in seeing is not the eschatological beatific vision *(visio beatifica)* but its earthly secular counterpart. This of course, even when it mirrors the gospel, belongs to the realm of the law and will be perfected by God the creator through the last judgment.

Theology, understood as a science, an academic discipline, also belongs to this realm of the political use of the law *(usus politicus legis)*. It therefore has its legitimate place in a state university, as is the case in Germany today. However, there are two aspects to theology, which correspond to the two different modes of questioning *(quaerere)*. If we approach theology from the standpoint of the academy, the question is: What makes theological science "science"? On the other hand, if we approach it from the angle of the divine service, the question rather is: What makes theological science theology?

Finally, a comparison between Luther's understanding of theology and that of Anselm of Canterbury and his programmatic formula "faith seeking understanding" *(fides quaerens intellectum)* highlights the understanding of theology that we have promoted in this book. The answer to the question about the relationship of Anselm's understanding of theology to Luther's is already contained in the distinction between the two types of questioning. The first, the elementary questioning, is magnificently exemplified by Luther as an Old Testament scholar. Although he was a professor of biblical studies, he never scorned or denied the education provided by the faculty of arts. He appreciated the art of philosophical and scholarly inquiry, the art of asking the right question. But for him this was purely secondary and had only regulative significance in that it did not constitute the subject matter of theology. On the other hand, he attributed constitutive significance to monastic liturgical spirituality with its focus on meditation in the divine service. Theology, then, is a way of life that is stamped by prayer, the study of scripture, and spiritual attack *(oratione, meditatione, tentatione)*. And to this we can also add death. By the same token, the theologian — and every Christian is a theologian — is a person under attack seeking certainty *(tentatus quaerens certitudinem)*. This formula, which picks up Anselm's programmatic formula and turns it inside out, illustrates the difference between Luther and Anselm in their understanding of theology.

Not that Anselm has nothing to say about the experience of spiritual attack *(Anfechtung)*. But for him it means something else. It prevents us from knowing clearly. This, we know from his philosophical and scientific inquiry, is of decisive importance for him. Certainly, Anselm does not claim that beauty *(pulchritudo)* has already made him aware of the insight given by the light of glory and with it of the righteousness and justice of God, who in his terrible hiddenness hurls us into the deepest spiritual crisis, where he himself becomes our enemy. What Anselm knows by reason alone *(sola ratione)*, what he "sees" in contemplation, is not the unveiled face of the triune God. He knows and sees what he believes, but not by virtue of the beatific vision *(visione beatifica)*.

However, in contrast to Luther, Anselm's philosophical and scientific inquiry is largely detached from the existential situation of spiritual attack *(Anfechtung)*. Furthermore, Anselm plays down the secular and profane nature of this questioning and with it the understanding *(intelligere)* that comes by reason alone *(sola ratione)*, because for him this understanding is the means by which the human spirit ascends to the vision of God.

We have seen that theology has two sides that must be clearly understood. First, there is its monastic aspect with its tradition of liturgical spirituality. This is constitutive in that it provides theology with its content. This includes the elementary questioning, the lament, and, most of all, the divine service of the church in which God speaks to us in meditation and we respond to him in prayer, which embraces the speaking of the heart to God in petition and intercession, thanksgiving, and adoration. True theology always begins and ends with the divine service. Secondly, there is the scientific, scholastic, academic side of theology that attends to matters of theological methodology (prolegomena). This regulates theology by ordering, analyzing, defining, and reflecting on its subject matter and by making the necessary connections and distinctions. It is important that the methods used by theology are allowed to retain their secular and worldly character. Theology does not need to elevate and transfigure them. Its methodology does not need to be spiritualized.

From the standpoint of its methodology, theology is an academic discipline, a scholarly pursuit. As such, it belongs to the realm of the law. This realm is not only marked by constraint, but it also has its own earthly, secular freedom and beauty.

Soli Deo Gloria

Endnotes

Notes to the Introduction

1. See Ulrich Köpf, *Die Anfänge der theologischen Wissenschaftstheorie im 13. Jahrhundert, BHTh* 49 (Tübingen, 1974).

2. Plato, *The Republic,* trans. H. D. P. Lee (London: Penguin, 1955), p. 118 (translation altered).

3. Plato, *The Republic,* p. 121 (translation altered).

4. Plato, *The Republic,* p. 118 (translation altered).

5. Plato, *The Republic,* p. 119.

6. See Godo Lieberg, "Die *'theologia tripertita'* in Forschung und Bezeugung," *Aufstieg und Niedergang der römischen Welt,* ed. Hildegard Temporini, I 4 (Berlin: De Gruyter, 1973), pp. 63-115.

7. See below note 11.

8. "In theology the decisive impulse for the 'scholastic' development of the twelfth century came from the *quaestio,* whose content and method were developed into scholastic theology, while the authority *(auctoritas)* for the 'content' of the doctrinal question went back to the pre-scholastic tradition" (Martin Anton Schmidt, *Scholastik, HKG* [Göttingen: Vandenhoeck & Ruprecht, 1969], p. 75).

9. See especially Athanasius, *Epistula ad Marcellinum in Interpretationem Psalmorum* (*MPG* 27, 11-46). See part one: note 235. For the wider context, see Heinrich Holze, *Erfahrung und Theologie im frühen Mönchtum. Untersuchungen zu einer Theologie des monastischen Lebens bei den ägyptischen Mönchsvätern, Johannes von Cassian und Benedikt von Nursia, FKDG* 48 (Göttingen: Evangelischer Verlagsanstalt, 1992).

10. See part one: section 3.

11. Jean Leclercq, *The Love of Learning and the Desire for God: A Study of Monastic*

Culture, trans. Catherine Misrahi, 3rd ed. (New York: Fordham University Press, 1961, 1982).

12. Leclercq, *The Love of Learning and the Desire for God,* p. 191.

13. Leclercq, *The Love of Learning and the Desire for God,* p. 193.

14. See Ulrich Köpf, *Religiöse Erfahrung in der Theologie Bernhards von Clairvaux,* *BHTh* 61 (Tübingen: Mohr Siebeck, 1980); Köpf, "Wesen und Funktion religiöser Erfahrung — Überlegungen im Anschluß an Bernhard von Clairvaux," *NZSTh* 22 (1980): 150-65.

15. See Gerald Hanratty, "The Origin and Development of Mystical Atheism," *NZSTh* 30 (1988): 1-17.

16. See Ernst Kapp, *Greek Foundations of Traditional Logic* (New York: AMS Press, 1942).

17. Dialectics was the study of philosophy, which included logic, metaphysics, and ethics.

18. I am also confirmed in this opinion by Ulrich Köpf, "Monastische Theologie im 15. Jahrhundert," *Rottenburger Jahrbuch für Kirchengeschichte,* vol. 11 (Sigmaringen, 1992), pp. 117-35, esp. 126f.

19. See Ernst Koch, "Therapeutische Theologie. Die *Meditationes sacrae* von Johann Gerhard (1606)," *Pietismus und Neuzeit. Ein Jahrbuch zur Geschichte des Neueren Protestantismus,* ed. Martin Brecht et al., vol. 13 (1987), pp. 25-46.

20. See part one: section 3, note 105.

21. See Oswald Bayer, *Theologie,* HST vol. 1 (Gütersloh: Gütersloher Verlaghaus, 1994), part A II, section 1, note 2.

22. See Oswald Bayer, *Theologie,* part A II, section 6.

23. See part one: section 4, note 370.

24. See Oswald Bayer, "Vernunftautorität und Bibelkritik in der Kontroverse zwischen Hamann und Kant," *Autorität und Kritik. Zu Hermeneutik und Wissenschafts-theorie* (Tübingen: Mohr Siebeck, 1991), esp. p. 80, n. 116.

25. See also the article *"Theologie"* which Bayer co-authored with Albrecht Peters in *Historischen Wörterbuch der Philosophie,* vol. 10, cols. 1080-95, ed. Joachim Ritter and Karlfried Gründer (Darmstadt: Wissenschaftliche Buchgesellschaft, 1998).

26. Gabrielis Biel, *Collectorium circa quattuor libros Sententiarum I: Prologus et Liber primus,* Coll. Martino Elze et Renata Steiger, ediderunt Wilfridus Werbeck et Udo Hofmann (Tübingen: Mohr Siebeck, 1973), p. 8.

Notes to Part One

1. WABR 1:217, 60-63 (Letter to Karlstadt, Oct. 14, 1518).

2. See the Introduction: "Important Moments in the Understanding of Theology: 3. The Main Problems with the Philosophy of Science."

3. WA 40/II:316, 5ff.: "This was called a penitential psalm. That is how it was used in all the churches . . ."; see LW 12:304.

4. WA 40/II:316, 13ff.: "Since they do not understand the definition of sin, neither do they understand grace . . ."; see LW 12:305. Luther also mentions these "two parts" in the wider interpretation: 327, 26-28: "When these [sins] are felt like this in the heart, then the other part of knowledge ought to follow which also should not be speculative but entirely practical and sensory, that people may learn and hear what grace is . . ."; see LW 12:316f.

5. WA 40/II:328, 2-5.

6. WA 40/II:369, 19f.: For here sin is not to be understood either metaphysically or historically, but theologically. . . ." That means (with Luther himself, according to Rörer's transcript) "it is revealed by the divine word alone" (369, 9f.; see the "but through the word"; 369, 11). See Luther's later reflection on the changes the Reformation brought to his theology in which the mode and medium of revelation are now crucial: "the righteousness of God is revealed by the gospel" (LW 34:337; WA 54:186, 6f.; Preface to the Complete Edition of Luther's Latin Writings, 1545). On "metaphysically" and "morally," see the *Lectures on Romans*: LW 25:330; WA 56:334, 3f. and 14f.

7. WA 40/II:373, 5-7: *"per promissiones et leges divinas, non per humanam regulam, id est: 'ut habeas veritatem in sermonibus tuis.'"* Note: We will follow the versification of the English Bible. Verse 4 in the English translations is verse 6 in the Hebrew Bible.

8. WA 40/II:319, 8f.; see LW 12:305.

9. "The psalm should be understood to be speaking about universal sin; not only David's adultery but also that of the monk . . ." (WA 40/II:362, 6f.). See Oswald Bayer, *Schöpfung als Anrede. Zu einer Hermeneutik der Schöpfung*, 2nd ed. (Tübingen: Mohr Siebeck, 1990), pp. 67f.

10. See WA 40/II:365, 8-10: "Take here in this way also sin in general: 'Against you, have I sinned' etc. 'I know my sin,' that is, I acknowledge that in your sight I am nothing but a sinner"; 365, 11: "Not to understand about actual sins but about universal sin . . ." and esp. 366, with an emphatic reference to Paul: "Paul rightly interprets the following universally: We are all condemned" (366, 9).

11. WA 40/II:333, 8f.; see LW 12:315.

12. WA 40/II:328, 1f.: *"subiectum Theologiae homo reus et perditus et deus iustificans vel salvator."* To define the subject matter of theology in this way is thoroughly consistent with the fact that the one single phrase in the entire Bible that Luther highlights by printing it in all capitals is Romans 3:25: "he forgives sins" *(SVNDE VERGJBT)*. In a marginal gloss on this phrase he calls it "the principal part" and "the center-piece of this epistle and of the whole of Scripture" (see WA 40/II:385, 9: *"principalis locus nostrae Theologiae"*). On that, see Martin Schloemann, "Die Mitte der Schrift. Luthers Notabene," in *Theologie und Aufklärung*. Festschrift für Gottfried Hornig zum 65. Geb., ed. W. E. Müller and H. H. R. Schulz (Würzburg: Königshausen & Neumann, 1992), pp. 29-40, esp. 34-36.

13. Luther's translation (1545). The passive formulation, "when you are judged,"

which is so important for his theology, does not follow the Masoretic text (as reflected in the Vulgate "when you judge" [*cum iudicaveris*]), but the Septuagint (which in Latin would be *"cum iudicaris"*).

14. WA 40/II:330, 1.

15. WA 40/II:330, 12.

16. WA 40/II:330, 17.

17. WA 40/II:326, 36.

18. See Luther's sermons on Gen. 32. On Gen. 31 and 32: WA 14:433-42 (March 19, 1524); Gen. 32: WA 14:443-50 (March 20, 1524); Gen. 32: WA 24:566-81 (no date); Gen. 32-34: WA 14:450-57 (April 10, 1524). See also WA 44:93-116.

19. WA 40/II:329, 7.

20. It is "the sermon or the gospel, through which he [Christ] comes to you or you are brought to him" (WA 10/I/1:13, 21; Ein klein Unterricht . . . , 1522). The general context of the *Kleinen Unterricht* shows the close connection, if not identity, between Christology and the doctrine of the word.

21. Oswald Bayer, *Promissio. Geschichte der reformatorischen Wende in Luthers Theologie,* 2nd ed. (Darmstadt: Wissenschaftliche Buchgesellschaft, 1989), pp. 326-29, esp. 327f. See *Promissio,* p. 308: "The doctrine of the two natures is for Luther identical with the doctrine of Christ the Mediator."

22. WA 40/II:354, 3f.

23. In the doctrine of the Trinity, Augustine had already made the category of relation the main category: *On the Trinity* VIII, Introduction.

24. It has become customary to speak of "relational ontology" since Wilfried Joest, *Ontologie der Person bei Luther* (Göttingen: Vandenhoeck & Ruprecht, 1967) (see esp. pp. 14, 37, 362), and Gerhard Ebeling, *Dogmatik des christlichen Glaubens,* 3 vols. (Tübingen: Mohr Siebeck, 1979) (see esp. I, pp. 215, 219-24, 233; II, pp. 102, 330, 335, 346, 500; III, pp. 91, 142). On the abiding necessity to distinguish between "relational ontology" and "substance ontology," see below, notes 420 and 421.

25. BC 356, 3f.; BSLK 512, 25-30; WA 30/I:299, 17-22.

26. WA 31/I:511, 28 (see below, note 29).

27. See WA 56:227, 7f. (on Rom. 3:4f.); LW 25:211 (translation altered): "When God is justified, he justifies, and when he justifies, he is justified." See Bayer, *Promissio,* pp. 122f.

28. WA 31/I:511, (26-31) 30f.: *"Damnatur [verbum dei] ab iis, qui volunt iusti esse, Iustificatur a peccatoribus."* It comes to the fore especially in his preparatory notes for his interpretation of Psalm 51 (1532) that the sinful human and the God who justifies exist together within a framework of mutual recognition. This is the starting point for an idealist interpretation of Luther such as we find, for example, in Joachim Ringleben, "Die Einheit von Gotteserkenntnis und Selbsterkenntnis: Beobachtungen anhand von Luthers Römerbrief-Vorlesung," *NZSTh* 32 (1990): 125-33.

29. WA 40/I:360, 5f. (on Gal. 3:6, 1531): *"Fides est creatrix divinitatis, non in persona, sed in nobis."*

30. LW 26:227; WA 40/I:360, 25 (printed version, 1535): *non in substantia Dei, sed in nobis.*

31. WA 40/I:360, 8: *quam ut faciam deum.*

32. BC 386, 2; BSLK 560, 16f.: *alleine das Trauen und Gläuben des Herzens machet beide: Gott und Abgott.* Luther himself knows that this is a *topos:* "as I have often said" (BC 386, 2; BSLK 560, 15; the same theme comes up in WA 28:679ff., 700 [Predigten über das 5. Buch Mose, 1529]).

33. BC 386, 3; BSLK 560, 21f.

34. WA 40/I:360, 8f., 11. See LW 26:227: "Nor does God require anything greater of us than that we attribute to him his glory and his divinity" (translation altered).

35. LW 36:42 (The Babylonian Captivity of the Church, 1520) (translation altered); WA 6:516, 30-2: *"Neque enim deus . . . aliter cum hominibus unquam egit aut agit quam verbo promissionis. Rursus, nec nos cum deo unquam agere aliter possumus quam fide in verbum promissionis eius."*

36. See the Introduction: "Important Moments in the Understanding of Theology: 3. The Main Problems with the Philosophy of Science."

37. Aristotle, *Nicomachean Ethics* X, 1178a 31-b17.

38. "But virtue is determined according to this distinction. We say of them, these are rational but these are moral" (Aristotle, *Nicomachean Ethics* I, 1103a 3-5; cited according to Thomas Aquinas, *In decem libros Ethicorum Aristotelis ad Nicomachum Expositio,* ed. R. M. Spiazzi, 3rd ed. [Turin: Marietti, 1964], p. 63).

39. WA TR 2:56, 22f. (no. 1340) or 464f. (no. 2444) or 1:72f. (no. 153); LW 54:22; see WA TR 5:384, 16f. (no. 5867): "Theology ought to be practical."

40. AWA 2:137, 1f.; WA 5:85, 2f.: *"ne vita activa cum suis operibus et vita contemplativa cum suis speculationibus nos seducant."*

41. Above all, Luther's polemic is aimed at the combination of these two principles: A "practical" way of thinking like, "I have acted wickedly; therefore I will be damned," Luther regards as speculative: WA TR 2:56, 20-22 (no. 1340), 1532. See WA TR 1:72, 17-19; LW 54:22 (no. 153), 1532; WA 40/II:329, 3-332, 7 (on Ps. 51:3) and note 208.

42. The phrase *"vita passiva"* can be found in AWA 2:302, 15; 303, 5; WA 5:165, 35f.; 166, 11. See Christian Link, "Vita passiva. Rechtfertigung als Lebensvorgang," *EvTh* 44 (1984): 315-51.

43. However, we should not simply lament this as an "inconsistency"; rather, we can welcome it insofar as the use of this adjective provides an arena, so to speak, in which the definition of "practice" can be fought out. In any case, we cannot do without the verb "to do or act" (Latin: *agere;* see above, note 35) in connection with the definition of faith.

44. Eckhart's Sermon on Mary and Martha in *Meister Eckhart: Teacher and Preacher,* ed. Bernard McGinn (New York: Paulist Press, 1986), sermon 86: 338-45. See Dietmar Mieth, *Die Einheit von vita activa und vita contemplativa in den deutschen Predigten und Traktaten Meister Eckharts und bei Johannes Tauler* (Regensburg: Pustet, 1969), esp. pp. 182-233.

45. For the reference to Tauler (see below, note 46) against the *Commentaries of Dionysius Concerning Mystical Theology* (WA 5:163, 25f.): WA 5:163, 17-171, 24. Luther of course does not find the emphasis on promise *(promissio)* in Tauler.

46. WA 5:166, 11

47. WA 5:158, 3-177, 27; AWA 2:283, 1-321, 5.

48. WA 5:163, 28f.; AWA 2:296: *"Vivendo, immo moriendo et damnando fit theologus, non intelligendo, legendo aut speculando."* Luther of course is speaking hyperbolically here, for he does not exclude understanding and reading, as the parallel in WA 39/I:421, 4f. Shows.

49. We should note that Luther did not oppose the Aristotelian definition of "righteousness" as such *(Nicomachean Ethics* V), but only the importing of it into the doctrine of sin and grace. What Aristotle writes in his ethics and politics Luther happily applies to ethics. See below, section 5: "Philosophy and Theology."

50. LW 44:72 (Treatise on Good Works, 1520) (translation altered); WA 6:244, 3-6.

51. LW 35:370 (Preface to the Epistle of St. Paul to the Romans, 1522) (translation altered); WA DB 7:10, 6-8.

52. WA 40/I:41, 2-5 (The Argument of Galatians, 1531): "righteousness which comes from us is not Christian righteousness, for we do not become good through it. Christian righteousness, on the contrary, is passive, which we can only receive, where we can work nothing, but only let someone else work in us, namely God. This is not understood by the world: 'It is hidden in mystery [1 Cor. 2:7]'"; see LW 26:4.

53. LW 31:55 (translation altered); WA 1:363, 28-36 (Heidelberg Disputation, 1518): *"qui nondum est destructus, ad nihilum redactus per crucem et passionem, sibi tribuit opera et sapientiam, non autem Deo . . . Qui vero est per passiones exinanitus, iam non operatur, sed Deum in se operari et omnia agere novit . . . hoc est, quod Christus ait Johan. 3. oportet vos renasci denuo, Si renasci, ergo prius mori."*

54. See below, note 104 (on the theology of the regenerate). For pietism's appeal especially to Luther in his *Preface to the Epistle to the Romans* (1522), see esp. Martin Schmidt, "Luthers Vorrede zum Römerbrief im Pietismus," in *Wiedergeburt und neuer Mensch,* AGP 2 (Bielefeld: Luther-Verlag, 1969), pp. 299-330.

55. LW 44:78 (Treatise on Good Works, 1520) (translation altered); WA 6:248, 26f.

56. LW 35:370 (Preface to the Epistle of St. Paul to the Romans, 1522) (translation altered); WA DB 7:10, 9-12. Regarding faith, which is "always active," see Galatians 5:6.

57. LW 31:53 (Thesis 21 of the Heidelberg Disputation, 1518): *"Theologus gloriae dicit Malum bonum et bonum malum. Theologus crucis dicit id quod res est."*

58. LW 2:123; WA 42:348, (37-42) 38; 1536. See Luther's interpretation of the first commandment in the *Large Catechism* (BC 386-92; BSLK 560-72).

59. Calvin follows Luther in calling the human heart a perpetual idol factory: *"hominis ingenium . . . esse idolorum fabricam"* (*Institutes of the Christian Religion,* trans.

Ford Lewis Battles, ed. John T. McNeill, vol. XX of *The Library of Christian Classics* (Philadelphia: Westminster, 1960), I, ii, 8, p. 108.

60. LW 31:52f. (Heidelberg Disputation, 1518) (translation altered); WA 1:362, 11-13: *"Ita ut nulli iam satis sit ac prosit, qui cognoscit Deum in gloria et maiestate, nisi cognoscat eundem in humilitate et ignominia crucis."*

61. LW 37:72 (That These Words of Christ, "This is My Body," etc., Still Stand Firm Against the Fanatics, 1527) (translation altered); WA 23:157, 30-2.

62. LW 35:370 (Preface to the Epistle of St. Paul to the Romans, 1522); WA DB 7:10, 3. The parallel to this is: "the human notion and dream" (LW 35:370; WA DB 7:8, 30).

63. LW 35:370 (translation altered); WA DB 7:8, 33f.

64. Compare the first question of Biel or William of Ockham (see the Introduction: "Important Moments in the Understanding of Theology: 3. The Main Problems with the Philosophy of Science") and Thomas Aquinas, *STh* I q.Ia.2: *"Utrum sacra doctrina sit scientia"* (whether sacred theology is a science). For an English edition of the *Summa*, see *The Summa Theologiae of St. Thomas Aquinas,* literally trans. Fathers of the English Dominican Province, 2nd rev. ed. (London: Burns, Oates & Washbourne Ltd., 1920).

65. WA 9:98, 21 (Randbemerkungen zu Taulers Predigten, c. 1516). For the later period, see Luther's interpretation of Psalm 51:2 (1532): "The knowledge of God and of humans is divine wisdom and true theology" (Enarratio Psalm LI. "Miserere mei Deus . . ."; WA 40/II:327, 11) and Thesis 20 of the *Disputation Concerning Man,* 1536: "But theology from the fullness of its wisdom . . ." (LW 34:138 [translation altered]; WA 39/I:176, 5). See below, section 3.4.1.

66. See *Metaphysics* XII (on this see the Introduction: "Important Moments in the Understanding of Theology: 1.1.2. Aristotle"). Here we have to keep in mind of course that for Aristotle "nothing can be demonstrated except from its own peculiar causes" (*Posterior Analytics* I, 9 75b 37f.) so that "every science has its own principles" (Otfried Höffe, "Einführung in die Wissenschaftstheorie der Zweiten Analytik," in *Aristotles, Lehre vom Beweis oder Zweite Analytik,* PhB 11 [Hamburg: Felix Meiner, 1990], XXV). "From the standpoint of the history of science, this is an extremely significant insight. It turns away from systematic thinking or the scientific quest for a philosophical unity of all things, and prepares the way for an approach to science that focuses on the particular rather than the general" (ibid.). Of course, Höffe also emphasizes that this insight in no way implies the rejection of the first philosophy *(prima philosophia)* but presupposes that "it is a fundamental science" (ibid.). But that raises the question of how the plurality of individual sciences and their principles relate to the *one* principle of the first philosophy *(prima philosophia),* which culminates in the theologic science.

67. With regard to the distinction between "vague and indefinite experience" *(experientia vaga),* on the one hand, and "ordered experience" *(experientia ordinata),* on

the other, see Dietz Lange, *Erfahrung und die Glaubwürdigkeit des Glaubens,* HUTh 18 (Tübingen: Mohr Siebeck, 1984), p. 17.

68. Aristotle, *Metaphysics* XII:10, 1076a 3f.; the quotation within the quotation comes from Homer's *Iliad* 2:204.

69. William of Ockham, *Prologus in expositionem super VIII libros Physicorum:* "no one thing is the subject of all, but different things are subjects of different parts." The question, what is the subject of natural philosophy — and also of logic, metaphysics, mathematics, and moral philosophy — "is the same as the question, who is the king of the world, because, just as no one is king of the world, but someone is king of one realm and another is king of another realm, so also the same holds true for the subjects of the different parts of science" (William of Ockham, *Texte zur Theorie der Erkenntnis und der Wissenschaft,* German/Latin edition, ed. and trans. with commentary by Ruedi Imbach [Reclam 8239] [Stuttgart: Reclam Verlag, 1984], p. 202).

70. We will come back to this when we discuss the relation between philosophy and theology (see below, section 5).

71. When Luther, in his definition of the subject matter of theology, makes a sharp distinction between the content of theology and that of the secular sciences and the arts (WA 40/II:328, 1-9), he reflects the influence of Ockham (see above, note 69).

72. *STh* I q. 1.

73. *STh* I q. 1a. 2.

74. *STh* I q. 1a. 4: "It is therefore more contemplative than practical."

75. *STh* I q. 1a 7 corp.

76. *STh* I q. 1a 5: "Now insofar as sacred theology is a practical science, its aim is eternal happiness."

77. See above, note 65.

78. WA 40/III:63, 17f: *"Theologia est infinita sapientia, quia nunquam potest edisci."*

79. WA 40/III:63, 18-64, 7.

80. Here it is necessary to distinguish between an individual (individuating) experience and a generalizing one. For the latter, see Aristotle, *Posterior Analytics* II, 19.

81. However, see below, note 335 and 336.

82. See above, section 2.1.

83. See, for example, WA 40/II:327, 28 (sensory knowledge: *cognitio sensitiva*).

84. WA 40/II:328, 12.

85. WA 40/II:326, 37: "I feel, I experience. For that is what the Hebrew word really means."

86. Plato, *The Republic,* 379-83. See the Introduction: "Important Moments in the Understanding of Theology: 1. Christian Theology between Metaphysics and Mythology."

87. *The Republic,* 380e, trans. H. P. Lee (London: Penguin, 1955), p. 119.

88. *The Republic,* 381a, c.

89. Aristotle, *Metaphysics,* XII:9, 1074b 32f.

90. Aristotle, *Metaphysics*, XII:9, 1074b 33-35.

91. WA TR 1:57, 44f. (no. 135): *"Primum ens videt se ipsum; si extra se videret, videret mundi molestias. In eo loco tacite negat Deum."* See WA TR 1:73f. (no. 155), esp. 73:22-4. See below, note 202.

92. WA TR 1:73, 32 (no. 155) (translation altered).

93. See the formulations in WA 18:706, note 2.

94. WA TR 1:73, 19-74, 16. Against Aristotle (*Metaphysics* XII:7, 1073a 4f.: "There is a being which is eternal and immovable and separate from sensible things"), Luther thinks of God this way: If God does not see the calamities external to himself, then he is not real; he is a God who "does not care about us" (WA TR 1:74, 11), a God who "sleeps" and "snores" (WA 18:706, 22f.; LW 33:171 in context; see LW 33:291; WA 18:785, 7-9); he is a God who can be compared with a drunken maid who should be watching the child but who does not notice it fall out of the cradle (WA TR 1:73, 29-31 and LW 34:143; WA 39/I:179, 30-4). Let Aristotle deny the "immortality of the soul and divine providence" (WA TR 1:73, 25).

95. *Metaphysics* VI:1 and *Topics* 145a 15f.

96. See further, Oswald Bayer, "Glauben und Wissenschaft," in *Autorität und Kritik. Zu Hermeneutik und Wissenschaftstheorie* (Tübingen: Mohr Siebeck, 1991), pp. 136f. (Wissenschaft und Theodizee).

97. "Allocutio, qua in Collegio Denkendorfino A. 1741 d. 24. Apr. valedixit Johann Albrecht Bengel," in Eberhard Nestle, *Bengel as Gelehrter. Ein Bild für unsere Tage; mit neuen Mitteilungen aus seinem handschriftlichen Nachlaß* (Tübingen, 1893), pp. 103-6, esp. 105). In the tradition of Bengel, Magnus Friedrich Roos (1727-1803) writes that Philipp Friedrich Hiller (1699-1769), "following the instructions of Dr. Luther himself, became an enlightened theologian through *prayer, meditation,* and *spiritual attack,* which many people today despise and neglect." Here, life and doctrine are intertwined. Roos emphasizes "that true Christian worship requires above all a right and thorough understanding of the truth, which God has revealed for our salvation. . . . People who are really committed to pure evangelical doctrine must experience its healing effect in their soul." Magnus Friedrich Roos, *Christliches Haus-Buch, welches Morgen- und Abendandachten . . . enthält* (Th. 1.2, Stuttgart, 1783), V-VI.

98. Johann Albrecht Bengel, "Wolgemeinter Vorschlag / wie ein Cursus Theologicus in vier bis fünf Jahren zu verrichten seyn möchte, auf wiederholtes Begehren entworfen (1742)," in Oscar Wächter, *Johann Albrecht Bengel, Lebensabriß, Character, Briefe und Aussprüche; nebst einem Anhang aus seinen Predigten und Erbauungsstunden nach handschriftlichen Mitteilungen* (Stuttgart, 1865), pp. 146-49, esp. 146 (§2f.): "Experienced theologians praise three things: *oratio, meditatio, tentatio.* We could also reverse the order: *Tentatio,* a person is roused initially by mild [spiritual] attacks that make the person search, and that in turn leads to prayer. *Tentatio* is not within our power but it will appear soon enough. *Oratio* needs to be practiced and learned in your own room. *Meditatio* is not as subtle as the other two; here we can really serve each other with honest and faithful advice."

99. Bengel stood in the tradition of Matthias Hafenreffer whose *Loci Theologici* (1st ed., Tübingen, 1600), which reached as far as Sweden, was the standard theological textbook in the Lutheran province of Württemberg for over a century. Its introduction is titled "Prolegomena for a felicitous study of theology, both for beginning and advanced students," although this does not appear in 1st ed. but, for example, in 5th ed. (Stuttgart, 1662), pp. 1-22. It is organized around the triad *oratio, meditatio, tentatio* (and Ps. 119!). See also Johann Valentin Andreae, *Christianopolis*, original text 1619, trans. David Samuel Georgi, 1741, intro. and ed. R. v. Dülmen (Stuttgart: Calwer, 1972), §77 *(theologia practica: orare, meditari, tentari)*, after §76 *(theologia scholastica)*.

100. Spener writes with regard to the method of studying theology described by Luther's triad *oratio, meditatio, tentatio,* that "until now, normally all our theologians followed him in recognizing that these things are necessary for theologians." Philipp Jacob Spener, *Die allgemeine Gottesgelehrtheit aller glaubigen Christen und rechtschaffenen Theologen,* vol. 1 (Frankfurt, 1680), p. 187; see vol. 2 (Frankfurt, 1680), p. 97. I thank Johannes Wallmann for this helpful reference.

101. See for example August Hermann Francke, "Einfältiger Unterricht," in *Öffentliches Zeugnis vom Werk/Wort und Dienst Gottes,* vol. 2 (Halle, 1702/3), 7. Also Erhard Peschke, *Studien zur Theologie August Hermann Franckes,* vol. 2 (Berlin: Evangelische Verlag, 1966), pp. 114-17.

102. See Johannes Wallmann, "Spener und Dilfeld. Der Hintergrund des ersten pietistischen Streites," in *Theologie in Geschichte und Kunst. Walter Elliger zum 65. Geburtstag,* ed. S. Herrmann and O. Söhngen (Witten: Luther-Verlag, 1968), pp. 214-35.

103. Hegel was also suspicious of the pectoral theology of Tholuck (see Georg Wilhelm Friedrich Hegel, "Enzyklopädie der philosophischen Wissenschaften im Grundrisse [1830], Vorrede zur 3. Ausgabe," in *Werke in 20 Bänden* (Theorie-Werkausgabe), vol. 8 (Frankfurt: Suhrkamp, 1970), pp. 32-38. Johann August Wilhelm Neander (1789-1850) used the phrase "the heart makes the theologian" *(pectus est, quod theologum facit)* as a motto for his book *Allgemeine Geschichte der christlichen Religion und Kirche,* 6 vols. (Hamburg, 1826-52).

104. See Wallmann, "Spener und Dilfeld," p. 220, note 29.

105. Johann Salomo Semler, *Erster Anhang zu dem Versuch einer Anleitung zur Gottesgelersamkeit, enthaltend eine historische und theol. Erleuterung des alten Ausspruchs "oratio, meditatio, tentatio faciunt theologum," in einer Zuschrift an seine Zuhörer, worin er seine Vorlesungen anzeigt* (Halle, 1758, 174 pages).

106. Semler, *Erster Anhang,* p. 89.

107. WA TR 3:312, 11-13 (no. 3425): "What makes the theologian: 1) the grace of the Spirit *(gratia Spiritus);* 2) trial and spiritual attack *(tentatio);* 3) experience *(experientia);* 4) opportunity *(occasio);* 5) diligent reading *(sedula lectio);* 6) knowledge of the liberal arts *(bonarum artium cognitio)."*

108. Semler, *Erster Anhang,* pp. 56-61, 67-69, 83-89, 127.

109. What Luther managed to keep together broke apart later into historical

scholarship and private piety or spirituality. See the discussion of the problem in the introduction to part two: The Problem.

110. See below, note 235.

111. But see Gerhard Ebeling, *Studium der Theologie. Eine enzyklopädische Orientierung* (Tübingen: Mohr Siebeck, 1975), pp. 176-78 (epilogue). Rolf Schäfer, "Oratio, meditatio, tentatio. Drei Hinweise Luthers auf den Gebrauch der Bibel," in *Gotteslehre und kirchliche Praxis. Ausgewählte Aufsätze,* ed. U. Köpf and R. Rittner (Tübingen: Mohr Siebeck, 1991), pp. 245-51.

112. We find these in the *oratio* and *meditatio*. However, the omission of the *tentatio* — or its vaporization into intellectual doubt — makes the two common elements qualitatively different. See below, note 212; also part two: section 7.3.

113. See above, note 103. Pectoral theology, a theology of the heart, emphasizes the emotions in contrast to the rationalist theology of neo-orthodoxy.

114. This is evident in Barth even at the point where he seems to come closest to Luther in his "introduction to evangelical theology." See Karl Barth, *Evangelical Theology: An Introduction* (London: Weidenfeld & Nicolson, 1968; German original: Zurich: EVZ-Verlag, 1962), pp. 133-44 (§12: Temptation). See below, note 339.

115. See Eberhard Jüngel, *Glauben und Verstehen. Zum Theologiebegriff Rudolf Bultmanns. Sitzungsberichte der Heidelberger Akademie der Wissenschaften, Philosophisch-historische Klasse* (Jahrgang 1985, Bericht 1) (Heidelberg: Winter, 1985).

116. Jüngel does not touch on this matter in his work. Yet the key to answering some "critical questions" that Jüngel addresses to Bultmann lies right here (Jüngel, *Glauben und Verstehen,* pp. 68-78).

117. Thomas Aquinas, *STh* I q.1 a.7): "But in sacred science all things are treated under the aspect of God; either because they are God himself; or because they refer to God as their beginning and end. Hence it follows that God is in very truth the object of this science."

118. Wolfhart Pannenberg, *Wissenschaftstheorie und Theologie* (Frankfurt: Suhrkamp, 1973), esp. pp. 299-348. Translated by Francis McDonagh under the title *Theology and Philosophy of Science* (London: Dartman, Longman & Todd, 1976), esp. pp. 297-345 (Chapter 5: "Theology as the Science of God"). Pannenberg, p. 298, refers expressly to the *"sub ratione dei"* (see above, note 117).

119. For Schleiermacher's distinctions, see part two: section 5: "Theology and Methodology."

120. Semler, *Erster Anhang,* p. 20.

121. See below, note 285.

122. LW 33:28 (The Bondage of the Will, 1525); WA 18:609, 5; see below, section 3.4.2.

123. See WA 24:17, 29-18, 16 with the paragraph about the twofold clarity of scripture in *The Bondage of the Will* (LW 33:28; WA 18:609, 4-12).

124. See above, note 123.

125. See Gottfried Hornig, *Die Anfänge der historisch-kritischen Theologie. Johann*

Salomo Semlers Schriftverständnis und seine Stellung zu Luther (Göttingen: Vandenhoeck & Ruprecht, 1961). We have to consider in this context the evidence presented by Wallmann, that Semler stands mainly in the tradition of Melanchthon. See Johannes Wallmann, "Johann Salomo Semler und der Humanismus," in *Aufklärung und Humanismus,* ed. Richard Toellner (Heidelberg: Schneider, 1980), pp. 201-17, esp. 207f.

126. LW 34:285 (WA 50:658, 29–659, 4). This is the only place in the whole of Luther's writings where this triadic formula appears. The reference to it in WA 48:276: *"Meditatio, Tentatio, Oratio* make a theologian" is not a second occurrence, but merely "an excerpt from Luther's preface" (idem.). But Luther uses the idea of the triad elsewhere. See LW 54:143; WA TR 2:67, 32-40 (no. 1353).

127. Martin Nicol fails to consider this in his *Meditation bei Luther* (Göttingen: Vandenhoeck & Ruprecht, 1984).

128. LW 34:285 (WA 50:659, 1-4).

129. LW 34:327-38; WA 54:(179-87) 176; see below, esp. note 151.

130. See WA TR 1:141-45 (no. 349).

131. See Jörg Baur, "Luther und die Philosophie," *NZSTh* 26 (1984): 13-28.

132. See below, section 2.

133. Luther's instruction prompted the development of a new literary genre. Representative of this is Johann Gerhard, *Methodus studii theologici publicis praelectionibus in Academia Jenensi Anno 1617 exposita* (Jena, 1620).

134. Luther's translation of the Bible strengthened the use of the German word *"Auslegung"* (interpretation). To understand the way in which it was used, see *Deutsches Wörterbuch,* ed. Jakob and Wilhelm Grimm, vol. 1 (Munich, 1854; reprint 1984), pp. 907f. See also WA 31/I:(1-31) 5, 35-6, 2 (Ps. 119:15), 10, 34f. (Ps. 119:48), 15, 5f. (Ps. 119:78), 17, 34-18, 2 (Ps. 119:99), 25, 17-19 (Ps. 119:148). See below, section 3.4.2, esp. note 242.

135. We need to give attention to the writing that appeared in the same year as the preface, *On the Councils and the Church* (*Von den Konziliis und Kirchen;* LW 41:3-178; WA 50:509-653) in order to understand the wider context. See below, note 174 and also notes 351-53.

136. For the editorial history of Luther's works, see Julius Köstlin and Gustav Kawerau, *Martin Luther. Sein Leben und seine Schriften,* 2 vols. (Berlin: Duncker, 5th ed., 1903), pp. 428-30. See also *Der Briefwechsel des Justus Jonas. Gesammelt und bearbeitet von Gustav Kawerau,* ed. Historische Commission der Provinz Sachsen, vol. 1 (Hildesheim: Georg Olms, 1964; reprint of the Halle ed., 1884), pp. 198f. WA 38:133, 8–134, 10 (1533); WABR 7:433, 36-64 (no. 3038; Letter from Capito, June 13, 1536); 435-37 (for background); WABR 8:99, 5-8 (no. 3162; Letter to Capito, July 9, 1537); LW 50:171; WA TR 4:84, 36–85, 6 (no. 4025; Sept. 29, 1538); LW 54:311 esp.: "Men [printers] in Augsburg and Wittenberg urged Luther to allow them to publish his collected works. He replied, 'I'll never consent to this proposal of yours. I'd rather that all my books would disappear and the Holy Scriptures alone would be read. Otherwise we'll rely on such writings and let the Bible go.'" For more, see below, note 139.

137. As we assess Luther's dismissal of the plan, we should take into account the rhetorical *topos* of modesty.

138. See the list in note 150 below.

139. LW 54:274; WA TR 3:622, 36-623, 1 (no. 3797), 1538: *"29. Martii [1538] Argentinenses petierunt veniam et catalogum certum librorum Lutheri in ordinem et tomos redigendorum."*

140. LW 54:274f.; WA TR 3:623, 2-7: *"Respondit Lutherus: Ego vellem omnes meos libros extinctos, ut tantum sacrae literae in biblia diligenter legerentur. Denn von den Büchern fellet man auf ander, sicut in primitiva ecclesia factum est, ubi a bibliae lectione ad Eusebii, deinde Ieronymi, deinde Gregorii, postremo scholasticorum et philosophorum lectionem se verterunt. Also wird's uns auch gehen."* See the following passage from Luther's Genesis commentary (on Gen. 19:29), which probably dates from the same time: "For this reason I myself hate my books and often wish that they would perish, because I fear that they may detain the readers and lead them away from reading Scripture itself, which alone is the fount of all wisdom. Besides, I am frightened by the example of the former age. After those who had devoted themselves to sacred studies had come upon commentaries of human beings, they not only spent most of their time reading the ancient theologians, but eventually they also busied themselves with Aristotle, Averroes, and others, who later on gave rise to the Thomases, the Scotuses, and similar monstrosities. For this reason books should be limited in number, and among these books only those which lead the reader into a correct understanding of the Scripture should be given approval. And in the books of the fathers themselves we should value nothing that is not in agreement with Scripture; it alone should remain the judge and teacher of all books. To be sure, it is profitable to hear the confessors, whether they are dead and teach in their writings or are living and teach by word of mouth. Nevertheless, there should be a limit. And one should always observe this rule: that we read those who expound Scripture" (LW 3:305f.; WA 43:93, 40-94, 14).

141. See WA 50:657f. (LW 34:283f.) and WA 50:660f. (LW 34:287f.) with WA 38:133, 8-134, 2 (Preface to "Catalogus oder Register aller Bücher und Schriften D. Martini Lutheri durch ihn ausgelassen . . . ," 1533). "For my part, I would like to see all [my books] destroyed, for my sole purpose in writing was to bring Holy Scripture and divine wisdom to light. . . ." See WA 10/II:329, 20f.: "Let all my books perish! – that is my earnest plea to any booksellers who may happen to hear me" (1522) (see WA 38:133, note 1).

142. LW 34:283; WA 50:657, 12f.

143. LW 54:275; WA TR 3:623, 7-9 (no. 3797), 1538: *"Propter historiam mallem illa conservari, ut homines viderent ordinem et congressum cum papa, qui olim formidabilis, nunc suspendibilis est"*; [see WA TR 3:588, 23-7 (no. 3749)]. See above, note 140. On Luther's victory over the pope by mouth and pen, see *A Sincere Admonition by Martin Luther to All Christians to Guard against Insurrection and Rebellion* (LW 45:57-74; WA 8:676-87; 1522). Recollections about the beginning of the gospel (*"Initio evangelii . . ."* LW 54:341f.; WA TR 4:316, 28 [no. 4446], 1539) are found frequently in the Table Talk of 1539: WA TR

4:316, 19-26 (no. 4445); 316, 27-317, 9 (no. 4446); LW 54:341; WA TR 4:320, 2-4 (no. 4451); LW 54:342; WA TR 4:320, 30-321, 5 (no. 4452); 321, 5-13 (no. 4453); 321, 28-33 (no. 4454); 339, 9-23 (no. 4487); LW 54:346. They all talk about the fight against the pope.

144. WA TR 4:311, 25-312, 1 (no. 4436), 1539: "They want to stop the spread of the Gospel among us *(cursum euangelii)* [2 Thess. 3:1], but that is not within our power, just as we cannot prevent the grass and the flowers growing in the fields." See also LW 2:334; WA 42:501, 4-7 ("the fate of the word") regarding Genesis 13:4.

145. WA TR 5:168, 18-169, 7 (no. 5468); 317, 11-318, 5 (no. 5677); LW 54:476. See WA TR 1:29, 7-10 (no. 76), 1531 and WA TR 4:491, 6f. (no. 4777). See also Oswald Bayer, "Vom Wunderwerk, Gottes Wort recht zu verstehen. Luthers Letzter Zettel," *Kerygma und Dogma* 37 (1991): 258-79.

146. Luther, quoting Statius, calls the Bible the "divine Aeneid" (WA TR 5:168, note 7). It is the book that records what people experienced and achieved and as such it can be the source of new experiences and achievements. It contains not only the things of the past but also of the future. Regarding its inexhaustibility, see Luther's polished words from the Leipzig Debate: ". . . divine Scripture, whose wisdom is greater than the capacity of the entire human race" (WA 2:309, 35f.). See the marginal note on Lombard (1509/10): "For the wisdom of this Scripture is greater than the capacity of any human genius" (WA 9:66, 9f.).

147. WA 38:134, 5-8 (see above, note 141). See also LW 54:440; WA TR 5:204, 30-32 (no. 5511).

148. See *Martini Lutheri praefatio in postillas,* 1527 (WABR 4:190-92 [no. 1093]); *Vorrede zum Catalogus oder Register aller Bücher und Schriften,* 1533 (WA 38:133f.); *Preface to the Wittenberg Edition of Luther's German Writings,* 1539 (LW 34:283-88; WA 50:657-61); *Vorrede zur Hauspostille,* 1544 (WA 52:1f.); *Preface to the [First Volume of the] Complete Edition of Luther's Latin Writings,* 1545 (LW 34:327-38; WA 54:179-87); *Preface to the Second Volume of the Wittenberg Edition of Luther's German Writings,* the substance of which is accredited to Luther, 1548 (WA 54:468-77).

149. These kinds of prefaces are different from the prefaces written for dedications. For the latter, see Helmar Junghans, "Die Widmungsvorrede bei Martin Luther," in AWA 5:39-65.

150. LW 54:274-75 (no. 3797), 1538; WA TR 3:622, 35-623, 9; LW 54:311 (no. 4025), 1538; WA TR 4:84, 36-85, 6; 4:87, 26-34 (no. 4029), 1538; LW 54:361 (no. 4691), 1539; WA TR 4: 432, 13-25; 691, 22-5 (no. 5168), 1540; WA TR 5:661, 21-662, 2 (no. 6439); 662, 23-665, 2 (no. 6442).

151. WA 54:187, 3-7 (English based on Bayer's translation; see LW 34:338; texts cited are Acts 12:24; 19:20; Rev. 12:12; and Phil. 1:6): *"ora pro incremento verbi adversus satanam, quia potens et malus est, nunc etiam furentissimus et saevissimus, sciens, quoniam breve tempus habet et regnum sui papae periclitatur. Confirmet autem Deus hoc in nobis, quod operatus est, et perficiat opus suum, quod incepit in nobis, ad gloriam suam. Amen."*

152. See above, notes 145f.

153. *Zweite Vorrede auf den Psalter* (1528): WA DB 10/I:98, 22-100, 2.

154. See LW 35:256 (Prefaces to the Old Testament: Preface to the Psalter 1545/ 1528); WA DB 10/I:104, 5, 9.

155. WA 38:134, 6f. See above, note 147.

156. Johann Georg Hamann reads "his own life's history" "in the history of the Jewish people" (Johann Georg Hamann, "Gedanken über meinen Lebenslauf," in *Sämtliche Werke*, ed. J. Nadler, vol. 1 [Vienna: Thomas-Morus-Press (Herder), 1950], p. 40). "If anyone wants to compare the map of Israel's journeys with my life, they will see how much they have in common" (p. 42). Of course we should not overlook the historical difference between Hamann and Luther. Nevertheless, the point of agreement is that both see their lives interpreted by scripture and it is this that enables them to make the connection between individuality and universality.

157. Hans-Joachim Kraus, *Psalms 60–150: A Commentary*, trans. Hilton C. Oswald (Minneapolis: Augsburg Fortress, 1989), p. 414: "Psalm 119 is a collection of statements of the individual Torah piety of postexilic times."

158. Nowhere else in the biblical writings do we find as many nouns used for God's word as in this psalm: precepts, commandments, law, testimonies, statutes, etc.

159. WA 8:140, 11f. (see below, note 164). See WA 4:311, note 2. For more on the daily offices mentioned by Luther, see: *Leiturgia. Handbuch des evangelischen Gottesdienstes*, ed. K. F. Müller and W. Blankenburg, vol. 3 (Kassel: J. Stauda-Verlag, 1956), pp. 160, 244f.

160. "This phrase, which is common in Luther research and in Lutheran theology, that the church is a 'creature of the word' *(creatura verbi)*, cannot be found in the index to Luther's works in German" (Otto Hermann Pesch, "Luther und die Kirche," *Lutherjahrbuch* 52 (1985): 127, note 28). WA 6:560, 33–561, 2; LW 36:107 ["the church, being a creation"] has to be added to those Luther texts mentioned by Pesch that come close to this phrase. See especially WABR 5:591 (lines 44-57, esp. line 55: "The church [*Christenheit*] is a creature, made by God's word").

161. WA 8:140, 18-21 (see below, note 164). See also the "two parts" of the epilogue to the Psalter of 1525 (to that, see below, note 354).

162. Luther to Karlstadt, Oct. 14, 1518, from Augsburg: WABR 1:217, 62 (no. 100). For the context and importance of this testimony, see Bayer, *Promissio*, p. 183.

163. WA 35:235-48; see LW 53:304f. The German hymn writer Nicolaus Selnecker replaces the reference to pope and Turk with the devil (*Evangelisches Gesangbuch* [Stuttgart: Gesangbuchverlag, 1996], #207:4). [*Lutheran Book of Worship* (Minneapolis: Augsburg Publishing House, and Philadelphia: Board of Publication, Lutheran Church in America, 1978), #230:1, "curb those who by deceit or sword . . . ," drops the reference to the devil.]

164. WA 8:129-204 (Von der Beicht, ob die der Papst Macht habe zu gebieten. . . . Der hundert und achtzehend Psalm [Ps. 119], 1521), esp. 133, A. [The treatise was dedicated to Francis von Sickingen; for the letter of dedication, see LW 48:244-47. See also LW 48:225, 231, 254.]

165. On this, see Heinrich Bornkamm, *Luther in Mid-Career 1521-1530*, ed. with

foreword by Karin Bornkamm, trans. E. Theodore Bachmann (Philadelphia: Fortress Press, 1983), pp. 609-30. See Martin Brecht, *Shaping and Defining the Reformation 1521-1532*, trans. James L. Schaff (Minneapolis: Fortress Press, 1990), pp. 325-34, 361-68.

166. The interpretation of 1529 picks up the formulations of 1521, for the most part literally, and explains them in greater detail.

167. WA 31/I:1-33. Compare Luther's words here, "that God would preserve us in his word," with the words of his hymn, "Lord, keep us steadfast in your word." (See above, note 163).

168. WA 31/I:3, 23-27.

169. See above, note 145.

170. Luther's final note is indirectly a document about his teaching on the three basic orders in creation *(Dreiständelehre)*. In the quote from Virgil *(Georgics/ Bucolics)*, Cicero, and Statius (in reference to Virgil's *Aeneid*), the economic order (the household), the political order (civil government), and the ecclesiastical order (the church) are mentioned. See Bayer, "Vom Wunderwerk," 268-71.

171. See better LW 33:61f.; WA 18:626, 8-40 (The Bondage of the Will, 1525).

172. See above, note 168.

173. WA 31/I:11, 9f.

174. LW 41:164f.; WA 50:641, 35–642, 21.

175. WA 31/I:31, 1-3.

176. WA 31/I:28, 5.

177. WA 31/I:28, 1-3.

178. WA 31/I:29, 1-4 (on Ps. 119:174). Luther fought against the spiritualists as much as against Rome. Psalm 119:113 gives us an excellent example of how he identifies specific contemporary enemies of God's word *(Die gantze Heilige Schrifft Deudsch,* Wittenberg 1545): "Ich hasse Fladdergeister/Und liebe dein Gesetze" ("I hate the high-flying spirits, but I love your law").

179. LW 34:285; WA 50:659, 3f.

180. LW 34:285f. (translation altered); WA 50:659, 5-21. Passages in the section *"Oratio"* that are not referenced all come from this opening citation. For a parallel to this as well as for a summary of what Luther has in mind overall with the triadic formula *oratio, meditatio, tentatio,* see WA TR 2:67, 32-40 (no. 1353), 1532: "We should not measure, judge, understand or interpret the Holy Scripture according to our reason, but we should consider it carefully and meditate on it prayerfully. Thus temptations and Satan are further reason for us to learn to understand it little by little through practice and experience; otherwise we will not understand anything of it, in spite of the fact that we hear and read it. The Holy Spirit must be the only master and teacher who instructs us, and the student should not be ashamed to learn from this teacher. When I am being attacked spiritually or am being tried and tested [*angefochten*], I take hold of a text or a passage in the Bible that shows me Jesus Christ, that he died for me, and then I am comforted."

Notes to Pages 43-45

181. See with WA 50:639, 20 ("Esopus Fabeln") WA 51:243 note 1 and below note 187.

182. See with WA 50:659, 20 ("Marcolfus") WA 50:288, note 3, WA 28:500 (note to 454, 10 or 37) and WA 49:800, 10.

183. See below, note 185. [German has two words for fools: *Narren* (Rom. 1:22) and *Toren* (Ps. 14:1). English makes no distinction.]

184. See the next note, esp. WA 18:609, 8f. (*sentire, cognoscere, credere* = to experience, to know, to believe).

185. LW 33:28 (translation altered); WA 18:609, 4-12: "*Duplex e[s]t claritas scripturae, sicut et duplex obscuritas, Una externa in verbi ministerio posita, altera in cordis cognitione sita, Si de interna claritate dixeris, nullus homo unum iota in scripturis videt, nisi qui spiritum Dei habet, omnes habent obscuratum cor, ita, ut si etiam dicant et norint proferre omnia scripturae, nihil tamen horum sentiant aut vere cognoscant, neque credunt Deum, nec sese esse creaturas Dei, nec quicquam aliud, iuxta illud Psal. 13. Dixit insipiens in corde suo, Deus nihil est [Ps. 14:1]. Spiritus enim requiritur ad totam scripturam et ad quamlibet eius partem intelligendam.*" It is clear from the phrase "darkened heart" (*obscuratum cor*) (see Rom. 1:21), that Luther understands the Psalm 14:1 passage against the background of Romans 1:18-20. Paul uses Psalm 14 (or Ps. 53) to articulate his radical understanding of sin (Rom. 3:10-12), which Luther also shares. Luther's use of Psalm 14:1 stands in stark contrast to that of Anselm in his *Proslogion,* ch. 2ff., translated and introduced by Thomas Williams under the title *Anselm, Monologion and Proslogion with the Replies of Gaunilo and Anselm* (Indianapolis/Cambridge: Hackett Publishing Company, 1996) [hereafter cited as *Proslogion*], pp. 99ff.

186. WA 40/II:328, 8f.: "*Theologia non pertinent ad hanc vitam, sed est alterius vitae.*" See the *Disputation Concerning Man,* Theses 3, 14, 19, 23, 35; LW 34:137-39; WA 39/I:175-77.

187. LW 13:199 (translation altered); WA 51:242, 36f. (in the context of 242, 1-243, 35) on Psalm 101:5 (1534/35). Luther is not making a general judgment; what he says does not apply for example to the ancient authors who speak contemptuously about marriage; their words are "the words of blind heathen" (LW 45:36; WA 10/II:293, 8; The Estate of Marriage, 1522). "Now observe that when that clever harlot, our natural reason (which the pagans followed in trying to be most clever), takes a look at married life . . ." (LW 45:39; WA 10/II:295, 16f.). Luther refers to the *Attic Nights* of Aulus Gellius, I vi, 1f. (noted by Reinhard Schwarz, "Beobachtungen zu Luthers Bekanntschaft mit antiken Dichtern und Geschichtsschreibern," *Lutherjahrbuch* 54 [1987]: 20, note 51).

188. LW 34:137, *Disputation Concerning Man,* Thesis 4; WA 39/I:175.

189. See with LW 34:285 ("eternal life"; WA 50:659, 6), *Disputation Concerning Man* (1536), LW 34:137-40, and the interpretation of Psalm 51 (1532), especially WA 40/II:327, 11f. as an interpretation of 328, 8f. See also WA TR 1:27, 19-26 (no. 76): Luther speaks about the power of Holy Scripture, "which far exceeds all the other arts of philosophers and lawyers. Good and necessary as they are, they are as good as dead when compared with God's word and as far as eternal life is concerned. Therefore we should not look at the Bible in the same way as we look at lawyers' books and the other arts.

For any one who does not go beyond reason and deny the self will certainly not properly understand Holy Scripture. The world cannot understand it because it does not know or understand anything at all about mortification and the killing of the old Adam, things that are clearly spoken about in God's word."

190. LW 19:54f.; WA 19:206, 31-207, 13 [on Jonah 1:5], 1526; Luther emphasizes that "reason is unable to identify God properly; it cannot ascribe the Godhead to the One who is entitled to it exclusively. It knows that there is a God, but it does not know who or which is the true God. It shares the experience of the Jews during Christ's sojourn on earth. When John the Baptist bore witness of his presence in their midst, they were aware that Christ was among them and that he was moving about them; but they did not know who it was. It was incredible to them that Jesus of Nazareth was the Christ. Thus reason also plays blind man's buff with God; it consistently fumbles in the dark and misses the mark. It calls that God which is not God and fails to call him God who really is God. Reason would do neither the one nor the other if it were not conscious of the existence of God or if it really knew who or what God is. Therefore it rushes in clumsily and assigns the name God and ascribes divine honor to its own idea of God. Thus reason never finds the true God, but it finds the devil or its own concept of God, ruled by the devil. So there is a vast difference between knowing that there is a God and knowing who or what God is. Nature knows the former — it is inscribed in everybody's heart; the latter is taught only by the Holy Spirit" (translation altered).

191. LW 19:55; WA 19:207, 4.

192. Johann Georg Hamann renewed Luther's diagnosis and protest in the context of the Enlightenment; in his *"Letzten Blatt"* (Last Paper), he emphasized the paradigmatic character of God's descent into humble humanity to counteract the philosophical ascent to a "supreme rational being." See Oswald Bayer and Christian Knudsen, *Kreuz und Kritik. Johann Georg Hamanns Letztes Blatt. Text und Interpretation,* BHTh 66 (Tübingen: Mohr Siebeck, 1983), esp. pp. 63 (text), 69-82 (interpretation).

193. This *topos* has fixed elements but their constellation changes. See WA 9:98, 33f. (marginal note to Tauler's sermons, 1516): "It ascends into heaven with Lucifer and will perish with him." Later we read of the natural human quest for God: "It does not grasp the God who is concealed behind a mask or clothed in the form of a person to accommodate himself to us, but it lays hold of God in his absolute majesty" (WA 40/II:330, 10-13 on Ps. 51:3, 1532). See below, note 209. See further WA 10/I/2:297, 9f. (on John 3:1-15); WA 23:732, 26 ("to ascend and to seek above"); WA 25:106, 29f.; LW 16:54-56 (on Isa. 4:6, 1532/4); WA 29:672, 1-5; WA 45:496, 2-14; LW 24:39f. (on John 14:5f., 1538).

194. WA 9:406 (13-22), 17-20. See Bayer, *Promissio,* p. 311.

195. WA TR 2:56, 26-57, 2 (no. 1340), 1532: "In sum, all skills, both domestic and political, have been lost because of speculation. . . . Thus Christian the goldsmith probably got involved in that speculation hoping to make a considerable profit from his wares. . . ." See WA TR 2:57, 28-33, esp. 31f.: "A speculative person may have good

ideas and plans, but when it comes to putting them into practice, it is a different story."

196. Luther claims to be able "to discuss it [faith], if not more elegantly, certainly more to the point, than those learned and skillful disputants have previously done, who have not even understood what they were discussing" (LW 31:344, The Freedom of a Christian, 1520 [translation altered]; WA 7:49, 18f.). See WA TR 2:468, 11 (no. 2457), 1532: "However, the scholastic teachers do not even have a knowledge of the catechism."

197. LW 37:72 (translation altered); WA 23:157, 30-32.

198. WA TR 1:72, 33f. in the context of the complete Table Talk (no. 153, 1532): "The mystical theology of Dionysius is nothing more than mere fantasy and lies, just as Plato also fabricates stories. . . ." For Luther's reference to the *mystica theologia* of the Areopagite and his refutation of it (LW 25:287; WA 56:299, 28), see Bayer, *Promissio*, pp. 60f. and Link, *Vita passiva*, p. 323; see below, section 3.4.3, esp. note 312.

199. WA 9:448, 34-36 (Sermo de testamento of Christi, 1520): "*ut humana natura certius comprehenderet deum et ad unum aliquod signum defigeretur, quo comprehenderet deum, ne vagaretur aut fluctuaret in suis speculationibus.*"

200. WA TR 2:57, 19-21 (no. 1340).

201. "*Speculatio*" is the term most frequently used in the scholarly discussion of the academy. Apart from Gabriel Biel's *Collectorium*, which Luther studied, see Thomas Aquinas, *STh* I q.1 a.1, 4.

202. WA TR 1:57, 44f. (no. 135, 1531) gives us Luther's report and judgment on *Metaphysics* XII: "The first being sees [only] itself; if it looked outside itself it would see the misery of the world. In that passage he [Aristotle] denies God." See also WA TR 1:73, 31f. (no. 155, 1532): "I say the opposite: If God only looks at himself, he is the most miserable being." The connection with Luther's polemic against speculation would be clear even if the two Table Talk discourses (no. 135 and no. 155) had been handed down to us separately (but see WA TR 1:73, note 1). For a parallel see LW 33:291; WA 18:785, 7-9 (in relation to lines 5f.: "Here even the greatest minds have stumbled and fallen, denying the existence of God"). The *Disputation Concerning Man*, LW 34:143; WA 39/I:179, 29-34 (1536), speaks polemically against the God of metaphysics, who is completely self-absorbed and does not address humans in a sensory and physical way. Here Luther has in mind especially the God of Aristotle. See also WA TR 1:73, 29-31: "What sort of a God is that, who does not accept us and does not care for us?"; 74, 10f. (no. 155). See above, notes 91-94.

203. WA 4:608, 32-609, 1. Since God is the God who is with us, Immanuel, Luther regards reason *(ratio)* as "something divine, so to speak" *(divinum quiddam)* (see above, note 188) in the very area in which Aristotle, by his own admission, does not: in the area of poiesis and praxis!

204. This is how the Lutheran Johann Georg Hamann saw the relation and made this note in his *Biblische Betrachtungen* [*Biblical Meditations*]: "The inspiration of this book is as much an act of divine condescension and self-abasement as is the cre-

ation by the Father and the incarnation of the Son. Therefore, humility of the heart is the only appropriate frame of mind for reading the Bible and an indispensable preparation for it." See Hamann, *Londoner Schriften. Historisch-kritische Neuedition,* ed. O. Bayer and B. Weißenborn (Munich: C. H. Beck, 1993), pp. 59, 6-10. It was a good move on the part of Friedrich Immanuel Niethammer to introduce his collection of selected writings of Luther *(Die Weisheit D. Martin Luthers,* edited jointly with Friedrich Roth in Nuremberg, 2nd ed., 1818) with a selection from Hamann's *Biblische Betrachtungen.* For an introduction to the *London Writings,* see John R. Betz, "Hamann's London Writings: The Hermeneutics of Trinitarian Condescension," *Pro Ecclesia* 14, no. 2 (Spring 2005): 191-234.

205. Anselm, *Proslogion,* Prologue, 93 *("sub persona conantis erigere mentem suam ad contemplandum Deum").*

206. See below, esp. notes 211-28 and 319-21.

207. WA TR 3:671, 10 or 673, 31f. (no. 3868, 1538).

208. WA 40/II:330, 1f. on Psalm 51:3 (1532), *"nudus deus . . . cum nudo hominis,"* in the context of 329, 3-332, 7). We should give special attention to the term *Deus absolutus* (the absolute God) in 330, 17 (see below, note 209). It marks the beginning of the exposition of what is the real topic and subject matter *(subiectum)* of theology: "the sinful and lost human being and the justifying or saving God" *(homo reus et perditus et deus iustificans vel salvator;* 328, 1f.; see section A.2.1). With regard to the traditional question about the "subject matter of theology" *(subiectum theologiae),* see Biel's, *Collectorium* (see note 20 and the introductory section of the book that discusses important moments in the understanding of theology).

209. WA 40/II:329, 3-330, 15 on Psalm 51:1 (1532): When we pray "mindful of God's promise that Christ is with us," we speak differently than those people who "manufacture" a god "and with their speculations ascend into heaven to speculate about God." "If we want to be saved, let us leave the God of majesty behind, because such a God is an enemy of all human beings. On the other hand, let us take hold of that God of whom David speaks, who is clothed with his promises that Christ is present. . . . That is the God we must have, lest the naked God comes face to face with the naked human being." In his writing *Das Wesen des Glaubens im Sinne Luthers* (1844), Ludwig Feuerbach underlined this crucial point in Luther's theology. See Oswald Bayer, "Gegen Gott für den Menschen. Feuerbachs Lutherrezeption," in *Leibliches Wort. Reformation und Neuzeit im Konflikt* (Tübingen: Mohr Siebeck, 1992), pp. 223-27, esp. note 63.

210. See above, section 2.2.2.

211. Anselm, *Proslogion,* Prologue, 93.

212. In his *Proslogion,* ch. 1, "A rousing of the mind to the contemplation of God" *(excitatio ad contemplandum Deum),* 97-99, Anselm like Luther is at home in the language of the psalms and makes special use of those words of the prayer that speak about "seeking" the God who stands over against us and addresses us (for example, "Teach me how to seek you . . . ," *Proslogion,* 99). The decisive difference between the

way in which Anselm and Luther use scripture, which at first glance seems the same, is that Anselm understands the affects of the psalms cognitively and interprets the episodes of spiritual attack *(Anfechtungssituation)* intellectually rather than existentially. Furthermore, Anselm's understanding of faith is completely different from that of Luther. Therefore, where Anselm distinguishes between "the knowledge of faith and the understanding of faith" (Ingolf U. Dalferth, "Fides quaerens intellectum. Theologie als Kunst der Argumentation in Anselms Proslogion," *ZThK* 81 [1984]: 104), the real distinction is between knowledge and faith. At the center of Luther's theology, however, is not the *fides quaerens intellectum* (faith seeking understanding) but the *tentatus quaerens certitudinem* (the person under attack seeking certainty). We get a hint of the question to be put to Anselm from Luther in Anselm's question to the soul: "What is it that you do not feel?" (Anselm, *Proslogion,* ch. 14, 108). Edmund Schlink points this out in "Anselm und Luther. Eine Studie über den Glaubensbegriff in Anselms Proslogion," in *Welt-Luthertum von heute* (Göttingen: Vandenhoeck & Ruprecht, 1950), pp. 269-93. What Anselm says in his *Proslogion* is certainly comparable with what he says elsewhere: "Let my heart feel what my mind understands" *(sentiam per affectum quod sentio per intellectum)* (Anselm of Canterbury, "Orationes sive meditationes," in *Opera,* ed. P. F. S. Schmitt, vol. 2 [Stuttgart: Friedrich Frommann Verlag, 1984], pp. 91, 197). See part two: section 7.3.

213. Luther gave grammar first place in the trivium: "Among all the sciences that people have discovered, grammar is especially useful for teaching theology" (WA 6:29, 7f.; 15 Theses on the Question of Whether the Books of the Philosophers Are Useful for Theology or Not, 1519). See WA 2:267, 32-35 and AWA II/2:29, 4; WA 5:27, 8 on Psalm 1:1 (1519-21): "First, let us look at grammar, which is truly theology." After grammar Luther highly esteems rhetoric, including the "poets and historians" (LW 45:370; WA 15:46, 18, To the Councilmen of All Cities in Germany That They Establish and Maintain Christian Schools, 1524), which are more important to him than dialectics ("that devil's dung, the philosophers and sophists," LW 45:370; WA 15:46, 20), which runs dry and leads us astray without language and history. Therefore, Luther insists on learning and paying attention to grammar and rhetoric *before* dialectics. "Deceived by a premature application of logic, . . . the sophists did not first take into account the rules of grammar or the science of words. If someone wants to know something about logic before he becomes familiar with grammar, and to teach before he listens and judge before he can speak, surely nothing good will come of it" (LW 37:301; WA 26:443, 8-12, Confession Concerning Christ's Supper, 1528). For Luther's efforts with dialectics, see WA 60:140-62, (Dialectica, ca. 1540?).

214. In his correspondence with Eobanus Hessus, Luther dismisses fears that the reform movement would be hostile to the sciences (the liberal arts): "I myself am convinced that without the knowledge of the [humanistic] studies, pure theology can by no means exist" (LW 49:34; WABR 3:50, 21f. [no. 596, March 29, 1523]). However, on the ambivalent value of a "knowledge of the liberal arts" *(bonarum atrium cognitio),* see WA TR 1:192, 15f., 19f., 27f. (no. 430, 1533); LW 54:71: "Reason that is under the devil's

control is harmful, and the more clever and successful it is, the more harm it does." "On the other hand, when illuminated by the Holy Spirit, reason helps to judge [interpret] the Holy Scriptures" and "takes all its thoughts from the word and also judges them according to the word" (translation altered).

215. WA TR 2:468, 24f. (no. 2457), 1532: *"Miror autem me hanc scientiam non discere."* See WA TR 2:470, 24f. According to WA 40/II:327, 27f., on Psalm 51:3 (1532), knowledge *(cognitio)* "should not be theoretical *(speculativa),* but entirely practical and sensory *(tota practica et sensitiva),* that people may hear and learn it. . . ."

216. See for example WA 34/I:53, 16-21 (Sermon on Heb. 13:4; 1531): "I have read it often and learn by saying it, but it is an art that I still have not mastered, and I am not ashamed to learn from it daily, even though I am an old doctor. The words are quickly learned. . . . But that is the art which I say we can regard as certain and indubitable."

217. See WA 40/II:326, 34-327, 16 on Psalm 51:3 (1532): "Further, this knowledge of sin is not some speculation or idea that my mind invents, but it is a true feeling, a real experience, and a grave struggle in the heart, as Scripture testifies when it says: 'I know my transgression,' that is, 'I feel it, I experience it.' For the same Hebrew word properly means to feel and experience the intolerable weight of God's wrath, and not, as the pope teaches, to think over what you have done, and what you have failed to do. The knowledge of sin is itself the feeling of sin. A sinner is a person who is pressured by his or her conscience and who is anxious and troubled, not knowing which way to turn." WA 40/II:327, 10f.: "There can be no dispute: The proper meaning of *agnosco* [to know] is 'to feel.'" The words can be changed or added to; hence consistency in terminology is obviously not achievable. See 40/II:328, 30-33 on Ps. 51:3 (1532): *cognoscere, scire, sentire, experiri.* See below, note 218.

218. WA 40/II:326, 37 on Psalm 51:1 (1532). See Siegfried Raeder, *Das Hebräische bei Luther untersucht bis zum Ende der ersten Psalmenvorlesung,* BHTh 31 (Tübingen: Mohr Siebeck, 1961), p. 269. Raeder, *Grammatica theologica. Studien zu Luthers Operationes in Psalmos,* BHTh 51 (Tübingen: Mohr Siebeck, 1977), p. 262 (biblical terms for thinking), pp. 267ff. *(docere),* p. 268 *(intellectus).* Already in the *Dictata super Psalterium* (1513-15), Luther emphasizes the affective aspect of knowledge.

219. WA 40/II:328, 1f. on Psalm 51:1 (1532): "The subject matter *(subiectum)* of theology," properly speaking *(proprie),* or its "theme" *(argumentum),* is "the sinful and lost human being and the God who justifies or the Savior" *(homo reus et perditus et deus iustificans vel salvator).*

220. Luther's disputation on the "subject matter of theology," which warrants being called classical, is to be found in his *Disputation Concerning Man* (1536; see above, note 186). There it states paradigmatically that Luther's clearly exclusive definition of the "object" of theology (WA 40/II:328, 2f.: "Anything sought outside this theme or subject matter [see above, note 219] constitutes a clear error or falsehood in theology") is in no way intended to isolate theology. On the contrary, the conflict with philosophy is essential to his concept of theology. See below, section 3.4.3 for Luther's use of the term *principium primum.* For more, see below, section 5.

221. For Descartes, only the knowledge that is clear and certain and that exists in the timeless present is true. See *The Philosophical Works of Descartes,* trans. Elizabeth S. Haldane and G. R. T. Ross, vol. 1 (Cambridge: Cambridge University Press, 1969), p. 237 ("Principles of Philosophy," Part I, principle XLV): "I term that clear [perception] which is present and apparent to an attentive mind, in the same way as we assert that we see objects clearly when, being present to the regarding eye, they operate upon it with sufficient strength." On the whole question of Descartes and his problems, see Oswald Bayer, "Descartes und die Freiheit," in *Leibliches Wort,* pp. 181-83.

222. WA TR 2:57, 31, 24 (no. 1340), 1532. See above, note 200.

223. LW 34:286 (translation altered); WA 50:659, 22-35. Passages in the section *"Meditatio"* that are not referenced all come from this opening citation.

224. See WA TR 2:56, 24 (no. 1340), 1532: "spiritualistic, that is, speculative" *(spiritualiter, id est, speculative)*. At the end of the previous paragraph of the preface, Luther had spoken of the "fanatics" or "factious spirits" *(Rottengeistern,* LW 34:286; WA 50:659, 18).

225. In contrast to present-day German usage, the word in Luther's time means not only something outer but also external *(externum): Deutsches Wörterbuch* (see above, note 134), vol. 1 (1854), p. 1035. [See the translator's footnote: LW 34:286 note 12.]

226. BC 322, 3; *BSLK* 454, 4-6; WA 50:245, 9-11.

227. See above, note 207.

228. BC 323, 9-11; *BSLK* 455, 27-456, 5; WA 50:245, 20-29. For a definition of spiritual "enthusiasm," see BC 322, 3; *BSLK* 453, 20-454, 3; WA 50:245, 5-9. See also BC 322, note 144. Luther says of the "enthusiasts, that is, the spirits, that they boast of having the Spirit without and before the word, and that accordingly they judge, interpret, and stretch the Scriptures or the oral word as they please."

229. LW 37:366 (Confession Concerning Christ's Supper, 1528); WA 26:506, 8-12.

230. Nicol, *Meditation bei Luther,* p. 63.

231. On this point Nicol is illuminating and full of information.

232. Nicol, *Meditation bei Luther,* p. 64.

233. Nicol, *Meditation bei Luther,* pp. 73-75, describes how appreciation for praying aloud declined in the late Middle Ages and made room for mental prayer *(oratio mentalis).* With Luther it is different: "The external, oral word is never heard without the participation of the heart; by the same token, the wordless thoughts and prayers of the heart always remain connected to that external word" (p. 81).

234. See below, note 235.

235. AWA 2/II:15, 10-12; WA 5:23, 30-3 (Operationes in Psalmos: Widmungsvorrede an Kurfürst Friedrich, 1519): *"nobis et verba et affectus praeparat hoc libro, quibus patrem caelestem alloquamur et oremus de iis, quae in reliquis libris facienda et imitanda esse docuerat, ne quid homo desiderare possit, quo ei ad salutem suam opus esset."* AWA 2/II:13 (note 66); 14f. (note 77) point here to the *Epistula ad Marcellinum in interpretationem psalmorum* of Athanasius (*MPL* 27, 11-46).

236. LW 35:254 (Preface to the Psalter, 1545/1528); WA DB 10/I:99, 24f.: "ein kleine Biblia."

237. AWA 2/II:15, 2 (see above, note 235). See WA 7:205, 1 (cited below in note 269).

238. See Emmanuel von Severus, "Das Wort 'Meditari' im Sprachgebrauch der Heiligen Schrift," *Geist und Leben. Zeitschrift für christliche Spiritualität* 26 (1953): 365-75.

239. See below, section 3.3.

240. See Severus, *"Meditari,"* pp. 365-75.

241. The following sentence of the preface of 1539 serves as a summary of this approach: "Thus you see in this same Psalm how David constantly boasts that he will talk [Ps. 119:15, 46, 48, 78, 98, 99, 148], meditate, speak, sing, hear, read, by day and night and always, about nothing except God's Word and commandments" (LW 34:286).

242. See especially the interpretation of Psalm 119 from 1521: WA 8:187, 15; 196, 13 (to that 197, 4); 196, 18; 202, 10 (to that 202, 19). See above, note 134.

243. In his Bible translation Luther consistently renders "to meditate/meditation" in Psalm 119 with "to speak" (see *Die gantze Heilige Schrifft Deudsch* [Wittenberg, 1545]). This is in line with the summarizing reference to the psalm in the preface (see above, note 241).

244. WA 8:188, 1-4 (1521).

245. LW 52:46; WA 10 I/1:188, 6 (see lines 7-17) on John 1:1-14 (Church Postil, 1522). See also Bayer, *Promissio,* pp. 19f. and 29, esp. note 87. See Birgit Stolt, "Luther, die Bibel und das menschliche Herz," *Die Zeichen der Zeit* 37 (1983): 295-302.

246. Friedrich Schleiermacher, *On the Glaubenslehre: Two Letters to Dr. Lücke,"* trans. James Duke and Francis Fiorenza, American Academy of Religion, Texts and Translations Series, 3 (Atlanta: Scholars Press, 1981), p. 40.

247. WA 8:204, 13 (1521). In the later Bible translation, Luther has: "My tongue will make its conversation from your word." See also Psalm 19:15.

248. See above, section 3.3.

249. See above, note 244.

250. Against Nicol, *Meditation bei Luther.* See above, note 230.

251. Nicol, *Meditation bei Luther,* p. 63; see above, note 230 and note 232. It is clear from this that Nicol does not take into account Luther's Reformation insights, or at least he fails to appreciate them, because he is more interested in Luther's continuity with tradition ("Kontinuität," *Meditation bei Luther,* p. 89) than his break with tradition.

252. See Botho Ahlers, *Die Unterscheidung von Theologie und Religion. Ein Beitrag zur Vorgeschichte der Praktischen Theologie im 18. Jahrhundert* (Gütersloh: Mohn, 1980).

253. As Nicol, *Meditation bei Luther,* p. 170 does.

254. Nicol, *Meditation bei Luther,* p. 170. As his article shows ("Meditation II," *TRE* 22:345f. Nicol agrees with this criticism (*Lutherjahrbuch* 55 [1988]: 38-45).

255. In the Table Talk quoted above (see note 207), Luther opposes the spiritualism of Zwingli and others who, by anticipating modern subjectivity, define the word "not according to the God who speaks, but according to the person who re-

ceives" *(non secundum dicentem Deum, sed secundum recipientem hominem)* (WA TR 3:670, 18f. [no. 3868], 1538).

256. LW 34:285; WA 50:659, 10 (Preface, 1539).

257. See above, note 144.

258. See above, note 105.

259. LW 34:286; WA 50:659. See also the "New Preface" to the *Large Catechism* from 1530 according to which God "solemnly enjoins us in Deuteronomy 6 [6:7-8] that we should meditate on his precepts while sitting, walking, standing, lying down, and rising, and should keep them as an ever-present emblem and sign before our eyes and on our hands" *(BC* 382, 14; *BSLK* 551, 2-6; WA 30/I:127, 34-36).

260. WA 28:76, 22-26 on John 17:1 (Sermon from August 8, 1528, as edited by Cruciger). The following passage comes from WA 28:77, 26-35. See 75, 32: "to hear and handle God's word physically" *(Gottes Wort leiblich hören und handeln).*

261. See the parody in WA 28:75, 23-8: "But that is true: if babbling or crying is purely an external gesture – as when people stood in the church all day long, counting the beads of the rosary, turning pages, howling and carrying on in the sanctuary – then it could certainly not be called prayer, since it happens without heart and soul, and nobody seriously thinks of asking God for anything."

262. On the fundamental significance of *Augsburg Confession,* Article 5, see Oswald Bayer, *Living by Faith: Justification and Sanctification,* trans. Geoffrey W. Bromiley (Grand Rapids, Michigan/Cambridge, U.K.: Eerdmans, 2003), pp. 44f.

263. Friedrich Schleiermacher, for example, not only takes *Augsburg Confession,* Article 14 as evidence of the "public Ministry of the word, as a definite office committed to men under fixed forms," but he also places *Augsburg Confession,* Article 14 in direct parallel to Article 5 (Schleiermacher, *The Christian Faith,* ed. H. R. Mackintosh and J. S. Stewart, English translation of the second German edition, 1989, first published in English 1921 [Edinburgh: T. & T. Clark, 1976], p. 614 [§134]), although he knows that all Christians have the ministry of the word. For the whole problem, see Oswald Bayer, "Wortlehre oder Glaubenslehre? Zur Konstitution theologischer Systematik im Streit zwischen Schleiermacher und Luther," in *Autorität und Kritik. Zu Hermeneutik und Wissenschaftstheorie,* pp. 156-68, esp. 167f.

264. WA 41:11, 9-13: "We are all theologians, that is, every Christian. . . . We all speak as theologians, as do all Christians. . . ."

265. For Melanchthon's understanding of this "idea of the world" in theology, see Oswald Bayer, *Theologie,* HST vol. 1 (Gütersloh: Gütersloher Verlagshaus, 1994), Part A II, note 85.

266. LW 5:76 (translation altered); WA 43:481, 34f., 33 on Genesis 26:24f., 1541: *"nos tales creaturas esse, cum quibus velit loqui Deus usque in aeternum et immortaliter" "sive in ira, sive in gratia."*

267. See above, notes 190f.

268. For more details and references, see Oswald Bayer, *Schöpfung als Anrede,* pp. 54f. See also part two: section 1.1.1

269. WA 7:205, 1 (Eine kurze Form der 10. Gebote. Eine kurze Form des Glaubens. Eine kurze Form des Vaterunsers, 1520).

270. According to the *Brief Instruction on What to Look For and Expect in the Gospels* (1521), "the preaching of the gospel is nothing else than Christ coming to us, or we being brought to him," LW 35:121; WA 10/I:1, 13, 21f. This "being brought to him" does not exclude the point Luther made earlier that whatever is given to us must be "desired, picked up and brought to us" (see above, note 269), but it gives it room — room to speak and breathe. For more clarity on this, see Martin Tetz, "Athanasius und die Einheit der Kirche. Zur ökumenischen Bedeutung eines Kirchenvaters," *ZThK* 81 (1984): 217-19.

271. See above, notes 107 and 213.

272. See above, notes 213 and 214 as well as LW 45:360; WA 15:38, 7-21 (To the Councilmen of All Cities in Germany That They Establish and Maintain Christian Schools, 1524).

273. LW 33:28 (translation altered); WA 18:609, 5: *"Externa [claritas] in verbi ministerio posita."*

274. LW 33:28 (translation significantly altered); WA 18:609, 12-14: *"Si de externa dixeris, Nihil prorsus relictum est obscurum aut ambiguum, sed omnia sunt per verbum in lucem producta certissimam et declarata toto orbi quaecunque sunt in scripturis."* See 606, 24-39.

275. See above, section 3.3

276. See above, note 171.

277. See above, notes 183-85.

278. BC 355, 6; BSLK 511, 46f.; WA 30/I:250, 2f. (Explanation of the Third Article of the Creed in the Small Catechism).

279. Regarding "teacher," see LW 34:286; WA 50:659, 16 (Preface, 1539); regarding "student," see WA 30/I:128, 21; BC 382, 16 (Martin Luther's Preface); BSLK 552, 9 and WA TR 1:26, 29-27, 2 (no. 76), 1531; LW 54:143; WA TR 2:67, 32-40 (no. 1353), cited above in note 180.

280. This is something that humans cannot do themselves. See for example WA TR 1:28, 31-29, 6 (no. 76), 1531. [The word *Anfechtung* is difficult to render into English. It can mean trial, testing, temptation, challenge, or attack. The precise meaning it has in a given place will depend on the context. Usually we have translated it as spiritual attack, but often other nuances are present also. See LW 63 note 32.]

281. See esp. the "Preface" of 1545: LW 34:338; WA 54:186, 25-29 (see note 285). Nicol is right in pointing to WA 54:186, 1: *"pulsare"* = "to knock" (see LW 34:337 "to beat importunately") and 186, 3: *"meditabundus dies et noctes"* (LW 34:337 "meditating day and night") (*Meditation bei Luther,* pp. 175-81: "The Tower Experience as Meditation on Rom. 1:17"). The polemic against those who read the Bible only one time and "want to absorb everything at once" is found frequently (LW 14:46; WA 31/I:67, 7f.; Preface, Psalm 118, 1530).

282. See above, note 221.

283. See below, note 285.

284. WA 54:186, 3 *("meditabundus dies et noctes")*. See also 186, 1 *("pulsare"* = "to knock" is a technical term from the meditation tradition; see Nicol, *Meditation bei Luther,* pp. 25-8) and 186, 2 *("ardentissime sitiens scire"* = LW 34:337 "most ardently desiring to know"). See above, note 281.

285. LW 34:338 (translation altered); WA 54:186, 26-29: He is one *"ex illis, qui (ut Augustinus de se scribit) scribendo et docendo profecerint, non ex illis, qui de nihilo repente fiunt summi, cum nihil sint, neque operati, neque tentati, neque experti, sed ad unum intuitum scripturae totum spiritum eius exhauriunt."* Quoted is Augustine, Epist. 143, 2; *MPL* 33, 585 = *CSEL* 44, 251. From 1543 onwards, Calvin concludes the preface to every edition of his *Institutes of the Christian Religion* with these words. See Oswald Bayer, *Theologie,* part A III, note 71.

286. Gotthold Ephraim Lessing, "Eine Duplik (1778)," in *Werke in 8 Bänden,* ed. H. G. Göpfert, vol. 8 (Munich: C. Hanser, 1979), pp. 32f.

287. *BC* 362, 5-6; *BSLK* 520, 24-30; WA 30/1:316, 14-20.

288. Psalm 119:109 ("My life is continually in my hands") could be taken to mean that I have myself in hand and that I am the captain of my own life. But careful exegesis shows that exactly the opposite is meant: that my life is in danger, threatened by forces beyond my control (I thank Hartmut Gese for pointing this out in a private conversation on June 29, 1989).

289. The opposite view is held particularly by Karl Rahner, who stands in the tradition of the Ignatian exercises (Rahner, *Grundkurs des Glaubens,* 11th ed [Freiburg: Herder, 1976], p. 422; translated by William V. Dych under the title *Foundations of the Christian Faith: An Introduction to the Idea of Christianity* [London: Darton, Longman & Todd, 1978], p. 440): ". . . wherever people living in themselves and in full possession of themselves risk themselves in freedom, they are not actualizing a moment in a series of mere nothings, but they are reaping the harvest of time . . ." (translation altered). On the Jesuit tradition mentioned above, see Ernst Wolf, "Menschwerdung des Menschen? Zum Thema Humanismus und Christentum," in *Peregrinatio,* vol. 2 (Munich: Kaiser, 1965), p. 127: *"anima mea in manibus meis semper"* (Ps. 119:109: My life is continually in my hands) as "a Jesuit Motto." If we are going to see in this motto a modern understanding of freedom, we need to consider that it is bound up with the notion of Ignatian "indifference" or "detachment" *(indifferentia):* the active willingness to make room for God's word and will, to choose what God has chosen.

290. LW 43:193-211; WA 38:351-75.

291. It is one of the great merits of Nicol's monograph, *Meditation bei Luther,* pp. 153-67, to have shown this for the first time in a detailed and comprehensive way.

292. LW 43:209 (translation altered); WA 38:373, 1-3.

293. LW 43:198 (translation altered); WA 38:363, 9-16. See LW 43:201-2; WA 38:366, 10-15; it is no accident that Psalm 119 [v. 18] is cited there.

294. David Friedrich Strauss, *Die christliche Glaubenslehre in ihrer geschichtlichen*

Entwicklung und im Kampfe mit der modernen Wissenschaft, vol. 1 (Tübingen and Stuttgart, 1840; unaltered reprint, Darmstadt, 1973), p. 136.

295. This interweaving of the outer and the inner is especially clear in the preface to the *Large Catechism:* one should "read it daily and make it the subject of meditation and conversation. In such reading, conversation, and meditation, the Holy Spirit is present and bestows ever new and greater light and devotion, so that it tastes better and better and is digested" (*BC* 381, 9; *BSLK* 549, 6-13; WA 30/I:127, 1-4).

296. See above, note 228 (in the general context of *BC* 322, 3-323, 13; *BSLK* 453, 16-456, 18; WA 50:245, 1-247, 4).

297. *BC* 322, 5; *BSLK* 454, 15; WA 50:245, 21.

298. The German word *treiben,* which basically means "drive," and which we have translated "work at," could mean, rather than "repeat" (see LW 34:286; WA 50:659, note 3) "move back and forth" (*Deutsches Wörterbuch,* vol. 22, 45) or "act" (= *agere;* op. cit., 54). See the preface of the *Large Catechism* where *"meditari"* (Ps. 1:2) is rendered with *"handeln"* (*BSLK* 549, 25-7; WA 30/I:127, 7-12). "Rub" (Latin: *terere;* German: *reiben;* WA 50:659, note 4) is a technical term from the meditation tradition, and refers to the act of rubbing the text [to release its meaning] like one would rub an herb; see Nicol, *Meditation bei Luther,* p. 62, note 135.

299. LW 34:286f. (translation altered); WA 50:660, 1-16. Passages in the section *"Tentatio"* that are not referenced all come from this opening citation.

300. See the revision to the 1531 Psalter at Psalm 46:7: "'The heathen rage': *ferdinandus, Dux Georgius"* (WA DB 3:46, 20).

301. See Luther's writing *Against Hans Wurst* (1541), LW 41:185-256, esp. 197f.; WA 51:461-572, esp. 484, 12-15.

302. See above, note 144.

303. [Note 304 in the German original.] See for example WA 56:299, 28 on Romans 5:2; 374, 16 on Romans 8:24.

304. [Note 303 in the German original.] *Theologia mystica,* which the ancients distinguished from *theologia propria* (= *historica*) and *symbolica,* "teaches that we should seek God in a negative way" *("docet Deum quaerere negative"):* WA TR 1:26, 18-20 (no. 75), 1531. See AWA 2/II:294, 19f.; WA 5:163, 17f. (Operationes in Psalmos, excursus on Ps. 5:12: *de spe et passionibus*). This threefold division of theology goes back to Gerson *(De theologia mystica),* who refers to the Areopagite: AWA 2/II, 295 (note 17). For more on Gerson, see Ulrich Köpf, "Erfahrung III/1," *TRE* 10:113. See LW 29:179 (WA 57/III:179, 6-13) on Heb. 5:12, 1518. See further, Bayer, *Promissio,* p. 65. See note 312. On the Aeropagite, see Oswald Bayer, *Theologie,* part B III, note 5.

305. See above, note 171.

306. See these words of the preface with LW 54:50; WA TR 1:146, 16 (no. 352), 1532: The devil "would teach them [the spiritualists and sects] well." The context (LW 54:50; WA TR 1:147, 3-13) is as follows: "I didn't learn my theology all at once. I had to ponder over it ever more deeply, and my spiritual trials and attacks [*Anfechtungen*] were of help to me in this, for one will never understand Holy Scripture without prac-

tice and spiritual attacks. This is what the spiritualists and sects lack. They don't have the right adversary, the devil. He would teach them well" (translation altered; the rest of this passage is not included in LW). "St. Paul also had a devil that beat him with fists and drove him through his attacks to a diligent study of the Scriptures. In the same way, I had the pope, the universities and all the scholars on my back — and with them the devil; they chased me into the Bible so that I had to read it diligently with the result that now at last I understand it properly. When we don't have such a devil, we are only speculative theologians who deal merely with our ideas and speculate with our reason."

307. See the beginning of the first Invocavit Sermon (1522): "The summons of death comes to us all, and no one can die for another. Each of us must fight our own battle with death alone. We can shout into another person's ears, but each of us must be individually prepared when death comes, [. . .]" (LW 51:70, translation altered; WA 10/III:1, 7-10). See also the "I — I, myself — I" in the *Confession Concerning Christ's Supper* (1528): LW 37:363; WA 26:503, 32, which is spoken with utter seriousness and full awareness of our apocalyptic responsibility in view of the final judgment.

308. See above, note 183 and notes 265-68.

309. See above, notes 211-16.

310. See instead of many Table Talk discourses only WA TR 5:384, 5f. (no. 5864): "A theologian needs to be made by trial and testing and by practice, not only by reading sacred texts" *("Theologum oportet fieri experimentis et usu, non lectione tantum sacrarum rerum").*

311. AWA 2/II:296, 10; WA 5:163, 28f.: *"Vivendo, immo moriendo et damnando fit theologus, non intelligendo, legendo aut speculando."* See above, note 48.

312. The adoption and correction of this tradition can be seen very clearly from AWA 2/II:294, 19-296, 11 (see the detailed notes 16-21); WA 5:163, 17-29. Luther rejects the negative theology that followed in the wake of Dionysius the Areopagite (see note 198) at the point where it becomes mere speculation without being lived: "But they held to the opposite of negative theology, that is, they chose neither death nor hell" (AWA 2/II:296, 3f.; WA 5:163, 22f.). See AWA 2/II:318, 11-319, 3; WA 5:176, 22-33.

313. This is not considered, for example, in Köpf's article (see note 304), pp. 113-15, which is otherwise very rich in material and highly nuanced.

314. That is clear especially from the excurses *de spe et passionibus* and *de fide et operibus* in *Operationes in Psalmos* (AWA 2/II:283-321; WA 5:158, 4-177, 28 and WA 5:394, 20-408, 13).

315. LW 31:343f.; WA 7:49, 7-19.

316. Emanuel Hirsch's reinterpretation is a good example of such an attempt to weaken this connection. See the essay "Drei Kapitel zu Luthers Lehre vom Gewissen," in his *Lutherstudien*, vol. 1 (Gütersloh: Bertelsmann, 1954), pp. 136f., note 4: "The unity between the conscience's experience of the present and the last judgment, as Luther experienced it in his trials and spiritual attacks *(Anfechtungen)*, is an extremely remarkable phenomenon when viewed from the perspective of the history of religions.

It represents the reemergence of early Christian piety, long submerged, in all its immediacy and power, and at the same time it forms the basis and starting-point of all modern attempts to transform the Christian myth into the inner experience of subjectivity. Both aspects are important: the original as well as the new, which has taken the form of a genuine breakthrough born of the passionate concentration of the individual soul on the divine mystery, before which it stands exposed."

317. Dietz Lange, *Erfahrung und die Glaubwürdigkeit des Glaubens*, p. 13. A text that speaks against such a reduction and that is also typical of Luther is LW 33:51-3 (WA 18:626, 8-40). See above, note 171.

318. WA TR 4:490, 24-491, 6 (no. 4777; the date cannot be earlier than 1537 because of the allusion to Agricola). "If I were destined to live longer, it would give me great pleasure to write a book about times of trial, testing, and spiritual attack *(tentationibus)* for without them we can know nothing about Holy Scripture or faith, nor can we know anything about the fear and love of God; moreover, we cannot even know anything about hope if we have never experienced times of trial, testing, and spiritual attack. Our John Agricola is just such a person who is arrogant in many ways because he has never been tried and tested by spiritual attack *(non tentatus)*. He is sure to cause havoc after my death. O, dear God, it is so hard for him to learn to read the Scriptures properly! There are three words we should learn properly and we should remain pupils of these three words for three years: What it is to love God, to have faith in him, and to fear him." If Luther's apocalyptic understanding of time and experience is nothing else than the first commandment and the theater of conflict associated with it, and if, as the catechism claims, it represents the witness of the whole Bible (WA TR 1:358 [no. 751]; see BC 382, 17f.; BSLK 552, 16-33; WA 30/I:128, 22-30), then this understanding transcends all distinctions based on the history of forms and traditions.

319. See *"probare"* ("to test or prove"), for example, WA 7:49, 9 (see above, note 315). [This emphasis does not come out in LW 31:343 where the phrase *nullo experimento eam probaverunt* is rendered "they have not experienced it."]

320. On the etymology, see: *Deutsches Wörterbuch*, vol. 3, 1862, pp. 788-91; Köpf, "Erfahrung III/1," pp. 109f.; Lange, *Erfahrung*, p. 8.

321. See the parallelism between "to experience and to become certain" (*BSLK* 553, 7f., Preface to the *Large Catechism*, 1530; see BC 383, 19) in the context of a reflection on meditation ("reading, teaching, learning, thinking and meditating [= *meditari*]," *BSLK* 553, 5f.).

322. By scratching metal alloys with a "touchstone" *(lapis lydeus)*, we can determine the genuineness of any gold that may be present.

323. Luther translates in the tradition of the Vulgate (*"tantummodo sola vexatio intellectum dabit auditui"*; see Psalm 118:67 and 75). See also WA 25:189, 15-39 (Jesajavorlesung z.St.; 1532/4) and Leonhard Hutter, *Compendium Locorum Theologicorum* (Wittenbergae, 1610), locus XXIV (De Cruce et Consolationibus), 1.1; translated by H. E. Jacobs and G. F. Spieker under the title *Compend of Lutheran Theology. A Summary*

of Christian Doctrine, Derived from the Word of God and the Symbolical Books of the Evangelical Lutheran Church (Philadelphia: Lutheran Book Store, 1868).

324. Of the two meanings of the word "experience" (see above, note 320), the active and the passive, the passive is for Luther the more important theologically.

325. LW 28:81; WA 36:506, 21 (Sermon on 1 Cor. 15:3, esp. the words "according to the Scriptures"). The above interpretation follows from the context (WA 36:499-507), which explains what is "scriptural."

326. Besides the text mentioned in note 325, see also WA 30/II:673, 13-17 (de loco iustificationis, 1530).

327. LW 14:46; WA 31/I:67, 10-12 in the context of lines 3-14, in which Luther explicates his understanding of meditation. [The play on the German words *Lesewort* and *Lebewort* cannot easily be reproduced in English.]

328. LW 54:7; WA TR 1:16, 13 (no. 46), 1531: *"Sola experientia facit theologum."* The context of this Table Talk discourse deals with the proper way in which the "Doctor of Scripture" (*doctor bibliae,* line 6) should use scripture. See WA 25:106, 27 (Jesajavorlesung, 1532/4): *"experientia, quae sola facit Theologum."*

329. This is evident from the context of the parallel to Table Talk no. 46 (see above, note 328): WA 25:106, 26-107, 19.

330. WA 7:97, 23 (Assertio omnium articulorum, 1520) in context (97, 23-35): Holy Scripture is "of itself certain, simple, and intelligible; it is its own interpreter, testing, judging, and illuminating everything, as it is written in Ps. 119: 'Either the declaration, as the Hebrew writer properly has it, or the opened door of your words, gives light and understanding to the simple' [v. 130]. Here clearly the Spirit has granted illumination and teaches that understanding is given through God's word alone, as through an opened door or first principle (as they say), from which we must begin in order to move towards the light of understanding. Again, the principle or head of your words is truth [v. 160]. You see, here also truth is not given except by the head of God's words, that is, unless you give his words first place and use them as a first principle for judging all words. And what do those eight words [law, promise, decrees, statutes, word, etc.] do? They take us, who have been condemned because of the perversity of our desires, and call us back to our origins; they teach us that the first and only things we should pursue are God's words and that the Spirit will come of his own accord and will drive our spirit out that we may do theology without danger." See the quotation of Psalm 1:2: WA 7:97, 10f. Psalm 119 and the understanding of meditation based on Psalm 1:2, in the context of all three rules, are significant for Luther's "Scripture principle." However, to the best of my knowledge, this connection has not yet been investigated.

331. WA 7:98, 11-13: *"verba divina esse apertiora et certiora omnium hominum . . . verbis, ut quae non per hominum verba, sed hominum verba per ipsa doceantur, probentur, aperiantur, et firmentur."*

332. See above, section 2.2.

333. Schleiermacher, *The Christian Faith*, 12-26 (§4f.).

334. WA 9:97, 12-14 (Randbemerkungen zu Taulers Predigten, 1516): *"Nota, quod divina pati magis quam agere oportet, immo et sensus et intellectus est naturaliter etiam virtus passiva."* Note how the passage continues (lines 15f.): "We are purely material, God is the maker of form, for God works all things in us" *(Nos materia sumus pura, deus formae factor, omnia enim in nobis operatur deus).*

335. See Aristotle, *De anima* II: 5, 416 b 33f.; II: 11, 424 a 1; III: 4, 429 a 13-18 and Theo Dieter, "Amor hominis — Amor crucis. Zu Luthers Aristoteleskritik in der probatio zur 28. These der 'Heidelberger Disputation,'" *NZSTh* 29 (1987): 241-58, esp. note 5.

336. See Dionysius the Areopagite, *De divinis nominibus* (*MPG* 3, 648): "he is taught by suffering [i.e., by undergoing the experience of] divine things, not only by learning about them" *(doctus est non solum discens, sed et patiens divina),* quoted by Thomas Aquinas, *STh* I q.1 a.1, 6 (ad tertium).

337. With Lange, *Erfahrung und die Glaubwürdigkeit des Glaubens,* p. 78.

338. For an explanation of this thesis and its comprehensive systematic significance, see Oswald Bayer, "Systematische Theologie als Wissenschaft der Geschichte," in *Autorität und Kritik,* pp. 181-200; Bayer, "Wortlehre oder Glaubenslehre?" in *Autorität und Kritik,* pp. 156-68.

339. See for example WA TR 4:491, 21-5 (no. 4777): "It is something deeper than despair on account of sin, as are the trials and spiritual attack *(Anfechtung)* spoken of in Psalm 8: 'You will let him be forsaken by God for a little while,' and Ps. 22: 'My God, my God, why have you forsaken me?' As if he wants to say: You are my enemy for no reason and although there was no sin."

340. Instead of the many references, see only LW 33:139 (WA 18:685, 3-24).

341. See above, after note 308.

342. See above, notes 330f.

343. WA 7:97, 28, 31 (in the plural: 98, 4, 9). See esp. Aristotle, *Metaphysics* VI: 1025b-1026a.

344. The relevant parts of the Analytics, Topics, Rhetoric, Physics, and Metaphysics are briefly mentioned in *Nicomachean Ethics* VI: 1139b 12-35.

345. Aristotle, *Nicomachean Ethics* VI: 1139b 22-4, trans. H. Rackham, *Aristotle in 23 Volumes,* vol. 19: *The Nicomachean Ethics* (Cambridge, Mass.: Harvard University Press, and London: William Heinemann, 1934), p. 333.

346. Luther in any case introduces the word "principle" with some reservations. He knows about its origin: "the first principle (as they say)" (WA 7:97, 28; see LW 33:91 [WA 18:653, 33f.]). In taking it up, he involves himself in something of a contradiction, not unlike the designation of faith as *opus operum* [a work worked by God] (WA 5:396, 32; excursus on Ps. 14:1, *de fide et operibus*).

347. It is necessary therefore to lift the question of the authority of scripture out of its ecclesial and theological ghetto and approach the interpretation of scripture as a critique of reason. See Oswald Bayer, "Schriftautorität und Vernunft — ein ekklesiologisches Problem," in *Autorität und Kritik,* pp. 56-58.

348. For the explication of what we can only hint at here, see Bayer, "Systematische Theologie als Wissenschaft der Geschichte," in *Autorität und Kritik,* pp. 193f. For the significance of Luther's understanding of theology for a responsible contemporary theory of science, see Bayer, "Glauben und Wissenschaft," in *Autorität und Kritik,* pp. 127-41.

349. See above, sections 3.2 and 3.3.

350. WA 39/II:176, 8f. (Promotionsdisputation von Johannes Macchabäus Scotus, 1542). See LW 28:302; WA 26:64, 2f. (on 1 Tim. 3:15; 1528): "The church is to be found where God's Word is taught in its purity" *(Si ibi verbum dei pure und ghet, est ecclesia).*

351. The first mark, "the holy word of God" (LW 41:148; WA 50:628, 29f.), is specified by the following four (LW 41:151-64; WA 50:630-41).

352. LW 41:164; WA 50:641, 20-34.

353. LW 41:164f.; WA 50:641, 35–642, 32.

354. WA DB 10/I:588-90 (Nachwort zum Psalter von 1525).

355. WA TR 5:384, 1-3 (no. 5863): *"Sathan vincitur tribus modis, et servatur ecclesia: 1. Fideliter docendo, 2. Serio orando, 3. Sedulo patiendo."*

356. LW 35:256-57 (translation altered); WA DB 10/I:104, 5-9, "Preface to the Psalter," 1545/1528.

357. WA 30/I:125, 4; *BC* 379, 2; *BSLK* 546, 6.

358. WA 30/I:125, 17-21; *BC* 380, 3; *BSLK* 546, 15-23.

359. Albrecht Peters, "Die theologische Konzeption des Kleinen Katechismus," *Pastoraltheologie* 73 (1984): 343.

360. See Karl Marx, *Selected Writings,* ed. David McLellan (Oxford: Oxford University Press, 1977), p. 69.

361. The German words *"zum Tode"* ("to death"), which come from the printed version (WA 10/III:1, 15; LW 51:70), must have been ringing in Heidegger's ears. See Martin Heidegger, *Sein und Zeit,* 9th ed. (Tübingen: Niemeyer, 1960), translated by John Macquarrie and Edward Robinson under the title *Being and Time* (London: SCM Press, 1962), §§46-53: "The possible Being-a-whole of Dasein and Being-towards-death."

362. LW 51:70 (translation altered); WA 10/III:1, 4-2, 3 (the smoothing out of the text done with an eye to the printed version). See the original preface to the *Large Catechism:* WA 30/I:129, 14-16; *BC* 383, 1f.; *BSLK* 553, 36–554, 4 ("a 'catechism' — that is, instruction for children. It contains what every Christian should know. Anyone who does not know it should not be numbered among Christians nor admitted to any sacrament.")

363. See above, note 196.

364. WA 7:49:18f. Luther says this especially in regard to the doctrine of the Trinity. This is clear from the parallel passages.

365. See the *Lectures on Romans:* "O pig-theologians!" (LW 25:261; WA 56:274, 14).

366. See above, section 3, esp. notes 183-85.

367. For more on reason as a "whore," see for example the sermon on *The Estate of Marriage* (1522): "that clever harlot, our natural reason" (LW 45:39; WA 10/II:295, 16). We should understand this term in the sense of Romans 1:18-33. The real issue is the perversion of the good use of reason.

368. See above, note 213.

369. WA 60:140-62.

370. WA 1:629-33.

371. WA TR 3:685, 15-18 (no. 3883), May 26, 1538.

372. WA TR 3:685, 7.

373. WA TR 3:685, 19-23. See 3:685, 4-12: *"Optimum consilium. Lutherus: Meum consilium est non esse disputandum in rebus arcanis, sed simpliciter in verbo Dei permanendum, praecipue in catechismo, nam ibi habetis exactissimam methodum totius religionis. Decalogum Deus ipse dedit, Christus ipsemet orationis dominicae formam praescripsit, Spiritus Sanctus symbolum exactissime composuit. Diese drei Dinge sind so gestellt, daß sie nicht feiner, tröstlicher und kürzer konnten gestellt oder gefaßt werden. Sed illa contemnuntur, quia res est levis, quia pueri et infantes illa quotidie pronuntiant."*

374. See above, note 362.

375. WA 53:64 (translation altered); WA 19:76, 2-11. The Ten Commandments played a special role only after the Fourth Lateran Council when confession was made a rule. See Johannes Meyer, *Historischer Kommentar zu Luthers Kleinem Katechismus,* vol. 1 (Gütersloh: Bertelsmann, 1929), p. 78.

376. *BC* 360-62; *BSLK* 517-19.

377. *BC* 363f. (translation altered) ; *BSLK* 521-23; *BC* has "blessing" instead of "prayer."

378. *BC* 365-67 (The Household Chart of Some Bible Passages); *BSLK* 523-27. The *Haustafel,* the Household Table, is often called the Table of Duties.

379. WA 7:194-229. The connection between the three parts of the catechism is formulated in the same way at the beginning of the explanation of the creed in the *Large Catechism: BC* 431f.; *BSLK* 646, 3-26. See WA 30/I:43, 27 (Katechismuspredigten, 1528).

380. WA 7:204, 7-11.

381. WA 7:204, 13-18.

382. WA 7:220, 1-5.

383. LW 43:200 (A Simple Way to Pray, 1535): "I think of each commandment as, first, instruction, which is really what it is intended to be, and consider what the Lord God demands of me so earnestly. Second, I turn it into a thanksgiving; third, a confession; and fourth, a prayer." Luther applies this fourfold meditation of the Decalogue to all parts of the catechism.

384. LW 43:200; WA 38:364, 31.

385. LW 43:209 (translation altered); WA 38:372, 26f.

386. *BC* 355, 2.

387. Since 1520 these four marks (command, promise, necessity, desire) charac-

terize Luther's understanding of prayer (see Bayer, *Promissio*, pp. 319-37); they are also determinative for his introduction to the Our Father in the *Large Catechism* (WA 30/I:193, 14-198, 2; *BC* 440, 1-445, 34; *BSLK* 662, 41-670, 21).

388. WA 30/I:129, 20; *BC* 383, 3; *BSLK* 554, 11; WA 30/I:130, 4; *BC* 384, 6; *BSLK* 554, 31; WA 30/I:185, 15f.; *BC* 650, 23; *BSLK* 650, 10f.

389. See above, section 3.4.2 and section 3.4.3.

390. WA TR 6:142, 26-30 (no. 6716).

391. LW 54:127 (translation altered); WA TR 2:4, 7-16 (no. 1234).

392. LW 54:443 (translation altered); WA TR 5:210, 15f. (no. 5518).

393. LW 19:56; WA 19:208, 21f. (Lectures on Jonah, 1526; translation altered). See LW 19:53-5; WA 19:206, 31-207, 13 for an exposition of this summarizing sentence.

394. WA 26:504, 30f.; LW 37:364: "The holy orders and true institutions established by God are these three: the order of the church *(status ecclesiasticus)*, the order of marriage *(status oeconomicus)*, and the order of government *(status politicus)*."

395. WA 26:505, 8; LW 37:365.

396. LW 37:365 (translation altered); WA 26:505, 16-21.

397. LW 34:137-44 (Theses and Disputation Fragment); WA 39/I:175-77 (Disputatio de homine).

398. WA 40/III:202-69 (1532/33); see WA 15:348-79 (1524).

399. For the four causes and their use, see Gerhard Ebeling, *Disputatio de homine II: Die philosophische Definition des Menschen. Kommentar zu These 1-19* (Tübingen: Mohr Siebeck, 1982), pp. 333-59.

400. WA 40/III:203, 24: "*Hanc causam pulcherrime et optime tractant.*"

401. WA 40/III:202, 30-33: "*Nam materialem et formalem causam solum tum Politiae, tum Oeconomiae norunt, finalem autem et efficientem causam non norunt, hoc est, nesciunt, unde veniant Politia et Oeconomia et a quo conserventur, item quo tendant.*"

402. WA 40/III:213, 12f.; see 237, 28-30 and *BC* 389, 26f.; *BSLK* 566, 12-37.

403. WA 40/III:222, 13; see 223, 5-9; 225, 9ff.

404. WA 40/III:222, 34f.; see 222, 13f.: "*Ex hoc: feci, vere [dona Dei] fiunt feces.*"

405. LW 41:167 (translation altered); WA 50:643, 29-31 (On the Councils and the Church, 1539).

406. LW 41:166; WA 50:643, 28f.

407. WA 39/I:229, 8-13 (Disputation Concerning Romans 3:28, 1537): "*una quaeque ars habet suos terminos et sua vocabula, quibus utitur, et ea vocabula, valent in suis materiis. Iuristae sua habent, medici sua, physici sua.*" This thesis highlights an important aspect of the Aristotelian view of science (on that, see above, note 66).

408. WA TR 1:141-45 (no. 349; Autumn 1532). On the different kinds and degrees of "certainty" discussed here, see the central theses of pre-Tridentine probabilism as summarized by Benjamin Nelson, *Der Ursprung der Moderne: Vergleichende Studien zum Zivilisationsprozeß*, 3rd ed. (Frankfurt: Suhrkamp, 1984), p. 167: "(1) It is foolishness to expect greater certainty than a given situation permits. (2) Mathematics yields demonstrable knowledge, but not physics. (3) Where certainty is not possible, philoso-

phers have the freedom to consider probable opinions. (4) In the moral and practical sphere (in contrast to the speculative), an individual who is confronted with opinions of varying degrees of probability, must give preference to the *more certain* and *more probable* opinion and act accordingly. The last two principles were later known by the terms "tutiorism" and "probabiliorism." See Oswald Bayer, *Theologie*, part A II, esp. 5.2.1.

409. WA 39/I:229, 16-19: *"Si tamen vultis uti vocabulis istis, prius quaeso illa bene purgate, füret sie mal zum Bade."*

410. See WA 39/I:231, 1-3: "All words become new when transferred from their own sphere to another" *(Omnia vocabula fiunt nova, quando e suo foro in alienum transferuntur)*. On recognizing the location of a word, see below, note 440.

411. WA 30/I:231, 18.

412. WA 30/I:231, 18.

413. WA 39/I:233, 11-16: *"Sunt duae diversae iustitiae, altera legis, viribus seu operibus nostris parta, altera divina misericordia per fidem nobis a Deo imputata. Sic oportet nos purgare has voces scholasticorum. Nummus valet, Wo er geschlagen ist. . . . Coram Deo opera sunt nihil valent, scilicet ad promerendam vitam aeternam. Coram et in mundo valent."*

414. WA 39/I:230, 2f.: *"Duplex est forum, theologicum et politicum."*

415. WA 39/I:229, 27-29: *"Theologi Parisienses detonant: Quod est verum in physica, est etiam verum in theologia."* See LW 38:243f.; WA 39/II:7, 9f., 25f.: "The Parisian theologians have concluded that the same thing is true in theology as in philosophy, and vice versa. . . . Neither can the same things all be true in the various fields of learning" *(Nam Parrhisienses theologi determinaverunt, esse idem verum in theologia, quod in philosophia, et e contra. . . . Neque enim possunt eadem omnia vera esse in diversis professionibus)*. See below, notes 423 and 426.

416. See especially theses 17ff. of the *Disputation Concerning Romans 3:28* (1537): WA 39/I:203f. The eschatology here is very distinctive. It gives us a much clearer picture of what the eschatological orientation means for Luther, with regard to progress, than we get in his *Disputation Concerning Man* (1536).

417. See WA 39/I:232, 7-233, 7 and Thesis 26: "Even more, the law itself will cease and be made void together with all knowledge and prophecy and the whole of Scripture" (203, 34f.).

418. LW 38:250; WA 39/II:15, 19-16, 3: *"omnes creaturae sunt pro Christo, ut sol, luna, et non contra Christum, quia omnia cooperantur piis in bonum, etiam ipse diabolus, mors, infernus. Sed inde tamen nondum fit verum et in theologia et philosophia, sed manebunt diversa specie et re."*

419. See Schleiermacher, *Der christliche Glaube* (see above, note 263), vol. 1, p. 112; see also Bayer, *Autorität und Kritik*, pp. 165f.

420. In soteriology and Christology, as well as in the doctrine of the Lord's Supper, it is necessary to think "not in terms of the category of substance but of relation" (WA 40/II:354, 3f.; see above, note 22). "A Christian is not inwardly and essentially *(intrinsece et formaliter)* holy. Neither is holiness a category of substance but of

relation *(praedicamento substantiae sed relationis); it* is given freely in mercy, simply by confessing and acknowledging that God is merciful to sinners" (354, 2-5; on Ps. 51:4; 1532). The very idea used here in the formula *"non in praedicamento substantiae, sed relationis"* is also central to Luther's positive argument that the Aristotelian concept of formal cause is inappropriate in soteriology: "The formal cause of our justification and salvation is divine mercy, imputation and acceptance. Without these, our newness or new obedience does not have a firm footing before God and does not please God; on the contrary, it is death and damnation" (39/I:228, 7-13).

421. See Baur, "Luther und die Philosophie."

422. LW 38:239-77; WA 39/II:1-33 (Disputation Concerning the Passage: "The Word Was Made Flesh" [John 1:14]). See besides Bengt Hägglund (see under note 427): Klaus Scholder, *Ursprünge und Probleme der Bibelkritik im 17. Jahrhundert. Ein Beitrag zur Entstehung der historisch-kritischen Theologie,* FGLP 33 (Munich: Kaiser, 1966), ch. 5, esp. pp. 118-24.

423. LW 38:243; WA 39/II:7, 10 *("esse idem verum in theologia, quod in philosophia, et e contra").* On the historical background, see Scholder, *Ursprünge und Probleme,* pp. 108ff., especially in regard to the condemnation by the Bishop of Paris on March 7, 1277, of the assertion of "two contradictory truths." This was condemned on the basis of 1 Corinthians 1:19 (108, note 9). Full reference: *Aufklärung im Mittelalter? Die Verurteilung von 1277. Das Dokument des Bischofs von Paris,* introduced, translated, and explained by Kurt Flasch (Mainz: Dieterich, 1989).

424. LW 38:269; WA 39/II:7, 32-36: *"quod idem non sit verum in theologia et philosophia. Scimus autem, aliud esse intelligere, aliud credere. Distinguitur ergo philosophia et theologia, philosophiae est intelligere sua ratione, theologiae vero credibile supra omnem rationem."* See WA 39/II:21, 10f.; LW 38:254: "We say: 'I believe in God,' not 'I understand God.'"

425. See the opening oration to the *Disputation Concerning Romans 3:28:* "sacred theology . . . is a divine gift; it is not the invention of human reason or of philosophy" (WA 39/I:260, 22f.); ". . . arrogant people confuse everything and do not distinguish between natural reason and this gift" [see Luke 21:15: "I will give you"] (39/I:261, 15f.). Luther does not distinguish between reflection understood as a task of civil righteousness and reflection understood as a task of revelation. Theology is the communicated revelation itself.

426. LW 38:242; WA 39/II:5, 31f. (Thesis 38): *"nunquam invenias, idem esse verum in omnibus."*

427. See Bengt Hägglund, *Theologie und Philosophie bei Luther und in der occamistischen Tradition. Luthers Stellung zur Theorie von der doppelten Wahrheit* (Lund: Gleerup, 1955).

428. LW 38:244; WA 39/II:8, 5-8: *"Nam ut Deus condidit sphaeras distinctas in coelo, sic in terra regna, ut unaquaeque res et ars suum locum et speciem retineat neque versetur extra suum centrum, in quo positum est."*

429. Here Luther differs from Schleiermacher; see Bayer, *Autorität und Kritik* pp. 164-66.

430. See for example LW 38:246f.; WA 39/II:11, 1-12, 10.

431. See LW 38:248; WA 39/II:13, 7; see also part two: section 2.3.4.

432. See, for example, the second thesis of the disputation "Whether the Books of the Philosophers Are Useful or Not for Theology" (1519?): "Of all the knowledge that human beings have acquired, grammar is especially useful for the teaching of theology" (WA 6:29, 7f.). See also WA 2:267, 32-5; 5:27, 8; LW 14:287; and WA 6:457f.; LW 44:200-2 (the reform of the universities, the dismissal of Aristotle, but "I would gladly agree to keeping Aristotle's *Logic, Rhetoric,* and *Poetics*": LW 44:201).

433. WA 39/II:105, 4-7: "*Creatura est in veteri lingua id, quod creator creavit et a se separavit, sed haec significatio non habet locum in creatura Christo. Ibi creator et creatura unus et idem est.*" See the continuation: "*Quia autem ambiguitas in vocabulo est et homines audientes hoc statim cogitant de creatura separata a creatore, ideo metuerunt eo uti, sed parce [!] licet eo uti ut novo vocabulo, sicut aliquando Augustinus dicit summa laetitia adfectus: Nonne admirabile mysterium? qui creator est, voluit esse creatura*" (Because there is an ambiguity in the term, and the people hearing it immediately think of a creature separate from the creator, they are afraid to use it, but it may be used sparingly [!] as a new term, as Augustine sometimes says with great joy: "Is this not a marvelous mystery? He who is the creator wanted to be a creature") (105, 7-11).

434. WA 39/II:104, 24: "*Spiritus sanctus habet suam grammaticam.*"

435. WA 39/II:104, 24-6: "*Grammatica omnibus modis valet, sed quando res maior est, quam ut comprehendi possit grammaticis et philosophicis regulis, relinquenda est.*"

436. WA 39/II:104, 10-18.

437. WA 39/II:112, 15-19: "*Est philosophicum argumentum. Nulla est proportio creaturae et creatoris, finiti et infiniti. Nos tamen non tantum facimus proportionem, sed unitatem finiti et infiniti. Aristoteles, si hoc audisset vel legisset, nunquam factus esset christianus, quia ipse non concessisset illam propositionem, quod eadem proportio sit finiti et infiniti.*"

438. WA 39/II:104, 18f.: "*Praescribuntur enim ibi nobis a Spiritu sancto formulae; in illa nube ambulemus.*" See 113, 1f.

439. Johann Georg Hamann, "Vermischte Anmerkungen . . . ," in Hamann, *Sämtliche Werke,* vol. 2, p. 129, 7-9. Hamann shares with his brother on 2/19/1760 from the preface of Bengel's *Gnomon* (1742) "a remarkable quote from our Luther," namely, "Theology is nothing but a grammar of the words of the Holy Spirit" (Johann Georg Hamann, *Briefwechsel,* vol. 2, ed. W. Ziesemer and A. Henkel [Wiesbaden: Insel Verlag, 1956], 10, 2-8). On the proximity of "gold" and "word" in Hamann, see Hamann, *Sämtliche Werke,* vol. 2, 129 and 59f. Think of the way Luther compares words with coins (WA TR 1:144, 16f. [no. 349]).

440. See Hamann, *Sämtliche Werke,* vol. 2, 60, 10-17; 71, 32-73, 9 ("Words derive their value, like place numbers, from their location. Like coins, the definitions and relationships of their terms will change according to place and time. . . .") Hamann may

have been the first to speak, as here, about the "role" of words. See also WA TR 1:144, 1-19 (no. 349); see above, note 407.

441. See WA 39/II:93, 5; 111, 14-16 etc.

442. In *Bondage of the Will,* Luther says of reason: "if she sees a thing happen once or twice, she immediately jumps to the conclusion that it happens quite generally and with regard to all the words of God and humans, making a universal out of a particular in the usual manner of her wisdom" (LW 33:121; WA 18:673, 31-33).

443. See esp. WA 39/II:93, 8-17.

444. WA 39/II:105, 6f. See above, note 433.

445. WA 39/II:105, 9 *("parce . . . uti").* See above, note 433.

446. WA 39/II:94, 20: *"Certum est tamen, omnia vocabula in Christo novam significationem accipere in eadem re significata."*

447. WA 39/II:94, 26: *"Homo sine literis, disciplinis, sine sensu quoque humano nescit discernere inter vocabula aequivoca."*

448. With Jörg Baur, "Luther und die Philosophie," *NZSTh* 26 (1984): 27.

449. LW 38:242; WA 39/II:5, 31f. (Thesis 38 of the Disputation Concerning John 1:14, 1539): *"Ita per singula artificia vel potius opera, si transeas, nunquam invenias, idem esse verum in omnibus."* Here we see Nominalistic presuppositions playing a role. See Bengt Hägglund, *Theologie und Philosophie bei Luther.*

Notes to Part Two

1. Hermann Fischer, "Luthers Sicht des Menschen im Spannungsfeld von philosophischer und theologischer Definition. Erwägungen zu Gerhard Ebelings Kommentar über Luthers Disputationsthesen 'De homine,'" *Theologische Rundschau* 57 (1992): 316.

2. For a summary, see Emanuel Hirsch, *Geschichte der neuern evangelischen Theologie im Zusammenhang mit den allgemeinen Bewegungen des europäischen Denkens,* vol. 4, 3rd ed. (Gütersloh: Gütersloher Verlaghaus, 1964), pp. 48-89.

3. See Hirsch, *Geschichte der neuern evangelischen Theologie,* pp. 88f. Also see section 5: "Theology and Methodology." On the relationship between Semler and Schleiermacher, see Gottfried Hornig, "Schleiermacher und Semler. Beobachtungen zur Erforschung ihres Beziehungsverhältnisses," in *Internationaler Schleiermacher-Kongress* (Berlin, 1984), ed. K. V. Selge (Berlin: De Gruyter, 1985), pp. 875-97, esp. 882-86.

4. See part one, note 264.

5. See part one: section 3.4.2: "Meditatio" (see above, note 4). (Note: "monastic" liturgical spirituality links daily work and the practice of piety with corporate involvement in the divine service.)

6. "No one denies that theology is only for teachers and scholars, whereas the Christian faith, or a summary of Christian teaching, which describes and promotes the Christian life and the happiness it brings, belongs to all Christians" (Johann

Salomo Semler, *Versuch einer freiern theologischen Lehrart. Zur Bestätigung und Erläuterung seines lateinischen Buches* [Halle, 1977], p. 192, cited in Trutz Rendtorff, *Church and Theology: The Systematic Function of the Church Concept in Modern Theology* [Philadelphia: Westminster, 1971], p. 33, translation altered). Here theology is "understood as a term for a specialist subject area that can be changed, corrected and developed. However, this cannot be done by Christians individually but only by the future teachers and pastors. Religion, on the other hand, designates the conviction of faith, spirituality and love of the neighbor that needs to be proved by all Christians. . . . The distinction between religion and theology, on the one hand, means that theology, which is alterable, should be free to criticize tradition, but on the other hand, it should also be released from the dubious claim that the results of its critique are binding on religion" (Gottfried Hornig, "Johann Salomo Semler," *Gestalten der Kirchengeschichte*, vol. 8, ed. M. Greschat [Stuttgart: Kohlhammer, 1983], pp. 272f.).

7. "The self-determination of private religion" means "that individual Christians with their faith in Christ and through their personal appropriation of salvation are bound neither to the doctrinal tradition of the church nor its authority. Private religion exists where Christians have found independent access to the basic truths of the Christian religion. . . . People become involved in it with their whole being, with their mind and conscience, their intellect and will, while for many the public religion of the church is nothing more than an external custom of Christianity without any inner involvement." See Gottfried Hornig, "Die Freiheit der christlichen Privatreligion. Semlers Begründung des religiösen Individualismus in der protestantischen Aufklärungstheologie," *NZSTh* 21 (1979): 200.

8. See Oswald Bayer, *Leibliches Wort. Reformation und Neuzeit im Konflikt* (Tübingen: Mohr Siebeck, 1992), pp. 66-68 ("Öffentlichkeit des Glaubens und 'Religion als Privatsache,'" pp. 57-72). On the need to fall back on a rational concept of what is generally human that claims to arbitrate the competing claims to validity on the part of positive definitions, see Bayer, *Zeitgenosse im Widerspruch. Johann Georg Hamann als radikaler Aufklärer* (Munich: Piper, 1988), p. 156 ("Geschichte und Vernunft," pp. 151-78).

9. "Some two hundred years ago, the concepts 'private religion' and 'private theology,' 'private faith' and 'private Christianity' entered the language of theology and eventually language generally through Semler's writings. Doubtless one of the long-range consequences of his conceptual scheme is the contemporary and widespread thesis that religion is a 'private matter' or 'private concern' of the individual. Although its significance is disputed, it has become something of a slogan" (Gottfried Hornig, "Die Freiheit der christlichen Privatreligion," p. 198). Hornig also notes, p. 211: "Semler's espousal of private religion might allow each Christian to retain his or her individuality and religious freedom, but it contributes either intentionally or unintentionally to the erosion of the church in Christianity."

10. This meta-critique critiques modern theology's own critique of the tradition. It is presented in a detailed way in Oswald Bayer, *Autorität und Kritik. Zu*

Hermeneutik und Wissenschaftstheorie (Tübingen: Mohr Siebeck, 1991); Bayer, *Freiheit als Antwort. Zur theologischen Ethik* (Tübingen: Mohr Siebeck, 1995) (the English translation to be published by Oxford University Press under the title *Responsive Freedom*); Bayer, "Vernunft ist Sprache. Hamanns Metakritik Kants," *Spekulation und Erfahrung* II, 50 (Stuttgart: Frommann-Holzboog, 2002), and in the two books referred to in note 8 above. For the best introduction in English to Hamann's later writings, especially his meta-critique of Kantian rationalism, see Gwen Griffith Dickson, *Johann Georg Hamann's Relational Metacriticism* (Berlin: De Gruyter, 1995).

11. See part one, note 439.

12. See Oswald Bayer, *Theologie*, HST vol. 1 (Gütersloh: Gütersloher Verlaghaus, 1994), B I, 11: "'Was uns unbedingt angeht'; die Entgegenständlichung des Gegenstandes der Theologie." [Translators' note: Part B has not been translated. However, for more on this, see Paul Tillich, *Systematic Theology*, vol. 1 (Chicago: University of Chicago Press, 1951), pp. 11-16, where he discusses the meaning of the term "ultimate concern."]

13. See Martin Luther, "Lectures on Genesis" (1535-45), LW 1:103 (translation altered); WA 42:79, 3: "*Haec est institutio Ecclesiae, antequam esset oeconomia et Politia.*"

14. LW 1:103; WA 42:79, 3: *sine muris.*

15. LW 1:105 (translation altered); WA 42:80, 2: *proponit ei verbum.*

16. LW 1:106 (translation altered); WA 42:81, 3f.: "*Hoc tantum vult, ut laudet Deum, ut gratias ei agat, ut laetetur in Domino. . . .*" Note how it continues: "*et ei in hoc obediat, ne ex vetita arbore comedat*" (that he obeys him by not eating from the forbidden tree), WA 42:81, 4.

17. Martin Luther, "Lectures on Jonah" (1526), LW 19:11 (translation altered); WA 19:208, 21.

18. Against Wolfhart Pannenberg, *Theology and the Philosophy of Science*, trans. Francis McDonagh (Philadelphia: Westminster, 1976), p. 361. However, note the important qualification on pp. 419-20.

19. Pannenberg, *Theology and the Philosophy of Science*, p. 361 (translation altered). However, see below, note 435.

20. See below, section 6.4: "Theology and Religious Studies."

21. See Martin Luther, "Against the Heavenly Prophets in the Matter of Images and Sacraments" (1525), LW 40:213f. (WA 18:204, 3f.). Accordingly, salvation is "achieved" on the cross *(sub Pontio Pilato)*, but it is "distributed" in the word (from the beginning of the world until its end).

22. Friedrich Schleiermacher understands the action of the divine service as "representative" (not "efficacious") activity. See *Die christliche Sitte nach den Grundsätzen der evangelischen Kirche im Zusammenhange dargestellt*, 2nd edition, ed. L. Jonas, Sämtliche Werke I-12 (Berlin, 1884), pp. 502-706 (esp. pp. 599-619) and *Die praktische Theologie nach den Grundsätzen der evangelischen Kirche im Zusammenhange dargestellt*, ed. Jacob Frerichs, Sämtliche Werke I-13 (Berlin: Reimer, 1850), pp. 68-82. For a critical reception

of the Schleiermacherian category of "representation," see Peter Cornehl, "Theorie des Gottesdienstes — ein Prospekt," *Theologische Quartalschrift* 159 (1979): 178-95.

23. See Karl Rahner, *Foundations of Christian Faith: An Introduction to the Idea of Christianity*, trans. William V. Dych (New York: Crossroad, 1984), p. 419.

24. On the understanding of the church as original sacrament, see Otto Semmelroth, *Die Kirche als Ursakrament*, 3rd ed. (Frankfurt: Knecht, 1963) and "Ursakrament," in *Lexikon für Theologie und Kirche*, vol. 10, pp. 568f.; Karl Rahner, "Kirche und Sakramente" (*Quaestiones disputatae* 10) (Freiburg: Herder, 1960), p. 17.

25. The exclusivity of the formulation refers only to the gospel. However, this does not contradict the fourfold way of describing the object of theology that we develop below (see section 2.1).

26. Martin Luther, *The Babylonian Captivity of the Church* (1520), LW 36:42 (translation altered) (WA 6:516, 30-32). (*"Neque enim deus, ut dixi, aliter cum hominibus unquam egit aut agit quam verbo promissionis. Rursus, nec nos cum deo unquam agere aliter possumus quam fide in verbum promissionis eius."*) See LW 36:39 (WA 6:514, 14); LW 36:42 (WA 6:517, 8f.). Schleiermacher reshapes this correlation between word and faith into a correlation between "God-consciousness" and the "immediate religious self-consciousness" and so fails to recognize its peculiarity. See Oswald Bayer, "Wortlehre oder Glaubenslehre? Zur Konstitution theologischer Systematik im Streit zwischen Schleiermacher und Luther," in *Autorität und Kritik*, pp. 156-68. Also see below, section 4.3.1: "The Existential Approach" (Schleiermacher).

27. LW 51:333 (WA 49:588, 15-18) (translation altered).

28. *Konfirmationsbuch der Evangelischen Landeskirche in Württemberg*, 10th ed. (Stuttgart: Quell-Verlag der Evang. Ges., 1962), p. 33 ("Answer to the Question: What Is Prayer?"). See Psalm 19:15 ("may the words of my mouth and the meditation of my heart be acceptable to you, Lord").

29. See Bayer, *Leibliches Wort*, pp. 66-68.

30. See Bayer, *Leibliches Wort*, pp. 289-305 and 306-13.

31. See Bayer, *Leibliches Wort*, pp. 62f.

32. A fuller description would explain the individual parts of the liturgy and their connections; I have used the "answered complaint" as an example, which focuses on the "Kyrie" and the prayer of intercession in the liturgy. See Bayer, *Leibliches Wort*, pp. 334-48.

33. See Martin Luther, *Babylonian Captivity of the Church* (1520), LW 36:48 (WA 6:520, 33-36).

34. LW 36:49 (WA 6:521, 29f.) (translation altered). The emphases are those of the author.

35. Compare LW 36:48 (WA 6:522, 27-29).

36. LW 36:51 (WA 6:523, 9) (translation altered).

37. Johann Georg Hamann, "Golgotha und Scheblimini," in *J. G. Hamann 1730-1788: A Study in Christian Existence* by Ronald Gregor Smith (New York: Harper & Brothers, 1960), pp. 229-30.

38. See *Concerning Christ's Supper. Confession* (1528), LW 37:36 (WA 26:505, 38–506, 7) and the *Large Catechism* (1529), BC 468:18–471:42 (WA 30/1:191, 28–192, 29 [*BSLK* 660, 18–661, 42]).

39. Ernst Käsemann, "Gottesdienst im Alltag der Welt. Zu Römer 12," in *Exegetische Versuche und Besinnungen,* vol. 2 (Göttingen: Vandenhoeck and Ruprecht, 1964), p. 201. Translated by W. J. Montague under the title "Worship in Everyday Life: A note on Romans 12," in *New Testament Questions of Today* (London: SCM Press, 1969), p. 191. For the correct understanding of Käsemann's thesis, see Karl-Adolf Bauer, *Leiblichkeit — das Ende aller Werke Gottes. Die Bedeutung der Leiblichkeit des Menschen bei Paulus,* Studien zum Neuen Testament, vol. 4 (Gütersloh: Gütersloher Verlaghaus, 1971), pp. 180f., note 27.

40. Against Ulrich Wilckens, *Der Brief an die Römer,* Evangelisch-Katholischer Kommentar 6/3 (Zürich/Einsiedeln/Köln and Neukirchen-Vluyn: Neukirchener Verlag, 1982), pp. 8f.

41. See above, note 39.

42. Martin Luther, *Treatise on Good Works,* LW 44:78; WA 6:248, 26f.: Interpretation of the third commandment (translation altered). [The German word *"Feier"* means a "festival day" and therefore a "holiday." To celebrate a festival *(feiern)* means to stop work. In this section, Luther is giving a Christian interpretation to the third commandment. In the Old Testament, the Sabbath day was a day of rest. People observed it by not working. Luther connects this with the Christian Sunday, the Lord's day, which we celebrate by having a "holiday" from work and attending divine service so that God can do his work. By going to worship, we put to death our old self by returning to our Baptism. In the divine service, we cease from our work of self-justification and instead receive by faith God's gift of justification in the receptive life *(vita passiva).*]

43. See Karl Barth, CD I/2:364 (KD I/2:400): Human being is that "being which is constantly realising its existence in acts of free determination and decision"; CD II/2:535 (KD II/2:594): "To exist as a man means to act. And action means choosing, deciding." Also, the "Christian faith is a free human *act*" (CD 4/1:757 [KD IV/1:846]; compare CD 4/1:769 [KD IV/1:859]. See Bayer, *Theologie,* B III, 2.3.4, notes 251-54 ("Der Mensch als Täter. Die der Theoretisierung korrespondierende Ethisierung") and B III, 2.4, notes 288-96.

44. See Rudolf Bultmann, "Grace and Freedom," in *Essays: Philosophical and Theological,* trans. James Greig (London: SCM Press, 1955): faith is obedience, a "free act of decision" (p. 176). "Such faith, embracing obedience and trust, is therefore man's *decision* against himself and for God, and as such, faith is an act" (p. 175).

45. Karl Marx, "Economic and Political Manuscripts," in *Selected Writings* (Oxford: Oxford University Press, 1977), p. 93. See also p. 95: "But since for the socialist *the whole of what we call world history* is nothing but the creation of man by human labour and the development of nature for man, humans have concrete and irrefutable proof that they created themselves, that they engineered their own *birth*" (translation al-

tered). Compare Hegel's thesis: "The *true being* of a human is bound up with . . . *his or her action;* this is what makes a person a *real* individual" (*Phenomenology of Spirit,* trans. A. V. Miller [Oxford: Oxford University Press], p. 193, translation altered).

46. On Bultmann's distinction between "work" and "act": "the less faith is a work, the more it is an act" ("Grace and Freedom" [see above, note 44], p. 175). Bultmann's understanding of faith as an act (of decision) reflects his understanding of the word of God as a demand (see below, notes 313 and 314).

47. See LW 36:59 (WA 6:528, 8-17).

48. *Lutheran Worship* 331:4 (*EG* 231:4) ("Here Is the Tenfold Sure Command"; on the third commandment).

49. Martin Luther, "Preface to the Epistle of St. Paul to the Romans," LW 35:370 (WA DB 7:10, 6-8).

50. See Martin Luther, *"Operationes in Psalmos"* (1519-1521) on Psalm 5:12 (WA 5:165, 33–166, 16). See part one: section 2.2. [Translators' note: "Receptive life" is a better translation of *vita passiva* than "passive life." Today the difference between the active and the passive voice in English grammar is no longer widely understood; "passive" is usually taken to mean "inactive" rather than "receptive." Hence, "receptive life" better conveys Luther's thought than "passive life."]

51. See the "Preface to the First Volume of the Wittenberg Edition of Luther's German Writings" (1539), LW 34:283-88 (WA 50:658, 29–661, 8) and the detailed interpretation of this text in part one: section 3: "The Three 'Rules': *Oratio, Meditatio, Tentatio.*"

52. See Bayer, *Autorität und Kritik,* pp. 156-68 ("Wortlehre oder Glaubenslehre? Zur Konstitution theologischer Systematik im Streit zwischen Schleiermacher und Luther").

53. Hegel, *Lectures on the Philosophy of Religion,* vol. 1, *Introduction and the Concept of Religion,* ed. and trans. Peter Hodgson (Berkeley: University of California Press, 1984), p. 84 (translation altered).

54. Hegel, Preface to the 2nd edition of *Science of Logic,* trans. A. V. Miller (Oxford: Oxford University Press, 1969), p. 42 (translation altered).

55. See below, section 4: "Transformations: the Problem of Secularization" — the ethical approach, the theoretical approach, the existential approach.

56. I take this approach to the doctrine of creation in my book *Schöpfung als Anrede.* There I have tried to develop a doctrine of creation, for example, from the morning hymn of Paul Gerhardt (Oswald Bayer, *Schöpfung als Anrede. Zu einer Hermeneutik der Schöpfung,* 2nd ed. [Tübingen: Mohr Siebeck, 1990], pp. 109-27) or from a section of the catechism (Bayer, pp. 80-108, translated in Oswald Bayer, "I Believe That God Has Created Me with All That Exists. An Example of Catechetical-Systematics," *LQ* 8 (1994): 129-61. Christology and the doctrine of the Trinity can be considered most appropriately on the basis of Luther's hymn "Dear Christians, One and All, Rejoice" (*LBW* 299; *Lutheran Worship* 353). On that, see Oswald Bayer, "The Being of Christ in Faith," *LQ* 10 (1996): 135-50. On the theological significance of the

complaint (which better translates *Klage* than "lament"), see Bayer, "Toward a Theology of Lament," in *Caritas et Reformatio*, ed. Carter Lindberg and David Whitford (St. Louis: Concordia Publishing House, 2002), pp. 211-20.

57. See below, section 3: "Promise and Faith" and see above, section 2.1: "The Object of Theology," where we demonstrate the need for a *fourfold* definition of the object of theology.

58. On "Catechetical Systematics" see part one: section 4. Calvin attempted to move in this direction in the first edition of his *Institutes* (1536), but later he gave up the idea. See Bayer, *Theologie*, A III, 5 and 6.

59. See part one: section 5.4: "The Grammar of the Holy Spirit" note 439. See also Ludwig Wittgenstein, *Philosophical Investigations*, trans. G. E. M. Anscombe (New York: Macmillan, 1958), §373, p. 116 ("Grammar tells what kind of object something is").

60. See below, section 4.1: "The Ethical Approach" (Kant).

61. See below, section 4.2: "The Theoretical Approach" (Hegel).

62. See below, section 4.3.1: "The Existential Approach" (Schleiermacher).

63. See Bayer, *Leibliches Wort*, p. 236, note 103, and see below, note 265.

64. See below, section 4.1: "The Ethical Approach" (Kant).

65. For more details, see Bayer, *Leibliches Wort*, pp. 328-30.

66. Martin Luther, *The Bondage of the Will* (1525), LW 33:140 (WA 18:685, 21-24 [translation altered]).

67. See the Introduction: "Important Moments in the Understanding of Theology. 2. Monastic and Scholastic Theology."

68. See Bayer, *Autorität und Kritik*, esp. pp. 128, 132, 138, and see below, section 2.3.4: "Science Is Wisdom Understood as Law" and section 7: "Faith and Sight," specifically, section 7.3: "Consequences."

69. Heinrich Scholz, "Wie ist eine evangelische Theologie als Wissenschaft möglich?" in *Theologie als Wissenschaft. Aufsätze und Thesen*, edited with an introduction by Gerhard Sauter (Munich: Kaiser, 1971), pp. 221-64.

70. See Wolfhart Pannenberg, *Theology and the Philosophy of Science*, trans. Francis McDonagh (Philadelphia: Westminster, 1976); Gerhard Sauter et al., *Wissenschaftstheoretische Kritik der Theologie. Die Theologie und die neuere wissenschaftstheoretische Diskussion. Materialien. Analysen. Entwürfe* (Munich: Kaiser, 1973); Oswald Bayer, *Was ist das: Theologie? Eine Skizze* (Stuttgart: Calwer Verlag, 1973). For an overview, see Gert Hummel, "Enzyklopädie theologische," *TRE* 9:716-42.

71. See especially *Handbuch der Fundamentaltheologie*, ed. W. Kern, H. J. Pottmeyer, M. Seckler, vol. 4 (Theologische Erkenntnislehre) (Freiburg, 1988); *Fides quaerens intellectum. Beiträge zur Fundamentaltheologie* (Max Seckler zum 65. Geburtstag), ed. M. Kessler, W. Pannenberg, and H. J. Pottmeyer (Tübingen: Francke, 1992).

72. See the Introduction: "Important Moments in the Understanding of Theology. 3. Problems with the Philosophy of Science."

73. Pannenberg, *Theology and the Philosophy of Science*, p. 299 (translation altered).

74. Pannenberg, *Theology and the Philosophy of Science,* p. 298 with explicit reference to Thomas (*STh* I, q. 1, art. 7); see also his *Systematic Theology,* vol. 1, trans. Geoffrey W. Bromiley (Grand Rapids: Eerdmans, 1991), p. 5.

75. Pannenberg, *Theology and the Philosophy of Science,* pp. 297-345, ch. 5 (the key chapter of the whole book): "Theology as the Science of God."

76. See part one: section 2.1: "The Subject Matter of Theology: The God Who Justifies and the Sinful Human."

77. See Bayer, *Leibliches Wort,* pp. 19-34 ("Rechtfertigung. Grund und Grenze der Theologie"), translated as "Justification as the Basis and Boundary of Theology," *LQ* 15 (2001): 273-92.

78. See my outline of systematic theology: *Living by Faith: On Justification and Sanctification,* trans. Geoffrey Bromiley (Grand Rapids: Eerdmans, 2003). On eschatology especially, see Oswald Bayer, "Die Zukunft Jesu Christi zum Letzten Gericht," in *Eschatologie und Jüngstes Gericht,* Bekenntnis. Fuldaer Hefte 32, ed. R. Rittner (Hannover: Lutherisches Verlag-Haus, 1991), pp. 68-99.

79. Pannenberg, *Theology and the Philosophy of Science,* p. 299 (translation altered).

80. Pannenberg, *Theology and the Philosophy of Science,* p. 299; this is taken up in Pannenberg, *Systematic Theology,* vol. 1, pp. 48-61 with reference to Gregory of Nyssa (395, 349, 350) and Descartes (106f., 113, 140, 350ff., 395).

81. Descartes, *Meditations on First Philosophy,* 3rd ed., trans. Donald Cress (Indianapolis: Hackett, 1993), pp. 77-79.

82. See part one: section 2.1. See also: LW 31:52 (WA 1:362, 1f.) (the "back" of God: *posteriora Dei*); compare Exodus 33:19-23.

83. "Then I saw myself with me alone in the Nothing" (August Klingemann, *The Night Watches of Bonaventure,* trans. and ed. Gerald Gillespie [Edinburgh: University of Edinburgh Press, 1972]), p. 213.

84. See Bayer, *Theologie,* B II, esp. notes 69, 82, and 96.

85. See Wolfgang Janke, "*Praecisio mundi.* Über die Abschnitte der mythisch-numinosen Welt im Schatten der Götzendämmerung," in *Mythos und Religion. Interdisziplinäre Aspekte,* ed. O. Bayer (Stuttgart: Calwer, 1990), pp. 31-57.

86. The distinction between law and gospel must in fact be *taught.* However, teaching about the distinction is one thing, making it is another. To actually make the distinction in a crucial situation (such as spiritual attack) in a way that is truly beneficial or salvific is not within our power, but it is solely the work of God. See *Leibliches Wort,* pp. 42f. ("Die Unverfügbarkeit der Unterscheidung").

87. See Ludwig Wittgenstein, *Tractatus Logico-Philosophicus,* trans. D. F. Pears and B. F. McGuinness (London: Routledge & Kegan Paul, 1974), p. 74: "What we cannot speak about we must pass over in silence."

88. See below, section 4.2: "The Theoretical Approach" (Hegel).

89. A "definition of the essence" of Christianity as a "realization of essence" is advocated by Ernst Troeltsch, "What Does 'Essence of Christianity' Mean?" in *Ernst*

Troeltsch: Writings on Theology and Religion, trans. and ed. Robert Morgan and Michael Pye (Atlanta: John Knox, 1977), pp. 124-81.

90. See below, note 198.

91. See below, section 4.3.2: "The Existential Approach" (Bultmann).

92. See *Autorität und Kritik,* pp. 59-82: "Vernunftautorität und Bibelkritik," pp. 71-74: "Moralgesetz und Bibelkritik," and below, section 4.1: "The Ethical Approach" (Kant).

93. See below, section 4.3.2: "The Existential Approach" (Bultmann) and section 4.3.3: "The Existential Approach" (Jonas).

94. See Bayer, *Autorität und Kritik,* pp. 11-18: "Theologie im Konflikt der Interpretationen."

95. Friedrich Schleiermacher, *The Christian Faith,* trans. and ed. H. R. Mackintosh and J. S. Stewart (Philadelphia: Fortress, 1976), §15, p. 78 (translation altered slightly).

96. See below, section 4.3.2: "The Existential Approach" (Bultmann).

97. See below, section 4.3.1: "The Existential Approach" (Schleiermacher) and section 4.3.3: "The Existential Approach" (Jonas).

98. For more details, see below, section 5: "Theology and Methodology."

99. *Critique of Pure Reason,* trans. Paul Guyer and Allen Wood (Cambridge: Cambridge University Press, 1998), A 820/B 848, p. 684. To be more precise, the model used was the section "Opining, Knowing, and Believing" of the "Transcendental Doctrine of Method" in Kant's *Critique of Pure Reason.* See Hans Joachim Iwand, "Wider den Mißbrauch des 'pro me' als methodisches Prinzip in der Theologie," *EvTh* 14 (1954): 120-24 (= *Theologische Literaturzeitung* 79 [1954]: 454-58).

100. *Augsburg Confession,* Article 5.

101. For more details, see Oswald Bayer, "The Modern Narcissus," *LQ* 9 (1995): 301-13.

102. Immanuel Kant, *Religion within the Limits of Reason Alone,* trans. Theodore Greene and Hoyt Hudson (New York: Harper Torchbooks, 1960), pp. 50-84.

103. Schleiermacher, *The Christian Faith,* vol. 2, §§92-105.

104. For more details, see below, section 4.2: "The Theoretical Approach" (Hegel) and section 6.3: "The Problem of Natural Theology."

105. The classical document of "monarchical reason" (or the absolute rule of reason; to this: Oswald Bayer, *Zeitgenosse im Widerspruch,* pp. 62f.; see p. 179) is Aristotle, *Metaphysics* XII, the concluding sentence: "That which exists does not want to be ruled badly. 'The rule of many is not good; therefore, let one be the ruler!'" (*Iliad* II, 204).

106. Emmanuel Levinas, *Time and the Other,* trans. Richard A. Cohen (Pittsburgh: Duquesne University Press, 1990); Levinas, *Humanism of the Other,* trans. Nidra Poller, introduced by Richard A. Cohen (Urbana and Chicago: University of Illinois Press, 2003); Levinas, *Die Spur des Anderen. Untersuchung zur Phänomenologie und Sozialphilosophie,* 2nd ed., trans. with an introduction by Wolfgang Nikolaus Krewani (Freiburg/Munich, 1987).

107. "For that reason, however, the absolute is the identity of identity and non-identity; both opposition and unity indwell it at one and the same time." See *The Difference between Fichte's and Schelling's System of Philosophy*, ed. H. S. Harris and Walter Cerf (Albany: State University of New York Press, 1977), p. 156; see also p. 159. See Hegel, *Science of Logic: Objective Logic*, trans. A. V. Miller (London: George Allen & Unwin, 1969), pp. 411-16, esp. 412f.

108. LW 33:140 (translation altered); (WA 18:685, 21-23). The most important biblical texts testifying to this are listed in Bayer, *Theologie*, B II, note III.

109. WA 20:380, 9f. (Sermon on John 16:23ff. for Rogate, 1526): *oppone promissionem suam et tuam necessitatem.*

110. See section 7: "Faith and Sight."

III. See the Introduction, "Important Moments in the Understanding of Theology. 3. Problems with the Philosophy of Science," note 25.

112. Immanuel Kant, *Critique of Pure Reason*, A 832, p. 691.

113. There is also another way in which we can speak of the threefold understanding of the object of theology, and that is to approach it from the standpoint of God, the world, and the self. For this, see below, section 2.3.2: "Meta-Critical Wisdom." Both approaches are complementary.

114. For more details, see Bayer, *Leibliches Wort*, pp. 2f.

115. If we take as our guide Aristotle's proposition that "being has several senses" (*to on legetai pollachos; Metaphysics* VII: 1028a), we can cautiously define the object of theology in a fourfold way, which would avoid a monism as well as a dualism. Furthermore, just as Aristotle elevated the category of substance, the gospel should be privileged above the other ways of specifying the object of theology because it is the definitive word and work of God — although, of course, these other ways cannot be understood as accidents of the gospel. I owe this insight to Dr. Theo Dieter.

116. Thus Eberhard Jüngel argues against Wolfhart Pannenberg: "There are two approaches in contemporary theology to learning how to think God again. The one way, pursued by Wolfhart Pannenberg with impressive consistency, is to begin thinking God in a way that presupposes that God has been removed from the equation *(remoto deo)* in order to arrive at a concept of God that can also function as the framework for an understanding of God that is uniquely Christian. This book will take the opposite approach. Our thinking here pursues a path which, one might say, goes from the inside to the outside, from the specifically Christian experience of faith to a concept of God that claims general validity. The goal of our thinking in this book is not to demonstrate that we can think God on the basis of general anthropological considerations, but that we can indeed think God as well as humanity on the basis of the event of God's self-disclosure that leads to the experience of God, and thus to demonstrate that the Christian truth is generally valid on the basis of its inner power" (*God as the Mystery of the World: On the Foundation of the Theology of the Crucified One in the Dispute between Theism and Atheism*, trans. Darrell L. Guder [Grand Rapids: Eerdmans, 1983], p. viii, translation significantly altered).

117. See above, note 80. "Philosophical reflection on the human necessity to be able to think the infinite and absolute can no longer offer a theoretical proof of the existence of God, but it still retains the critical function of the natural theology of antiquity relative to every form of religious tradition by imposing minimal conditions for any discourse about God that wants to be taken seriously. But this still leaves us with nothing but a *'general philosophical concept* for that which merits being called "God"' [Jüngel]. Without recognizing this possibility, Christian talk about God cannot advance any solid claim to universality" (Wolfhart Pannenberg, *Systematic Theology*, vol. 1, p. 107, translation significantly altered). See above, also note 18.

118. See below, section 6: "Specificity and Breadth."

119. Schleiermacher, *The Christian Faith*, p. 5 (translation altered).

120. Schleiermacher, *The Christian Faith*, pp. 12-18.

121. Ulrich Köpf, *Die Anfänge der theologischen Wissenschaftstheorie im 13. Jahrhundert (BHTh* 49) (Tübingen: Mohr Siebeck, 1974), p. 199, especially notes 221f. on Albert Magnus (p. 201, note 231: *"Scientia proprie est affectiva"* = "knowledge is properly speaking affective"). [Translators' note: affective knowledge is the same as poetic knowledge, which is altogether different than scientific knowledge. See James L. Taylor, *Poetic Knowledge: The Recovery of Education* (Albany: State University of New York Press, 1998).]

122. Ulrich Köpf, *Die Anfänge*, p. 203 note 238 (Bonaventure, *Commentary on the Four Books of the Sentences*, Q. 3: *". . . ad affectum, sic perficitur ab habitu medio inter pure speculativum et practicum, qui complecitur utrumque";* translation: ". . . as for the affects, it [the intellect] is thus perfected by a middle habit, between the purely speculative and practical, which embraces both").

123. WA 5:165, 33-166, 16 (on Ps. 5:11). On Tauler: WA 5:165, 18-20.

124. WA 5:85, 2f. (= AWA 2, 137, 1f.) (on Ps. 3:3): *"ne vita activa cum suis operibus* et *vita contemplativa cum suis speculationibus nos seducant";* translation: "so that we are not led astray by the *active life* with its works, or by the *contemplative life* with its speculations." See part one: section 2.2.

125. Aristotle, *Nichomachean Ethics* X, 7-8.

126. Aristotle, *Nichomachean Ethics* VI, 2, 1139a 35-63.

127. Eckhart's Sermon on Mary and Martha in *Meister Eckhart: Teacher and Preacher*, ed. Bernard McGinn (New York: Paulist Press, 1986), sermon 86: 338-45. See Dietmar Mieth, *Die Einheit von vita activa und vita contemplativa in den deutschen Predigten und Traktaten Meister Eckharts und bei Johannes Tauler*, Untersuchungen zur Struktur des christlichen Lebens (Regensburg: Pustet, 1969), pp. 186-233.

128. See Bayer, *Autorität und Kritik*, pp. 127-41 ("Glauben und Wissenschaft"), esp. pp. 129-31.

129. It is surprising that Pannenberg, both in his philosophy of science *(Theology and the Philosophy of Science)* and in his *Systematic Theology* (Grand Rapids: Eerdmans, 1991-1998), which builds on the former, does not even bother with the question of the receptive life *(vita passiva)* but attends only to contemplation.

130. LW 44:78 (translation altered); WA 6:248, 26f. (see above, note 42).

131. In his own way Kant took up the question himself, especially in the *Critique of Pure Reason:* "Thus I had to deny *knowledge* in order to make room for *faith*" (B 30).

132. See below, section 4.2: "The Theoretical Approach" (Hegel) and section 7: "Faith and Sight."

133. The Lutheran philosopher and theologian Johann Georg Hamann (1730-88) brilliantly defended this Pauline perspective. See Oswald Bayer and Christian Knudsen, *Kreuz und Kritik. Johann Georg Hamanns Letztes Blatt. Text und Interpretation* (*BHTh* 66) (Tübingen: Mohr Siebeck, 1983), pp. 100-14 ("Revelation and Passion"), esp. pp. 110-14. For an introduction to Hamann, see below, note 177.

134. See LW 26:228 (WA 40/1:362, 15): "faith slays reason and kills it" *(fides rationem mactat et occidit).*

135. See below, section 6.3: "The Problem of Natural Theology."

136. Karl Marx, "Economic and Political Manuscripts."

137. See the Introduction: "Important Moments in the Understanding of Theology. 1. Christian Theology between Metaphysics and Mythology."

138. For more detail, see *Autorität und Kritik,* pp. 201-5 ("Kontemplative und aktive Theodizee").

139. "Science and human power coincide; for where we do not know the cause we cannot produce the effect" *("Scientia et potentia humana in idem coincidunt, quia ignoratio causae destituit effectum")* (*Novum Organum,* Aphorisms III, *The Works of Francis Bacon,* new facsimile edition of Spedding, Ellis, and Heath [London 1857-74, 14 volumes], vol. 1, 1963, p. 157).

140. See below, section 4.2: "The Theoretical Approach" (Hegel).

141. See below, section 4.1: "The Ethical Approach" (Kant).

142. See below, section 4.3.1: "The Existential Approach" (Schleiermacher–Feuerbach).

143. For more details, see below, section 4.3.1.

144. See above, note 95. The standard translation is slightly altered.

145. When Luther (WA TR 3:669-74 [No. 3868, from May 10, 1538], esp. 670, 18f.) says polemically of the enthusiasts that "they do not define and consider the word according to the God who speaks but according to the human recipient" *("definiunt verbum non secundum dicentem Deum, sed secundum recipientem hominem,"* 673, 3f.), he criticizes a principle of epistemology that is both ancient and modern: "What a recipient receives is determined by the recipient's disposition" *("receptum est in recipiente per modum recipientis")* (Aquinas, *STh* I, q. 84, art. 1). However, the reversal of this principle does not mean that we would not be involved in faith through the God who speaks *(deus dicens),* for in making its confession, faith is in fact empowered to attribute to God what is his and so in this way it becomes the creator of the Deity *("creatrix divinitatis"),* but of course only "in us." On the idea that faith is the creator of the Deity, see part one: section 2.1 ("The Subject Matter of Theology"), note 29.

146. *Critique of Practical Reason,* trans. Mary Gregor (Cambridge: Cambridge University Press, 1997), A 291f., 134-35 (translation altered).

147. *Critique of Pure Reason,* A 850, p. 701.

148. *Critique of Practical Reason,* A 291, 134 (translation altered).

149. *Critique of Pure Reason,* A 835, p. 693 (translation altered).

150. *Critique of Pure Reason,* B xiii, p. 109.

151. Immanuel Kant, *The Conflict of the Faculties,* trans. Mary Gregor (Lincoln: University of Nebraska Press, 1992), p. 67 (translation altered).

152. Kant, *The Conflict of the Faculties,* pp. 71f. (translation altered). See Bayer, *Autorität und Kritik,* pp. 71-74 ("Moralgesetz und Bibelkritik"). In contrast to an "intelligible" faith, that is, one "relevant to our moral destiny," Kant holds that this cannot be established and understood but at most explained "by a critical knowledge of the ancient languages, philology and a knowledge of the ancient world." We see this from his reference to Herder's *Interpretation of Genesis* (1774): Kant, "Der Streit der Fakultäten" (1798), in Immanuel Kant, *Werke in 10 Bänden,* ed. W. Weischedel, vol. 9 (Darmstadt: Wissenschaftliches Buchgesellschaft, 1970), p. 80, note 116.

153. See Wolfgang Janke, *"Praecisio mundi."* The phrase *praecisio mundi,* which literally means "cutting off the world," refers to Bultmann's demythologization of the New Testament which cuts out the mythological world of the biblical narrative that he believes is extraneous to a purely existential interpretation. For this, see below, section 4.3.2.

154. Bultmann's Letter of May 25, 1922, to Barth in *Karl Barth — Rudolf Bultmann. Briefwechsel 1922-1966,* ed. B. Jaspert (Karl Barth GA V, vol. 1 [Zurich: Theologische Verlag, 1971, Letter number 2]). See letters no. 46 (of May 26, 1928) and no. 47 (of June 8, 1928). Further, Rudolf Bultmann, "The Problem of Hermeneutics" in *Essays: Philosophical and Theological,* trans. James Greig (London: SCM Press, 1955), pp. 259-61.

155. Insofar as philosophy refers to the "cosmic aspect" (the *Weltbegriff* as distinct from the *Schulbegriff* or "the scholastic aspect"), it is "a teaching of wisdom" (Immanuel Kant, *Logic,* trans. Robert S. Harman and Wolfgang Schwarz [Indianapolis: Bobbs-Merrill, 1974], p. 30; translation altered).

156. See Bayer, *Autorität und Kritik,* pp. 71-74.

157. Rudolf Bultmann, *Theology of the New Testament,* one volume edition, trans. Kendrick Grobel (New York: Scribner's Sons, 1955), p. 241.

158. Immanuel Kant, "Speculative Beginning of Human History" (1786), "The End of All Things" (1794) in *Perpetual Peace and Other Essays,* trans. Ted Humphrey (Indianapolis: Hackett, 1983) and Kant, *Religion within the Limits of Reason Alone,* pp. 115-38.

159. Kant's criticism does not end the history of the interplay between dogmatism and skepticism, as he claimed, but further promotes it. For this thesis, see Oswald Bayer, "Kants Geschichte der reinen Vernunft in einer Parodie. Hamanns Metakritik im zweiten Entwurf," *Kant-Studien* 83 (1992): 1-20.

160. See Bayer, *Autorität und Kritik,* pp. 74-76.

161. Kant, *The Conflict of the Faculties,* pp. 118f. See Bayer, *Autorität und Kritik,* p. 73.

162. "He who hates science but loves wisdom all the more is called a misologist" (Kant, *Lectures on Logic,* trans. and ed. J. Michael Young [Cambridge: Cambridge University Press, 1992], p. 539). See Plato, *Laches* 188c 6; *Phaedo* 89d 1-4; *Republic* 456a 4. The sense in which wisdom is not acquired through science, but at the same time does not despise it, will be explained below (see section 2.3.4: "Science Is Wisdom Understood as Law").

163. See above, notes 123 and 124.

164. See above, note 85 on the concept of *praecisio mundi.*

165. See Proverbs 1:7; 15:33; Psalm 111:10; Job 28:28; Sirach 1. On "wisdom" and "wisdom poetry," see Hartmut Gese's articles in *Die Religion in Geschichte und Gegenwart,* vol. 6, 3rd ed. (1962), pp. 1574-81.

166. See below, section 4.3.2: "The Existential Approach" (Bultmann).

167. See, for example, Proverbs 8.

168. See Bayer, *Autorität und Kritik,* pp. 89-95 ("Erklärung und Erzählung").

169. On the problem of methodological atheism in theology, see Adolf Schlatter, "Atheistische Methoden in der Theologie" (1905), in Schlatter, *Zur Theologie des neuen Testaments und zur Dogmatik. Kleine Schriften,* ed. and intro. Ulrich Luck (*Theologische Beiträge* 41) (Munich: Kaiser, 1969), pp. 134-50.

170. See above, section 2.1: "The Object of Theology," and see also part one: section 2.1: "The Subject Matter of Theology."

171. See *Soliloquia* I, 7, 1 (*MPL* 32, 8872): "I desire to know God and the soul. Nothing more? Nothing at all" (*"Deum et animam scire cupio. Nihilne plus? Nihil omnino"*).

172. Rudolf Bultmann, "What Does It Mean to Speak of God?" (1925) in *Faith and Understanding: Collected Essays,* ed. Robert W. Funk, trans. Louise Pettibone Smith (London: SCM Press, 1969), pp. 53-65 and *Theology of the New Testament,* p. 241: "Every sentence about God is at the same time a sentence about humanity and vice versa."

173. See, for example, Proverbs 9.

174. See the Introduction: "Important Moments in the Understanding of Theology. 1. Christian Theology between Metaphysics and Mythology."

175. Johann Georg Hamann, "Aesthetica in Nuce," in *German Aesthetic and Literary Criticism: Winckelmann, Lessing, Hamann, Herder, Schiller, Goethe,* ed. H. B. Nisbet, trans. Joyce Crick (Cambridge: Cambridge University Press, 1985), p. 150 (translation slightly altered). The texts cited are Ecclesiastes 12:13 and Revelation 14:7.

176. See above, note 171.

177. Johann Georg Hamann, *Londoner Schriften. Historisch-kritische Neuedition,* ed. O. Bayer und B. Weißenborn (Munich: Beck, 1993), pp. 304, 8-10 ("Biblical Meditations of a Christian," 1758, on 1 Pet. 4:11). For an introduction to these *London Writings,* see John R. Betz, "Hamann's London Writings: The Hermeneutics of Trinitarian Condescension," *Pro Ecclesia* 14, no. 2 (Spring 2005): 191-234. Betz's intention is "to reintro-

duce Hamann's theological aesthetics, which consists chiefly in his understanding of beauty in terms of *kenosis,* i.e., as the radiance of divine condescension" (194).

178. Martin Luther, marginal note on Peter Lombard's *Books of Sentences* (1509/ 11): *"Major est enim hujus scripturae authoritas quam omnis humani ingenii capacitas"* (WA 9:66, 9f.). The Holy Scriptures appear as the "divine Aeneid" in Luther's last note. See Oswald Bayer, "Vom Wunderwerk, Gottes Wort recht zu verstehen. Luthers Letzter Zettel," *Kerygma und Dogma* 37 (1991): 258-79. See also part one: section 3.2 ("The Place of the Formula"), note 146.

179. See *Autorität und Kritik* (see above, note 10), pp. 83-107 ("Wahrheit oder Methode?").

180. See part one: section 2.3 ("Science or Wisdom?"), note 65. On the infinite richness of theology as "experiential wisdom" *("sapientia experimentalis"):* WA 40/ III:63, 17: "Theology is infinite wisdom because it can never be fully learned" (*"Theologia est infinita sapientia, quia nunquam potest edisci";* on Psalm 121:2 [1532/33]).

181. This follows Francis Bacon's threefold classification of science (see *Autorität und Kritik,* pp. 83-107 ["Wahrheit und Methode?"], esp. pp. 97-99 ["Wahrheit als Tochter der Zeit"]). However, this threefold approach to science appears already in a work by the Spanish physician and psychologist Juan Huarte, *Examen de ingenios para las ciencias* [An Examination of Human Intelligence] (1575), who follows Aristotle in distinguishing between "memory" *(memoria),* "reason" *(entendimiento),* and "imagination" *(imaginativa)* as the three faculties of the mind, where memory relates to the past, reason to the present, and imagination to the future. This book, which attempts to show the connection between psychology and physiology, became enormously popular in Europe and was first translated in English with the title *The Examinations of Men's Wits* (1596). The author discusses memory, reason, and imagination in part 5 of the book and then in part 8, in a very significant move, he ascribes these three basic anthropological faculties to the sciences.

182. See Hamann's attempt (*Autorität und Kritik,* pp. 22-26 ["Gesetz und Freiheit"]). However, it has two appreciable weaknesses. First, Hamann identifies the coercion of the law in its political mode *(usus politicus legis)* (see below, note 192) with that function by which it convicts us of sin *(usus elenchticus legis)* and acts as a "disciplinarian until Christ comes" (Gal. 3:24). Secondly, Hamann speaks solely of the freedom of the gospel and neglects to clearly distinguish it from the freedom that is one of the effects of the political function of the law, besides its work of compulsion.

183. See below, section 6.3: "The Problem of Natural Theology."

184. Since it is the nature of theology, understood as an academic discipline, to engage in conflict and dispute (hence the German *Konfliktwissenschaft*), it must engage critically with the problems of modernity. One useful way of doing this would be to use wisdom informed by the law-gospel distinction as a criterion for analyzing Lessing's critique of theology and reason. See Johannes von Lüpke, *Wege der Weisheit. Studien zu Lessings Theologiekritik* (GTA vol. 41) (Göttingen: Vandenhoeck & Ruprecht, 1989).

185. See above, notes 167 and 173.

186. *To this extent,* we agree with Lonergan, who finally focuses his question of theological methodology on the subject who pursues theology; see Bernard J. F. Lonergan, *Method in Theology* (New York: Herder & Herder, 1972). But insofar as he accepts the basic insights of transcendental philosophy, we have to disagree with him. We must insist that the self-critical subject, without which critical knowledge is impossible, can only be established by law and gospel, and this cannot be brought into the unity sought by transcendental thinking.

187. Johann Georg Hamann, *Briefwechsel,* vol. 5, ed. A. Henkel (Frankfurt/Main: Lang, 1965), pp. 333, 16-19, to Friedrich Heinrich Jacobi (January 23, 1785).

188. Immanuel Kant, *Critique of Pure Reason,* B 131, p. 246.

189. See above, section 2.2, especially the reference to Romans 14:23. For a strong case in favor of the inclusion of the doctrine of sin in the philosophy of science and hermeneutics, see Michael Trowitzsch, *Verstehen und Freiheit. Umrisse zu einer theologischen Kritik der hermeneutischen Urteilskraft (ThSt* 126) (Zurich: Theologischer Verlag, 1981).

190. Martin Luther, *The Disputation Concerning Man* (1536), Thesis 5: LW 34:137 (translation altered); WA 39/I:175, 11-13.

191. Luther, *The Disputation Concerning Man,* Thesis 9: LW 34:137; WA 39/I:175, 20f.

192. For the sake of brevity, we use Luther's terminology. See especially LW 26:308f. (WA 40/I:479, 17-480, 31), especially LW 26:308 (WA 40/I:479, 30).

193. See above, note 68.

194. See below, section 7.3.

195. Against Karl Barth, see Bayer, *Theologie,* B III, 2.3.2: "Die Einheit von Evangelium und Gesetz."

196. See above, section 2.1: "The Object of Theology."

197. But there is a place where we must say that God and faith are inaccessible and beyond our grasp: *Leibliches Wort,* pp. 42f. ("Die Unverfügbarkeit der Unterscheidung").

198. See Falk Wagner, "Aspekte der Rezeption Kantischer Metaphysik-Kritik in der evangelischen Theologie des 19. und 20. Jahrhunderts," *NZSTh* 27 (1985): 25-41, esp. 31-34 ("On the problem of the non-objectifiability of God").

199. This is one of the points on which the earlier and later Wittgenstein agreed.

200. Martin Heidegger, *Being and Time,* trans. John Macquarrie and Edward Robinson (New York: Harper & Row, 1962), p. 62. The exact passage (in translation) that is being referred to is this: "Philosophy is universal phenomenological ontology, and takes its departure from the hermeneutic of Dasein (existence), which as an analytic of *existence,* has fastened the end of the connecting thread of all philosophical enquiry at the point from which it *arises* and to which it *returns*" (translation altered).

201. Ludwig Wittgenstein, *Philosophical Investigations,* trans. G. E. M. Anscombe

(Oxford: Basil Blackwell, 1976), p. 5: "I shall also call the whole, consisting of the language and the actions into which it is woven, the 'language game'" (§7). To understand Wittgenstein, of course, we must observe this limitation: "the *speaking* of language is part of an activity or form of life" (§23).

202. "Performative-Constative" is the title of a paper originally presented by J. L. Austin in French (with the title "Performatif-Constatif") at a (predominantly) Anglo-French conference held at Royaumont in March 1958. The English translation was published in *Philosophy and Ordinary Language,* ed. Charles E. Caton (Urbana, Chicago, London: University of Illinois Press, 1963), pp. 22-33. The discussion that followed is recorded on pages 33-54.

203. Austin, "Performative-Constative," p. 33 (translation significantly altered).

204. Aristotle, *Peri hermeneias* 5, 17 a 8.10.12.15. (Note that *Peri hermeneias* means *Peri logou apophantikou:* Concerning [the forms of] declarative sentences. The *logos apophantikos* is a *logos* [statement] that involves an *apophansis,* a manifestation that lets something be seen from itself, literally a "showing-from," like the Latin *"demonstratio."* The declarative sentence expresses the claim that what it is showing corresponds to what is the case in reality. However, it may be either true or false.) See, on the other hand, Plato's indemonstrable *logos (logos anapodeiktos)* (see *Definitiones* 415 b 10) mentioned by Schleiermacher in *On the Glaubenslehre: Two Letters to Dr. Lücke,* trans. James Duke and Francis Fiorenza, American Academy of Religion, Texts and Translations Series, 3 (Atlanta: Scholars Press, 1981), pp. 42-43.

205. See *Wörterbuch der philosophischen Begriffe* (*PhB* 255), ed. J. Hoffmeister, 2nd ed. (Hamburg: Meiner Verlag, 1955), under "judgment" *(Urteil):* "originally that which is allotted, then narrowed down very early to the verdict (Latin *decretum*) handed down by a judge and until the 17th century used only in this sense as a legal term; Leibniz, however, employed it for the Greek *apophansis,* Latin *enuntiatio,* scholastic *judicium,* which is the declaration that forms part of a syllogism. . . . The logical judgment is expressed linguistically by a statement or assertion that consists of the subject (S), the predicate (B) and the copulative expressing the relation between them."

206. Austin, "Performative-Constative," p. 23.

207. Austin, "Performative-Constative," p. 23 (translation altered).

208. See Franz Wieacker, *Zur praktischen Leistung der Rechtsdogmatik: Hermeneutik und Dialektik. Hans-Georg Gadamer zum 70. Geb.* vol. 2 (Tübingen: Mohr Siebeck, 1970), pp. 311f., note 2.

209. Ian T. Ramsey gives a fine overview in "Theologie und Philosophie im angelsächsischen Bereich," *Die Religion in Geschichte und Gegenwart,* 3rd ed., vol. 6, pp. 830-38. See Lars Bejerholm/Gottfried Hornig, *Wort und Handlung. Untersuchungen zur analytischen Religionsphilosophie* (Gütersloh: Gütersloher Verlaghaus, 1966); Ingolf U. Dalferth, ed., *Sprachlogik des Glaubens. Texte analytischer Religionsphilosophie und Theologie zur religiösen Sprache* (*BevTh* 66) (Munich: Kaiser, 1974).

210. See Oswald Bayer, *Promissio. Geschichte der reformatorischen Wende in Luthers Theologie,* 2nd ed. (Darmstadt: Wissenschaftliche Buchgesellschaft, 1989), esp. ch. 4.

211. The same is true of the blessing that Luther accurately describes as a "constitutive" or "performative" speech act: "the blessings of a promise, of faith, and of a gift" (*"benedictions promissionis et fidei et praesentis doni"*) are "more than mere wishes; they are indicatives and performatives; they actually bestow and bring about what the words say" (*"non imprecativae tantum, sed indicativae et constitutivae, quae hoc ipsum, quod sonat re ipsa largiuntur et adferunt"*) (LW 5:140, translation altered [WA 43:525, 3-5; 10f. on Gen. 27:28f.]). See also LW 4:154-55 (WA 43:247, 22-26).

212. Bayer, *Promissio*, chapters 5-10.

213. LW 8:193 (translation altered) (WA 44:720, [28-36]30-36). See Oswald Bayer, "Die reformatorische Wende in Luthers Theologie," *ZThK* 66 (1969): 119.

214. LW 26:387 (translation altered) (WA 40/I:589, 25-28 [on Gal. 4:6]). The theological prolegomena *(Prinzipienlehre)* of Johann Gerhard, which is essentially his doctrine of Holy Scripture *(de scriptura sacra),* is "nothing other than the counterpart in the philosophy of science to the statement that God does not lie" (Konrad Stock, *Annihilatio mundi. Johann Gerhards Eschatologie der Welt* [Munich: Kaiser, 1971], p. 58). See Numbers 23:19; 1 Samuel 15:29; Hebrews 6:18. On the idea of certainty in Luther, see Karl-Heinz Zur Mühlen, *Nos extra nos: Luthers Theologie zwischen Mystik und Scholastik* (Tübingen: Mohr Siebeck, 1972).

215. See Thomas Aquinas, *STh* I, q. 16a.1c; a2 ob.2. Truth is the consonance between the intellect or understanding and its object *(veritas est adaequatio rei et intellectus).* This is usually referred to as the correspondence theory of truth.

216. Compare Vico's idea of the interchangeability of what is true *(verum)* and what is made *(factum),* which is captured in his basic proposal that knowing and making are one *(verum et factum convertuntur).* We can put this famous *verum — factum* principle (formulated in 1710) another way: the things we know best are the things we make. The principle states that truth is verified through creation or invention and not, as Descartes held, through observation. "The criterion and rule of what is true is to have made it. Accordingly, our clear and distinct idea of the mind cannot be a criterion of the mind itself, still less of other truths. For while the mind perceives itself, it does not make itself" (Giambattista Vico, *On the Most Ancient Wisdom of the Italians,* trans. L. M. Palmer [London: Cornell University Press, 1988], p. 31). This criterion of truth would later shape the history of civilization in Vico's opus, *The New Science* (1725), since civil life, like mathematics, is wholly constructed. See Karl Löwith, *Vicos Grundsatz: verum et factum convertuntur. Seine theologische Prämisse und deren säkulare Konsequenzen, Sämtliche Schriften,* vol. 9 (Stuttgart: Metzler, 1986), pp. 195-227.

217. *Criticism of Hegel's Philosophy of Right* (Introduction), trans. Annette Jolin and Joseph O'Malley (Cambridge: Cambridge University Press, 1970); Feuerbach is presupposed.

218. Feuerbach's philosophical manifesto "Preliminary Theses on the Reform of Philosophy" (1842) appears as the final section in *The Fiery Brook: Selected Writings of Ludwig Feuerbach,* trans. Zawar Hanti (New York: Anchor, 1972), p. 173. See Bayer, *Leibliches Wort,* p. 58.

219. Luther opposes "those who imagine that faith is a quality latent in the soul" *(somniantes eam [= fidem] esse qualitatem latentem in anima)* that can be described and actualized. His answer is this: "When the word of God says what is truth and the heart clings to it in faith, the heart is imbued with this same truth of the word and through the word of truth is made true and is verified" *(Verum quando verbum dei sonat, quod veritas est, et cor ei adhaeret per fidem, tunc cor imbuitur eadem veritate verbi et per verbum veritatis verificatur).* (Explanation of Thesis 12 of the Disputation *de fide infusa et acquisita* held on February 3, 1520: WA 6:94, 9-12).

220. Bayer, *Leibliches Wort,* esp. pp. 46-48, 64f.

221. On that, see the article referred to in note 101 above and in section 4.2 below, translated as "The Modern Narcissus," *LQ* 9 (1995): 301-13.

222. The problem of an uncritical use of Feuerbach's critique of religion would have to be dealt with in a discussion with, say, Hans-Martin Barth ("Glaube als Projektion. Zur Auseinandersetzung mit Ludwig Feuerbach," *NZSTh* 12 [1970]: 363-82).

223. Jürgen Habermas, *Knowledge and Human Interests,* trans. Jeremy J. Shapiro (Boston: Beacon, 1971), p. 235, note 35 (translation altered).

224. Plato, *Meno* 80d5-86c3.

225. Kant, *Critique of Practical Reason,* A 287, p. 132 (translation altered).

226. See below, section 4.3: "The Existential Approach."

227. Rolf Schäfer, "Welchen Sinn hat es, nach einem Wesen des Christentums zu suchen?" *ZThK* 65 (1968): 344. See his article "Christentum, Wesen des" in *Historisches Wörterbuch der Philosophie* I, 1008-16.

228. Wittgenstein, *Philosophical Investigations,* §371, p. 116. See Luther ("The Grammar of the Holy Spirit"; see part one: section 5.4), Hamann (see part one, note 439), and Johann Gerhard: "Our theology in this life is almost entirely grammatical" *("theologia nostra in hac vita fere tota est grammatica")* (*Loci theologici,* Locus II, §20). See Stock, *Annihilatio mundi,* p. 128, note 4.

229. Wittgenstein, *Philosophical Investigations,* esp. §§371ff, pp. 116f.

230. Without it being "a mystical *pragmatology,*" as Feuerbach assumes in the programmatic formulation of his hermeneutics; see the preface to the 1st edition of his *Das Wesen Christentums* [*The Essence of Christianity*] (Stuttgart: Reclam, 1971), p. 8. Feuerbach has to hold that view because for him "the essential difference between religion and philosophy" has to do with the image and not, as we would say, with the word. Therefore, he holds that it is a self-evident truth of religion that "the image *as image* is central" (p. 8), while Christian theology, as outlined above, must say that it is the word as such that is central.

231. For the exceptionally clear formulation of the principles of existential interpretation by Hans Jonas, see below, section 4.3.3. The unbridgeable gulf between the hermeneutic of Schleiermacher and that of Luther is seen with the clarity of an almost ideal type in Schleiermacher's definition of the relationship between religion and the (scriptural) word, at least as he presents it in his early period: "The religious

person is not one who believes in a sacred writing but one who has no need of it and could well produce one himself" (Friedrich Schleiermacher, *On Religion: Speeches to Its Cultured Despisers,* trans. Louise Pettibone Smith [Philadelphia: Fortress, 1987], p. 91 [translation altered]).

232. See in brief Rudolf Bultmann, *Theology of the New Testament,* one-volume edition, trans. Kendrick Grobel (New York: Scribners, 1951, 1955), "Epilogue" to the First Section ("The Relation between Theology and Preaching").

233. See Wilhelm Herrmann, "Die Wirklichkeit Gottes" (1914), *Schriften zur Grundlegung der Theologie,* vol. 2 (*Theologische Beiträge* 36/II), ed. P. Fischer-Appelt (Munich: Kaiser, 1967), p. 314: "The only thing we can say about God is what he does with us" (cited by Rudolf Bultmann, "What Does It Mean to Speak of God?" in *Faith and Understanding* [Philadelphia: Fortress, 1987], p. 63 (translation altered).

234. See Wilhelm Herrmann, "Grund und Inhalt des Glaubens," in *Ges. Aufsätze,* ed. F. W. Schmidt (Tübingen: Mohr Siebeck, 1923), pp. 275-94.

235. See below, sections 4.3.1, 4.3.2, and 4.3.3.

236. See above, section 1: "Divine Service and Theology" (esp. 1.1.2: "The Particular Divine Service") and: *Leibliches Wort,* esp. pp. 289-305 and 306-13.

237. Emanuel Hirsch, Preface to *Die Umformung des christlichen Denkens in der Neuzeit. Ein Lesebuch,* 1938 (reprint Tübingen: Katzmann [u.a.], 1985, with an afterword and bibliographical introduction, ed. H. M. Müller). See also Hirsch, *Geschichte der neuern evangelischen Theologie im Zusammenhang mit den allgemeinen Bewegungen des europäischen Denkens* (1949) (Gütersloh: Gütersloher Verlaghaus, 1960), vol. 5, pp. 621-26.

238. Bayer, *Leibliches Wort,* pp. 6-15 ("'Methode': Kommunikative Urteilsform").

239. Bayer, *Leibliches Wort,* pp. 1-6.

240. See Bayer, *Theologie,* B III, 2.3.2: "Die Einheit von Evangelium und Gesetz" and 2.3.4, excursus: "Der Mensch als Täter."

241. Wilhelm Herrmann, *Ethik* (1901), 6th ed. (Tübingen, 1921).

242. See below, section 6.3: "The Problem of Natural Theology."

243. Herrmann, *Ethik,* V (preface to the first edition).

244. For a detailed discussion of the problem, see Oswald Bayer, "Die Gegenwart der Güte Gottes. Zum Verhältnis von Gotteslehre und Ethik," chapter in *Leibliches Wort,* pp. 314-33.

245. Wilhelm Herrmann, "Kants Bedeutung für das Christentum" (1884), in *Schriften zur Grundlegung der Theologie,* Section I, ed. P. Fischer-Appelt (*TB* 36/I) (Munich: Kaiser, 1966), p. 122. See Herrmann, "Unsere Kantfeier," *Christliche Welt* 18 (1904): 145-49.

246. Immanuel Kant, *Lectures on Metaphysics,* trans. Karl Ameriks and Steve Naragon (Cambridge: Cambridge University Press, 1997), p. 301.

247. Kant, *Religion Within the Limits of Reason Alone,* p. 5.

248. Helmut Peukert, *Science, Action, and Fundamental Theology: Toward a Theology*

of Communicative Action, trans. James Bohman (Cambridge, Mass., and London: MIT Press, 1984).

249. Peukert, *Science,* esp. p. 238 (translation slightly altered).

250. See above, note 248. [Translators' note: Peukert applies Jürgen Habermas's theory of communicative action to recent developments in theology. He attempts to formulate a foundational theory of theology in response to the challenges of the theories of science and action in the last century.]

251. See Oswald Bayer, *Zugesagte Freiheit. Zur Grundlegung theologischer Ethik* (*Gütersloher Taschenbücher* 379) (Gütersloh: Gütersloher Verlaghaus, 1980) and *Freiheit als Antwort.*

252. *Critique of Practical Reason,* trans. Mary Gregor (Cambridge: Cambridge University Press, 1997), p. 48. See Immanuel Kant, *Metaphysics of Ethics,* trans. H. W. Cassirer, ed. G. Heath King and Ronald Weitzman (Milwaukee: Marquette Press, 1998), p. 34.

253. Georg Wilhelm Friedrich Hegel, *Lectures on the Philosophy of Religion,* vol. 3, *The Consummate Religion,* ed. Peter Hodgson et al. (Berkeley: University of California Press, 1985), p. 132.

254. Georg Wilhelm Friedrich Hegel, *Sämtliche Werke,* ed. H. Glockner, vol. 20 (Stuttgart: Frommann, 1958), pp. 445-50.

255. See Hegel, *Sämtliche Werke,* p. 449. See also Karlfried Gründer, "Die Einsicht des Spitalsweibs," in *Archiv für Begriffsgeschichte* 26 (Bonn: Bouvier, 1982), pp. 221-27.

256. For an appreciation of Hegel's respect for the sound content of the Christian faith, see Bayer, *Theologie,* B III, 1.2.3 (*"Gewinn der Anselmwende: 'Sache', 'gediegener Gehalt'"*).

257. See further Oswald Bayer, "The Being of Jesus Christ in Faith," *LQ* 10 (1996): 135-50.

258. See below, section 7: "Faith and Sight."

259. For evidence of this, see Bayer, *Leibliches Wort,* pp. 63f.

260. See Oswald Bayer, "The Modern Narcissus," *LQ* 9 (1995): 301-13.

261. Georg Wilhelm Friedrich Hegel, *Lectures on the History of Philosophy,* vol. 2, trans. E. S. Haldane and Frances H. Simson (Atlantic Highlands, N.J.: Humanities Press, 1955), p. 150.

262. Georg Wilhelm Friedrich Hegel, *Lectures on the Philosophy of Religion,* vol. 1: *The Concept of Religion,* ed. Peter C. Hodgson (Berkeley: University of California Press, 1984). See the sections on the relationship between religion and philosophy and between representation *(Vorstellung)* and concept *(Begriff).*

263. Preface, *The Essence of Christianity* (1843), 2nd ed., in *The Selected Writings of Ludwig Feuerbach,* trans. Zawar Hanti (New York: Anchor, 1972), p. 248 (translation altered).

264. Ludwig Feuerbach, "Vorwort zur ersten Gesamtausgabe" (1846), in *Werke,* ed. W. Bolin and Fr. Jodl, vol. 2 (Stuttgart: Frommann, 1959), p. 409.

265. Franz Overbeck, *Über die Christlichkeit unserer heutigen Theologie* (1873), 3rd

ed. (Darmstadt: Wissenschaftliche Buchgesellschaft, 1963), p. 35. Although his polemical thrust is the same as that of Feuerbach, Overbeck is fundamentally different in the way he emphasizes that there is an essential interconnection between linguistic and literary forms, on the one hand, and "reflection on life," on the other (see Franz Overbeck, *Über die Anfänge der patristischen Literatur* [*Historische Zeitschrift* 48 (1882): 417-72], ed. Wissenschaftliche Buchgesellschaft as vol. XV of "Libelli" [Darmstadt, 1966]). In other words, Overbeck stresses the inseparability of linguistic forms and the situations that they reflect (see the correspondence between "early literature" and "the eschatological reflection on life," *Über die Anfänge der patristischen Literatur*). It is here that his insights must continue to point the way ahead for theology. The existential interpretation stresses one of these two aspects too one-sidedly, at the cost of the other which attends to an analysis and critique of the forms.

266. Feuerbach, Preface to the 1st edition of *The Essence of Christianity*, p. 8; see also pp. 5f. On this, see Bayer, *Leibliches Wort*, pp. 205-41 ("Gegen Gott für den Menschen. Feuerbachs Lutherrezeption," p. 210, note 21.

267. Feuerbach, Preface to the 1st edition of *The Essence of Christianity*, p. 11. On this, see Bayer, *Leibliches Wort*, p. 228, note 71.

268. For the details, see Bayer, *Leibliches Wort*, esp. pp. 235-40 ("Gegen die idealistische Identitätsprämisse: das sinnlich-konkrete Wort als Urdatum der Theologie").

269. See Bayer, *Theologie*, B III, 1.2.2.1: "*Barths Verhältnis zu Schleiermacher*," note 56.

270. For the broader context of the argument that follows, see: "Wortlehre oder Glaubenslehre? Zur Konstitution theologischer Systematik im Streit zwischen Schleiermacher und Luther," in Bayer, *Autorität und Kritik*, pp. 156-68.

271. Here and in what follows we cite the second edition of his systematic theology: Friedrich Schleiermacher, *The Christian Faith*, trans. and ed. H. R. Mackintosh and J. S. Stewart (Philadelphia: Fortress, 1976). Where only the paragraph number is given (§), the lead proposition is cited. [Translators' note: *Frömmigkeit* is a key word for Schleiermacher. Older translations often render it as "piety." We will translate it as "spirituality."]

272. Schleiermacher, *First Letter to Dr. Lücke* (see above, note 204), p. 40.

273. Wilfried Brandt, *Der heilige Geist und die Kirche bei Schleiermacher* (*SDGSTh* 25) (Tübingen: Mohr Siebeck, 1968), p. 173; he cites here the first edition of the *Glaubenslehre* (1821/22), vol. 2 (1822) §142, p. 449. Note here the characteristically modern split between spirit and nature.

274. Schleiermacher, *The Christian Faith* §19, p. 92. See *The Christian Faith* §16, p. 79: "Then we shall not be able to take either the poetic or the rhetorical form of expression as the predominating, or even as the really primary and original, form of His self-proclamation. These have only a subordinate place in parabolic and prophetic discourses."

275. See below, section 4.3.3: "Jonas."

276. See especially the *Lectures on the Essence of Religion* (1848 and also 1851), particularly the fourth lecture in *Werke*, vol. 8 (Stuttgart: Reclam, 1960), pp. 31-40.

277. We should note here that the "social praxis" is unspecified because under this heading Marx "reduces" interaction to work and therefore "communicative action to instrumental action": Jürgen Habermas, "Arbeit und Interaktion. Bemerkungen zu Hegels Jenenser 'Philosophie des Geistes' " (in *Technik und Wissenschaft als 'Ideologie,'* 4th ed. [Frankfurt: Suhrkamp, 1970], p. 45, in the context especially of pp. 44-46). See Habermas, *Knowledge and Human Interests*, trans. Jeremy Shapiro (Boston: Beacon, 1968), esp. ch. 3.

278. See above, notes 119 and 120.

279. Feuerbach, *The Essence of Christianity* (see above, note 263), p. xxxvi (Preface to the 2nd edition) (translation altered).

280. See especially "Ludwig Feuerbach" (in Karl Barth, *Die Theologie und die Kirche. Ges. Vorträge,* vol. 2 [Zurich: Zollikon, 1928], pp. 212-39), the section on Feuerbach in *Protestant Theology in the Nineteenth Century: Its Background and History* (London: SCM Press, 1959, 1972), pp. 534-40, and the expansive perspective that appears in the epilogue to the book *Schleiermacher — Auswahl von Schleiermacher bis zur Bultmannschule*, which was the responsibility of Heinz Bolli (*Gütersloher Taschenbücher* 419, 3rd ed. [Gütersloh: Gütersloher Verlaghaus, 1983], pp. 290-312, esp. pp. 298-303). See John Glasse, "Barth zu Feuerbach," *EvTh* 28 (1968): 459-85. See also Bayer, *Theologie* B III, 1.2.2.1: *"Barths Verhältnis zu Schleiermacher."*

281. See above, note 8.

282. The following argument is used in my discussion of Tillich in *Theologie*, B I, 7.3: *" 'Mystisches Apriori' — das Problem der Fundamentaltheologie."*

283. It is transcendent but is ascertained transcendentally.

284. *Dialektik,* ed. L. Jonas (Berlin, 1839), p. 150 (= *Die Umformung des christlichen Denkens in der Neuzeit,* p. 210).

285. *"Non 'potest homo naturaliter velle deum esse deum,' Immo vellet se esse deum et deum non esse deum"* (Martin Luther, "Disputation against Scholastic Theology" [1517], thesis 17: LW 31:10 [translation altered]. In the note to this in BoA 5:321, 24f., the polemical reference is supported by the proposition of Duns Scotus and Gabriel Biel that Luther takes up in this thesis and debates).

286. LW 31:350 (translation altered); WA 7:54, 11-15 (*The Freedom of a Christian,* 1520).

287. WA 7:25, 16-18 (German version of *The Freedom of a Christian,* 1520). Compare the interpretation of the first commandment in the *Large Catechism, BC* 386:1-390:29 [*BSLK* 560-72]).

288. Compare §11 with §13 in *The Freedom of a Christian* (1520), WA 7:12-38; LW 31:343-77) and the *Treatise on Good Works* (1520), which is clearly taken up here, LW 44:15-114; WA 6:202-76, in its interpretation of the first commandment, as well as that of the *Large Catechism* (see above, note 287).

289. Friedrich Schleiermacher, *Brief Outline of Theology as a Field of Study,* trans.

Terrence N. Tice (Lewiston/Queenston/Lampeter: The Edwin Mellen Press, 1990), §29, p. 17. Unless otherwise noted, Tice's translation of the *Brief Outline* always follows the 2nd ed., 1830, and is based on the critical edition of Heinrich Scholz (Leipzig: Deichert, 1910): "Ethics" is "the science of the principles of history." Compare *The Christian Faith* (see above, note 271), §2, Postscript 2, p. 5: "By Ethics is here understood that speculative presentation of Reason, in the whole range of its activity, which runs parallel to natural science."

290. BC 388:22–389:23 (*BSLK* 564, 40–565, 14): it is "a false worship and highest idolatry," if the conscience "seeks help, comfort and blessedness in its own works" and "relies and presumes on them, as if it did not want to receive anything as a gift from him [God], but rather wanted to earn it by itself." That would amount to "deeming oneself to be God and usurping his place" (translation altered).

291. BC 384:3 (*BSLK* 560, 16f.). See above, note 287.

292. Schleiermacher, *Brief Outline,* §33. On the "above" [in the sense of a general concept] of §33 in the *Brief Outline* ("The point of departure of philosophical theology, therefore, can only be taken 'above' [!] Christianity, in the logical sense of the term . . ."): Hendrik Johan Adriaanse, "Der Herausgeber als Zuhörer. Ein Schleiermacher-Kollegheft von Ludwig Jonas," in *Schleiermacher und die wissenschaftliche Kultur des Christentums,* ed. G. Meckenstock (Berlin: De Gruyter, 1991), pp. 117-19.

293. Included in Gerhard Ebeling, *Wort und Glaube,* vol. 2, *Beiträge zur Fundamentaltheologie und zur Lehre von Gott* (Tübingen: Mohr Siebeck, 1969), pp. 396-432.

294. For example, from the linguistic phenomenon of "responsibility." On that, see Georg Picht, "Der Begriff der Verantwortung," in *Wahrheit. Vernunft. Verantwortung. Philosophische Studien* (Stuttgart: Klett, 1969), pp. 318-42.

295. "And by assertion . . . I mean a constant adhering, affirming, confessing, maintaining, and an invincible persevering" (Martin Luther, "The Bondage of the Will" [1525], LW 33:20 [WA 18:603, 12f.]). A demonstration calls for understanding whereas an assertion *(assertio)* calls for agreement and assent. An "assertion" is an external, oral word that can hold its own ground in public debate — in contrast to an "axiom," whose truth is self-evident; it is experienced intuitively through immediate, inner evidence; it is not heard but is clear. The assertion and axiom can be combined insofar as the word allows us to see.

296. See above, note 233 (translation altered).

297. Our discussion will essentially stick to the following text, which is representative of his position: Rudolf Bultmann, *New Testament and Mythology,* ed. and trans. Schubert M. Ogden (Philadelphia: Fortress, 1984).

298. See the Introduction: "Important Moments in the Understanding of Theology: 1. Christian Theology between Metaphysics and Mythology."

299. *New Testament and Mythology,* p. 41.

300. *New Testament and Mythology* (see above, note 297), pp. 7-8. See also pages

25-27, 31. On "self-understanding," see page 15; see also pages 39f. Self-understanding is "the understanding of being" (see pages 21f., 23-25, 32).

301. Bultmann, *New Testament and Mythology*, pp. 16, 23, 24, 26-29, 32.

302. Kant, *Critique of Pure Reason* A 445, p. 485 (translation altered).

303. Kant, *Critique of Pure Reason* A 448, p. 486.

304. The importance of the idea of the "moment," which Bultmann took over from Kierkegaard, can hardly be overestimated. However, a separate study would be needed to show the full significance that this concept has for Bultmann.

305. Rudolf Bultmann, "Der Begriff der Offenbarung im Neuen Testament," in *Glauben und Verstehen*, vol. 3 (Tübingen: Mohr Siebeck, 1960), p. 30.

306. Bultmann, *New Testament and Mythology*, pp. 9 and 15.

307. Bultmann, *New Testament and Mythology*, p. 9: "The real point of myth is not to give objectivizing representations but the understanding of existence expressed in them" (translation significantly altered). See p. 15. This disjunction is a clear expression of Kantian dualism.

308. Bultmann, *Glauben und Verstehen*, vol. 3 *(Wissenschaft und Existenz)*, p. 117.

309. Bultmann, *New Testament and Mythology*, p. 11 (translation slightly altered).

310. See above, section 2.3: "Theology Understood as Wisdom." Further, see Henning Luther, *"Subjektwerdung zwischen Schwere und Leichtigkeit — (auch) eine ästhetische Aufgabe?" NZSTh* 33 (1991): 183-98.

311. Bultmann, *New Testament and Mythology*, p. 29. See Rudolf Bultmann, "Grace and Freedom," in *Essays*, pp. 171-2.

312. Johann Georg Hamann, *Briefwechsel*, vol. 4, ed. A. Henkel (Wiesbaden: Insel-Verlag, 1959), p. 391, 16-18; to Johann Friedrich Reichardt [June 17, 1782]. See Oswald Bayer and Christian Knudsen, *Kreuz und Kritik*, p. 111.

313. Rudolph Bultmann, "New Testament and Mythology," in *Kerygma and Myth: A Theological Debate*, ed. Hans-Werner Bartsch, trans. Reginald H. Fuller (London: SPCK, 1972), p. 36: "By giving up Jesus to be crucified, God has set up the cross for us." See page 37: "The preaching of the cross as the event of redemption challenges all who hear it to appropriate this significance for themselves, [and hence] to be willing to be crucified with Christ." Bultmann has no place for understanding the appropriation of Christ's action for us as a promise. The gift (see above, note 311) is immediately a task, the indicative immediately an imperative, a "demand" (see below, note 314), and it is by fulfilling this demand, through the act of the decision of faith, that the significance of the cross as the event of salvation is "appropriated." Bultmann cannot *let* the promise of salvation *be* what it is: a promise that is bestowed and that simply wants to be savored (see above, note 312).

314. Bultmann, "New Testament and Mythology," p. 40: "This word [the apostolic preaching] therefore is 'added' to the cross and makes its saving efficacy intelligible by demanding [!] faith and confronting each of us with the question whether we are willing to understand ourselves as those who are crucified and risen with Christ" (translation altered). See above, note 313.

315. See above, note 154.

316. Bultmann, "New Testament and Mythology," p. 4. See page 3 ("stripping the Kerygma from its mythological framework").

317. Kant wants to adopt "a procedure similar to that of *chemistry*," the art of separation, and to try to "*separate* the empirical from the rational" (*Critique of Practical Reason*, A 291, 167). He sets "the rational in opposition to the empirical" (*Critique of Pure Reason* A 835, 693).

318. Immanuel Kant, *Anthropology from a Pragmatic Point of View*, trans. Victor Lyle Dowdell (Carbondale, Ill.: Southern Illinois University Press, 1978), p. 84. See Bayer, *Autorität und Kritik*, pp. 71-74: "Moralgesetz und Bibelkritik."

319. See above, notes 310, 312, and 313.

320. Such understanding is not something purely cognitive and contemplative, but a "practical" understanding in which I "know something," similar to that "knowing" of which Paul speaks in Romans 7:7.

321. Heidegger, *Being and Time*, p. 63: "Higher than actuality stands *possibility*."

322. Rudolph Bultmann, *Theology of the New Testament*, vol. 2 (London: SCM Press, 1955), p. 241 (epilogue).

323. "The formal structures of existence, which are demonstrated in the ontological analysis, are 'neutral,' that is, they are valid for all existence" ("Das Problem der 'natürlichen Theologie'" [*Glauben und Verstehen*, vol. 1, 4th ed. (Tübingen: Mohr Siebeck, 1961)], p. 312 — in the context of pp. 305-12). See Rudolf Bultmann, "Die Geschichtlichkeit des Daseins und der Glaube. Antwort an Gerhardt Kuhlmann," *ZThK* 11 (1930): 339-64. For the counter-thesis, see Karl Löwith, "Phänomenologische Ontologie und protestantische Theologie," *ZThK* 11 (1930): 365-99. On this problem: Dietrich Bonhoeffer, *Act and Being* (1931), trans. Bernard Noble (New York: Harper & Row, 1961), pp. 73-76.

324. Kant speaks of metaphysics "as actually given with *the natural structure* of human reason" ("Prolegomena to Any Future Metaphysics," trans. Gary Hatfield in *Theoretical Philosophy after 1781*, ed. Henry Allison and Peter Heath (Cambridge: Cambridge University Press, 2002), p. 150; as a parallel to this, see *Critique of Pure Reason* A VII. Note Ecclesiastes 3:11: "He has also set eternity in people's hearts. . . ."

325. See above, note 272.

326. See the concise and pregnant characterization in Habermas, *Arbeit und Interaktion*, p. 31: "Cassirer takes the dialectic of representation [namely, through symbols and language, as Hegel, following Herder, developed it in his Jena *Philosophy of Spirit/Mind*] as a connecting thread in his Hegelianizing interpretation of Kant, which is at the same time the basis of his philosophy of symbolic forms."

327. The analysis of existence and linguistic analysis are one in their polemic against "quasi-material concretions." If linguistic analysis fights against the "metaphysical," "hypostatizing 'question of essence,'" then it will help us recognize "a particular ontological approach from the way that it restricts itself to the existence of physical things and excludes the analogous treatment of mental phenomena" (Karl-

Otto Apel, "Wittgenstein and Hermeneutical Understanding," in *Towards a Transformation of Philosophy*, trans. Glyn Adey and David Frisby [London: Routledge & Kegan Paul, 1980], p. 18 [translation altered]).

328. See above, section 4.3.1: "Schleiermacher."

329. See Bayer, *Autorität und Kritik*, esp. pp. 11-18.

330. See above, note 272.

331. See Oswald Bayer, "Neuer Geist in alten Buchstaben," in *Gott als Autor: Zu einer poietologischen Theologie* (Tübingen: Mohr Siebeck, 1999), pp. 209-20.

332. See Bayer, "Laut und Buchstabe — Raum und Zeit. Hamanns Metakritik der transzendentalen Ästhetik Kants," in *Religione, Parola, Scrittura*, ed. M. M. Olivetti (Padua: Cedam, 1992), pp. 449-57.

333. See part one: section 5.4 ("The Grammar of the Holy Spirit"), note 439.

334. See above, note 289. [Translators' note: Theology in Schleiermacher's day was normally studied as an academic discipline in the university and was regarded as a science. Its scientific character is most evident in its quest for an appropriate method and its use of various analytical tools. See the translators' preface.]

335. On the two elements in the Schleiermacherian concept of science, see, for example, the explanation of §24, 25 in the *Brief Outline*: the term "philosophical theology" "is justified partly by the connection of its task with ethics and partly by the very nature of its content, in that a large part of its work has to do with defining concepts."

336. See Thomas Aquinas, *STh* I, q.16 a.1c; a.2 ob.2. Further: *STh* I, q.21 a.2. See already Albertus Magnus, *Summa Theologiae* I, 25, 2 *(adaequatio rerum et intellectus)*.

337. *Logic of Scientific Discovery* (New York: Harper, 1959), p. 53.

338. See above, note 284.

339. On the relation between the context of justification and the context of discovery, see Hans Albert, *Treatise on Critical Reason*, trans. Mary Varney Rorty (Princeton, N.J.: Princeton University Press, 1985), pp. 48-54.

340. *The Christian Faith*, §15, p. 79.

341. *The Christian Faith*, §15, p. 83.

342. *The Christian Faith*, §15, p. 84 (translation altered).

343. Noted in the apparatus of the German edition of Schleiermacher's *Der christliche Glaube*, ed. M. Redeker, 2 vols., 7th ed. (Berlin: 1960), p. 114. Science is an instrument, not an end in itself. See thesis 4.112 from Wittgenstein's *Tractatus Logico-Philosophicus* cited in note 199 above.

344. See, for example, the concluding sentence of §15 of *The Christian Faith*: "the doctrines in all their forms have their ultimate ground so exclusively in the emotions of the religious self-consciousness, that where these do not exist the doctrines cannot arise" (p. 78).

345. *The Christian Faith*, §33, p. 133.

346. *The Christian Faith*, §33, p. 133.

347. This linkage of individuality and universality has formally an exact equiva-

lence in Sartre's concept of freedom. See especially his essay "L'Existentialisme est un Humanisme" (1946); on this, see Hans-Georg Geyer, "Norm und Freiheit," in *Das gnädige Recht Gottes und die Freiheitsidee des Menschen*, ed. A. Falkenroth (Neukirchen: Neukirchener Verlag, 1967), pp. 47-52, summarized on p. 51: "The most individual human act is at the same time the most universal. Only the act of the most solitary freedom does not lose sight of human community."

348. Friedrich Engels, "Ludwig Feuerbach and the Outcome of Classical German Philosophy," in Karl Marx and Friedrich Engels, *Selected Works in Two Volumes*, vol. 2 (Moscow: Foreign Languages Publishing House, 1949), p. 360 (translation altered) (Engels's definition of "ideology").

349. *The Christian Faith*, p. 85 (translation altered). This critical point aims at "overcoming the apparent contradictions that arise from the poetic and rhetorical realms and compensating for the consequences" (Schleiermacher's handwritten note; see ibid. [in the German original], apparatus [translation altered]). Hans Jonas has gone into the matter in his considerations *Über die hermeneutische Struktur des Dogmas*, especially in his treatment of the questions of compatibility that arise in thinking about dogma. See above, section 4.3.3: "Jonas."

350. This criticism of Schleiermacher is not disposed of by propositions such as this: "since the dogmatic procedure has reference entirely to preaching, and only exists in the interests of preaching" (*The Christian Faith*, §19, p. 88), because "preaching" for Schleiermacher is the "presentation," the "expression" of a Christian self-consciousness that lies behind it. See above, section 4.3.1: "Schleiermacher."

351. Explanation of §5 in the *Brief Outline*. On the other hand, he writes in §135 in *Der christliche Glaube* 2/1, p. 315 [not in the English edition]: "only a very superficial view of Christianity can reduce the Christian community to family life and quiet, private relationships, without the public dimension." However, this does not do anything to change Schleiermacher's concept of theology and the way he understands the relationship between the word and faith.

352. Paul's words in 2 Corinthians 4:13 ("I believed; therefore I have spoken"), if they are taken in the context of his theology and the psalm he cites (Ps. 116), do not constitute any objection to this. Conversely, a sentence from Schleiermacher such as the statement that "faith comes only from preaching" (*The Christian Faith*, §121, p. 564; see Rom. 10:17), taken in the general context of his theology, does not change the basic intent of what he says in proposition §15, which is determinative for his thinking. See above, section 4.3.1 and note 231.

353. *Brief Outline*, §5.

354. Therefore, 1 Corinthians 4:7, or a proposition like it, is an alternative to the claim "No one gives me anything!" In the same way, as part of homiletics, we should draw up a list of sayings from everyday life, giving special attention to the language of advertising (e.g., "it's everyone for themselves," "everyone has to bear his own burdens," "there's nothing you can do about it," etc.). They should then be analyzed to see how they shape our lives. To complete the exercise, we need to describe and evalu-

ate the parallel speech acts that the church enacts in the name of Jesus to counter these slogans.

355. Gerhard Sauter has thoroughly investigated this question. In addition to the publication mentioned above in note 70, see Gerhard Sauter, *In der Freiheit des Geistes. Theologische Studien* (Göttingen: Vandenhoeck & Ruprecht, 1988); see also the additional literature listed on pages 199f.

356. On the question: What does it mean to follow a rule? and the connection between Wittgenstein's *Philosophical Investigations* (§199) and Peter Winch's *The Idea of the Social Sciences and Their Relation to Philosophy* (London: Routledge & Kegan Paul, 1967), see Jürgen Habermas, *On the Logic of the Social Sciences* (Cambridge, Mass.: MIT Press, 1988); further, Karl-Otto Apel, "Wittgenstein und Heidegger: Die Frage nach dem Sinn von Sein und der Sinnlosigkeitsverdacht gegen alle Metaphysik," *Transformation der Philosophie*, vol. 1 (Sprachanalytik, Semiotik, Hermeneutik) (Frankfurt: Suhrkamp, 1973), p. 266.

357. When Luther speaks of the three "rules" for the study of theology (see part one: section 3: *"Oratio, Meditatio, Tentatio"*), he means something other than the way in which the term "rule" is used today, which basically assumes a Cartesian understanding. See part one, note 221 (context), *Autorität und Kritik*, pp. 83-107 *(Wahrheit oder Methode?)* and section 2.3 above, especially 2.3.3: "The Historical *A Priori:* The Understanding of Time and the Concept of Science."

358. See the following note.

359. In view of the comparatively high level of consistency and coherence between the way of formulating the question and the way of working, we could use the singular and speak of a "system," although this term is problematic for the reasons we have already mentioned.

360. Ernst Troeltsch, *Absoluteness of Christianity and the History of Religions* (Richmond: John Knox, 1971), p. 45.

361. I have attempted to do this for the historical critical method, as a discussion starter, in *Was ist das: Theologie? Eine Skizze* (Stuttgart: Calwer, 1973), pp. 103-16. We should not begin by limiting the technical-dialectical element to such an extent that there could no longer even be a dispute between it and that which, according to the argument above, takes the place of the transcendental-dialectical element. This dispute cannot be eliminated, either by failing to recognize the methods as content-laden and regarding them as nothing more than neutral techniques that cannot affect real "theology," or, like Ernst Troeltsch, by immediately giving the methods "the upper hand" (Ernst Troeltsch, "Über historische und dogmatische Methode in der Theologie," in Troeltsch, *Zur religiösen Lage, Religionsphilosophie und Ethik, Gesammelte Schriften*, vol. 2 [Aalen: Scientia, 1962], p. 734) and letting them completely determine the subject matter of theology.

362. See Frithjof Rodi who, in his article on Wilhelm Dilthey, formulates his task this way: "to return to Dilthey's theological beginnings and to see his hermeneutical works as the great process of secularization that begins with

Schleiermacher's first speech, or more precisely, with the sentence: 'You must transport yourselves into the interior of a religious soul and seek to understand its enthusiasm'" (*Tendenzen der Theologie im 20. Jahrhundert. Eine Geschichte in Porträts,* 2nd ed., ed. H. J. Schultz [Stuttgart: Walter, 1967], p. 17).

363. *Brief Outline,* §26 (1st ed.): "Philosophical theology is the root of all theology." See Schleiermacher's *Gelegentliche Gedanken über Universitäten in deutschem Sinn* (1808), which in the 4th section ("On the faculties") stresses the point that "all members of the university, irrespective of which faculty they belong to, must have their roots in it [that is, the philosophical faculty]" (*Die Idee der deutschen Universität. Die fünf Grundschriften aus der Zeit ihrer Neubegründung durch klassischen Idealismus und romantischen Realismus,* ed. E. Anrich [Darmstadt: Wissenschaftliche Buchgesellschaft, 1956], p. 260; see p. 261).

364. *Brief Outline,* §31 (1st ed.): "Practical theology is the crown of theological study."

365. See above, section 3.1: "Analysis of Existence or Analysis of Language?"

366. Schleiermacher uses this same formulation in his written opinion, dated May 25, 1810, on the establishment of the theological faculty in which he says of the individual theological disciplines that they can be theological "only through their interest in Christianity" (Appendix no. 31 in R. Köpke, *Die Gründung der Königlichen Friedrich-Wilhelms-Universität zu Berlin. Nebst Anhängen über die Geschichte der Institute und den Personalbestand* [Berlin, 1860], p. 211).

367. H. Scholz makes this very clear, for example, in the Introduction to his German edition of the *Brief Outline: Kurzen Darstellung,* pp. xxviii-xxxii.

368. We should consider the divergence of definitions in §§6f., on the one hand, and in §8, on the other, in the light of §5. The extra in this paragraph, so to speak, compared with the definitions in §§6f., must of course also be considered scientifically so that, in the light of that, we can say, with Scholz (see above, note 289) in his introduction, p. xxxii, "Theology is a postulate of faith that strives for methodical self-reflection on the widest scale possible."

369. See above, note 95.

370. See Popper, *Logic of Scientific Discovery,* p. 44.

371. See the translators' preface for the problem of calling theology a "science" (*Wissenschaft*).

372. Albert, *Treatise on Critical Reason,* p. 101: "Whoever adopts it [that is, critical philosophy] does not decide for an abstract principle with no existential significance, but for a way of life." See *Treatise,* p. 53: "The model of rationality found in critical philosophy is the outline of a way of life" (translation altered). This critical philosophy "even has a moral content" (*Treatise,* p. 101). According to Popper, the demand for critical rationalism can be met only on the basis of a "moral decision," indeed, an "irrational *faith in reason*" (Karl R. Popper, *The Open Society and Its Enemies,* vol. 2: *The High Tide of Prophecy: Hegel, Marx, and the Aftermath* [London: Routledge & Kegan Paul, 1966], pp. 232 and 231).

373. See above, section 2.3.4: "Science Is Wisdom Understood as Law" and below section 7.3: "Consequences."

374. Johann Georg Hamann, *Briefwechsel,* ed. W. Ziesemer/A. Henkel, vol. 1 (Wiesbaden: Insel, 1955), pp. 446, 33f. (Letter to Immanuel Kant, 1759). See also Bayer, "Poetological Theology: New Horizons for Systematic Theology," *International Journal of Systematic Theology* 1, no. 2 (1999): 163.

375. Karl Rahner, "Formale und fundamentale Theologie," *Lexikon für Theologie und Kirche,* vol. 4, pp. 205f. See below, note 429.

376. See below, note 383.

377. This priority comes out in the *Brief Outline* in a proposition like §33: "The point of departure of philosophical theology, therefore, can only be located 'above' [!] Christianity, in the logical sense of the term, that is, in the general concept of a religious community or fellowship of faith." On the word "above," see above, note 292.

378. See above, section 2.1.

379. See above, especially sections 1.1 and 2.3.2.

380. Johann Georg Hamann, "Golgotha und Scheblimini" (1784), in *Sämtliche Schriften,* ed. J. Nadler, vol. 3 (Vienna: Herder, 1951), pp. 305, 2f. (emphases deleted). On interpretation, see Bayer, *Zeitgenosse im Widerspruch: Johann Georg Hamann als radikaler Aufklärer,* pp. 166-74 and 214-29. See *Autorität und Kritik,* pp. 83-107 *(Wahrheit oder Methode?),* esp. pp. 97-107. [Translators' note: It is perhaps worth noting that the very title of this essay, "Golgotha und Scheblimini," reflects a theme that is central to Hamann's writings: the paradoxical identity of humility (Golgotha) and glory (Scheblimini). For him there is no Scheblimini (Ps. 110:1) apart from Golgotha (Matt. 27:33), no glory apart from abasement. This is expressed paradigmatically in the condescension and exaltation of Christ (see the Christ hymn in Phil. 2:6-11). However, as Betz points out (see above, note 177), not only did Hamann see "that glory and *kenosis* go hand in hand; he also perceived that this paradoxical identity (this *coincidentia oppositorum*), which is proper to Christ . . . is mysteriously proper to *all* the persons of the Trinity: that their shared glory consists precisely in their shared humility, their shared *kenosis,* which is but a figure, for the sake of the creature, of the kenotic life, the love they share, in eternity."]

381. We should compare this to Karl Barth's line of argumentation. Barth, of course, proceeds from the historical fact, an approach that brought the charge of "revelatory positivism" (see Bayer, *Theologie,* B III, 1.2.1); but then he turns around and inquires into the condition for the possibility of election, an event that occurs prior to time, in order to understand the historical event of the divine incarnation in the light of election. See Bayer, *Theologie,* B III, 1.2.2.1, esp. note 41.

382. See Friedrich Wilhelm Joseph Schelling, *Vorlesungen über die Methode des akademischen Studiums* [*Lectures on the Methods of Academic Study*] (given in 1802, first published in 1803), 8th Lecture *(Über die historische Konstruktion des Christentums)* and 9th Lecture *(Über das Studium der Theologie).* See Bayer, *Theologie,* B I, note 86.

383. *Brief Outline,* §32.

384. See above, section 1.2.

385. See above, note 177 in the context of section 2.3.3: "The Historical *A Priori:* The Understanding of Time and the Concept of Science."

386. Walter Kasper, "Votum zum Thema 'Vernunft und Geschichte,'" in *Menschenrechte. Aspekte ihrer Begründung und Verwirklichung,* ed. J. Schwartländer (Tübingen: Attempto, 1978), pp. 232f. Consider the topic of the whole volume, especially the contributions from the discussion: pp. 217-33.

387. See Walter Schulz, *Die Vollendung des deutschen Idealismus in der Spätphilosophie Schellings* (Stuttgart/Köln: Kohlhammer, 1955); Walter Kasper, *Das Absolute in der Geschichte. Philosophie und Theologie der Geschichte in der Spätphilosophie Schellings* (Mainz: Matthias-Grünewald-Verlag, 1965); Dietrich Korsch, *Der Grund der Freiheit: Eine Untersuchung zur Problemgeschichte der positiven Philosophie und zur Systemfunktion des Christentums im Spätwerk F. W. J. Schellings (BevTh 85)* (Munich: Kaiser, 1980); Hartmut Rosenau, *Die Differenz im christologischen Denken Schellings (Europäische Hochschulschriften, Theologie 248)* (Frankfurt am Main/Bern/New York: Lang, 1985).

388. The theme of this entire section is thoroughly dealt with in Bayer, *Zeitgenosse im Widerspruch. Johann Georg Hamann als radikaler Aufklärer,* pp. 151-78 *(Geschichte und Vernunft).* See also *Autorität und Kritik,* pp. 117-24 ("Das Wort vom Kreuz").

389. See the Introduction "Important Moments in the Understanding of Theology. 1. Christian Theology between Metaphysics and Mythology."

390. See Jörg Jeremias, *Der Prophet Hosea* (Altes Testament Deutsch 24/1) (Göttingen: Vandenhoeck & Ruprecht, 1983), pp. 143-47 ("The Overturning of God's Heart"). See Jeremias, *Die Reue Gottes* (Biblische Studien 65) (Neukirchen: Neukirchener Verlag, 1975), pp. 52-59.

391. On the significance of this tension for Christology and soteriology, see Oswald Bayer, "The Being of Jesus Christ in Faith," *LQ* 10 (1996): 135-50.

392. See the speech on the study of theology *(De studiis theologicis)* written by Melanchthon (not 1521: contra CR 11:41) and given by Justus Jonas in 1538 (Otto Clemen, *Studien zu Melanchthons Reden und Gedichten* [Leipzig: Heinsius, 1913], pp. 33f.); see also CR 11:41-50, esp. 44f. (Latin text is reproduced in Bayer, *Theologie,* p. 143, note 85).

393. LW 31:41 (translation altered); WA 59:409, 20f.

394. LW 31:41 (thesis 29) (translation altered); WA 59:409, 3f.

395. WA 59:409, 6f.

396. See Ecclesiastes 3:11.

397. LW 31:40 (translation slightly altered); WA 1:362, 21f.

398. For the "definition" of a human as "a rational animal with a fabricating heart" *(animal rationale habens cor fingens),* see Bayer, *Autorität und Kritik,* p. 105, note 94.

399. John Calvin, *Institutes of the Christian Religion* (1559), I, 11, 8.

400. LW 31:52-53 (translation altered); WA 10/I:362, 11-13.

401. WA 10/I, 2:297, 7-10.

402. See below, chapter 7.3.

403. Gerhard Ebeling, *Disputatio de homine*, vol. 1, *Text und Traditionshintergrund* (Tübingen: Mohr Siebeck, 1977), p. 33.

404. However, even Thomas's theology is not without conflict: Thomas contradicts the Aristotelian thesis of the eternity of the world. See Anton Antweiler, *Die Anfangslosigkeit der Welt nach Thomas von Aquin und Kant*, 2 vols. (vol. 2: *Quellentexte*) (Trier: Paulinus Verlag, 1961).

405. See Jörg Baur, "Weisheit und Kreuz," in *Zugang zur Theologie. Fundamentaltheologische Beiträge. Festschrift für Wilfried Joest zum 65. Geburtstag*, ed. F. Mildenberger and J. Track (Göttingen: Vandenhoeck & Ruprecht, 1979), pp. 33-52; Jörg Baur, "Weisheit und Kreuz," *NZSTh* 22 (1980): 33-44. For a note on the critical and polemical function of theology, see above, note 184.

406. Dietrich Bonhoeffer, *Ethics*, ed. Eberhard Bethge, trans. Neville Horton Smith (New York: Macmillan, 1965), p. 197: "There are not two realities, but *only one reality*, and that is the reality of God, manifest in Christ, in the reality of the world" (translation altered). See Oswald Bayer, *"Christus als Mitte. Bonhoeffers Ethik im Banne der Religionsphilosophie Hegels?"* in *Leibliches Wort*, pp. 245-64.

407. The Theological Declaration of Barmen, 8.11; *Church Dogmatics* IV/3, §69.

408. See above, note 116.

409. See Bayer, *Theologie*, B III, note 125.

410. Günter Gawlick, "Hermann Samuel Reimarus," in *Die Aufkärung (Gestalten der Kirchengeschichte*, ed. M. Greschat, vol. 8) (Stuttgart: Kohlhammer, 1983), p. 300.

411. Gawlick, "Hermann Samuel Reimarus," p. 302.

412. See Friedrich Mildenberger, "Der Glaube als Voraussetzung für ein wahres Denken Gottes. Zu Kant und dem Problem von Theologie und Ökonomie," *NZSTh* 32 (1990): 152, note 40.

413. Mildenberger, "Der Glaube als Voraussetzung," p. 152 ("following 1 Tim. 3:16 and other biblical texts, it was customary to speak of the divine mysteries that reason cannot conceive). *"Articuli fidei puri sunt partes doctrinae Christianae de mysteriis divinis captu rationis humanae sibi relictae superioribus, divinitus tamen revelatis"* (David Hollaz, *Examen theologicum acroamaticum* [1707], Darmstadt Reprint, 1971, I, 57).

414. Mildenberger, "Der Glaube als Voraussetzung," p. 152.

415. See Oswald Bayer, *Autorität und Kritik*, pp. 117-24: "Das Wort vom Kreuz," pp. 119f., notes 10 and 11.

416. Bayer, *Autorität und Kritik*, p. 120, notes 13 and 14.

417. See Martin Luther, "De divinitate et humanitate Christi" (1540) (WA 39/II:93, 2-19).

418. Think of the way the New Testament uses the term, especially Ephesians 3:9 *(oikonomia tou mysteriou)*, Ephesians 1:9f., and Ignatius, *Ephesians* 18:2. Further, see above, note 413.

419. See above, note 406.

420. See above, note 409.

421. Friedrich Schleiermacher, "Second Letter to Lücke" (see above, note 204), pp. 55-89.

422. The comparison between the outline of Schleiermacher's dogmatics and Bultmann's account of Paul has been outlined above (4.3.2).

423. This is something formal and ontological, which we only ever meet in real concrete historical situations. But, as a fundamental anthropological unity, it must, according to Schleiermacher at least, be thought — "presupposed" or "assumed."

424. See above, section 4.3.2, note 322, together with the context.

425. Schleiermacher of course is more cautious than Barth insofar as he makes the *antithesis* of the consciousness of sin and grace constitutive for the main part of his dogmatics while Barth proceeds monistically.

426. The essential features of this concept have been developed above, apart from the introductory section ("Divine Service and Theology"), in section 4.3.1 in the context of a critical comparison between Schleiermacher and Luther.

427. Carl Heinz Ratschow, *Die Religionen* (HST 16) (Gütersloh: Gütersloher Verlaghaus, 1979), pp. 119f.

428. Ratschow, *Die Religionen*, p. 119.

429. Karl Rahner, "Der eine Jesus Christus und die Universalität des Heils," in *Universales Christentum angesichts einer pluralen Welt*, ed. A. Bsteh (Mödling: St. Gabriel, 1976), pp. 57-85. See Ratschow (see above, note 427), pp. 108-12. See further, Karl Rahner, "Über die Heilsbedeutung der nichtchristlichen Religionen," in *Schriften zur Theologie* XIII (Zurich: Benziger, 1978), pp. 341-50. A summary is given in Rahner, *Foundations of Christian Faith: An Introduction to the Idea of Christianity*, trans. William V. Dych (New York: Crossroad, 1984), pp. 311-16 ("Jesus Christ in Non-Christian Religions").

430. See above, section 6.1, especially note 374.

431. See above, section 3: "Promise and Faith."

432. See *Autorität und Kritik*, pp. 117-24 ("Das Wort vom Kreuz").

433. See above, section 6.1.

434. See Oswald Bayer, *Umstrittene Freiheit. Theologisch-philosophische Kontroversen* (UTB 1092) (Tübingen: Mohr Siebeck, 1981), pp. 152-61. See also Bayer, "Theologie I, evang. Sicht," in *Ökumene-Lexikon. Kirchen, Religionen, Bewegungen*, ed. H. Krüger, W. Löser, and W. Müller-Römheld (Frankfurt: Lembeck, 1983), pp. 1154f.; and *Leibliches Wort*, pp. 6-15. For more on the communicative form of judgment or discernment, see Bayer, "Poetological Theology: New Horizons for Systematic Theology," *International Journal of Systematic Theology* 1, no. 2 (1999): 159-61.

435. The important thing for Wolfhart Pannenberg is a unity that is bound up with a form of teleological thinking based on a process of development. See Pannenberg, "Toward a Theology of the History of Religions," in *Basic Questions in Theology*, vol. 2, trans. George H. Kehm (Philadelphia: Westminster, 1971), pp. 65-118; compare this to Ratschow, *Die Religionen*, pp. 103-8. On the other hand, a theology of pilgrims *(theologia viatorum)* does not attempt to fabricate a unity that does not exist, but it is aware of the painful differences and contradictions and is guided in this by the

distinction between law and gospel. At the same time, it will reject the idea of process thinking and will not make quantitative but only qualitative judgments, in line with the way we defined the subject matter of the theology (2.1), and only in this way will it achieve the "perspective of a history of world religions" (see above, note 19).

436. Johan Georg Hamann, "Zweifel and Einfälle" [Doubts and Ideas] (1776), in *Sämtliche Werke*, ed. J. Nadler, vol. 3 (Vienna: Herder, 1951), 192, 22-26; English translation in Smith, *Hamann* (see above, note 37), p. 259.

437. Hamann (see above, note 436), 191, 21-193, 8. On this, see *Autorität und Kritik*, pp. 197-99. What emerged earlier (6.1) as a question of the relation between history and reason must therefore be deepened by the question of the extent to which theology is a study of religion; this will also avoid Rahner's speculation (see above, note 429).

438. See above, section 6.1.

439. The "communicative form of judgment" (also see above, note 434) allows us to better understand the "basis of the Christian church's encounter with the non-Christian religions" (*Arnoldshainer Konferenz und Vereinigte Evangelisch-Lutherische Kirche Deutschlands, Religionen, Religiosität and christlicher Glaube. Eine Studie* [Gütersloh: Gütersloher Verlaghaus, 1991] pp. 117-32) and to use terms like "mission," "dialogue," and "conviviality" (i.e., living together with others in a way that transcends cultural and religious boundaries) more accurately in light of the distinctions and connections that emerge from such an encounter. But, most of all, the "communicative form of judgment" highlights the importance of the doctrine of sin and eschatology, which is not given the attention it deserves in the above study.

440. Thomas Aquinas, *Summa theologica* Suppl. q. 92 a.1 c: ". . . because, since understanding is an operation most proper to humans, it follows that their happiness must be held to consist in that operation when perfected in them." *(". . . quia, cum intelligere sit maxime propria operatio hominis, oportet quod secundum eam assignetur sibi sua beatitudo, cum haec operatio in ipso perfecta fuerit."* See the first sentence of Aristotle's *Metaphysics:* "All humans by nature desire to know."

441. Jürgen Habermas, *Theory and Practice*, trans. John Viertel (Boston: Beacon, 1971), p. 17. See Oswald Bayer, *"Zum Ansatz theologischer Ethik als Freiheitsethik,"* in *Freiheit als Antwort.*

442. See above, note 372.

443. Johann Gottlieb Fichte, *Die Anweisung zum seligen Leben*, ed. H. Verweyen (PhB 234) (Hamburg: Steiner, 1983), p. 83 (Lecture 5). Translated by William Smith under the title *The Popular Works of Johann Gottlieb Fichte*, vol. 2 (London: Trübner & Co. Ludgate Hill, 1889), p. 377.

444. "The Way towards the Blessed Life," in *Popular Works of Johann Gottlieb Fichte*, p. 378 (translation altered).

445. Paul Ricoeur, "Erzählung, Metaphor und Interpretationstheorie," *ZThK* 84 (1987): 251.

446. Søren Kierkegaard, *The Sickness unto Death*, ed. and trans. Howard and

Edna Hong (Princeton: Princeton University Press, 1980), p. 82 (translation significantly altered).

447. Søren Kierkegaard, *Fear and Trembling*, trans. Walter Lowrie (Princeton: Princeton University Press, 1941).

448. Thomas Aquinas, *Summa theologica* Suppl. q. 92, a.2 ob.2.

449. Hollaz, *Examen theologicum acroamaticum* I, 666 and 672.

450. See Revelation 22:4.

451. "God despises this apathy [of the Stoics] (*Deus detestatur apathiam illam* [*Stoicorum*]), LW 7:315 (Lectures on Genesis); WA 44:533, 16.

452. LW 33:292 (translation altered); WA 18:785, 35-37: *"lumen gloriae aliud dictat, et Deum, cuius modo est iudicium incomprehensibilis iustitiae, tunc ostendet esse iustissimae et manifestissimae iustitiae. . . ."* This conclusion to Luther's *De servo arbitrio*, if taken in the context of WA 18:783, 17-785, 38 — together with his preface to the Book of Job (1524; WA DB 10/I:4) — is to my mind the most accurate articulation of the crucial point of eschatology. In this sense, it is addressed in the last chapter (which deals with faith within the lawsuit with God) in my outline of dogmatics *Living by Faith*, pp. 69-80.

453. John 16:23 is equivalent to 1 Corinthians 13:12!

454. See *Autorität und Kritik*, pp. 199f. (*Systematische Theologie als Wissenschaft der Geschichte*, Section VIII: *"Sinn" der Geschichte?*)

455. Georg Wilhelm Friedrich Hegel, Preface to the 2nd ed., *Science of Logic*, trans. A. V. Miller (London: George Allen & Unwin, 1969), p. 42 (translation altered).

Bibliography: English Translations of Oswald Bayer

Compiled by Amy Marga

Articles

Bayer, Oswald. "Angels Are Interpreters." Translated by Christine Helmer. *Lutheran Quarterly* 13 (1999): 271-84.

———. "The Being of Christ in Faith." Translated by Christine Helmer. *Lutheran Quarterly* 10 (1996): 135-50.

———. "The Doctrine of Justification and Ontology." Translated by Christine Helmer. *Neue Zeitschrift für systematische Theologie und Religionsphilosophie* 43 (2001): 44-53.

———. "Does Evil Persist?" Translated by Christine Helmer. *Lutheran Quarterly* 11 (1997): 143-50.

———. "Freedom? The Anthropological Concepts in Luther and Melanchthon Compared." Translated by Christine Helmer. *Harvard Theological Review* 91 (1998): 373-87.

———. "God as Author of My Life-History." *Lutheran Quarterly* 2 (1988): 437-56.

———. "Hermeneutical Theology." Translated by Gwen Griffith-Dickson. *Scottish Journal of Theology* 56 (2003): 131-47.

———. "I Believe That God Has Created Me with All That Exists. An Example of Catechetical-Systematics." Translated by Christine Helmer, footnotes translated by Richard Bliese. *Lutheran Quarterly* 8 (1994): 129-61.

————. "Justification as the Basis and Boundary of Theology." Translated by Christine Helmer. *Lutheran Quarterly* 15 (2001): 273-92.

————. "Law and Morality." Translated by Christine Helmer. *Lutheran Quarterly* 17 (2003): 63-76.

————. "Luther as an Interpreter of Holy Scripture." Translated by Mark C. Mattes. In *The Cambridge Companion to Martin Luther*, ed. Donald K. McKim, pp. 73-85. Cambridge: Cambridge University Press, 2003.

————. "Luther's Ethics as Pastoral Care." *Lutheran Quarterly* 4 (1990): 125-42.

————. "The Modern Narcissus." Translated by Christine Helmer. *Lutheran Quarterly* 9 (1995): 301-13.

————. "Nature and Institution. Luther's Doctrine of the Three Orders." Translated by Luis Dreher. *Lutheran Quarterly* 12 (1998): 125-59.

————. "Notae ecclesiae." *Lutheran Contributions to the Missio Dei*, pp. 69-82. Geneva: Department of Church Cooperation of the Lutheran World Federation, 1984.

————. "Poetological Doctrine of the Trinity." Translated by Christine Helmer. *Lutheran Quarterly* 15 (2001): 43-58.

————. "Poetological Theology: New Horizions for Systematic Theology." Translated by Gwen Griffith Dickson. *International Journal for Systematic Theology* 1 (1999): 153-67.

————. "Report about the newly discovered Luther Manuscripts." *Luther and the Dawn of the Modern Era. Papers for the Fourth International Congress for Luther Research*, edited by Heiko A. Oberman. Publication of the SHCT, no. 8, pp. 117-26. Leiden: 1974.

————. "A Response to Richard McCormick." *Studies in Christian Ethics 1: Ethics and Ecumenism* (1988): 30-32.

————. "Rupture of Times: Luther's Relevance for Today." Translated by Christine Helmer. *Lutheran Quarterly* 13 (1999): 34-50.

————. "Self-Creation? On the Dignity of Human Beings." *Modern Theology* 20 (2004): 275-90.

————. "Social Ethics as an Ethics of Responsibility." Translated by Alan Suggate. *Worship and Ethics. Lutherans and Anglicans in Dialogue*, edited by Oswald Bayer and Alan Suggate, pp. 187-201. In Theologische Bibliothek Töpelmann, no. 70. Berlin and New York: Walter de Gruyter, 1996.

———. "Theology in the Conflict of Interpretations — Before the Text." Translated by Gwen Griffith-Dickson. *Modern Theology* 16 (2000): 495-502.

———. "Toward a Theology of Lament." Translated by Matthias Gockel. In *Caritas et Reformatio*, edited by D. Whitford, pp. 211-20. Saint Louis: Concordia Publishing House, 2002.

———. "With Luther in the Present." Translated by Mark A. Seifrid. *Lutheran Quarterly* (Spring 2007): 1-16.

———. "The Word of the Cross." Translated by John R. Betz. *Lutheran Quarterly* 9 (1995): 47-55.

———. "Worship and Theology." Translated by Alan Suggate. *Worship and Ethics. Lutherans and Anglicans in Dialogue*, edited by Oswald Bayer and Alan Suggate, pp. 148-61. Theologische Bibliothek Töpelmann, no. 70. Berlin and New York: Walter de Gruyter, 1996.

Books

———. *Living by Faith: Justification and Sanctification*. Translated by Geoffrey W. Bromiley. Grand Rapids: Eerdmans, 2003.

———. *Martin Luther's Theology: A Re-Presentation*. Translated by Thomas H. Trapp. Grand Rapids: Eerdmans, 2008.

———. *Theology the Lutheran Way*. Translated by Jeffrey G. Silcock and Mark C. Mattes. Grand Rapids: Eerdmans, 2007.

Bayer, Oswald, and Alan Suggate. *Worship and Ethics: Lutherans and Anglicans in Dialogue*. Theologische Bibliothek Töpelmann, no. 70. Berlin: Walter de Gruyter, 1995.

Index of Names

Abelard, Peter, 11
Aeschylus, 5
Aesop, 43, 133, 146
Agricola, John, 243n.318
Alber, Erasmus, 208
Albert, Hans, 182
Anselm of Canterbury, 34, 47-48, 211-12, 230n.185, 233n.212
Aristotle, 2, 6-7, 19, 21-22, 24, 28-32, 47-48, 64-65, 68, 75-78, 108-9, 112, 118, 127, 140, 161, 165, 189, 219n.49, 220n.66, 222n.94, 226, 232n.202, 232n.203, 250n.420, 261n.116, 266n.181, 284n.404
Athanasius, 34
Augustine, 8, 10, 34, 47, 58, 120-21, 129, 137, 163, 170, 251n.433
Austin, J. L., 126-30, 138
Averroes, 226n.140

Bacon, Francis, 266n.181
Barth, Hans-Martin, 270n.222
Barth, Karl, 34, 82, 92, 109, 116, 125, 142, 152, 164, 192-97, 224n.114
Bengel, Johann Albrecht, 33, 81, 222n.97, 223n.99, 251n.439
Bernard of Clairvaux, 11

Biel, Gabriel, 2, 13-14, 16-17, 21, 24, 29, 97-98, 105, 220n.64, 232n.201, 274n.285
Bonaventure, 107
Bonhoeffer, Dietrich, 82, 193, 196
Brunner, Emil, 194
Büchner, Georg, 112
Bultmann, Rudolph, 13, 34, 116-20, 126, 131, 138, 152, 159-68, 197, 256n.44, 257n.46, 264n.153, 276n.304, 276n.313, 276n.314

Calvin, John, 190, 219n.59, 258n.58
Cassirer, Ernst, 169, 277n.326
Cicero, 75-77, 229n.170

Demosthenes, 76
Descartes, Rene, 50, 58, 99, 119, 120, 163, 236n.221, 269n.216
Dilthey, Wilhelm, 138, 280-81n.362
Dionysius the Areopagite, 46, 232n.198, 242n.312
Duns Scotus, John, 226n.140, 274n.285

Ebeling, Gerhard, 157-59
Eckhart, Meister, 11-12, 23, 108-9
Eusebius of Caesarea, 37, 196

Index of Names

Ferdinand, King, 60
Feuerbach, Ludwig, 20, 94, 113, 132-33, 137-38, 147-48, 150-52, 233n.209, 270n.222, 270n.230, 273n.265
Fichte, Johann Gottlieb, 205
Freud, Sigmund, 113, 135, 151

George, Duke of Saxony, 60
Gerhard, Johann, 12, 225n.133, 269n.214
Gregory of Nyssa, 37, 259n.80

Habermas, Jürgen, 204, 277n.326
Hafenreffer, Matthias, 223n.99
Hamann, Johann Georg, 81, 87, 121, 163, 228n.156, 231n.192, 232n.204, 251n.440, 263n.133, 266n.182, 282n.380
Hegel, Georg Friedrich, 20, 27, 34, 82, 93-94, 100, 102-4, 110, 112, 126, 137, 142, 144-48, 150-51, 154, 159, 169, 181, 185, 191, 194-97, 204-5, 211, 223n.103
Heidegger, Martin, 126, 138, 164-65, 246n.361, 267n.200, 256n.45, 272n.256, 277n.326
Henry, Duke of Braunschweig, 60
Herder, Johann Gottfried, 277n.326
Herrmann, Wilhelm, 414, 453, 456-57
Hesiod, 3
Hessus, Eobanus, 234n.214
Hirsch, Emanuel, 139, 242n.316
Hollaz, David, 195, 205-6
Homer, 3, 5, 7
Hornig, Gottfried, 253n.9
Huarte, Juan, 266n.181
Hume, David, 117

Jerome, 37
Jonas, Hans, 138, 168-70, 270n.231, 279n.349
Jonas, Justus, 283n.392
Jüngel, Eberhard, 224n.116, 261n.116, 262n.117

Kant, Immanuel, 13, 91, 94-95, 103, 112,

115-18, 120, 123, 125-26, 135, 142-44, 160-64, 167-68, 186, 194-96, 204, 263n.131, 264n.152, 264n.159, 265n.162, 276n.307, 277n.317, 277n.324, 277n.326

Leclercq, Jean, 10-11
Lessing, Gotthold Ephraim, 58, 194-96, 266n.184
Levinas, Emmanuel, 104
Lombard, Peter, 2, 23, 46
Lonergan, Bernard J. F., 267n.186
Luther, Martin, 1, 3, 10, 12-13, 15-89, 91-93, 95-98, 103-7, 109-10, 112-13, 122-23, 128-30, 133, 137-38, 142, 145-47, 149-50, 152, 155-56, 159-60, 164, 181, 186, 189-92, 205-6, 210-12, 216n.4, 216n.6, 216n.12, 218n.41, 219n.49, 221n.71, 222n.94, 222n.97, 223n.109, 225n.126, 225n.133, 225n.134, 225n.136, 226n.140, 226n.141, 227n.146, 228n.160, 229n.170, 229n.178, 229n.180, 230n.185, 230n.187, 230n.189, 231n.190, 232n.196, 232n.202, 232n.203, 233n.209, 233n.212, 234n.213, 234n.214, 235n.220, 236n.228, 236n.233, 237n.255, 239n.270, 242n.312, 242n.316, 243n.318, 244n.324, 244n.330, 245n.346, 247n.383, 247n.387, 249n.416, 249n.420, 250n.425, 251n.439, 256n.42, 263n.145, 269n.211, 270n.219, 270n.231, 280n.357, 287n.452

Marx, Karl, 67, 92, 111-12, 126, 132, 151, 159, 274n.277
Melanchthon, Philipp, 12-13, 188, 192, 224n.125, 238n.265
Mörike, Eduard, 211
Mohammed, 51
Münzer, Thomas, 51

Neander, Johann A. W., 223n.103

Nicol, M., 237n.251, 240n.291
Niethammer, Friedrich Immanuel, 233n.204

Ockham, William, 14, 21, 28-29, 31, 80, 221n.69
Overbeck, Franz, 95, 147, 272-73n.265

Pannenberg, Wolfhart, 34, 97-99, 261n.116, 262n.129
Peukert, Helmut, 143, 272n.250,
Plato, 1, 4-7, 11, 31-32, 47, 55, 64, 103, 109, 111-12, 135, 161, 200, 268n.204
Popper, Karl, 172-73, 204, 281n.372

Rahner, Karl, 183, 199, 240n.289, 286n.437
Reimarus, Hermann Samuel, 194-95
Ringleben, Joachim, 217n.28
Roos, Magnus Friedrich, 222n.97

Sartre, Jean-Paul, 279n.347
Schelling, Friedrich W. J., 154, 164, 185-86
Schleiermacher, Friedrich, 35, 53, 83,

93-94, 101, 103, 107, 110, 112-13, 126, 131, 138, 142, 148-60, 165-66, 168-69, 172-83, 185-86, 196-97, 238n.263, 254n.22, 255n.26, 270n.231, 279n.350, 279n.351, 281n.362, 281n.366, 285n.423, 285n.425
Scholz, Heinrich, 97
Semler, Johann Salomo, 12-13, 33-36, 54, 83-84, 93, 253n.9
Socrates, 5, 135
Spener, Philipp Jakob, 223n.100
Statius, P. Papinius, 227n.146, 229n.170

Tauler, Johannes, 23, 107
Tholuck, Friedrich August, 34
Thomas Aquinas, 29, 34, 77, 97, 203-5, 224n.117, 263n.145
Tillich, Paul, 192
Troeltsch, Ernst, 280n.361

Varro, 8

Wittgenstein, Ludwig, 125-28, 137-38

Index of Subjects

Index of Scripture References

Boldface indicates that a passage is discussed without explicit citation of the chapter and verse (e.g., "the Ten Commandments," "the Lord's Prayer").

299

Index of Scripture References